The Complete Guide to

NEEDLEWORK

Techniques and Materials

The Complete Guide to NEEDLEWORK Techniques and Materials

Consultant Editor
Mary Gostelow

FRASER STEWART

Consultant editor
Mary Gostelow

Contributing editors
Julie Athill
Shiela Betterton
Doreen Burford
Hazel Chapman
Wendy Jackson
Beverley Marshall
Anna Pearson
The Textile Conservation Centre
Janice Williams

A QUILL BOOK

Published 1988 by
Fraser Stewart Book Wholesale Ltd
8 Market Place
Hertford, Herts
SG14 9DF

First published 1982

ISBN 1 85348 032 0

Published in the USA, its territories and dependencies and Canada by
Chartwell Books Inc, Secaucus, New Jersey.

This book was designed and produced by
Quill Publishing Limited
32 Kingly Court
London W1

Art director James Marks
Production director Nigel Osborne
Editorial director Jeremy Harwood
Senior editor Liz Wilhide
Editor Joanna Rait
Assistant editor Caroline Oulton
Designers Paul Cooper Steve Wilson
Art assistants Annie Collenette Janel Minors
Illustrators Marion Appleton Ray Brown Bob Byrnes Paul Cooper Nick Gibbard
Jim Marks Richard Prideaux Lorna Turpin Steve Wilson
Photographers James Abelson Clive Boden Philip de Bey Ian Howes
Paul Sawyer
Picture researcher Imogen Graham

Filmset in Great Britain by Front Page Graphics, London EC1.
Origination by Hong Kong Graphic Arts Limited,
Hong Kong.
Printed in Hong Kong by Leefung-Asco Printers Limited.

Quill would like to extend special thanks to
Shelagh Ford at The American Museum; Marion Appleton; Bogod Machine Company Limited; Elles and Farrier; Elna Sewing Machines (GB) Limited; Margaret Hall and Audrey Walker at Goldsmith's College; Laura Ashley Limited; The Lord Chamberlain's Office; Christine Risley; Jim Moeller at Silver Thimble; Anne Amos, Norma Clyde, Sherry Doyal, Dinah Eastop, Karen Finch, Maria Lamarca, Marion Lamb and Lois Singer at The Textile Conservation Centre.

Contents

Introduction

Needlework is both a necessary and a decorative art. The very act of stitching with a needle can hold two or more surfaces together, but at the same time embellish the surface of at least one of those materials. In the context of this book "needlecraft" is interpreted as decorative stitching, in some instances practical as well as attractive, and in other cases pure embellishment.

Techniques covered here use a single, eyed needle. Patchwork and quilting fall within this category; knitting and crochet do not. Machine decoration worked on an ordinary domestic sewing machine is also included. There are inevitably borderline areas which are difficult to categorize and new techniques will undoubtedly come to light in the near future. One surprising characteristic of needlecraft is, indeed, its vitality. Throughout the centuries, needleworkers have been quick to follow new trends; many of these developments will be carefully explained in the chapters that follow.

This introduction outlines the basic techniques that apply to all the different needlecraft forms included in the book. Subsequent chapters cover canvaswork, appliqué and raised work, patchwork and quilting, smocking, silk, bead and metal thread embroidery, machine embroidery, counted thread, crewel, whitework, and drawn and pulled work. The final chapter examines collecting, conservation and display. Each section is set out in a similar fashion, covering techniques, materials and the history of the particular form. Special stitches and patterns are explained and diagrammed.

Right *An exotic piece of nineteenth-century Indian embroidery worked in cotton on a woollen ground. The bodies of the animals and the figures have been blocked in with finely executed chain stitch, to give them weight against the looser background textures.*
Below *Crazy patchworks were very popular towards the end of last century, and a feature was made of the seams as well as the diversity of the shapes and fabrics. These seams were sewn in bright colours with decorative cross and herringbone stitches.*
Top right *An example of beadwork combined with raised or stumpwork, worked in the 1680s. It measures 10×13 inches (25×33 cm), and shows a king addressing his queen and attendants. The large beaded flowers and fruit in the background are very characteristic of this type of work, as are the unlikely proportions of figures and buildings to plants. The faces, hands and knees of the figures are all raised work.*

***Above** A detail from a large machine-embroidered cushion cover. The silky background fabric has been painted, and the embroidery worked subsequently. There is also some appliqué work within the design. The delicate use of colour within the abstract floral shapes, and subtle merging of embroidery with paint, demonstrates the kind of finesse that contemporary needlework can achieve.*

Our goal throughout has been to present not only a complete, but an excellent guide to needlecraft. Needlework cannot and should not be rushed. It is worth taking time to work stitches properly; a pattern should be exactly aligned and colour-balanced. It is essential to purchase the best materials you can: in terms of hours of stitching, investment in the best makes economic sense. This also applies to making up and displaying finished pieces.

For those of you who already stitch, may you enjoy this book. As well as aiming for perfection, enjoyment along the way is also important – nowadays no needlecraft should be a drudge. For those who are new to what can easily become a happy and worthwhile addiction, the following pages should answer some initial queries.

Basic Principles

Needlecraft is sewing, which implies taking a threaded needle in and out of a "ground" material, either a canvas with easily discernible mesh of warp and weft threads, a fabric, perhaps an evenweave, with easily visible warp and wefts, or a more closely woven fabric. Sewing on canvas, called variously canvaswork (as here), or needlepoint, or needlepoint "tapestry" (a misnomer since technically tapestry is woven decoration) has its own large and enthusiastic following. Many of the techniques worked on an evenweave are "counted thread", in which stitches are formed over a certain number of warp and weft threads. Other techniques, worked on evenweave or more closely woven fabric, take no account of the number of fabric threads over which a stitch is worked.

"Stitches" are formed by the threaded needle going in and out of the ground material. If both in-and-out are worked in one movement, it is technically "stitching", a word also used to imply any form of decorative sewing. If the needle goes in and then it is taken out, in two actions, it is known as "stabbing".

Basic Equipment

Before you begin, you need the tools with which to work. You need fabric, threads, needles, perhaps a frame or hoop, scissors, good light and comfortable surroundings.

Fabric

Regardless of which canvas or fabric you choose, you should work with the selvedge and warp threads vertical. A wide range of canvases and fabrics is available from good needlework suppliers; if you are a beginner, it is a good idea to ask advice from the expert at the shop. Make sure you buy enough fabric for your project before you begin – it is better to have a little too much than not enough.

Below *A selection of canvases with different sized meshes, from the coarse to the very fine. Each one shows a square inch of worked canvas with, left to right: 6, 14, 18 and 22 intersections or stitches to each inch of canvas. Select according to the type of texture required. The finest ones are not suitable for beginners.*

***Above** A canvas work cushion cover sewn in the latter part of the sixteenth century. The colours of the wools are predominantly pinks and greens, and both colour and design are very characteristic of canvaswork of the period. Cushions have been popular through the ages for most types of embroidery, but are particularly associated with canvaswork, a durable form of needlework.*

Right *It is a good idea to keep all sewing equipment in one place. That way it should stay clean and neat while remaining instantly accessible. The basket shown is both capacious and attractive; an unlined basket would be less satisfactory, as smaller items could slip out through the bottom and sides. Most needleworkers favour a container that is light and easily portable. Buttons should be kept in boxes or tins, and thread ends securely fastened to avoid tangles.*
Far right *A selection of needlework frames that can be used for embroidery, canvaswork and quilting. The advantage of the largest stand is that both hands are left free to work. The fabric must be laced into position, whereas on the square frame without a stand, tacks or drawing pins can be used. The smaller circular frames are only used for fine needlework. They are made from two loops that can be tightened by a screw, between which the fabric is trapped. Whenever a frame is being used, make sure that the fabric is evenly stretched with no wrinkles or buckling. The small palette can be used to keep lengths of thread tidy, separate and accessible.*

Thread

Beginners usually work with either woollen yarn or stranded cottons. Wool is generally used for canvaswork; stranded cotton for many of the other techniques.

Stranded cotton is variously called "floss" and "DMC", a brandname now often used generically. As the name implies, this thread consists of six cotton strands, loosely twisted with a Z-twist. Skeins contain 26 feet (8 m), and it is necessary to be careful when extracting just the right amount for stitching – say, a length of about 15 inches (38 cm). Some brands have a guide on the paper wrapper indicating which end of the skein's thread to pull. If there is no such guide, pull one of the ends out extremely carefully. If you pull the wrong end, the skein will become tangled, perhaps irretrievably so.

Some people prefer to cut an entire skein into suitable lengths before they begin to stitch. The easiest way of doing this is to cut a card to the required length (say, 15 inches/ 38 cm), then wind the thread round and round the card and cut through at both ends.

You can store cut lengths by looping them through the holes of a palette – the plastic rings of the top of a pack of beer cans make a good and inexpensive palette. You can also store cut or whole skeins in a clear-fronted tool cabinet or in the special looseleaf files with clear pockets available on the needlecraft market.

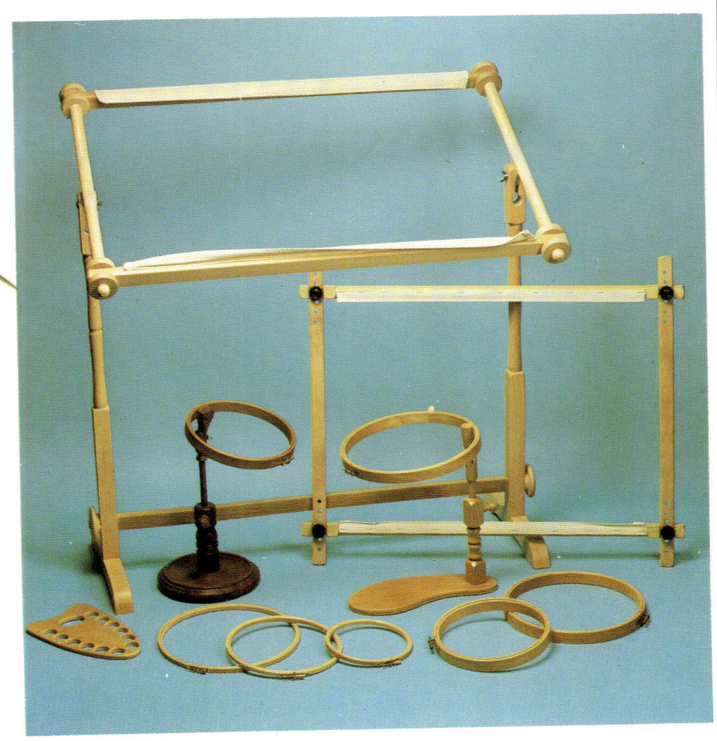

Above *A selection of threads for use in needlework. The colour and weight must obviously be taken into consideration when purchasing. The slightly thicker threads make excellent threads to be couched. They are twisted together, and cannot be divided up in the way that some embroidery silks can be stranded. Unless the stitches used to couch down a thread are a feature in themselves, they should be worked in a fine thread as inconspicuously as possible. Some whitework is also sewn with very fine thread. Experiment with different colours and textures to find the right balance with the background fabric and the design of the piece.*

You can stitch with one, two, three, four, five or all six strands of stranded cotton. Regardless of how many strands you require, you should always "strip" a cut length before stitching. This entails carefully extracting each strand, one by one, until all six strands have been separated. As many strands as are required can then be put back together again. This results in smooth, untwisted stitching and the thread will cover the ground fabric better.

Stranded cottons have no nap, so you can stitch from either end of a cut length. Wools, on the other hand, usually do have an easily discernible nap. If you cannot find it by any other means, you can pass the thread over your upper lip. When you have found the nap, make sure that you thread the needle so that the smoothness runs down from the needle along the main thread length.

Needles

Specific needle requirements are listed in each of the following chapters. Most experienced needlecrafters have their own favourite needles, and you will quickly discover which size needle, and which type, suits you best.

Today needles are made of stainless steel and should not tarnish easily. If they do discolour it should not affect the fabric or threads with which you are working.

Store the needle you work with most often with a length of thread through it. This way you will be able to find it more easily if it falls. It is not a good idea to store your needle in your mouth, even temporarily.

Frames

Frames and hoops form an essential part of many needleworkers' accessories. Today, frames are generally square or rectangular, whereas hoops are most often circular, sometimes oval. If you are working some counted thread forms, you do not necessarily need to have your material held taut on a frame or hoop; if you are concentrating on canvaswork, you definitely need a square or rectangular frame. In some other techniques it is a matter of your own personal preference whether you work with the piece held in your hand or with the material held taut.

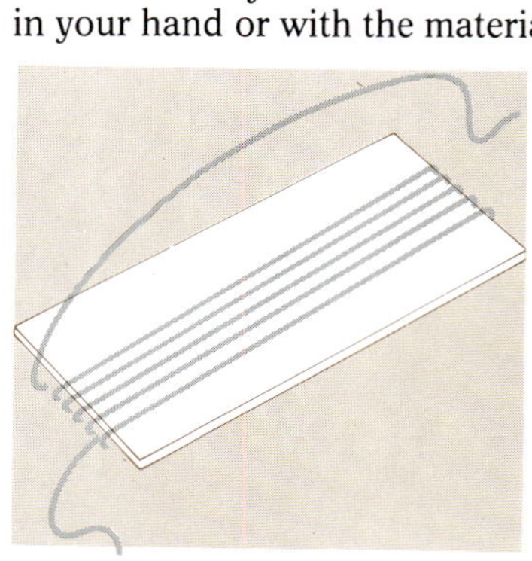

Measuring thread length.
1. *The optimum thread length for embroidery is approximately 15 inches (38 cm). Longer threads may become tangled.*

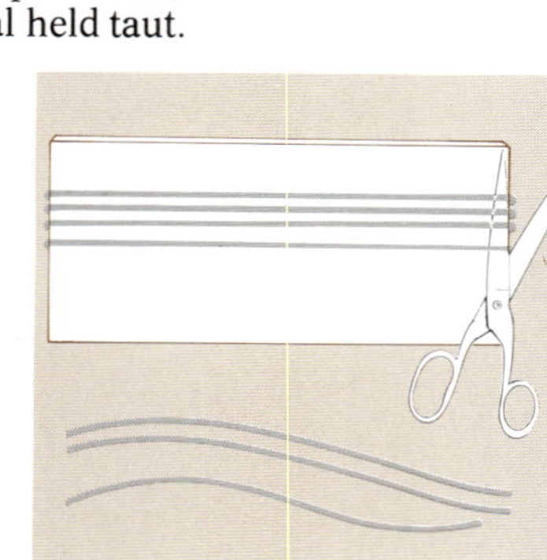

2. *Wind the thread round a card 15 inches (38cm) long as many times as the number of thread lengths required.*

***Above** A selection of wools for use in crewel and canvaswork. Select wools that are appropriate to the size of canvas mesh being used; when in doubt consult the supplier.*

In the past, canvas and other materials had to be laced in place on the square or rectangular frames, a painstaking process known as "dressing". Nowadays, a simple range of roller bar frames is available; another inexpensive alternative is to use pairs of artists' stretchers, hammered together. The canvas is held by staples or drawing pins.

When putting canvas or fabric on a frame, it is best to pin one centre point of one side first and then pin the centre point of the opposite side, followed by the centre points of the other two sides. Next, pin outwards from one central pin to a corner point; pin the diagonally opposite section in the same

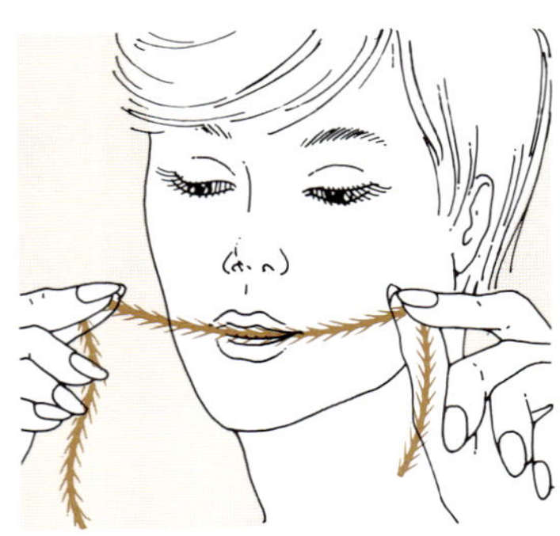

Finding the nap.
***1.** The easiest way to identify the direction of the nap on the thread is by passing a taut section between the lips both ways.*

***2.** In one direction the thread will feel much rougher. When sewing, make sure that the spines of the nap point are in the opposite direction to the needle.*

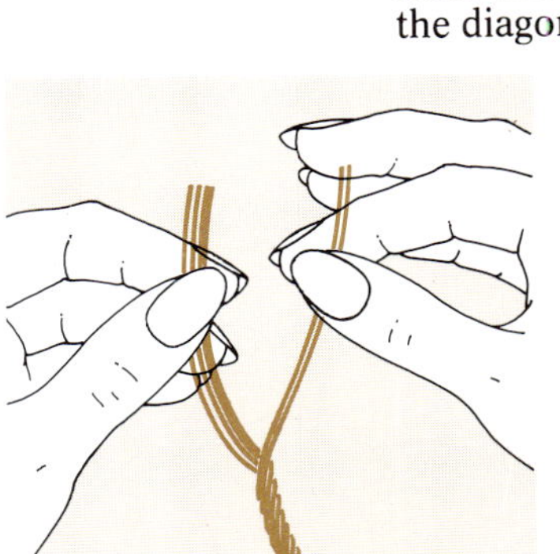

***3.** Cut through all the loops at either end, for a handy bunch of threads, all the same length.*

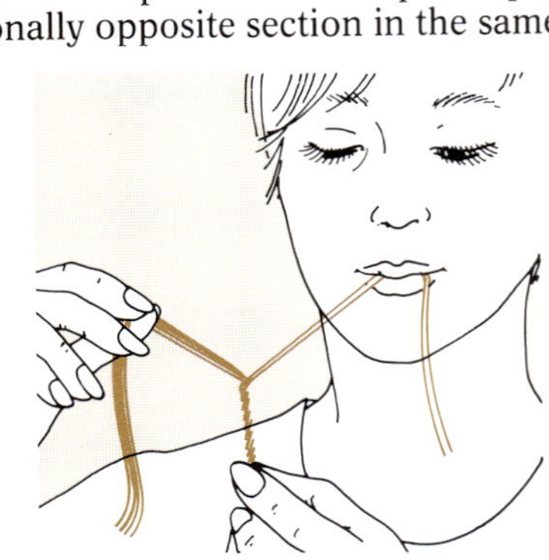

***Preparing thread** Work with as many strands of the thread as required, separating them out as shown. Do this even when using all the strands.*

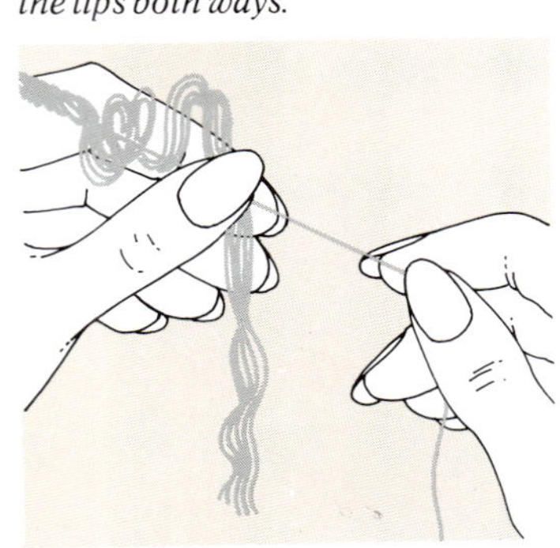

***Preparing wool yarn** Strands must be separated to obtain a smooth working thread.*

way and continue in this manner until all sections are held firmly. If you are using drawing pins, make sure they lean slightly away from the canvas.

One of the advantages of the two-ringed circular or oval hoop is that it can easily be moved along from one area of the fabric to another. The lightweight plastic hoops available today are particularly easy to set up. The smaller ring is placed beneath the fabric and the larger, screwed ring is placed above it. When the screw is tightened, the fabric is held taut between the ridge on the outside of the smaller hoop and the ridge on the inside of the larger hoop.

Scissors

Most needleworkers only need two pairs of scissors. One should be large dressmaking scissors with long enough blades to cut fabric and canvas. The other pair should have short, very sharp blades. Needlework scissors should be reserved for sewing and not used for any other purpose.

Working area

Good light and comfortable surroundings are all too often ignored, but both are essential for producing fine work. The best type of light is an anglepoise type, positioned so the light comes over the left shoulder (lefthanded people may find it better to have the light coming over their right shoulder).

An upright chair with good back support enables you to sit comfortably while you are stitching. If the chair has arms make sure they are not too high. Low and wide arms can conveniently hold pins, scissors and threads. It is quite tempting, when you are progressing well with a piece, to sit and stitch for a long time. Regardless of how comfortable your surroundings and how keen your enthusiasm, it is not a good idea to sit for too long. Try and force yourself at least to stand up and stretch every so often.

Other equipment

There are other pieces of equipment in which you could invest but they are not strictly necessary, as long as you have fabric, threads, needles and perhaps a frame or hoop, scissors and good surroundings. If

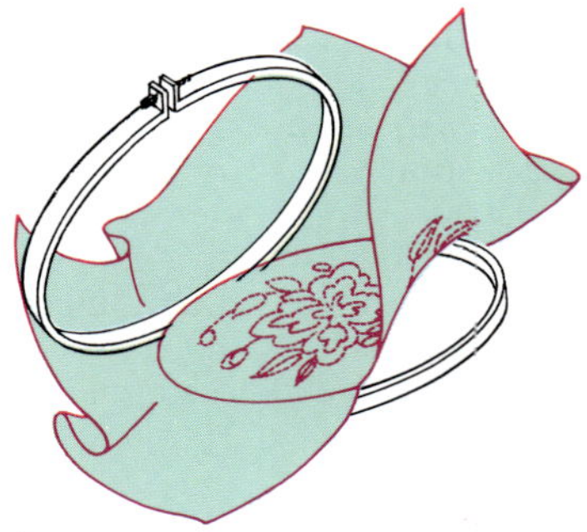

Framing embroidery 1. *Place fabric, pattern side up, over inner hoop as shown. Push outer hoop down over the inner one trapping the fabric.*

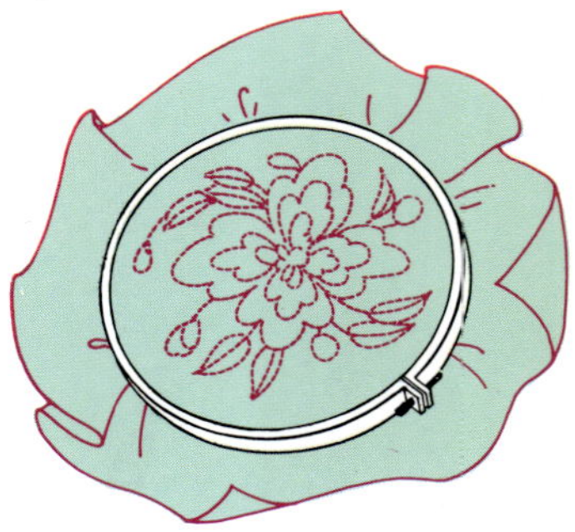

2. *The fabric should be taut within the frame without being strained or wrinkled. Use the screw to alter the tension in the frame as required.*

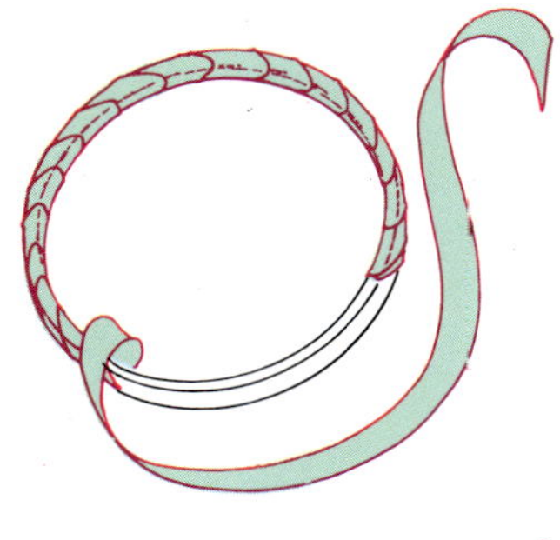

Frame binding *To protect very fine fabric from damage, wrap masking tape or bias binding tightly round the inner hoop and secure the ends.*

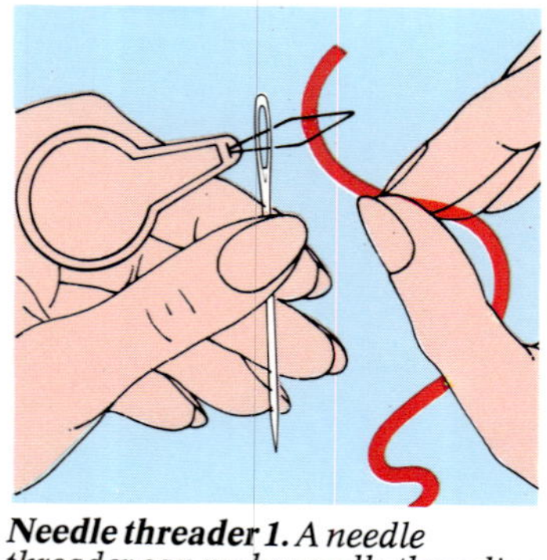

Needle threader 1. *A needle threader can make needle threading much easier. Thread the diamond of wire through the eye of the needle as shown above.*

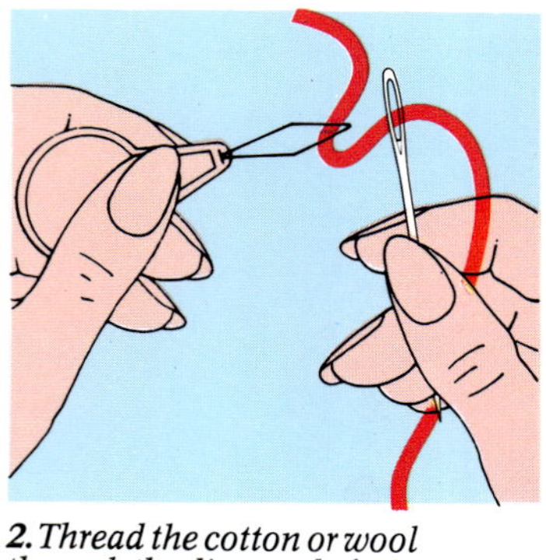

2. *Thread the cotton or wool through the diamond of wire. Draw the needle back over the wire diamond, and it will force the thread through.*

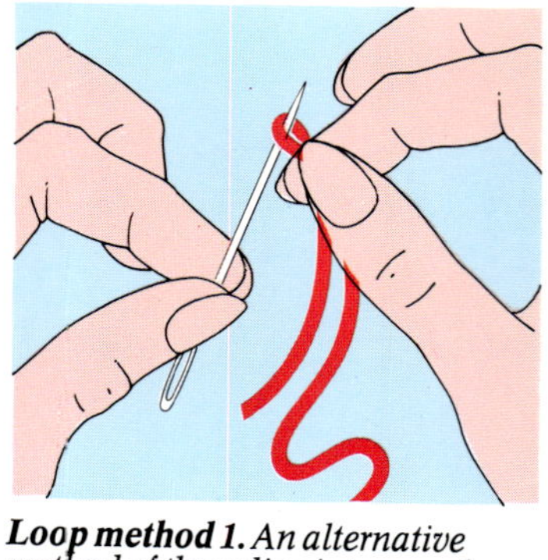

Loop method 1. *An alternative method of threading is to use a loop. Wrap the cotton or wool tightly round the eye of the needle in a loop.*

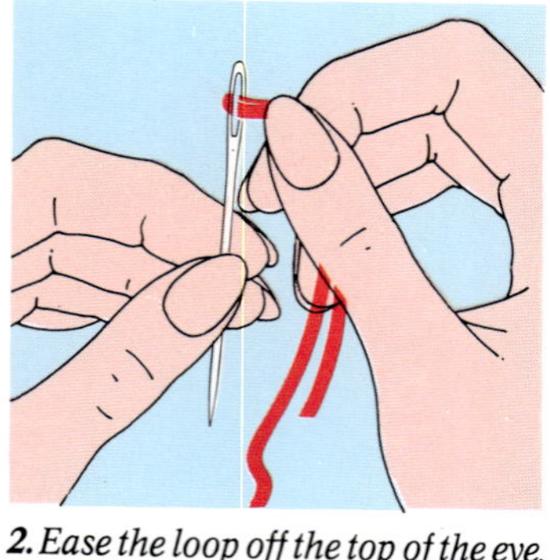

2. *Ease the loop off the top of the eye, and attempt to thread the needle loop-first. The loop will be stiffer and easier to thread than the limp end.*

you do want to add to your range of equipment, a needle-threader is useful, as is a neck-hanging magnifier or a floor-standing magnifying light. Frames and hoops can be held on gadgets that you sit on; at greater cost, some floor-standing models are available. A simpler and less expensive method is to hold the frame on a convenient table or ledge with a handyman's clamp.

You probably already have a container of dressmaking pins and sewing threads useful for tacking. You may even have a loop-turner, intended for turning narrow fabric cords and straps right side out. Pencils, a ruler and an eraser should also be to hand. If you are lefthanded, you should also have a mirror nearby. To follow diagrams, left-handed stitchers should simply look at the mirror's reflection of the diagrams, drawn here for righthanded needleworkers.

Left *A detail from a Chinese coat covered in silk embroidery. It is worked in very fine satin stitch throughout, and the muted colours of the flowers and leaves have been beautifully blended to set off the cream silk ground.*
Right *Good lighting is essential for all types of needlework. Anglepoise lights are favoured, but a small strip light and a ring neon filament have also been shown as they provide an equally clear strong light. The lamp used should have a flexible jointed stand.*

Left *A colour wheel can be consulted when colours are selected for a needlework design. Decide on the design before choosing the colours, and be prepared to adapt ideas to the fabrics and threads available.*
Right *A small selection of needles. There are many hundreds on the market, of every conceivable combination of length and thickness. The blunt-ended ones with large eyes are known as tapestry needles and are generally used for canvaswork. The long thin needles are beading needles. Several beads can be threaded onto the needle at once, before it is pulled through. It is impossible to work fine embroidery with a coarse needle, or to penetrate several layers of tough fabric with a needle that is too small, so it is important to select needles carefully.*

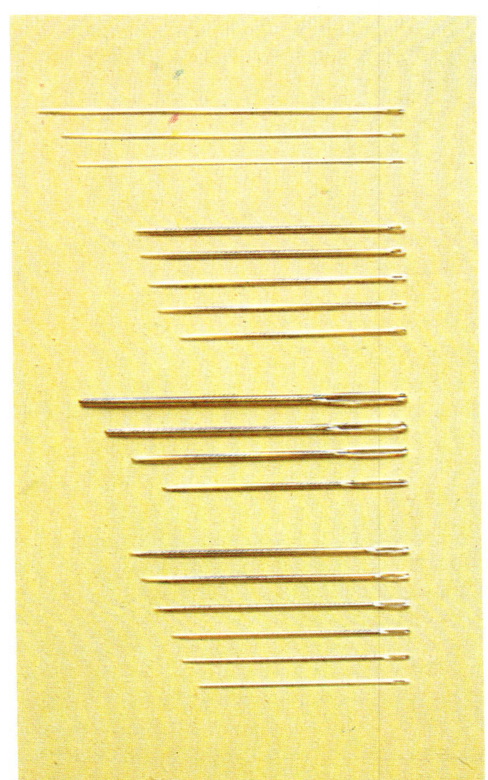

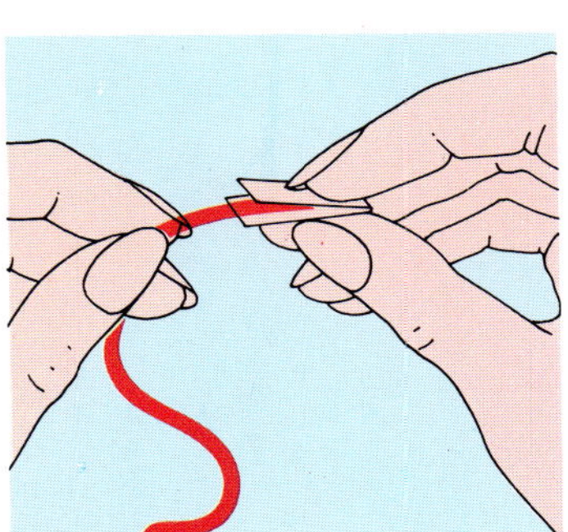

Paper method 1. *If there is no needle threader to hand, you can use the paper method. Place the end of the thread in a piece of folded paper.*

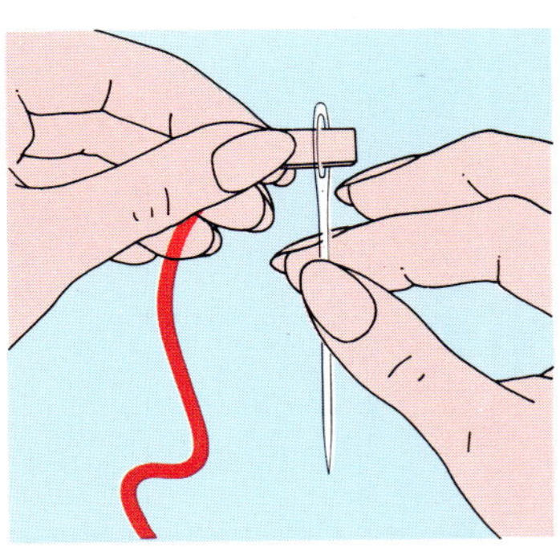

2. *The paper can then be pushed through the eye of the needle with the thread inside it. The paper must be small enough to fit and relatively stiff.*

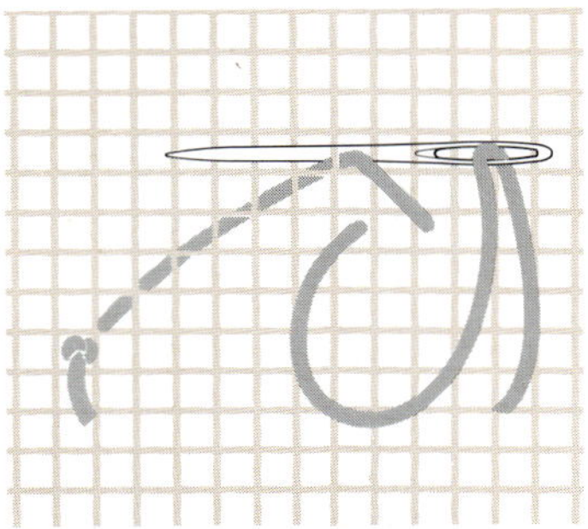

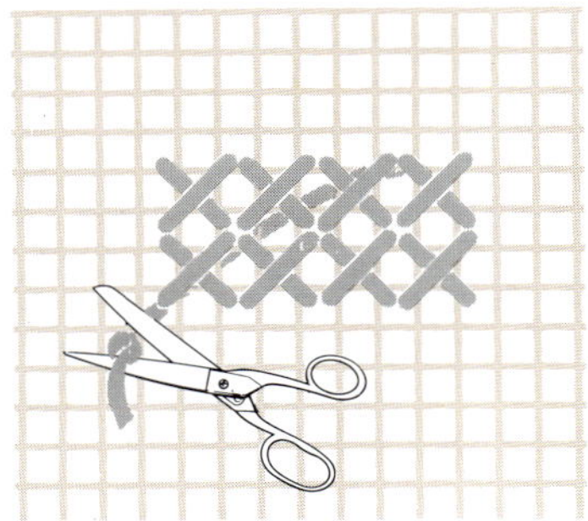

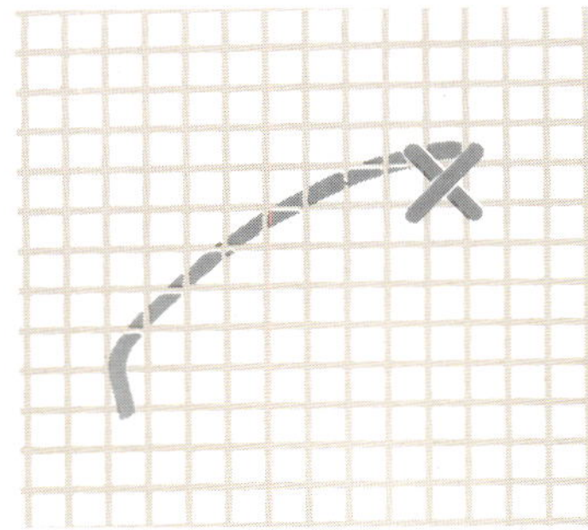

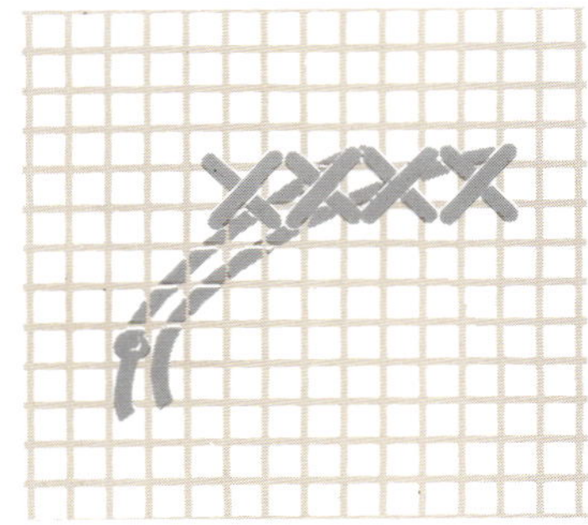

Starting and ending threads 1. *To secure the thread end when starting, make a knot and leave it on the right side of the fabric.*

2. *Make a long stitch from the direction in which you will work. The embroidery stitches will hold the thread and you can cut off the waste knot.*

3. *When ending a thread, secure it in a similar way, by making a waste tail and taking the tail to the area you will be covering with stitches.*

4. *The tail will not need knotting. It will be bound at the same time as the waste knot of the next thread by that thread's first stitches.*

Basic Techniques

Preparing the fabric

When you cut your canvas or fabric make sure to cut exactly between warp and weft threads. If you are cutting linen, you can withdraw a guide thread first to help you cut exactly.

Bind the edges of the cut material to prevent fraying or unravelling. Among the methods are machine zigzagging and binding with tape; either an overlocking machine or a professional tape binder is very useful for this operation. For projects such as tablecloths, it is often easier to mitre the corners of the fabric and hem the cloth before beginning the main decoration.

It is always helpful to find the centre of your area before you start to stitch. To do this, thread up a length of tacking thread, preferably in a pale colour that will not show if accidentally caught in subsequent stitching. Measure the halfway point across the top of your area and, from that point, tack from top to bottom of the area, making sure you do not cross any vertical warp threads. Similarly find the halfway point on one side of the area and, from that point, tack from one side to the other, making sure you do not cross any horizontal weft threads.

Stitch key

It is especially useful for canvaswork and counted thread techniques to work a large token stitch to act as a key. If you are going to work in tent stitch, make a large tent stitch in the upper righthand corner of your canvas. Constant glances back at this key stitch will ensure that subsequent tent stitches all face the same direction. Similarly, a large cross key will help you to cross all your cross stitches in the same way. (Keys should, of course, be removed when the piece is finished.)

Beginning and ending thread

It is better not to start stitching with a holding knot. You can secure the end of the thread with one or two little back or running stitches in a space that will subsequently be covered with stitching. An alternative method is to make a waste knot. A knotted thread is taken in from the front of the material, a short distance from where you will begin stitching. The subsequent stitching will then bind the holding thread on the reverse of the work so that the holding knot can be cut without having to turn the material over. Ending a thread can also be done with one or two little holding stitches, or with the waste tail method.

Waste knots and waste tails are particularly appropriate on canvaswork and other dense stitch techniques. If you finish off a thread by weaving in and out of the back of worked stitches, you are stretching those stitches. By forming waste knots and waste tails each subsequent stitch accommodates the extra thread.

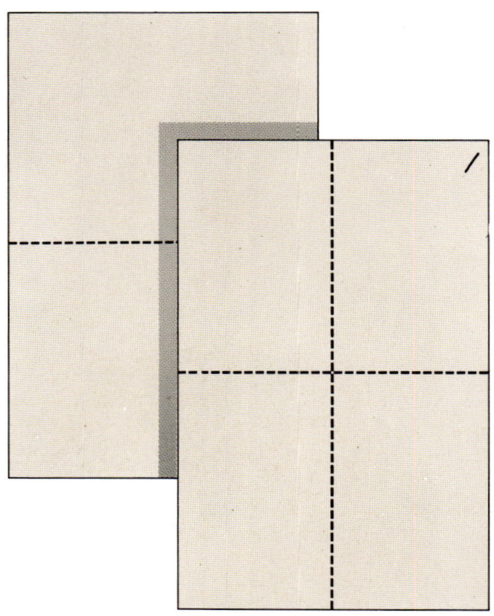

Above *It is often necessary to find the exact centre of the fabric in order to organise the design effectively. This can be done by folding the fabric lengthways and breadthways. The centre of the fabric will be where the two creases cross.*

Binding the fabric 1. *To prevent fraying while the piece is being worked, bind the edges temporarily with masking tape as shown.*

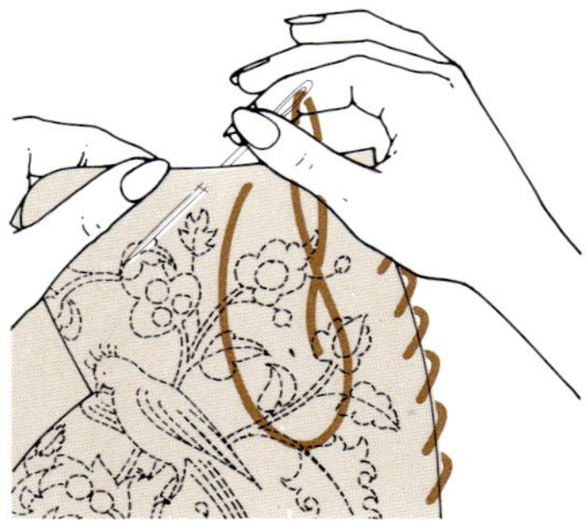

2. *Alternatively, raw edges can be neatly secured with overcast stitching. Overcast by hand, along each edge.*

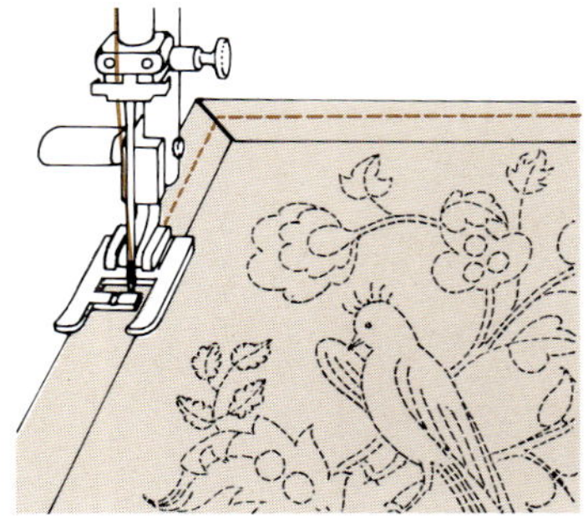

3. *A neater and more reliable way of binding the raw edges is to turn them over to the depth of 1 inch (2.5 cm) and machine stitch round on the wrong side.*

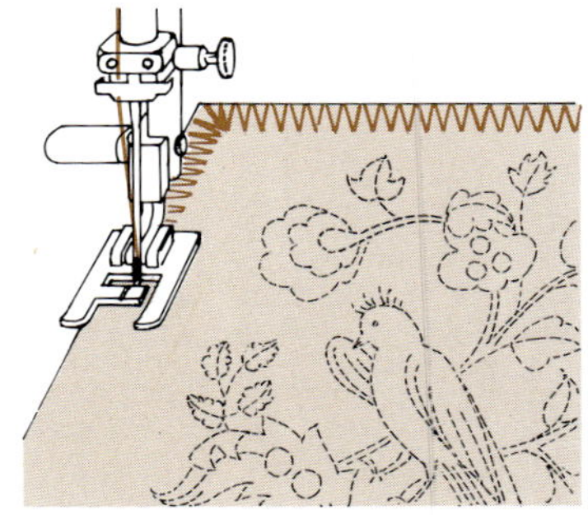

4. *If there is a hem, machine straight stitch can be used. Use machine zigzag stitches to bind raw edges if there is to be no turn-over.*

Left *An example of bad embroidery. This piece displays a multitude of errors that could very easily have been prevented. There are smudges of dirt and blood on the background fabric, most of the cross stitches have been worked back to front, the French knots are messy, tacking has been left in, and the original outline shows to the left of the church tower. The tension throughout is haphazard, and the threads used as well as the design itself are all unbalanced. The colours clash.*

Design

When first learning to embroider, it is wise to begin with a charted design, a transfer or even with a purchased kit. When stitching from a chart or graph, make sure that you read all instructions carefully before you begin. On some graphs one square equals one stitch. In other cases, one line equals one thread. Check on the size of the stitches (over one, two or more threads). If the chart is black-and-white, you will find it much easier to follow if you take time to colour it.

Transfer designs consist of a pattern on tissue paper. To transfer the design, lay the paper, design side down, above the chosen fabric, and apply a heated iron. Transfers are available as inserts in specialist and other magazines, and from needlework suppliers and other shops. They are used especially for crewel and other surface embroideries which do not need the warp and weft threads of the fabric to be exactly aligned.

Pencils are available for making your own transfer. Draw the reverse of your pattern on paper, lay the paper design side down, and iron it. An easier method of making a transfer pattern, however, is to draw the design the right way round on thin paper. Lay dressmakers' or carbon film paper (the type used in electric typewriters) above, carbon side down, and the tracing above. Make sure you do not pin through all three layers as pin marks will show carbon spots: cut the carbon to a smaller size than fabric and paper, pin the paper to the fabric along the top edges and loosely insert the carbon. Carefully press out the outline pattern, say with the end of a blunt needle.

Although some needleworkers object to commercial kits, for beginners such kits often make economic and practical sense. The complete package should include enough material, embroidery threads, needle and full instructions. As many materials are only available in standard widths, if you want to work a small piece of embroidery, buying your own fabric can be very wasteful. Beginners, too, are apt to misjudge the amount of thread required. Running out of thread may mean that you cannot get

__Below__ Find the centre of the background fabric and use it to plan the design. Avoid a concentration of heavy shapes too near the top or bottom of the design. Cut the proposed shapes out of paper, and move them around until satisfied.

__Right__ An early twentieth-century linen tablecloth worked by Ann Macbeth. She designed and worked a prodigious number of pieces, wrote books and articles about embroidery and was head of the needlework, embroidery and appliqué department at Glasgow School of Art 1910 to 1928.

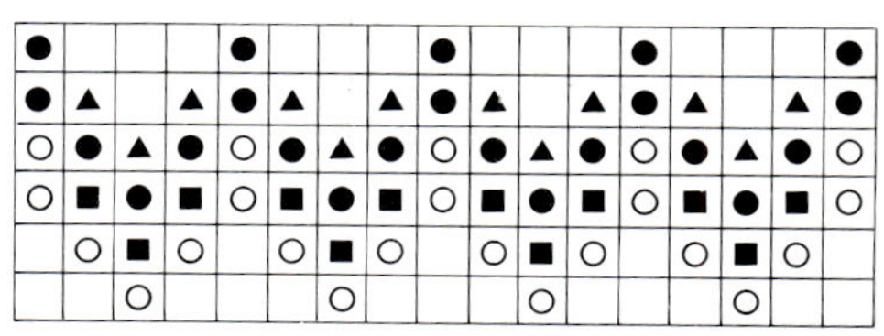

__Left__ Plot out the pattern on squared paper, using symbols for the different colours as shown. Repeat using different symbols for the stitches to gain a thorough understanding of the colours and textures of a design before embarking on the actual stitching. It is obviously much easier to make alterations at the drawing stage.

Transferring designs with carbon 1. *Place the carbon paper, carbon side down on the right side of the fabric. Pin the pattern down on top, design side up.*

2. *Trace over the lines of the pattern using a small tracing wheel. Try to avoid repeating areas as the final line may become blurred or messy. Remove carbon and pattern.*

Hot iron transfer 1. *Copy the design onto thick tracing paper, turn it over and trace round the outline again with a transfer pencil.*

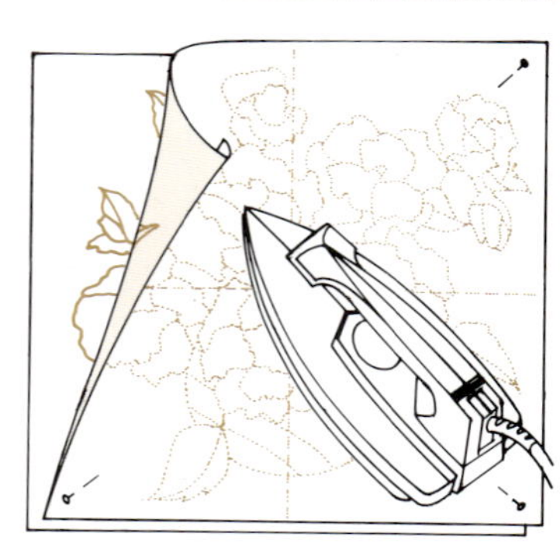

2. *Turn the tracing paper over again, place it on the fabric and iron the design into position with a cool iron. Iron ready-made transfers on in same way.*

more supplies from the same dye-lot. Another advantage of kits is that they can encourage you to have the confidence to progress to making your own designs.

Some of the techniques described in following chapters have special design instructions and ideas. Blackwork, for instance, has special affiliation with tiles and wrought-iron patterns. Needlepoint similarly has its own design inspirations. A wealth of other ideas can be taken from the patterns on furnishing, photographs in magazines and from nature.

Most embroidery techniques share some basic design considerations. Although some people stitch creatively without first planning a design, it is a good idea, unless you are utterly confident in your own talent, to make a preliminary sketch. When you are satisfied with a few basic shapes, cut these out of newspaper. Cut the same shape out several times from different parts of the newspaper, in order to vary the tone. Lay these shapes on a sheet of white paper and move them around until you achieve a balance in tone and composition. You will find that the darker shapes seem heavier and these should not all go at the top of the design. The bottom should be slightly heavier in tone than the top, while each side should be roughly equal in tone. If there is any unevenness, the eye will better accommodate it in the righthand side. When you have decided on the composition, fix the shapes to the paper with pins or tape.

Use a colour wheel to work out the colour scheme. Lay your chosen fabric next to a colour scheme that appeals to you. You will find that the two colour schemes either side will blend beautifully. If you stitch with any or all of the colours in these five schemes, the result will be harmonious. If you want a more striking effect, incorporate colours which contrast those in the scheme, which will be opposite on the wheel.

Decide which shape is to be which colour. Lay tracing paper over the paper collage and mark the outlines through. When the tracing is complete, colour the outlines in using the appropriate colours.

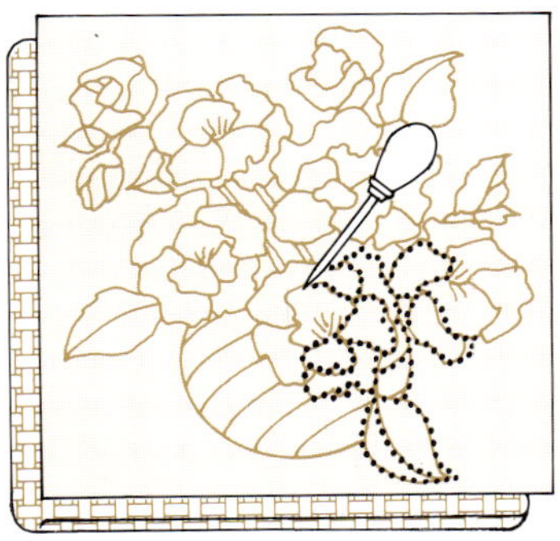

Pricking and pouncing 1. *Place the design on some newspaper or rags, and prick along the lines of the pattern with a pin or sharp implement.*

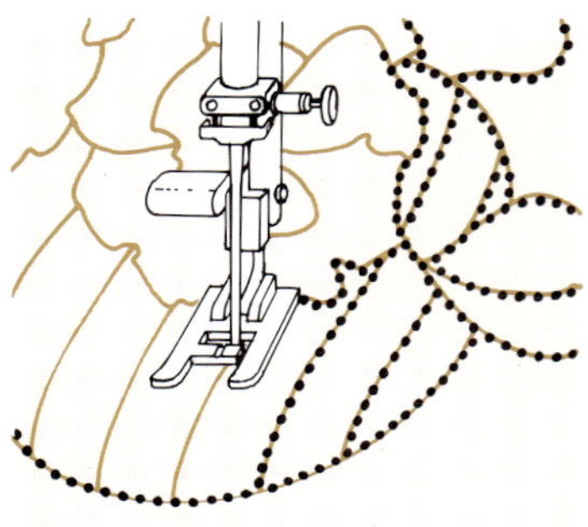

2. *The pricked holes must be fairly close together, so the process is time-consuming. It can be done more quickly with a threadless sewing machine.*

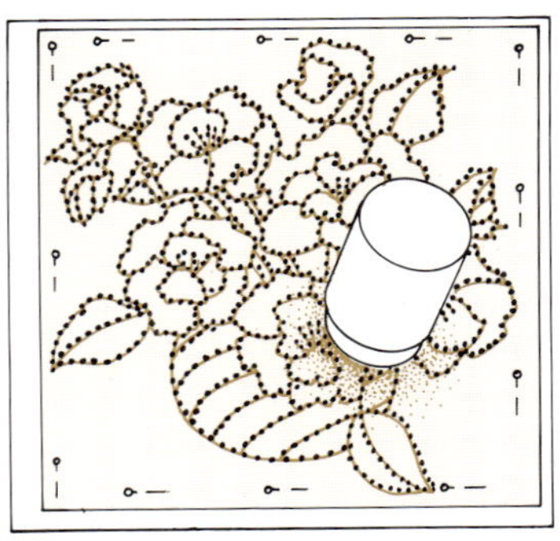

3. *Having pricked out the design on the pattern, pin it right side up onto the fabric. Use a small felt pad to rub special pounce powder over the holes.*

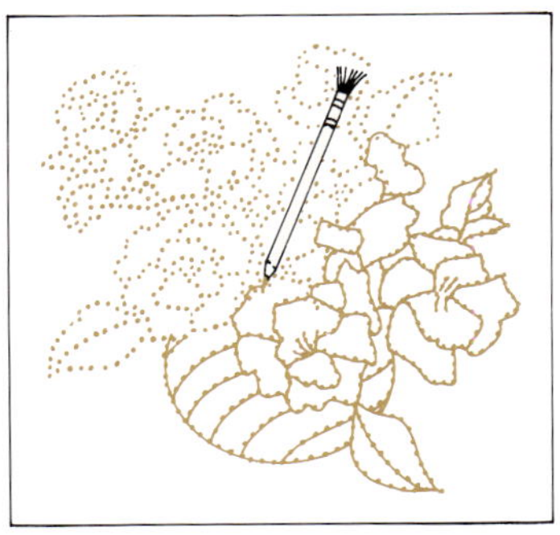

4. *Take the paper off very carefully so as not to blur the pounce powder. Join up all the small dots that have been marked with a dressmaker's pencil.*

Transpose this design to the fabric, either using the carbon method or the old-fashioned "prick and pounce" method. This involves making pinpricks around the outlines of the tracing, placing it above the fabric, and pushing a powder (pounce) through the outline holes.

Your design might not be the right size for your fabric. If this is the case, the most professional method of enlarging or reducing a design to the required size is with a pantograph, which can be obtained from an art supplier. This device is a complicated system of levers – follow the outline of your shape and, when the pantograph is set to the required size alteration, it draws the correct shape accordingly.

If you do not have a pantograph, you can use the blocking method of enlarging or reducing. Divide your drawing into quarters horizontally, and quarters vertically, to give sixteen equal shapes. Similarly, divide a piece of paper of the required size into sixteen shapes. Carefully copy the pattern in the top lefthand shape of the original pattern, drawing it in the top lefthand shape of the correctly sized paper. Continue until you transpose all the shapes' patterns.

If you want to transpose a freeform design to a chart, the easiest way is to lay a piece of graphed tracing paper over the drawing, and block off the design. A clear plastic sheet with marked graph can also be used instead of graphed tracing paper. Lay the plastic over the design and, noting where the pattern shows through the clear graph, copy it onto another piece of ordinary graph paper.

If you are making your own graphs, you might find curves and circles confusing. Use a compass or an appropriately shaped plate or saucer to draw the required curves and then block these off. If you are not sure whether to block off one or two squares at each "step" on the curve, it is better to do too few rather than make too many stitches. If you are still in doubt, stitch on the outside rather than the inside of the marked line.

To form a circle, first block off one-eighth of the whole. Segments either side of this first blocking are then mirror images of that blocking. Continue in this manner around the whole circle.

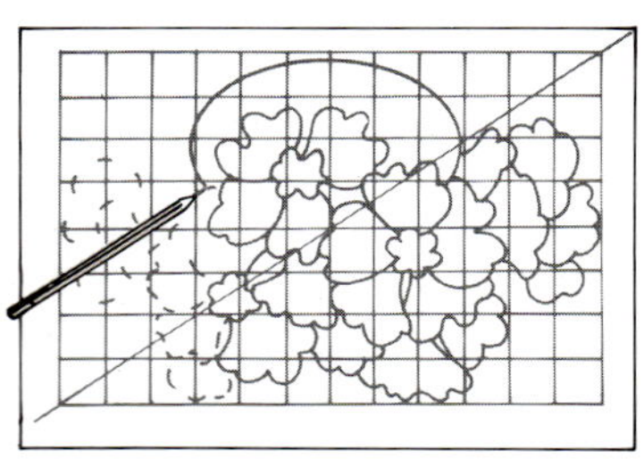

Enlarging and reducing patterns 1. *It is relatively easy to enlarge a pattern if it is on square paper. Box off the sides and draw in a diagonal as shown.*

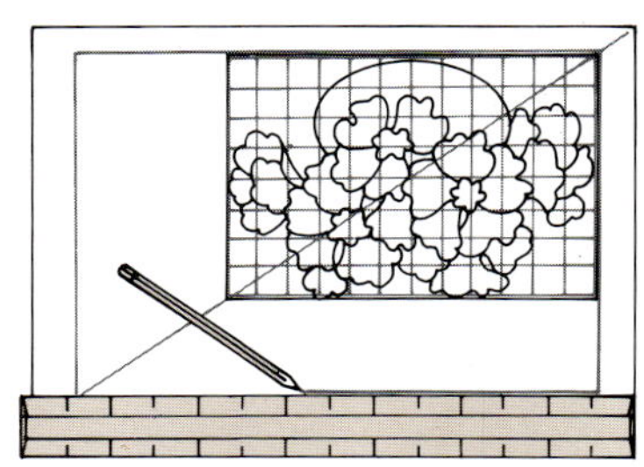

2. *Extend the diagonal to the new required height, and draw in the new sides to the design.*

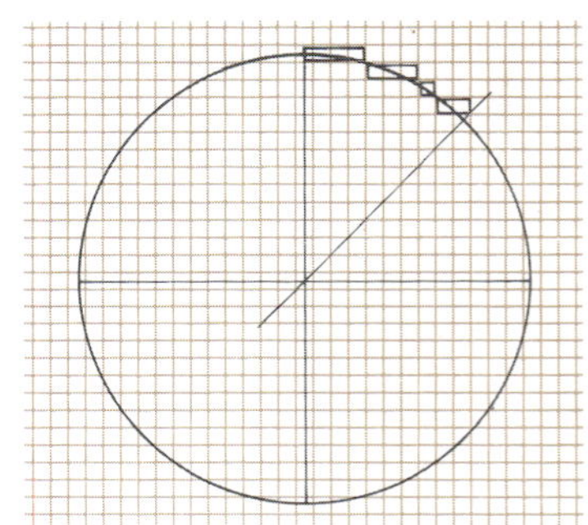

Curved designs 1. *Difficulties are often encountered in reproducing circular designs. Draw the proposed circle onto squared paper as eight segments.*

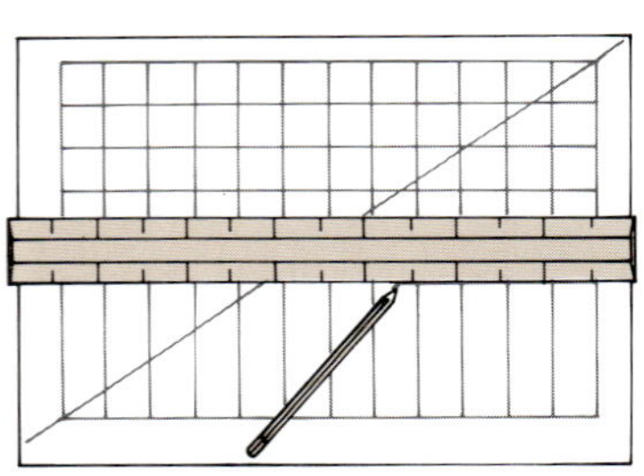

3. *Rule in the same number of squares as in the original design, and draw the design in square by square.*

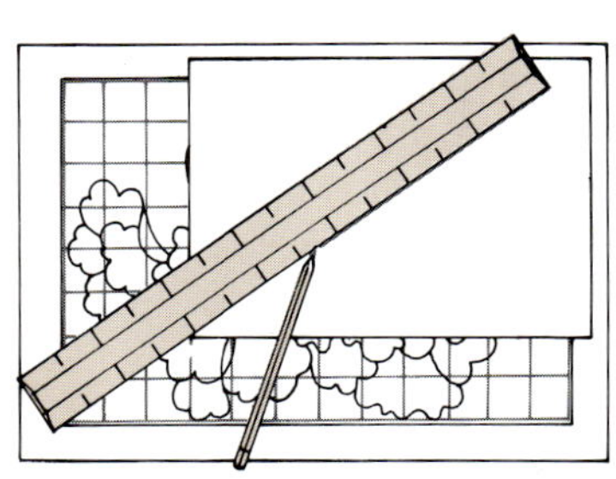

4. *Use the same procedure to reduce a pattern.*

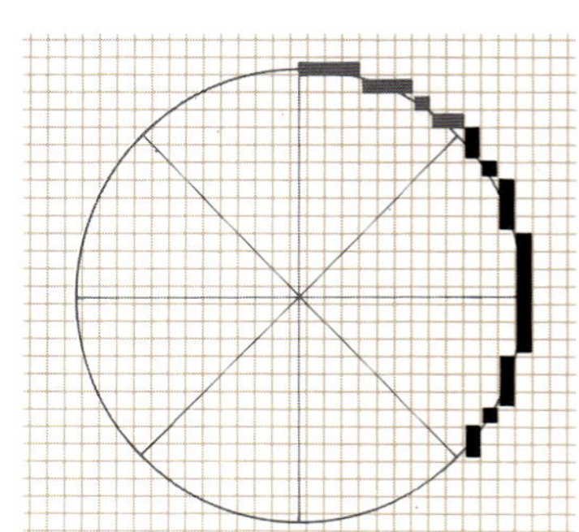

2. *Block round the curve, one section at a time, making each segment a mirror image of its opposite number. Block in less rather than more squares initially.*

Above *A silk cushion embroidered in orange and gold satin stitch on a black ground. The design is striking, and the leaves and petals have been executed with great fluidity.*

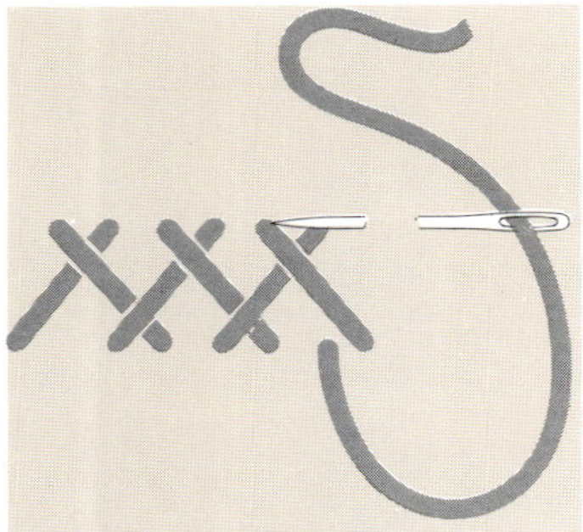

Herringbone stitch *Start at upper left and work rows of this stitch from left to right. Following rows fit neatly when worked directly below.*

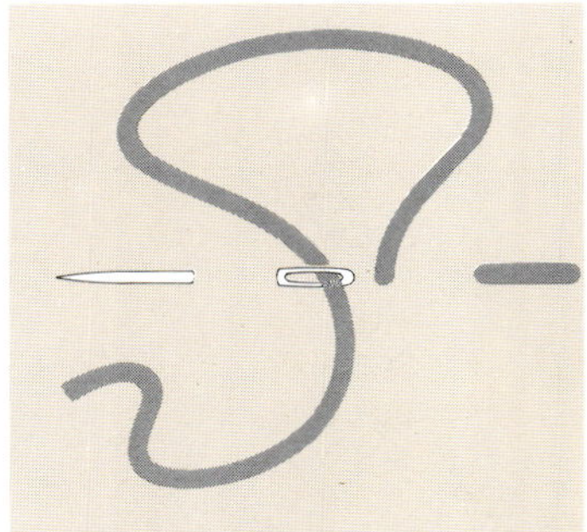

Running stitch *Work this from left to right. Several stitches can be picked up at once, before pulling the needle through.*

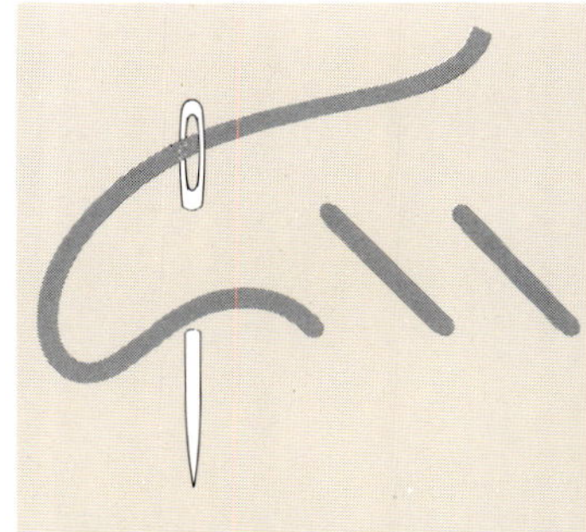

Cross stitch 1. *Work each row of cross stitches in two spans. First, stitch diagonal half crosses from right to left.*

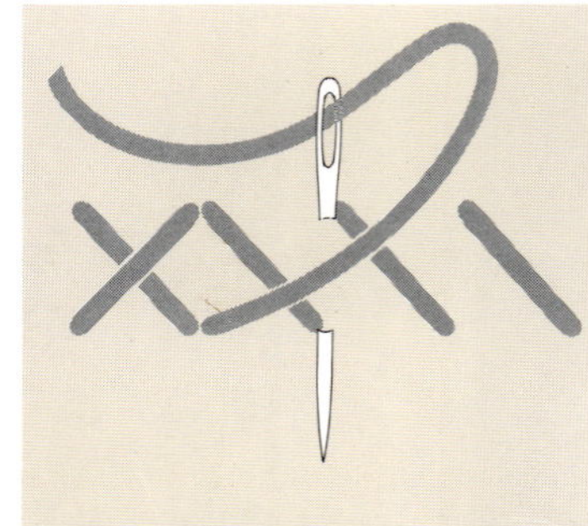

2. *Then work back from left to right, forming complete crosses. Stitch the next rows directly beneath the first.*

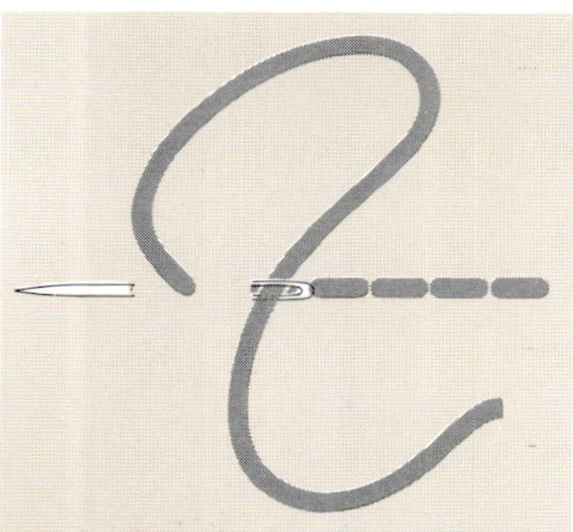

Back stitch *Having made a large stitch, begin the next halfway back along the line. Use the same stitch holes.*

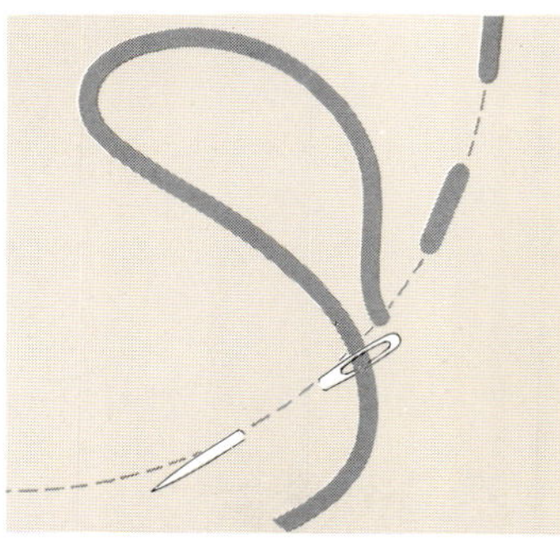

Double running stitch 1. *This is a simpler outline stitch, achieved with two lines of running stitch worked on top of each other.*

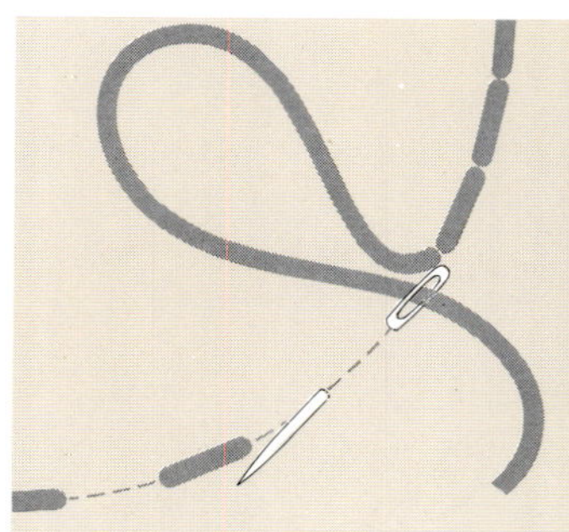

2. *The stitches of the second line on the right side of the material fill the gaps left by the first line.*

Chain stitch *Bring the needle through the fabric, reinsert it in the same hole and make a stitch with the thread caught under the needle point.*

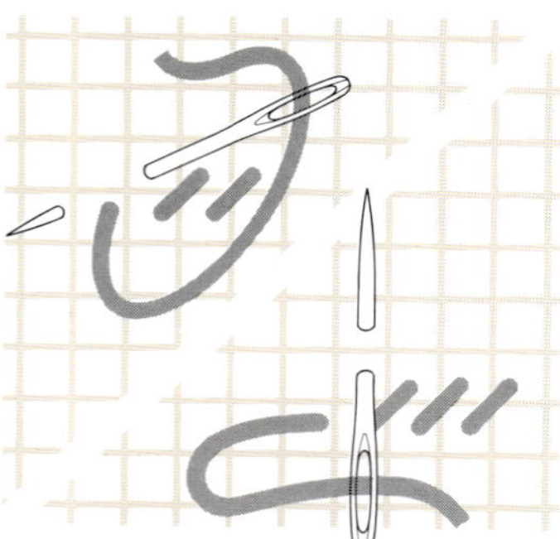

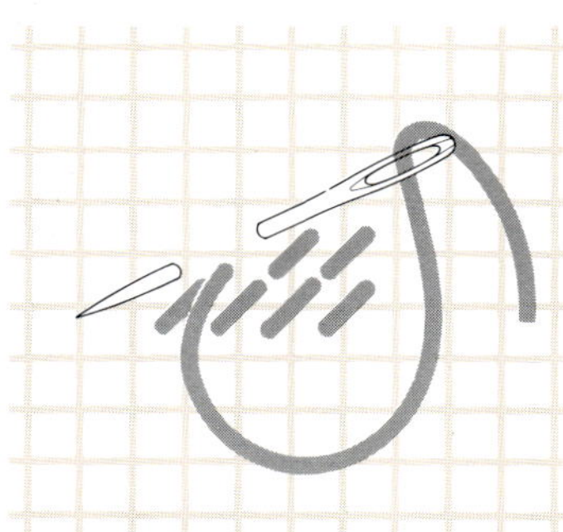

Tent stitch (horizontal) *Begin this canvaswork stitch at upper right, and work each row from right to left. At the end of each row, leave the needle vertical behind the canvas. Turn the canvas around, and stitch the next row directly in line with the previous row.*

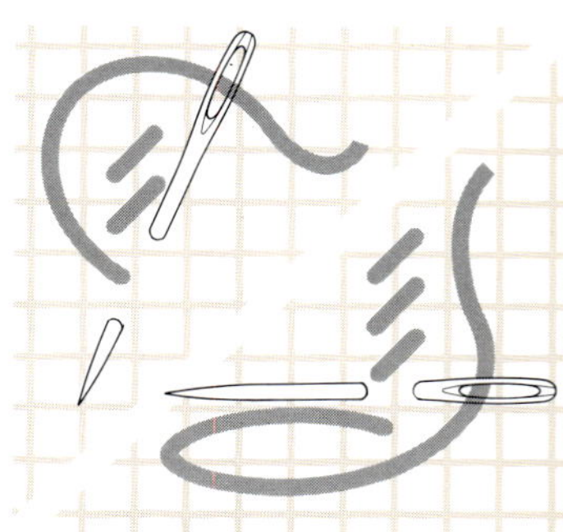

Tent stitch (vertical) *Begin at upper right and work down the canvas, row by row. At the end of each row, leave the needle horizontal behind the canvas. Turn the canvas around, and stitch the next row beside the first in the same way.*

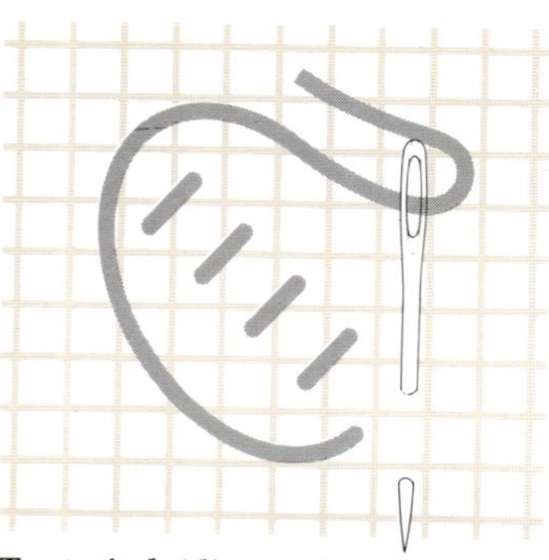

Tent stitch (diagonal) *Work this stitch alternately down and up the canvas. For downward stitches, hold the needle vertically between stitches.*

2. *Working up, hold the needle horizontally between stitches. Place stitches in diagonal rows, with one canvas hole between each.*

Satin stitch *Use this as a filling stitch, keeping stitches at an even tension. Work from left to right with the stitch slanting behind.*

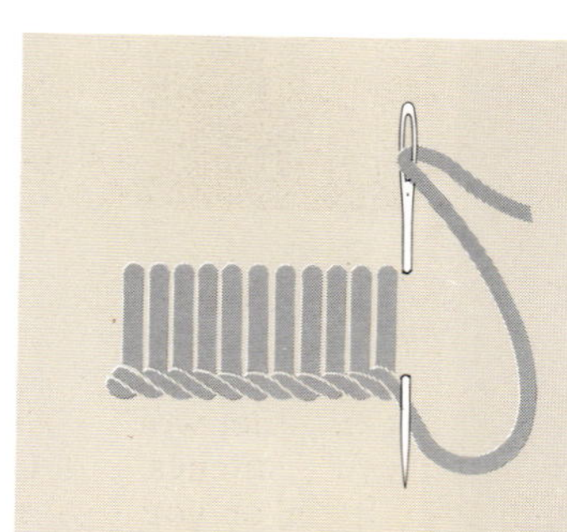

Buttonhole stitch *Work these stitches close together, from left to right. Make a downward stitch, looping the thread beneath the needle.*

Using a mirror *A small hand mirror can be used to convert instructions for righthanded needleworkers into lefthanded ones. Organize it as shown.*

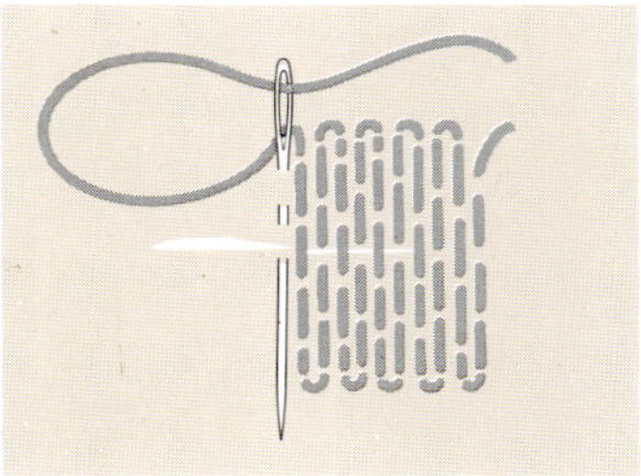

Mending *If there is a tear in your fabric, you can mend it with small tacking stitches worked up and down over it.*

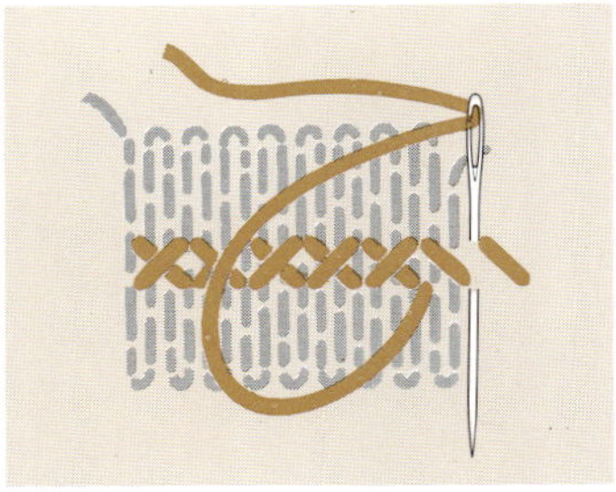

Once the tacking is in place, the desired stitches can be worked over the tacking.

Left *This canvaswork chair back is from one of a pair of eighteenth-century chairs at Belton House. Each animal, bird, leaf and branch has been beautifully outlined, and carefully shaded in muted greens.*

Mending

Many things can go wrong when you stitch. If you make an accidental snip in your fabric, you can either work one or two little holding darning stitches and subsequently stitch over them or you can add a small patch, either to the front or the back of the surface, and stitch over it. If you are working a crewel or raised work piece it might be better simply to add another motif, to cover the snip or hole.

Making up

If you have worked canvaswork pieces for a pair of slippers or panels for a fine evening bag, you should have these articles professionally made up. Simple canvaswork cushions can be made up at home.

For some other techniques, the sandwich method is ideal. After you have finished stitching, take the fabric off the frame or hoop and, depending on the type of stitching, press carefully. Lay the fabric on a backing of similar size, right sides in. Machine- or hand-stitch nearly all the way round the area, leaving a small area through which the shape can be turned right side out.

Such shapes turn much better right side out if you snip surplus off the seam corners before turning: snip almost but not quite to the stitching. If the shape is irregular or curved, cut small Vs in the surplus of any convex shape and simple slits in the surplus of concave parts.

Canvaswork

Left *The vast and impressive Bradford Table Carpet has a symmetrical central panel with a colourful border depicting a variety of scenes and figures from Elizabethan village life. Worked on fine canvas in silks, the carpet is sewn in tent stitch throughout.* **Above** *A detail from the carpet's border shows the lord and lady of the manor with their dog. The carpet is a fine example of early canvaswork, as well as affording fascinating historical insights.*

Canvaswork is any type of decorative needlework on canvas. It includes tent stitch, Florentine or Bargello and all forms of stitchery. "Needlepoint" is the usual term applied to canvaswork in the United States and is fast becoming the accepted word in Britain. However, needlepoint was originally a term applied in England to lace made with a needle rather than with bobbins.

"Tapestry" is a term frequently, and wrongly, applied to canvaswork, particularly pictorial pieces. Tapestry is basically a woven design.

History

In the sixteenth century, the Elizabethans started to adapt the designs of the medieval tapestries to canvaswork by working pictures in tent stitch using silks, wools and metal threads. Turkey work – wool knotted on a canvas ground and cut into a pile effect to give a hard-wearing luxury fabric – was one of the first techniques to be adapted by English needleworkers of the sixteenth century. The fabric was used to drape over long, plain oak tables and cupboards and for upholstering chairs. These table carpets and cupboard cloths, with their formal diaper patterns in traditional reds, blues and yellows, had previously been imported from the Near East, but they were extremely costly, and both professional and amateur needleworkers began to copy them with a needle on canvas. Very quickly, in the English adaptations, the stylized emblems within the diamond-shaped lozenges were softened and floral motifs introduced.

Contemporary inventories reveal that even large houses only had one or two chairs, kept for the master of the house and important guests. The rest of the household would have sat on wooden benches – hence, the large number of cushions, frequently embroidered on fine canvas, which also appear on the household lists of the period. Square cushions would have been used on chairs, long cushions on benches and window seats.

Tent stitch, with its strong construction covering every thread of canvas, was introduced at this time to simulate the expensive imported woven tapestries. Because of the inherent strength of this stitch, many pieces from this period have survived.

The great houses would have had at least one professional needleworker, probably a man, who would work the large pieces and also draw, prepare and help the ladies of the house with the smaller pieces, which they would work themselves as a pastime. Young girls were trained to embroider both as a practical skill and social accomplishment. Their standards were so high it is often difficult to decide whether work is from the needle of a professional or amateur.

Barbara Snook in *English Embroidery* raises a question as to the status of those who worked the Bradford Table Carpet:

"Has the central panel, worked in an all-over pattern of interlocking vines and grapes, been worked in a guild workshop and the wide borders, bursting with amusing detail of Elizabethan country life, been worked by members of the household for which it was destined?" The size – 13 feet 9 inches x 6 feet 9 inches (about 4 x 2 m) - and the fine canvas used (about 400 stitches to the square inch) means that working the carpet must have been a formidable task.

The border shows the fashionably dressed lord and lady of the manor, with their family and a church in the distance. Elsewhere in the border is the manor house surrounded by a moat, a charming picture of a shepherd chasing a wolf that is running off with a sheep, the mill with its water wheel and a man carrying a sack of flour to be ground, together with many other informative details of the period.

Moveable type printing had started in Germany in the fifteenth century and Elizabethan needleworkers were able to refer to herbals and bestiaries when planning a piece. The influence of these books can easily be seen in a great many pieces where the scale and proportion of animals and flowers have no relation to fact; the embroiderer obviously had never seen them.

The bed hangings of this period frequently had small canvas panels, worked with these flowers and animals in silk tent stitch, which

Top *The Judgement of Solomon as depicted on a canvaswork panel at Hardwick Hall in Derbyshire. It is one of a series, famous for the rich and beautiful French-style costumes worn by the figures. Although largely worked in tent stitch, buttonhole and satin stitch are also used to highlight some details on these costumes.* **Above** *Diana and Acteon, one of three panels also from Hardwick Hall, based on illustrations from Salomon's* La metamorphose de l'Ovide figurée. *Acteon surprises Diana bathing with her nymphs. She is angered and turns him into a stag.*

were then applied to large velvet panels with a border of couched metal thread to cover the edges. These hangings, such as the black velvet bed hangings at Hardwick Hall, proved popular. The ground fabric was much softer than canvas, they were faster to work and the newly available, rich Italian velvets set off superbly the detail of the small panels.

At this stage, certain pieces became associated with the name of the individual who worked them. Foremost among these was Mary, Queen of Scots, and although the vast majority of work attributed to Mary is unlikely to have been worked by her, the Oxburgh Hangings and two other pieces embroidered with her cypher survive. These were worked during the long period that she was held in captivity under the supervision of the Earl of Shrewsbury.

An inventory made in 1601 by Bess of Hardwick, the Earl's wife, and another famous needlewoman, lists all the items in the main rooms of Hardwick Hall; more than three and a half centuries later many of the things they prized still remain in the house. There are few comparable collections of Elizabethan embroidery. The majority of the items can be attributed to the workrooms if not the needle of Bess herself, as we know that she employed at least one professional embroiderer as well as a circle of ladies who would have stitched with her. The representation of Europa and the Bull, one of three long canvasworks with designs taken from Ovid's *Metamorphoses*, may have been worked by Bess as it has her cypher between the two figures on the right.

Bed hangings were important for keeping out the draughts in unheated rooms, and also because bedrooms were not the private places they are today. At the French court, the king's Levee was one of the social events of the day and in England too, the king and important statesmen would receive visitors in their bed chambers. In consequence, the bed linens, hangings and furnishings were grand and beautiful. They were frequently a family's most valuable possession.

The famous bed at Parham Park has a silk embroidered coverlet, headboard, headcloth and canopy dated 1585. These hangings were richly decorated in the Italian style, with coloured silks enriched by gold thread and pearls. The bed base, four outer curtains and three testers are in Hungarian point. These were worked in about 1615 using canvas only 9 inches (23 cm) wide; a charming barley-sugar stick design has been used to disguise the joins. The two designs, worked 30 years apart, blend extremely well together.

The Hungarian point wall hangings in the Green Anteroom in the same house, are worked on canvas 20 inches (51 cm) wide. It is possible to see the narrow strap design masking the joins in the canvas and the variation of the gold shade used for the background.

After the Restoration in 1660 when Charles II came to the throne, there was a period of good, if not luxurious, living. A new breed of gentlemen appeared; well-travelled and knowledgeable, they were keen to take part in the planning and decorative stages of the houses they built as

Right *Europa and the Bull, another of the three pieces now at Hardwick Hall based on Salomon's illustrations of Ovid. Jupiter disguised as a bull is abducting Europa, the King of Tyre's daughter. The initials on the righthand side of the panel are ES for Elizabeth Shrewsbury.* ***Far right*** *A formal garden at Villandry in France. Mazes and potagers (ornamental vegetable gardens) like this one lend themselves perfectly to canvaswork designs. Hedges and shrubs can be worked in stitches of differing textures, within the formal geometric shapes of the garden as a whole.*

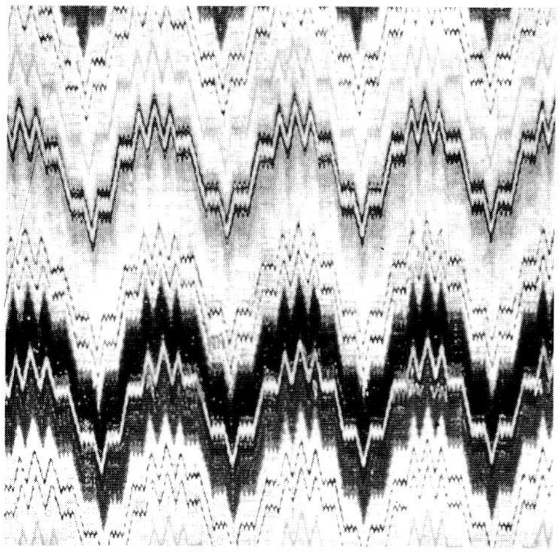

Far left *A detail from the bedhangings at Hardwick Hall that may have been worked by Mary, Queen of Scots.*
Left *A detail from the fine Hungarian Point wall hangings at Parham Park in West Sussex. Sewn on narrow strips of canvas, only 20 inches (51cm) wide, the joins are beautifully masked by the design.*

Above *A cushion from Hardwick Hall, generally thought to have been worked by Mary Queen of Scots. Herbals and bestiaries were often consulted by Elizabethan needleworkers as they planned their designs.*

suitable settings for the sculpture, paintings and curiosities they had acquired. The patronage of craftsmen was revived and the skills of builders and artisans increased rapidly.

Life became more comfortable and centred around the home. Fine furniture and silver was an investment; embroidery was the contribution of the ladies of the house. As furniture became more ornate, table carpets, used in early times to cover the plain oak furniture, started to be used as floor coverings.

Women of this period worked fancier projects than previously, such as firescreens, small pictures and seat covers. Woven fabrics had become more available and were used for larger furnishings. Biblical subjects taken from the Old Testament, with the people dressed in accurate representations of seventeenth-century costume, and the reigning monarch not infrequently portrayed as the main figure, became very fashionable to do.

When George I came to the throne in 1714, unable to speak any English, life at court changed. Gentlemen, other than the leading politicians, no longer needed to spend so much time in London and were free to expand their knowledge of art, literature and architecture. Travel to Italy increased, and more time was spent in the country houses, planning and decorating.

Some of the large houses had needlework rooms, where canvaswork panels, framed with elaborate carved mouldings were mounted on the walls. One such house, where fortunately the panels are still intact, is Wallington Hall in Northumberland. Lady Julia Calverley, who worked these panels, lived in Yorkshire and although one of the panels is dated 1717, they were not moved to Wallington until 1755. There is also a fine tent-stitch screen also worked by her with scenes from Hollar's engravings of Virgil's poems, the *Georgics* and *Ecologues*. The vast scale of the fruit compared to the figures in the foreground is amusing.

Thomas Chippendale (1718-1779) was only one of a number of excellent craftsmen working in London turning out fashionable designs. Together with a team of craftsmen, Chippendale made pieces of baroque furniture, then rococo designs introduced from France in the middle of the century, and, at the end of his career, he followed the architect Robert Adam's (1728-1792) neo-classical designs.

The Chippendale workshop sold carpets, stuffed mattresses and made upholstery. Chippendale also gave explicit instructions for the design of canvaswork he considered suitable for certain pieces. A chair in the Earl of Pembroke's collection has covers worked with figures in exotic costumes, animals, urns and flowers, closely following suggestions in the third edition of Chippendale's book, *The Gentleman and Cabinet Maker's Director* (1754). He also promised Lady Knatchbull, who had placed an order for some large "Barjair" chairs, that he would send a pattern for the seats in advance so that she could start on the needlework. He proposed using a green striped cotton for temporary coverings and suggested that these could be used to protect the needlework when it was fixed in place.

Towards the end of the eighteenth century, the designs of Robert Adam were fashionable. These were very delicate and feminine, with classical motifs. After 1780, he introduced painted furniture, especially in the "Etruscan" style; his Etruscan Room at Osterley Park has a red, green and black colour scheme, derived from the Greek vases that had been excavated at Pompeii shortly before.

George Hepplewhite brought Adam's designs to individual craftsmen everywhere in *The Cabinet-maker and Upholsterer's Guide* (1788) just as Chippendale's *Director* had earlier. He set out instructions for the upholstery, but with this lighter, carved and painted furniture, plain silks or simple stripes were more suitable than canvaswork.

In North America at this time, wives were expected to make a great many of the hangings and upholstered pieces used in their homes. As imports from England became unpopular after the War of Independ-

Above *One of the three Stoke Edith needlework hangings now in the Garden Room at Montacute House. The mountains in the background suggest a wild and more natural landscape outside the confines of the formal garden.*
Right *A detail from one of the panels in the needlework room at Wallington Hall. It was worked over a seven-year period by Lady Julia Calverley and her ladies, in Yorkshire, before being moved to Wallington in Northumberland.*
Far right *A coarser seventeenth-century piece that was probably worked by amateurs, with 40 stitches to the square inch.*

Above *An extremely solid wing chair, with canvaswork upholstery embroidered in 1760. The pattern is worked over the back of the chair and across the seat, and the colours have remained remarkably bright.*

ence, centres for fine furniture were set up in Philadelphia, Newport and Boston, creating a flourishing American industry.

By the end of the eighteenth century, a great many changes had taken place. Ready-made fabrics and furniture started to be available in greater quantities and, especially in the towns, people had a good choice of alternatives. Canvaswork was only used for firescreens, pictures and other small objects. The excellent training in all forms of needlework given to women in the past was no longer available, as other leisure pursuits took precedence.

From about 1815, Berlin woolwork became popular with the upper and middle classes on both sides of the Atlantic. Originally, Berlin woolwork was worked with soft, worsted wool on canvas, following a hand-coloured chart. As the craze grew, silks and beads were used to add highlights; turkey (plush) stitch was worked and then clipped to give a sculptural relief; chenille thread (a thick, furry thread) was used for special effects. Unfortunately, the standard of the materials and the subjects portrayed became increasingly poor. The canvas became coarser so women could increase their output of useless footwarmers, wall pockets and mantle borders (narrow pelmet-type shapes that were used to decorate the chimneypiece). With the introduction of aniline dyes after 1856 the colours grew markedly worse.

Not until 1862, when an International Exhibition was held in London, did good design reemerge in the traditional needlework crafts. At this exhibition, William Morris (1834-1896) exhibited publicly for the first time, and it was also the first time the Japanese had taken a stand at such an event to show their furniture and arts and crafts. In comparison with high Victoriana, these showed a simplicity and restraint which proved very influential.

William Morris had probably the greatest single influence on the regeneration of good design in domestic arts during the nineteenth century. With his associates, who included the artists Burne-Jones (1833-1898) and Rossetti (1828-1882), he developed a belief in the individual status of the artist and craftsman, and was determined to break down the barriers between those who practised fine and applied arts. The Aesthetic Movement, which grew from these beginnings, aimed to use craft processes rather than mass manufacture in fostering functional designs, and to make these views known to the general public.

In 1872, the School of Art Needlework (now the Royal School of Needlework) was founded in London by Queen Victoria's third daughter, Princess Christian of Schleswig-Holstein. One of its main aims was "restoring Ornamental Needlework to the high place it once held among the decorative arts". William Morris was among those who designed projects for the school.

In 1876, the Royal School of Needlework sent an exhibition to the Philadelphia Centennial. This prompted Candice Wheeler to set up the New York Society of Decorative Arts, with the help of Louis C. Tiffany, among others. Together with the newly formed Needlework and Textile Guild of Chicago, the Society provided encouragement to other arts and crafts groups throughout America, with the aim of creating a national and enduring style of needlework. About the same time, the Boston Museum of Fine Arts established a school for art needlework to promote the artistic aspects of the craft.

In 1900, Lewis F. Day (1845-1910) wrote a book called *Art in Embroidery* in which he stated that "Nothing is more futile than to put it [the art of needlepoint] to anything like pictorial purpose. The wonderfully wrought pictures in tent stitch, for example, bequeathed to us by the seventeenth century, are painful object-lessons in what not to do". He believed that canvaswork should be recognized and enjoyed for what it is, and used to its greatest potential as a geometric, angular art-form and its purpose should not be confused with that of art in painting.

In 1920, the Embroiderers' Guild was established in England; membership was open to embroiderers all over the world. The Guild initially had many members in the United States, but soon after, the Embroiderers' Guild of America was set up as an independent body.

The first president of the Embroiderers' Guild, Louisa Pesel, was also the leader of the Winchester Broderers who worked cushions and kneelers for Winchester Cathedral between 1931 and 1936. This project was the first of many church projects all over the world; other notable examples include the projects for Wells Cathedral and for Washington Cathedral in the United States.

Canvaswork has enjoyed a reawakening of interest in the last 20 years. Many guilds have become established and traditional techniques have been reexamined. A major feature of this renewal is the willingness to experiment with techniques, stitches and materials, often combining canvaswork with other forms of needlework in the same piece.

Above *One of the series of cushions and kneelers worked by the Winchester Broderers for Winchester Cathedral between 1931 and 1936. The project was organized by Louisa Pesel, who was president of the Embroiderers' Guild in the early 1920s. The background of this kneeler has been worked in long-legged cross stitch.*

Right *A detail from a canvaswork cushion cover at Hardwick Hall in Derbyshire. It is one of many pieces of Elizabethan needlework, beautifully worked and still in good condition, that can still be seen there.*

Materials and Equipment

Of all needlework techniques, canvaswork probably needs to be made the most hard-wearing as it is most often used for items which receive a great deal of use. A patchwork or appliqué bedspread can be folded up every evening, a dress with smocking or whitework will probably only be worn occasionally, silk embroidery often just hangs on the wall, but a piano stool, set of dining chairs, or even cushions worked in canvaswork, will be used constantly.

Always plan your projects carefully and buy the best possible materials. When you compare the cost of the canvas and wools with the number of hours that you will be stitching, the materials represent a small part of the result. By buying the best possible materials you will enjoy the project more, it will look better when complete and will last longer.

Canvas

Most canvas is made from cotton but there are exceptions. Linen canvas is available in 13 and 17 mesh and is the best for pulled thread stitches. Polyester canvas, though not widely available, is very soft and good for clothing or pieces that need to be gathered. Silk gauze, which is available in

Left *A charming piece of canvaswork, produced as a kit. The design is both droll and ingenious, and the overall effect is very pleasing. Such a kit would be ideal for needleworkers not sufficiently confident to draw up their own designs.*

Below *The designs on this cushion cover and box were inspired by the layout of the formal garden at Villandry in France. The cushion is worked in very muted tones of blue, cream and brown, while the box features brighter yellows, purples and pinks.*

guages up to 72 mesh, is the one to use for very fine work. Plastic or PVC canvas comes in 7 and 10 mesh sheets as well as circles, hexagons and squares. It is rigid, so that baskets or boxes can be made by joining pieces together. Children enjoy using plastic canvas because it is easy to hold.

The standard cotton canvas is available in white and ecru. White is more satisfactory for working with pale colours; ecru is better for dark colours because the canvas is not so likely to show through the yarn. With very dark colours it may be necessary to paint the canvas to match, to avoid any pale canvas threads showing.

Canvas comes in various widths; check the widths available in the mesh you need and take the most economical for the particular project, for example a yard (about 91 cm) of 36-inch (91 cm) or 40-inch (102 cm) wide canvas will make four good cushions, whereas a yard of 27-inch (69 cm) will not.

Look for canvas with tightly twisted round threads, and no knots or irregularities in the thickness of the threads. There are two main types of canvas: Penelope and Mono.

Penelope (double thread canvas) should be used when working a large piece of canvas and you wish to work the background and border in a large tent stitch over the double thread, and give finer detail to the main subject area by working small tent stitches over single canvas threads.

Penelope canvas is also used in kits that have been trammed, that is, when threads of the right colour have been run across each area to indicate the colour that the tent stitch should be worked on top. Some people believe this double thickness of wool makes the work wear better, but this is not necessarily the case.

Mono is a single thread canvas. It is available in evenweave and interlock constructions which have different uses. With evenweave (which is the canvas stocked by most suppliers), the single horizontal and vertical threads are woven over and under each other; this canvas has a certain amount of give and is the right choice for all upholstery, cushions and pulled thread work.

Interlock canvas has two vertical threads bonded, not woven, round each horizontal thread; it is more stable and can be trimmed very close to the finished work without unravelling. It is good for small objects, where the seams are bound with an overcasting stitch which is part of the pattern, or when the edges of the canvas are bound with another material.

The gauge of a canvas is the number of threads which can be stitched in an inch (2.5 cm); for example, 14 mesh canvas will have 14 threads to every inch. Larger mesh canvas has fewer threads to the inch and does not give so much detail in the same sized piece because the stitches are larger. On the other hand, 24 mesh, which is the finest of the readily available canvases, would be excellent for realistic shading or work in silks. If, when working from a chart, you use a larger mesh canvas than suggested, it will automatically increase the finished size; conversely, a finer canvas will reduce the size of the completed piece.

Thread

Wool The wools most widely available and suitable are Paternayan's Persian and Appleton's crewel. Persian yarn consists of three strands of two-ply wool, which is loosely twisted and can be separated easily. Appleton's crewel is produced in individual strands of one ply, each strand being slightly thinner than an individual strand of Persian yarn. Three strands of crewel are needed for

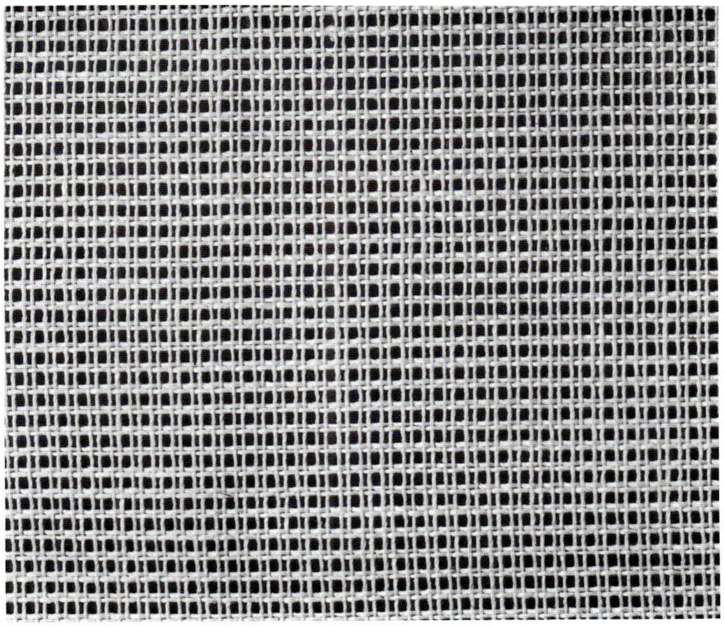

Far left *A selection of canvases, including: very fine silk gauze with 48 meshes to the inch, plastic canvas and interlock canvas. They are all pictured life-size. Beginners should not attempt to work a fine gauge canvas until confident on the medium meshes.* ***Above left*** *Mono canvas of the evenweave variety. It is very popular, and appropriate for most canvaswork items.* ***Below left*** *Penepole canvas. The double weave can be useful, if two different sized stitches are being used extensively in a piece of work.*

Left *Blunt tapestry needles of various sizes.*

as efficient a coverage as two strands of Persian yarn on the same mesh canvas. The number of strands to use depends on the size of the canvas mesh, and the type of stitch. The thread should always cover the canvas easily.

Look at both ranges, if possible, when selecting a colour scheme. Although Appleton's crewel wools tend to have a more muted range and Paternayan bolder colours, some crewels have exciting, clear hues and you may find some subtle shades of Persian yarns. Both types can be worked on the same canvas.

It is important to obtain the right amount of wool from the same dye lot because dye lots can vary and the difference will show in a large area of one colour. As a rough guide, 14 inch (36 cm) square sampler cushions take approximately 5 ounces (142 g) on 14 mesh canvas. When planning a large piece or a matching set of furnishings, it is worth working a test area in the stitch on the same mesh canvas and calculating the full amount you will need.

If it seems likely that the yarn will run out, despite careful planning, take the remaining hank of wool to the shop for matching. Having found the nearest colour match, introduce it gradually into the work, a strand at a time every so often. This will make the transition as unnoticeable as possible.

Crewels are sold by the ounce (28 g) and by the small skein; they are cheaper by the ounce if you need anything more than the

Left *A variety of stranded cottons from different manufacturers. They should always be stripped, that is separated out and reassembled in the required combination, to avoid a messy finish.* ***Below left*** *Embroidery silks should be dry-cleaned rather than washed. The two top skeins are Au Vere a Soie, that can be obtained in hanks of different weights. On the spools underneath, the twisted thread is Soie Oval, and the smooth is Soie Gobelin. These are available in a smaller range of colours than the Au Ver à Soie.*

Below *A detail from one of a pair of contemporary pieces, worked by Lady Mark Fitzalan Howard, to adorn antique ormulu bell-pull ends. Beads, metal threads and silk embroidery have been used, set off by areas of smooth diagonal tent stitch. The work is still in progress, but eventually antennae will be added to the larger butterflies.*

smallest quantities. By cutting a length at each end of the skein you have a working length for 14/18 mesh canvas. Paternayan is often already cut but about 30 inches (76 cm) is best to work with. If the canvas is fine, shorter lengths will be easier. Persian is sold by the ounce, the half ounce and, in some places, by the thread.

Medici wool is now also available in both the United States and Britain. Although it has a much smaller colour range, its muted shades can produce an unusually smooth finish.

Stranded cottons These are made of six strands of embroidery floss and can be used to highlight wool, or on their own. They always need stripping to enable the strands to lie flat and give good coverage when a suitable number of strands are combined. The number of strands to use varies with the mesh of the canvas. A length of about 25 inches (63 cm) is easiest to work with. Two-ply perle cotton is also available, and gives a light sheen to canvaswork.

Silks Like stranded cottons, silks should always be stripped before use. Three brands are now widely available. Au Ver à Soie is a seven-stranded silk, usually available in gramme measurements – in 2 g and 12 g skeins – in an extensive colour range with a choice of shades. This brand needs to be dry cleaned. A second brand, Gobelin, comes in 55 yard (50 m) tubes, and Oval, a third brand, in 33 yard (30 m) tubes. These both have the same range of 59 colours.

Metallic threads There is a great potential for experimenting while doing canvaswork; metallic threads provide an exciting challenge. Most of the metallic threads which can be used on fabrics can be successfully added to canvas work. Some of them can be stitched through, others need to be couched with a finer thread to the surface.

Before using any, consider the purpose of your work. Some metallic threads are washable and do not tarnish, but not all. Others are apt to unravel, but by using a needle-threader the head of the filament is not damaged and there is less chance of the whole length unwinding. Any metallic or twisted fabric lies more comfortably in a needle with a slightly larger eye, so take the next size up of tapestry needles to the size recommended for the particular canvas. If a particular metallic thread unravels despite these precautions, dip the head of the thread into clear nail-varnish and allow to dry before threading it.

Frames

Canvaswork is no exception to other forms of needlework: it is better to use a frame. The canvas is easier to see and does not get distorted, which is especially important when working different stitches on one piece, as they all have different stresses. Also the work stays cleaner and the finished piece looks infinitely better. If you choose a frame on a stand, you can use two hands which makes working faster and smoother because of the even pull on the thread.

Other equipment

Paletters are helpful when working in a close colour range. Palette shapes or simple rings in wood, plastic or stiff card can be used to give clear ideas of shade ranges and colour comparisons.

You will need a large pair of scissors for cutting the canvas and wool, and small sharp-pointed or curved scissors for the needlework. For cutting out, rippers are quick, but great care must be taken to avoid cutting canvas threads. It is easier to cut wools on the back of the canvas where there is more wool to get at. Once the stitches have been cut, a pair of tweezers will help to pull out the strands.

Needles

Tapestry needles are recommended for use in canvaswork, being specially made with blunt points to slip between the canvas threads without splitting them. Choosing the size from a range between sizes 14 and 26 depends on the mesh of the canvas and the thickness of the yarn. The needle must pass through the holes comfortably without dislodging them, and at the same time the yarn must pass through the eye easily to avoid friction and unravelling. During work, move the end of the yarn to different positions in the needle eye to avoid one section of the yarn going thin. A useful type of needle is a laying needle, which helps to make silks and stranded cottons look smooth.

Needle-threaders are handy and protect the ends of the threads. There are two types. One has a thin wire loop which is good for silks or threading a beading needle but not strong enough for wool; the other, more difficult to find in Britain, is a thin piece of metal with a small hole at either end, and is suitable for wool.

Left *Wools for canvaswork fall into three main categories: Fine wools such as Medici wool and Appleton's crewel (**left**); thick wools not easily divisible (**centre**); and wools such as American, Persian or Twilley's which can be divided (**right**).*

Guidelines for stitching a range of evenweave canvases

canvas mesh	available in plastic	available in interlock	resulting use	needle size	number of wool strands to use	number of stranded cotton strands to use	number of silk strands to use	number of strands of other threads
24			needle painting and shading	24	1 Persian or 1 crewel	3	2	1 Balger fine filament
18		yes	needle painting, shading and Florentine designs	22	1 Persian or 2 crewel	5	4	1 Balger 16
16			Florentine designs	20	Persian not satisfactory 3 crewel	6	5	1 Twilley's Goldfingering 1 Balger 16
14		yes	geometric designs	20	2 Persian 3 crewel	9	7	1 Twilley's Goldfingering 1 Coats soft cotton
12		yes	rugs	18	2 Persian 3 crewel			
10	yes	yes	children's work or quick decorative work	18	3 Persian 4 crewel			2 Twilley's Goldfingering
7	yes		children's work or quick decorative work	16	4 Persian 5 crewel			

Use an extra strand for straight stitches, and when working black strands on a white canvas.
Use a larger size needle when stitching with metallic threads or for pulled thread work.

Techniques

Design

Mrs. A.H. Christie in her book *Samplers & Stitches* (1920) states,

> In the art of embroidery, the question of design is so interwoven with that of technique that pattern planning, if approached in the right way, grows almost unconsciously out of the study of stitches. It will be found upon experiment that many stitches can introduce new ideas for design. The worker is urged, when thinking over a new piece of work, either simple or complex, to take some characteristic stitches and do what can be done with them, rather than to make a design with pencil and brush and then see what stitches can be adapted to working it out. The former method is fairly certain to result in a true embroidery design; the latter sometimes looks as if it had been stitched with difficulty, and would perhaps have been better if painted with the brush.

Sometimes, however, an embroiderer may particularly wish to copy a picture, or want to reproduce a scene from real life. This approach to design, called "needle painting", generally includes a naturalistic rendering of the motif, whether it is a flower, an animal or a rural scene. The "geometric" designs are often based on the contrast between stitches and textures, as well as the colours and patterns in which they are worked. Before choosing the stitches, and the design to suit the stitches, it is worth considering the purpose for the finished item. If it is to be a picture to hang on the wall, then the stitches may be of varying tensions and textures; if, however, it is to be a cushion cover, it probably needs to have more hardwearing stitches. The type of stitches used will influence the design; except in "pictorial" canvaswork they are the most important aspect of the embroidery.

Pictorial These designs are usually worked in tent stitch; a combination of different stitches can be used but if there is also a combination of different colours the

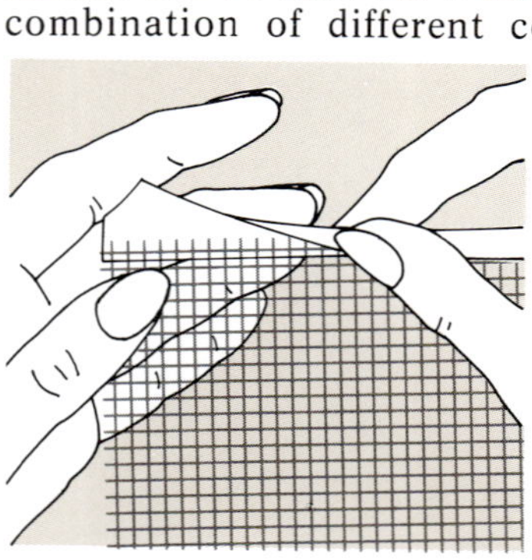

Binding the canvas *If the canvas has not been stretched onto a frame for working, the edges are liable to fray. This can be prevented by binding the edges with tape.*

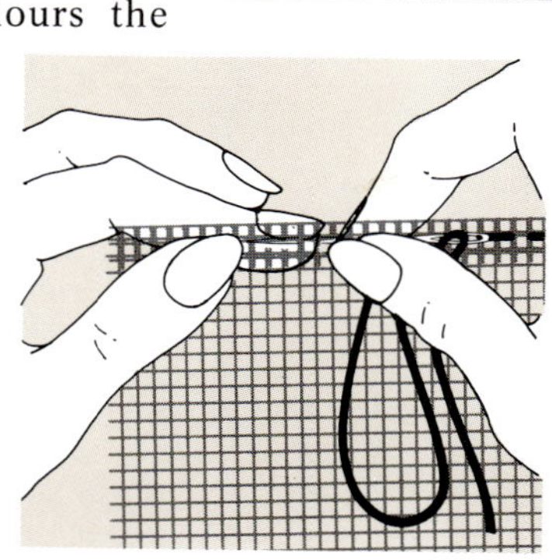

Tacking the canvas *Alternatively the edges of the canvas can be tacked down to prevent fraying. Fold the edges over and stitch them all the way round.*

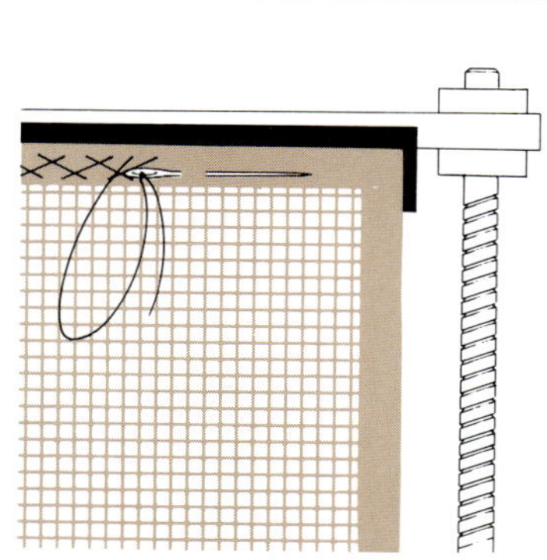

Mounting straight-sided frames
1. *It is important to get the canvas evenly stretched before starting the design. Sew the fabric onto the webbing of both rollers.*

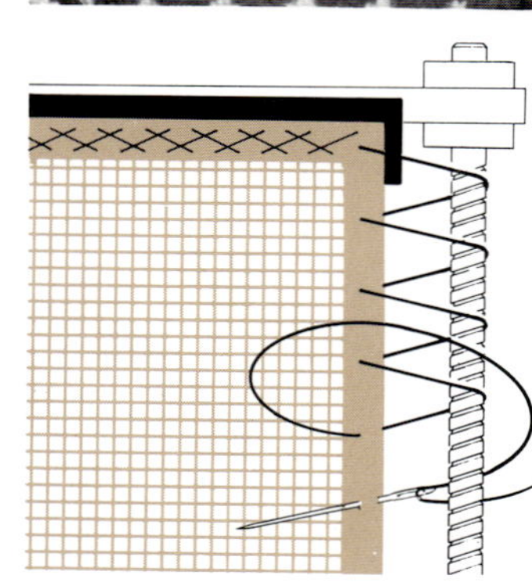

2. *Then fit the rollers into their slots and adjust until the canvas is taut. Use a needle and tough thread to lace the remaining two sides of canvas firmly onto the stand.*

finished motif may look overworked. Variations of stitchery are usually more successful on a "primitive" or stylist piece. Tent stitch is suitable for detailed, even realistic-looking embroideries, because of its even texture and the small size of these stitches, which allow outlines to look curved and soft.

If you are working from a painting, study the colours and shadows within the colours carefully. It may help to do an outline drawing of the subject, labelling leaves and petals for example, and marking patches of light and shade. Consider adjoining petals or other details, and if their outlines need emphasizing, it may be worth making the appropriate juxtaposing colours stronger or paler. A canvas with a fine mesh allows the outlines of the flowers to be soft and rounded, while the rigid structure of the canvas helps the design to be exactly balanced if desired.

If a floral design is desired, it is worth remembering, when stitching, to complete a flower at a time. In a leaf, the vein should be worked first. Petals, leaves and stems can all be stitched in the direction of their growth, which adds a touch of realism as well as producing a more interesting result due to the light catching stitches of different directions in different ways. The background, which should be worked last, can be stitched in skip tent, which is a stitch that only covers alternate threads of the canvas, adding a subtle sheen and texture to the canvas without appearing too heavy.

Left *A teaching piece that uses a wide variety of stitches and techniques to depict Anne Hathaway's cottage. The windows have been worked in pulled thread, with couched thrums (rug remnants) for the path and roof. Silk, beads and wool have all been incorporated.*
Far left *A detail from a hearth rug worked by Lady Mark Fitzalan. The insects are predominantly golds and yellows on a dark brown ground, and the piece demonstrates very clearly the use of a Penelope weave canvas for stitches of two different sizes.*

Shading is used to make the subjects look realistic. Having stripped all the yarns, soft colour changes can be made by mixing strands of lighter and darker shades in the needle at the same time. Never mix two contrasting colours as the result will be "tweedy" and obvious.

If you want to make a sampler for a special occasion, you can include the name of the recipient, or dates, or a picture of a house if it has a distinctive outline or features. A picture that hangs on the wall does not receive any wear so surface stitchery and beads can be added for special effects.

Geometric designs are perfect for textural or ornamental stitchery. Often they originate from squares, triangles, hexagons or columns; from patchwork patterns or Edwardian tiled floors. Geometric designs are formed either by the shapes of the stitches, the shapes of areas of stitches or the shapes of areas of colour. Where a single colour is used, it is important to balance and select the stitches, to create interesting contrasts and complements, and perhaps offset the design with panels of pulled thread. Where brighter colours are used, fewer different stitches are needed.

To learn techniques for this type of embroidery it is best to follow design charts, which allow the beginner to concentrate on the stitchery without worrying about the shapes of areas. When going on to design, it is important to remember a few basic points. Use small stitches when working a small area, and larger ones if there is a lot of space. Balance the shape as well as the scale of the stitches: square stitches for square areas, diamond (for example, diamond leaf) for diamond, and corner triangles can have their directional diagonal accentuated by Milanese or Oriental stitches. Textured areas are set off well by a background of diagonal tent. Stitches worked in one colour can be interestingly juxtaposed by two-colour areas. The whole design, its textures and colours, should look coordinated and balanced within itself.

More sophisticated designs can be found in oriental rugs, although, however complex

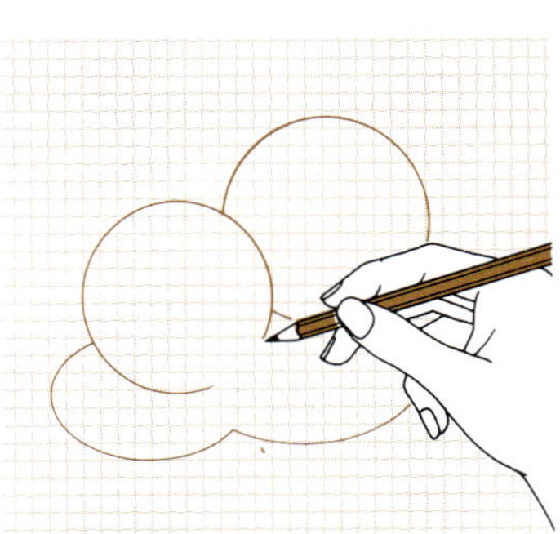

Marking a design on canvas 1. *You can mark the design directly on the canvas with a Nepo marker, paint or pencil.*

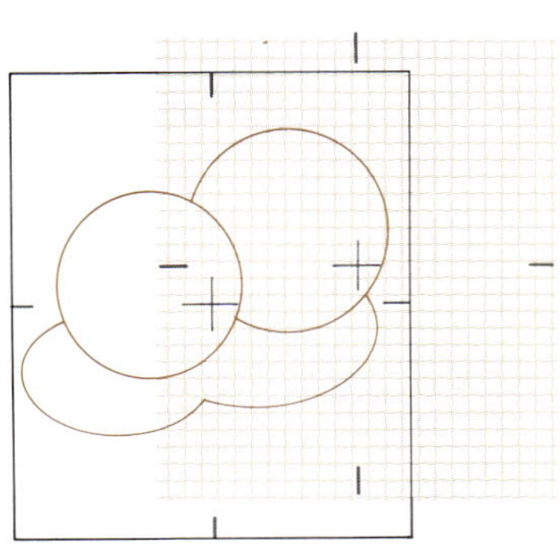

2. *Otherwise mark the canvas with the design underneath, visible through the canvas. First find the centre of the canvas.*

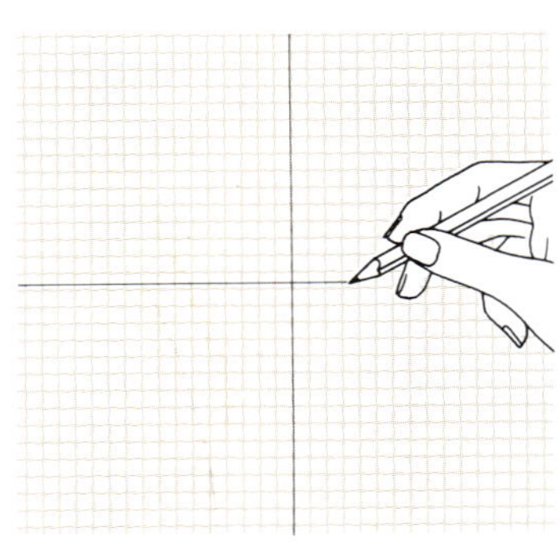

3. *Mark the centres of the canvas and the design and draw horizontal and vertical lines through them.*

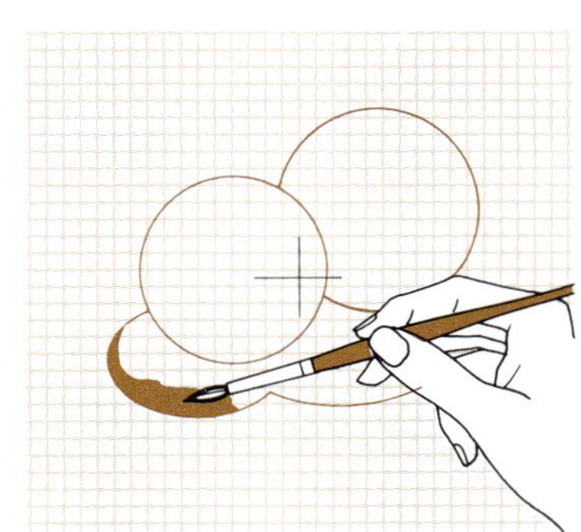

4. *Having placed the centres together, mark the design on the canvas using paints, a Nepo or thread.*

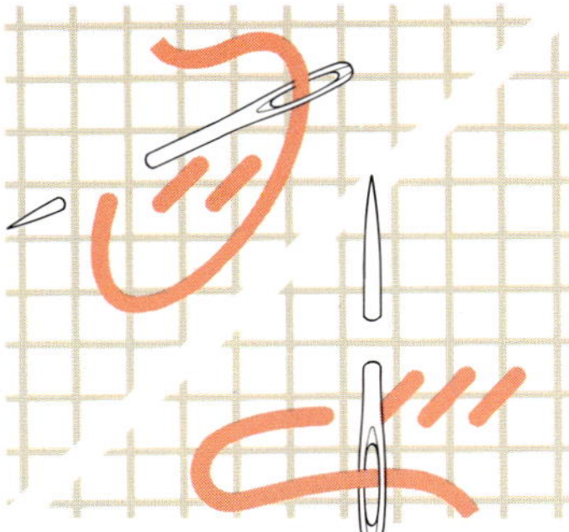

Tent stitch (horizontal) 1. *This stitch produces an even and closely shaded surface and is appropriate for a variety of different designs. Always work it from right to left.*

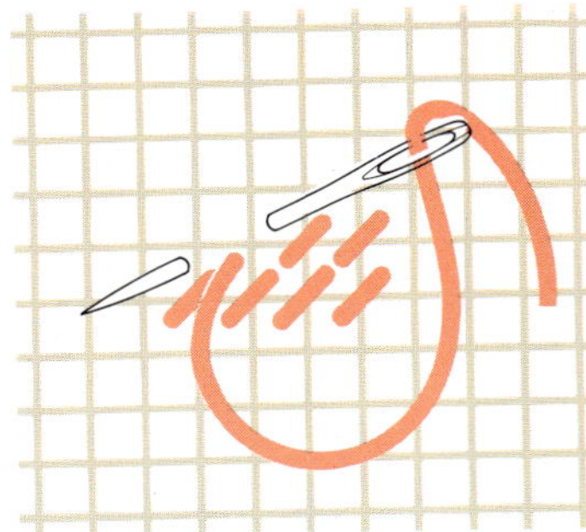

2. *When the first row has been completed, push the needle through to the back, turn the canvas through 180° and begin the second row. Repeat at the end of each row.*

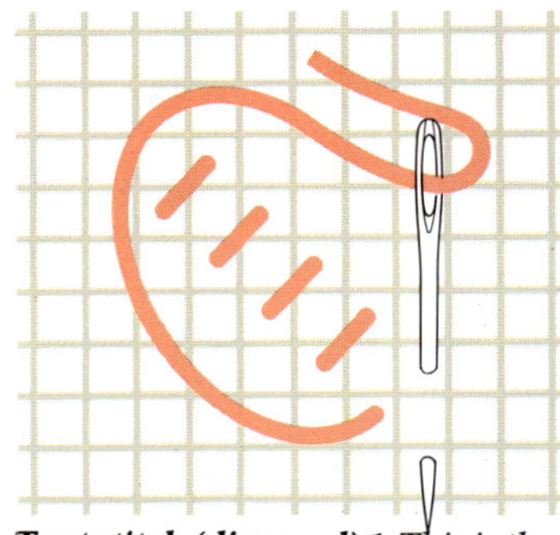

Tent stitch (diagonal) 1. *This is the most popular contemporary way of working tent stitch. Place the stitches diagonally down the first row, one canvas hole apart.*

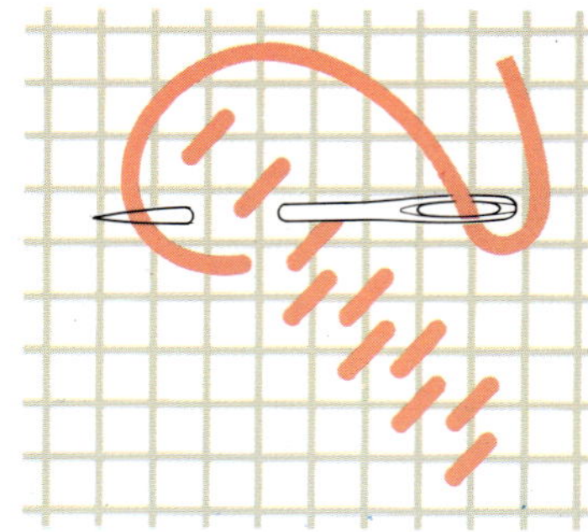

2. *For the second row, work diagonally back up the canvas, placing these stitches between those of the first row. Continue working rows down and then up the canvas.*

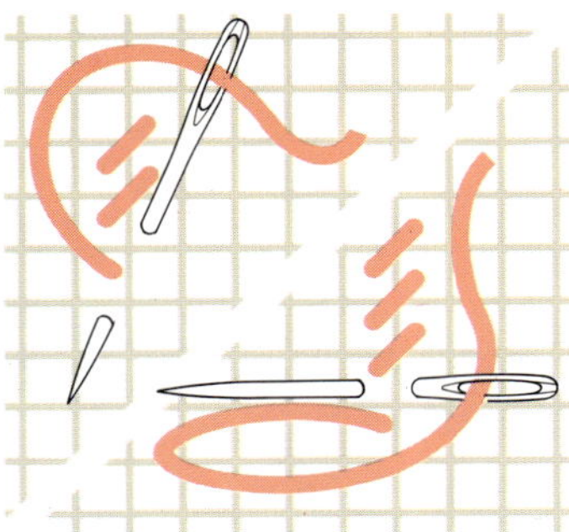

Tent stitch (vertical) 1. *The same stitch can also be worked downwards if this is preferred. At the end of each row the needle must be pushed through to the back.*

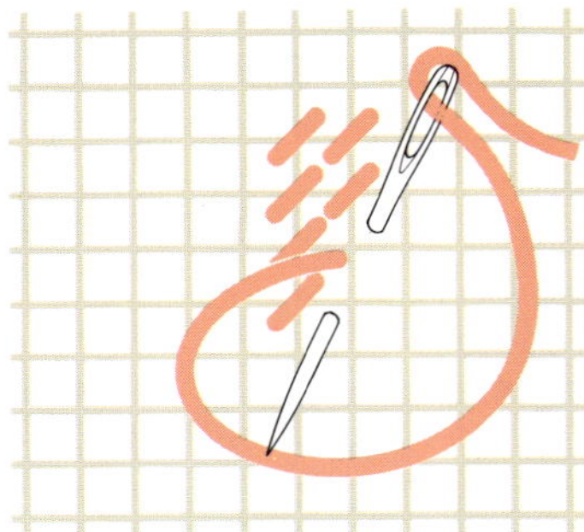

2. *Having completed the first row, the canvas must be turned through 180°, and the second row worked downwards like the first. Repeat for subsequent rows.*

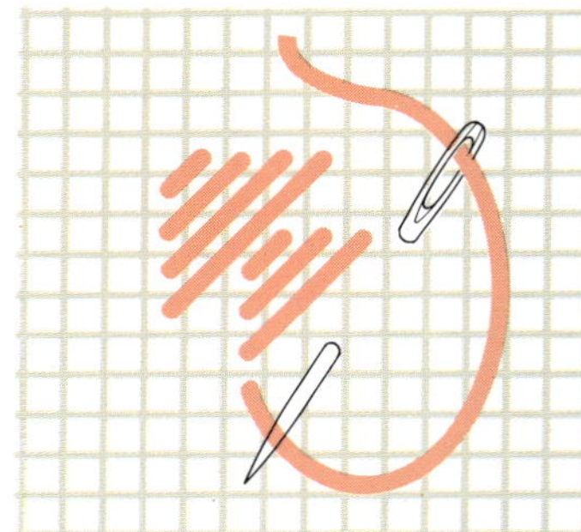

Milanese stitch 1. *This stitch is formed from interlocking rows of triangular-shaped blocks of four stitches. Work downwards diagonally from left to right.*

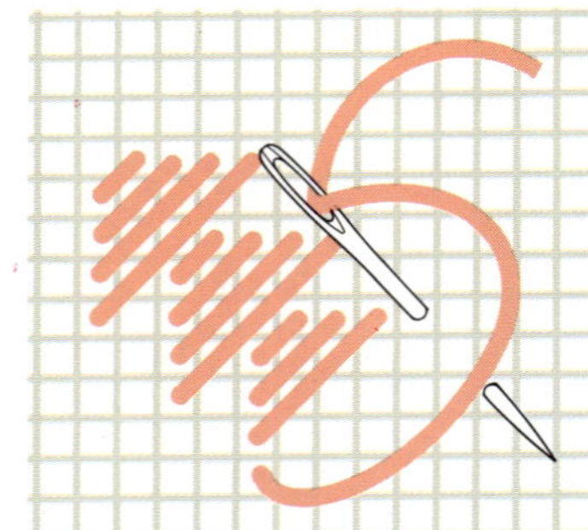

2. *Having completed the first row, stitch the next row back upwards to the right of it. In the second row, the triangles must be facing the opposite way to the first.*

the designs, rules of scale and stitch are usually followed. Rectangular borders, for example, are often filled with large square stitches, each one surrounded by a row of pulled thread to accentuate the raised texture of the stitch and give a bold edge to the completed piece. Diamond shapes down the centre can be filled with diamond-shaped stitches.

Parterres, knot gardens, mazes and potagers (ornamental vegetable gardens) all lend themselves perfectly to canvaswork designs, being beautifully ordered and outlined and filled with contrasting foliage. Stitches to represent the variety of foliage can be used – a neatly clipped yew may be represented in neat cross stitches; the profusion of colours and chaos of shapes and heights in the flower beds may be shown in a combination of more textured stitches. The outline of low balustrades and pavilions can also be incorporated.

Florentine is a general name for a whole range of wave-designs and lozenge-designs with large-scale or small-scale repeats. All Florentine designs use straight stitches placed parallel to the threads of the canvas. Florentine stitch, and variations of it, form the basic Florentine peak-and-valley design. Hungarian, Parisian and brick stitches are other straight stitches which may be used to fill designs.

Because different length stitches, and combinations of lengths can be used with any spacing rhythm in the rising and falling patterns of the basic Florentine stitch, there is a limitless number of possible designs. Wave designs are formed by peaks and valleys which may result in an even or uneven zigzag, depending on whether the peaks and valleys are of equal or unequal height and depth, or they may be stitched in a more rounded pattern. Rows of either shading or contrasting colours produce a harmonious or dramatic effect.

Lozenge designs consist of mirrored top and bottom rows, usually repeated, with straight stitches filling the enclosed areas. Four-way designs are produced by working four triangular sections at right-angles to each other, so forming a square block with the pattern worked out from the centre. For diagonal Florentine, the canvas is diagonally intersected, and the angle of stitching changed on the intersection.

All Florentine patterns are versatile, and are used in different ways for different purposes. Ribbon patterns are generally worked as a two-colour band going across the canvas, suitable for belts or curtain tie-backs. Petites Fleurs is an excellent choice for dining chairs and all-over cushions, as the stitches within this design are not too long. Pomegranate is a traditional design which repeats well over a large area, making an especially bold design if four are worked at

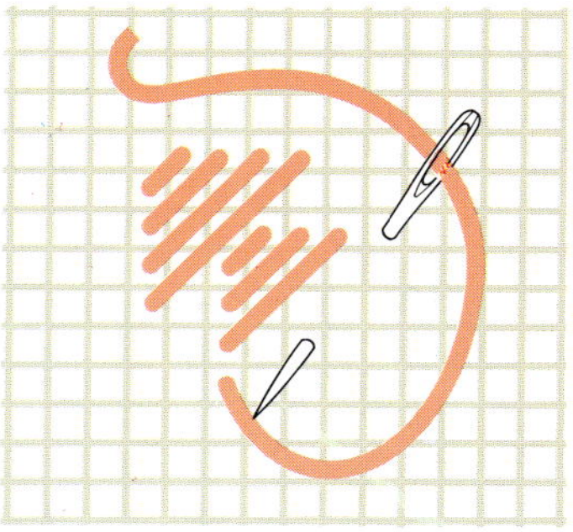

Oriental stitch 1. *Start off by working a row of triangular-shaped blocks, as for Milanese stitch. Again work diagonally down the canvas and then back up for the next row.*

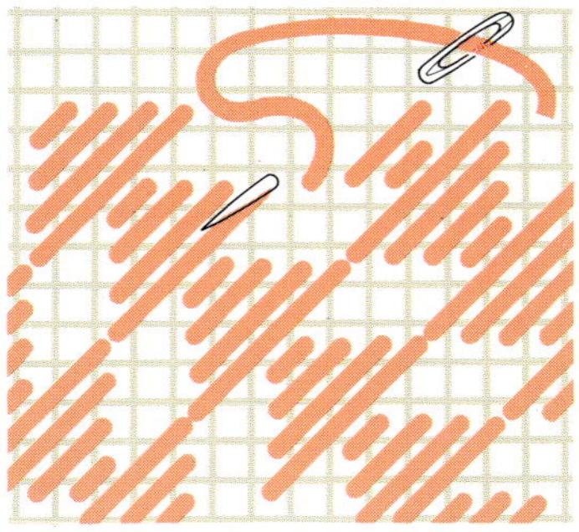

2. *The direction of the triangles must be alternated with each row, but for this stitch they must be arranged so that the bases of all the triangles are aligned.*

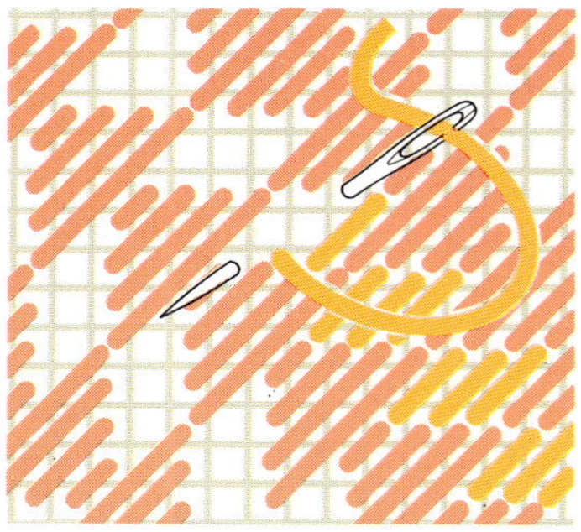

3. *This will leave diamond-shaped areas of canvas empty. These empty areas lie alternately lengthways and crossways between each row.*

4. *Fill all the gaps with blocks of three stitches slanting downwards from right to left. Use the same colour or a contrasting one.*

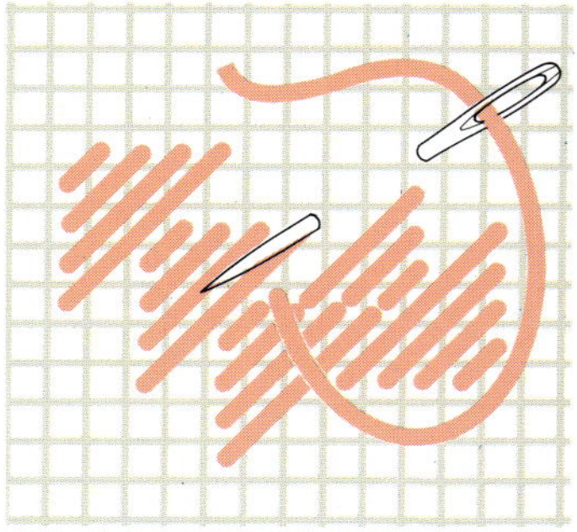

3. *Milanese stitch should result in a bold regular surface with each triangular fitting into the next. The triangles must face the same direction in alternate rows.*

Left *Three sampler cushions worked in wool on canvas, demonstrating different geometric designs worked in a variety of stitches.* ***Above*** *A modern Florentine cushion worked in wool, with a belt that has been stitched in an adaptation of the same design. The latter is worked in silks, into which fine gold filaments have been twisted. The attractive bell-shaped ends are made from silk.*

Right *A detail from a large floral piece worked in stranded cottons on linen canvas. Only four different colours have been used: cream, yellow, coral and deep coral, but by mixing the strands from the different coloured skeins, an extraordinarily wide range of colours has been produced to shade the rose. The area round this flower has been worked in skip tent stitch.*

right-angles, using the base of the lowest stitch as the common hole to all four repeats. This is a version of four-way Florentine. This and diagonal Florentine are useful for working over large areas of canvas. Choose the design carefully for the project's finished purpose; patterns that have long stitches will not wear as well as those with short ones. Start stitching in the centre of the canvas as this ensures a symmetrical design with the same number of pattern repeats either side.

Preparing the canvas

Either bind or sew all the cut edges of the canvas before starting work, using masking tape or by machining a double hem. When mounting the canvas on the frame fix it with drawing pins, which are more satisfactory than staples as they enable you to tighten the canvas from time to time. Always work with the selvedge on the left or right side of your work, and mark the top of the canvas so that you do not swing it round by mistake.

Allow plenty of canvas for the piece, and remember you will need at least 2 inches (5 cm) left unworked on all sides for stretching the finished work. Sometimes a more important border than at first planned looks exciting, and it is a shame if there is not enough space to work it. Take pieces of canvas you plan to join from the same roll. In the case of a rug with a number of flowers each worked on a separate panel, for example, which is to be joined when complete, make sure they are from exactly the same piece of canvas, otherwise the joins may not match satisfactorily. If you delay buying matching canvas you may even find the mesh has been discontinued.

Spraying canvas gold or silver can produce interesting results. Use ordinary paint spray sold for Christmas decorations and work on a frame. It is not as yet sure whether this effect will tarnish with time.

Marking the design

If furniture is to be covered by the canvaswork, make a template of the size in paper or calico. On any canvas, allow 2½ inches (6 cm) extra on all sides for turnings.

The method of marking depends on the

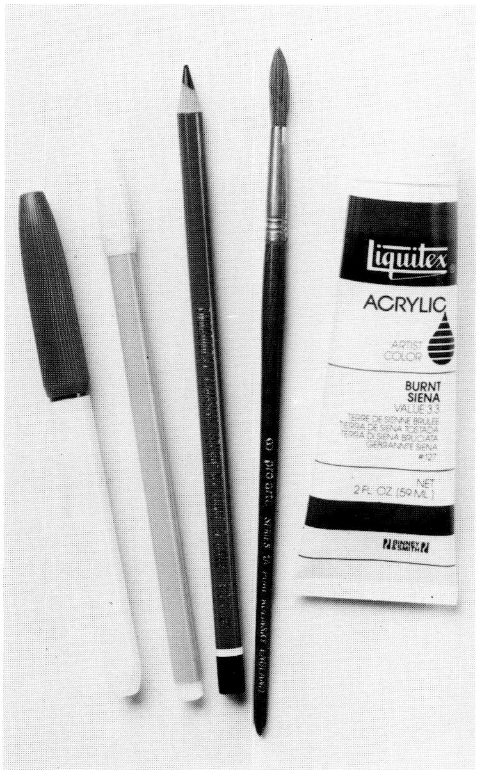

Above *For marking designs, use a Nepo marker, a water-soluble marker that should be used for delicate designs or those worked in silks; a pencil, ideal for geometric designs, or acrylic paint for scenic canvases. Oil paints are also good for painting onto a canvas.*

Right *The great bed at Parham Park in West Sussex. The curtains are beautifully worked in Florentine stitch.*
Far right *A detail from the bed curtain at Parham Park. They are made of strips of canvas no more than 9 inches (23 cms) wide that have been stitched together. The barley stick patterns ingeniously conceal these seams.*

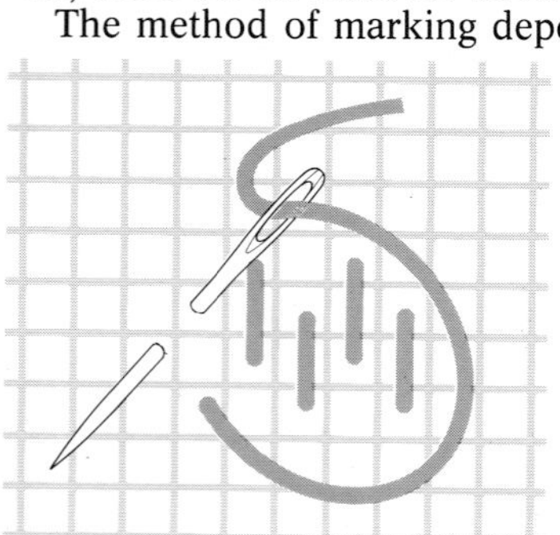

Brick stitch 1. *This is a popular stitch that is easy to master. Leave one canvas hole between adjacent stitches and change direction at the end of every row.*

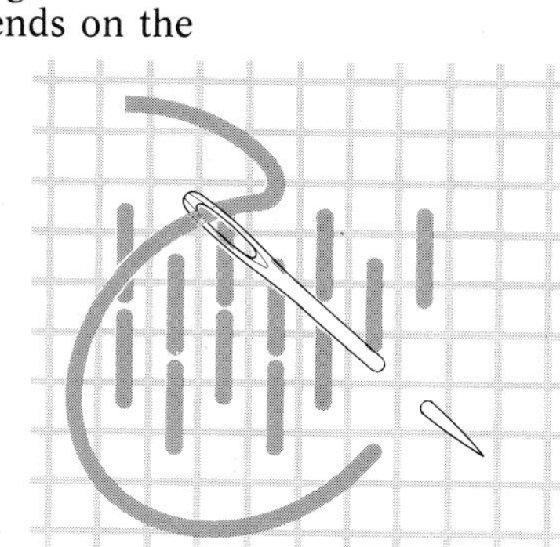

2. *Having completed the initial row, place the stitches of the next row underneath it, spanning alternate empty canvas holes. Align the third row with the first.*

Hungarian stitch 1. *This is similar to brick stitch but is worked in small diamond-shaped blocks of three stitches each. Change direction at the end of a row.*

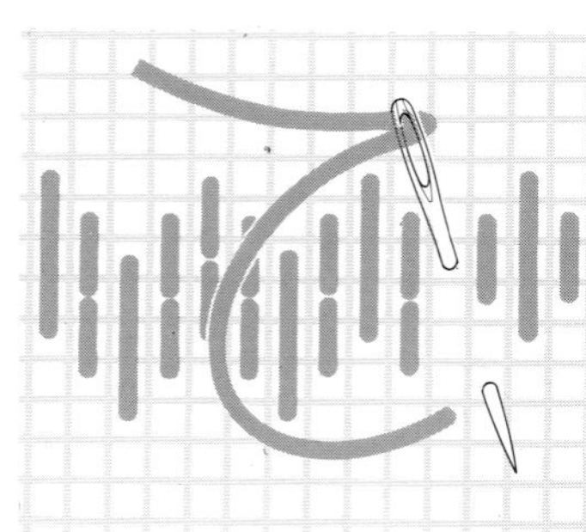

2. *Again a canvas hole must be left between each diamond unit, and the diamonds making up the second row must be placed in the gaps underneath the first row.*

type of design. When marking a geometric design it is quickest and easiest to use a very sharp pencil; its point will move along the channel between two threads and mark an accurate straight line. The graphite may come off on light-coloured wools during the stitching so rub over the marked canvas well with kitchen paper before starting work. The alternatives are to use a tacking thread or paint, or a Nepo marker which can be bought from most needlework suppliers. For pictorial designs, enlarge or reduce the chosen design onto paper, or, if the original size is suitable, just outline the details so they are easily visible through the canvas. Mark the centre of the design, and the centre of the canvas, then draw straight horizontal and vertical lines through the centre points. Pin the two centres together to a large board, with the design beneath the canvas, and working first on the weft thread and then the warp, pin the four line-ends to the board. Pinning alternately on opposite sides, attach the canvas and the design tautly to the board.

Nepo markers are the best choice when marking a curved design; they come in a range of colours either individually or in an assorted pack. The mid-grey is probably the most useful. When copying or adapting an original coloured picture, for example an oil painting in a museum, it is best to mark only the outlines onto the canvas with the Nepo and then, working from a postcard or colour reproduction, work out your own shading. When marking a piece for pulled thread or work which may finally have a partially bare canvas background, mark the minimum, using one of the markers that washes out with cold water. Increasing numbers of markers are coming onto the market, both permanent and water solvent.

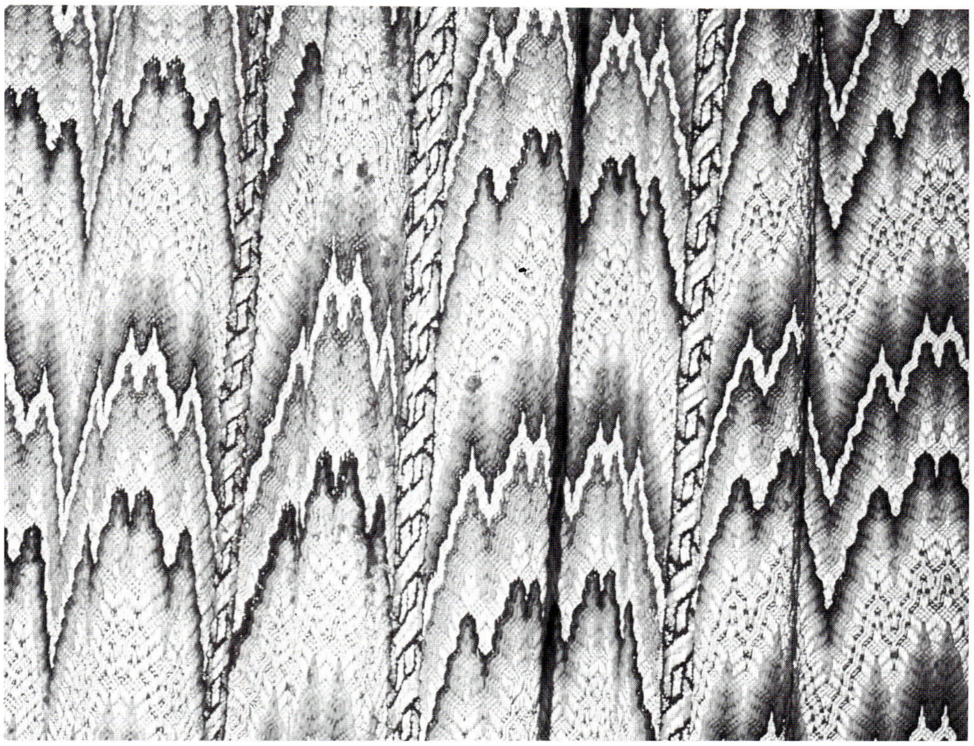

Parisian stitch 1. *Alternate long and short stitches for the first row working from right to left. The short stitches must span one canvas hole and the long ones four.*

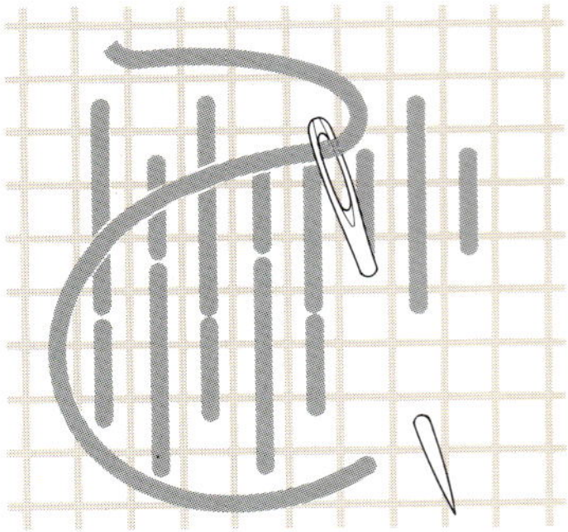

2. *Work the second row underneath from left to right, placing the long stitches directly under the short ones above and the short under the long.*

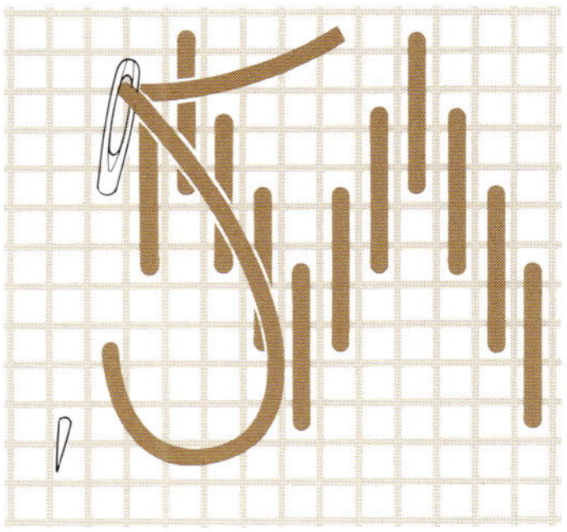

Florentine stitch 1. *There are endless variations of this stitch, generally consisting of closely parallel vertical stitches worked in rows to form zigzag shapes.*

2. *These stitches make up a jagged line, into which the rows above and below must fit. The peaks and valleys may be arranged at regular or irregular intervals.*

Check all markers carefully on the corner of the actual piece of canvas you intend to use to see that they do not run.

Stitches

The most commonly used canvaswork stitch is tent stitch. It is particularly suitable for pictorial work and shading, producing a very even texture. Diagonal stitches over one mesh can also be formed by half cross stitches, which are less durable than tent stitches and more liable to distort the canvas, but use less thread and may be strengthened by working over a laid thread. There are two types of tent stitch, the preferred being diagonal or basketweave because it is firmer and does not distort. Continental tent stitch should only be used when there is one single line of colour to be worked, which may be horizontal, vertical or diagonal.

For a more textured effect, there is a very wide variety of stitches to choose from. The choice partly depends on the size of stitches required by the design and the shape of the area to be filled. It is also worth considering the texture of the stitches; some may be flat but many have particular textures, for example leaf stitches show growth lines in obvious relief.

Diagonal stitches, which slant across the threads of the canvas, include tent and half cross stitches. Others are slanted gobelin, and encroaching gobelin, which both create neat textures, the former in rows, the latter uniform over the canvas. The amount of canvas threads to work the stitches over is a matter of choice depending on the requirements of the canvaswork. Byzantine stitch forms a jagged, diagonal texture across the canvas. Cushion stitch is worked to form a pattern of square blocks on the canvas, each block consisting of five diagonal stitches. A variation of cushion stitch, producing a more interesting, partly raised texture, is called chequer stitch, made by alternating squares of cushion stitch with squares of nine tent stitches. Two more diagonal stitches, Milanese and Oriental, create bold and highly textured triangular units, with the triangle tips running in opposite directions in alternate rows. As a guide, these diagonal stitches need three strands of crewel wool on a 14 mesh canvas for good coverage.

Florentine stitch (which is also called flame point) forms the bold zigzag patterns associated with Florentine canvaswork. The stitches are straight, and create the jagged effect by the rows being stepped in peak-and-valley designs. The variations in the length of the stitches and the height of the steps between one stitch and the next, create the degrees of jaggedness. It is important to ensure there is an even amount of thread at the back of the canvas when working peak-and-valley designs. When working up and down across the canvas, short stitches may result behind the lines ascending the peak

Above *Three progressive stages in a canvaswork piece, the design of which was adapted from an eighteenth-century New England bed-cover. The 18 mesh to the inch mono canvas was sprayed silver, before work was started on the flower, in silk, beads and metal threads.*

Right *Two jewellery rolls, with designs based on traditional Oriental patterns. The one in the foreground is worked in wool on 14 mesh to the inch canvas, and the other is worked on finer canvas, 18 mesh to the inch, in mixed threads. The latter also features pulled thread work.*

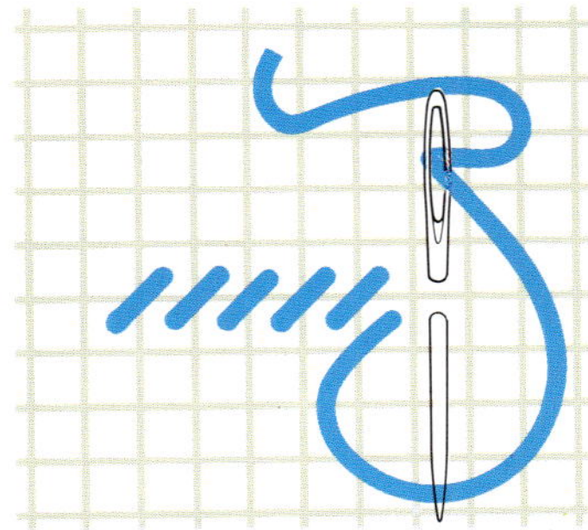

Half cross stitch (horizontal) *Work this stitch from left to right. When a row is complete, push the needle to the back, turn the canvas through 180° and begin again.*

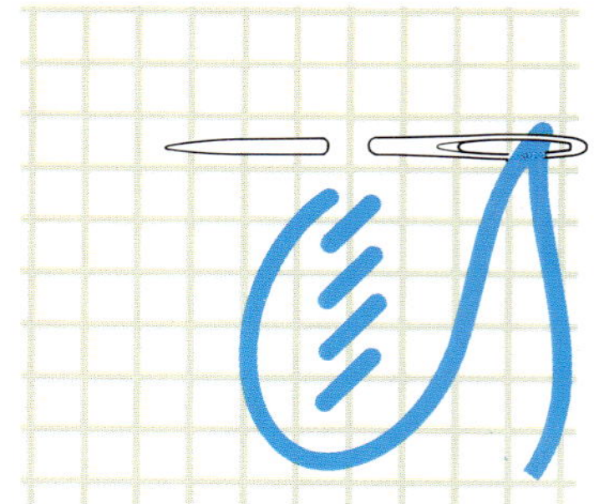

Half cross stitch (vertical) *This stitch can also be worked vertically. Always move downwards, turning the canvas through 180° at the end of each completed row.*

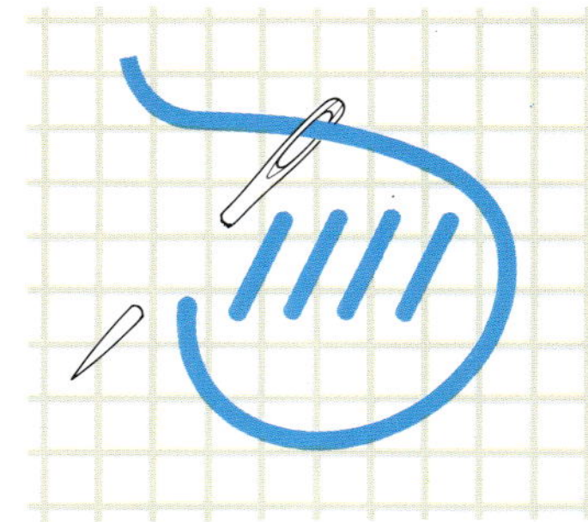

Slanted gobelin 1. *The length of stitch used as well as the width between the stitches can be varied. Work one row from right to left and then another from left to right.*

2. *Fit each stitch diagonally over the canvas intersections. The tip of each new stitch must fit between the two bases of the stitches in the row above.*

Byzantine stitch 1. *Each row consists of two units of either three or four stitches. Steps are formed by placing these units horizontally and then vertically.*

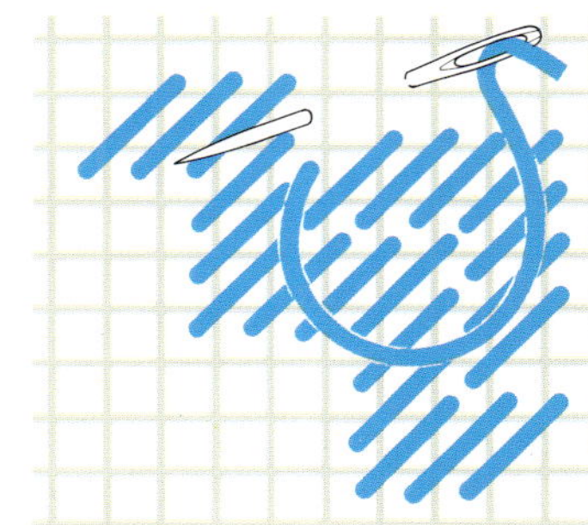

2. *Work alternately down and then up the canvas, fitting the step units into each other as shown. This stitch can also be worked using larger stitches.*

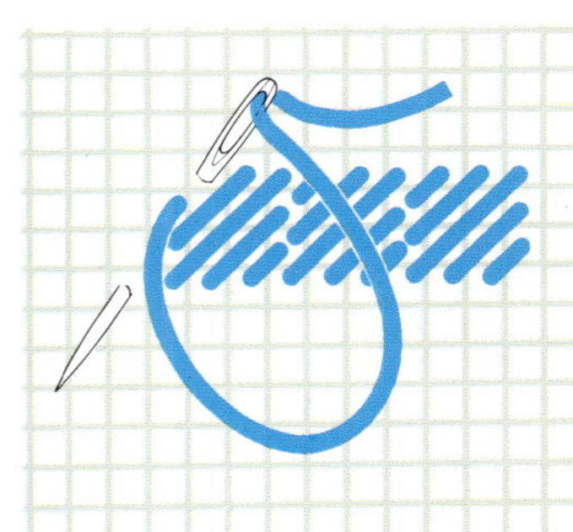

Scottish stitch 1. *Work a square-shaped block from five diagonal tent stitches as shown. Scottish stitch is made up of rows of these blocks side by side.*

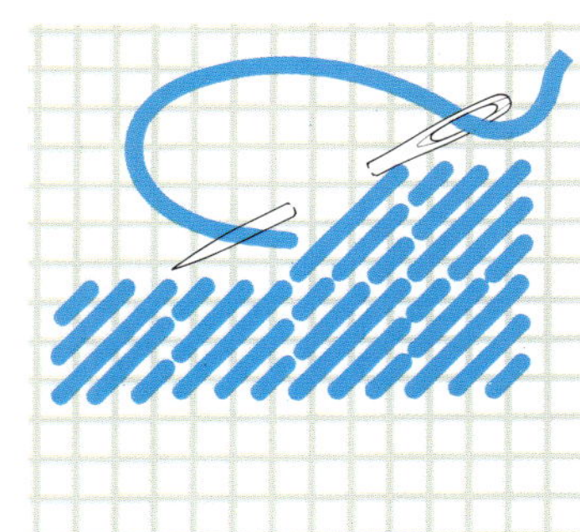

2. *At the end of each row turn the canvas through 180° and begin the next row directly underneath it. Each new block must be aligned with the one above it.*

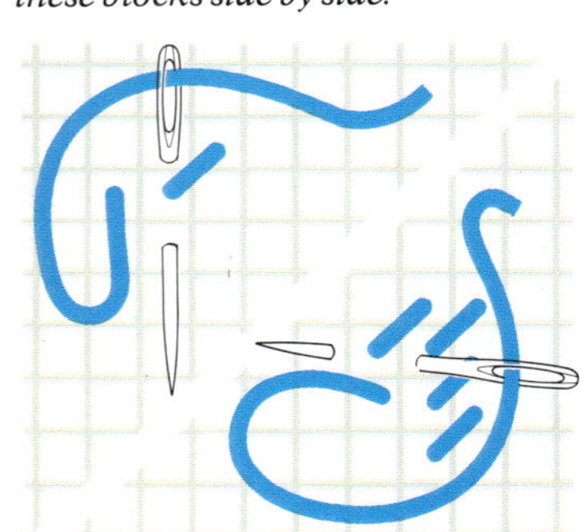

Chequer stitch 1. *Working from right to left, sew alternate blocks of Scottish stitch and small tent stitches as shown.*
All the blocks must be the same size.

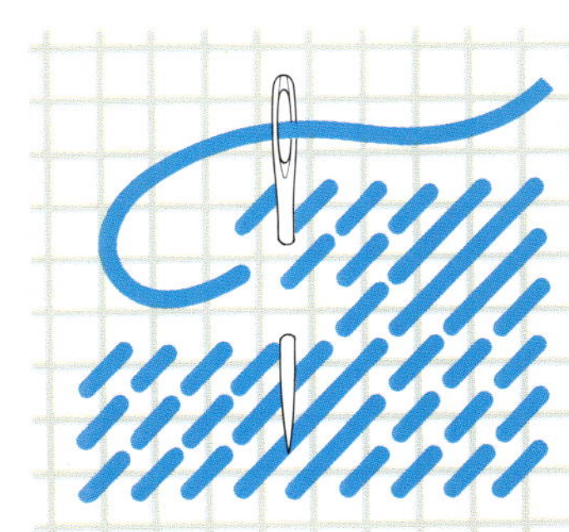

2. *When a row has been completed, turn the canvas through 180° to begin the next row. Align Scottish blocks with tent blocks and vice versa for chequered effect.*

and long stitches behind the descent. Over a whole canvas this can result in thick and thin patches which obviously will not wear evenly. The problem can be avoided by starting each line at the alternate end.

Other straight stitches include straight gobelin and straight encroaching gobelin; brick stitch, which looks much like its name; Hungarian, which produces a pattern of small diamond units; and Parisian, which produces a more complicated texture formed by interlocking rows of long and short straight stitches. All except Hungarian need four strands of crewel wool on 14 mesh canvas. Hungarian only needs three.

A number of stitches are formed by making crosses of various sizes in various directions. The following selection includes large and small, textured and flat cross stitches. The basic cross stitch consists of two diagonal stitches crossing at the centre over one mesh. It can be formed by making whole crosses, or by making a row of half-crosses and working back along the row to form the complete stitches. On single canvas the first method is best. Leviathan (which is also known as Smyrna) is a much larger cross stitch, formed by making a cross stitch over four canvas threads then a straight cross on top, also over four threads. Each unit is raised and square when complete.

A variation of this is the double cross stitch – a straight cross worked over four threads with a diagonal cross, worked over two canvas threads, on top. Having worked one row of these, the next row will dove-tail neatly with the taller ends of the straight crosses placed centrally in the spaces between two previous double cross stitches. Each unit is diamond-shaped and raised.

Large and straight cross stitch is made by a large diagonal stitch over four canvas threads, with small upright crosses over two threads placed in the diamond spaces between. This creates an unusual latticework pattern, made more interesting, as with many of these doubled stitches, by using two colours for the different crosses.

Long-legged cross stitch is useful for borders. The stitch is worked by starting with a cross stitch, then taking a diagonal across four canvas threads in order to form the first diagonal of the next stitch. The result is raised and plaited. Crossed corners are formed by large diagonal cross stitches over four threads of canvas, with stitches over two threads of canvas worked diagonally across the ends of each original diagonal.

Fern stitch, fishbone and rococo are further tied stitches. The former two are variations on the basic principle; the latter is different in that the top and bottom holes are the same for each group of four stitches, which cover four canvas threads, and each stitch is tied in the middle with a horizontal back stitch covering one canvas thread. The

Straight gobelin stitch *This simple stitch is worked from right to left, then left to right. The rows touch but do not overlap, and the stitch length can be altered.*

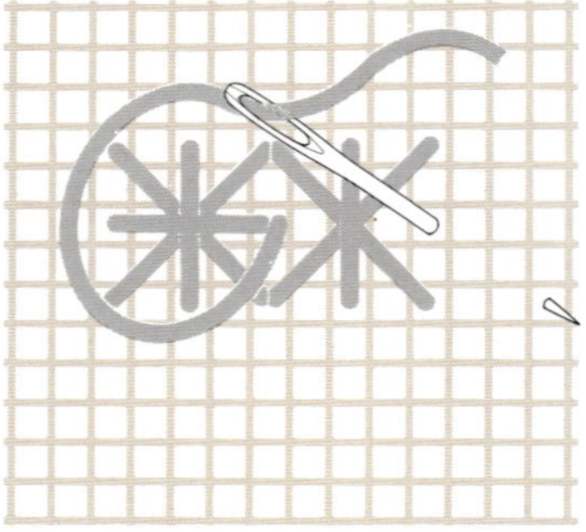

2. *Each individual stitch must cover four canvas meshes. Work the second row back underneath the first, making sure the new star tips fill the same canvas holes as the bases of the stars above.*

Long-legged cross stitch 1. *The small leg of the cross here spans two canvas threads, and the longer leg therefore spans four canvas threads.*

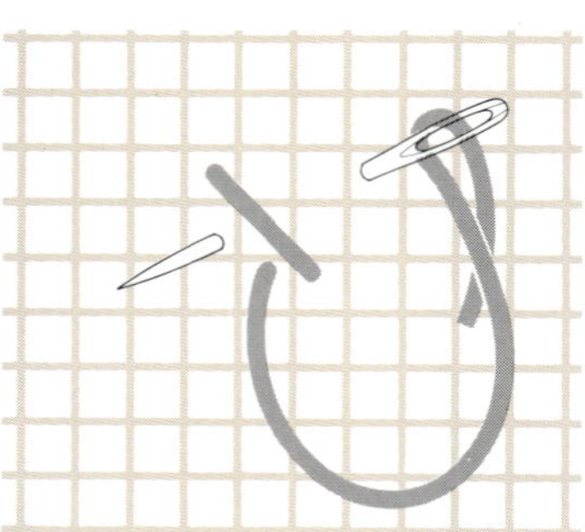

Fern stitch 1. *This stitch is made up of regular rows of top heavy crosses worked downwards. Each diagonal stitch spans two canvas mesh intersections.*

Right *A contemporary four-way Florentine flower design worked in wools on a piece of canvas that has been applied to a cushion cover. An unusual effect has been achieved by leaving the background of the border worked in triple cross bare.*

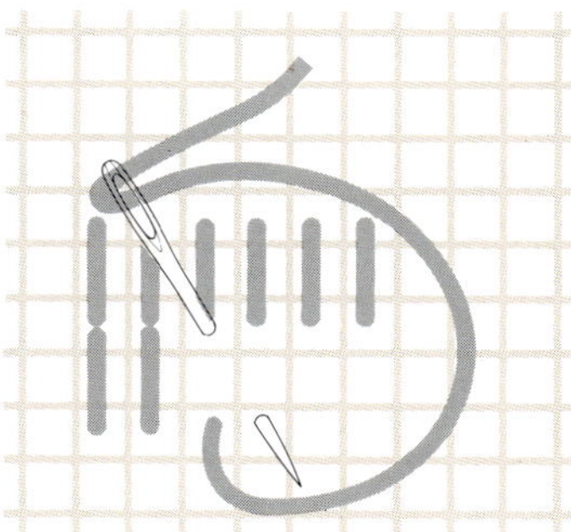

Encroaching straight gobelin *Again start off from right to left and change direction with each row. The tips of the new stitches overlap with the bases of the row above.*

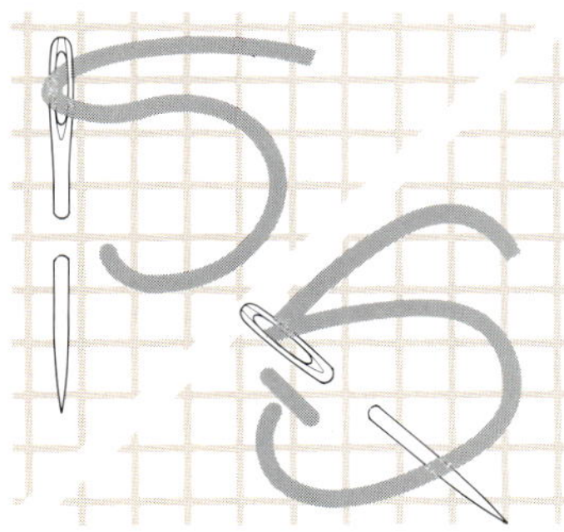

Cross stitch (horizontal) 1. *Work small crosses over the required number of mesh intersections, organizing the stitches as shown.*

2. *When a row has been completed from left to right, work the next row back from right to left. Align the new crosses with the previous crosses. Neighbouring stitches share holes.*

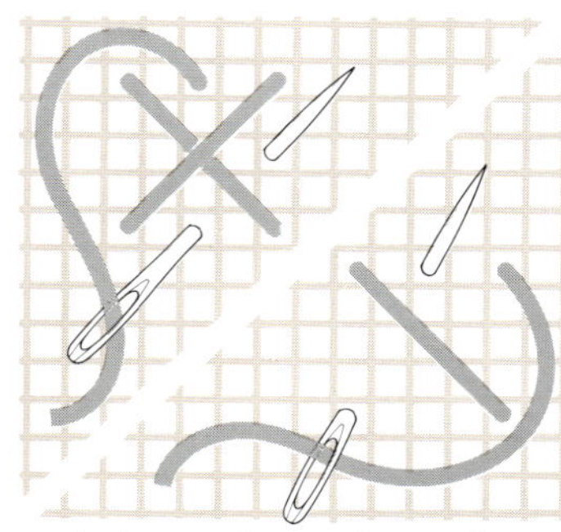

Leviathan 1. *This stitch is made up of rows of regularly arranged star-shaped units. Work a large basic cross stitch as shown, and sew an upright cross stitch over it.*

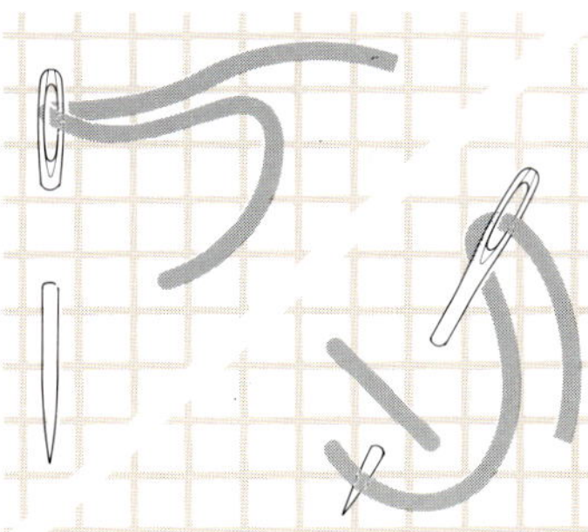

Double cross stitch 1. *This stitch is similar to leviathan, but the large upright cross stitch is worked first over four meshes, and a smaller basic cross stitch over two meshes worked on top.*

2. *The second row must be worked underneath the first in the opposite direction, but the units are not aligned with the ones above. The tips of the bottom row fit between the bases of the row above.*

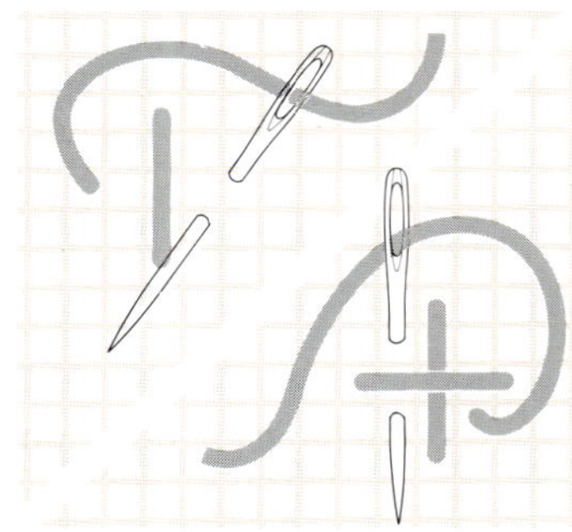

Large and straight stitch 1. *In this stitch, a large basic cross stitch is worked over four meshes alternating with a small upright cross stitch over two canvas meshes.*

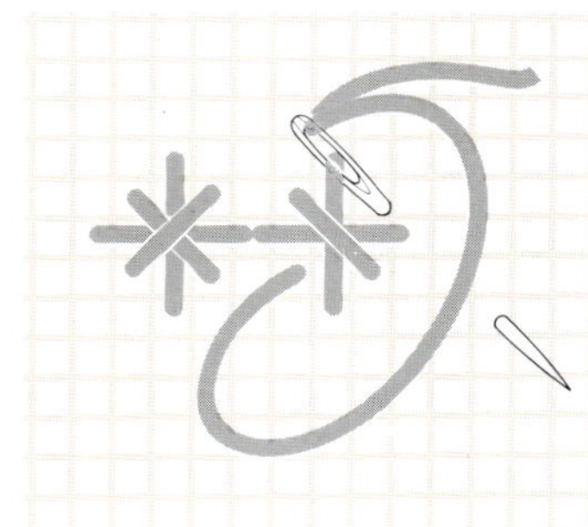

2. *Align the second row back under the first. The tips and bases of the large crosses share the same canvas holes and the gaps formed inbetween are filled with additional small crosses.*

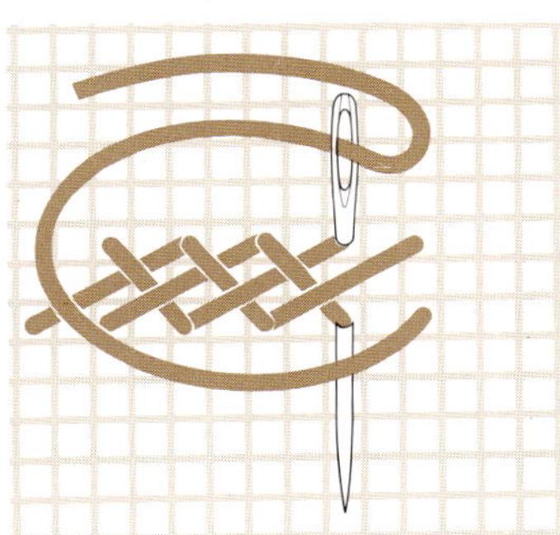

2. *When a row has been completed, turn the canvas through 180° and begin the next row. Align the rows so that the tips of adjacent crosses share a canvas hole with the previous row.*

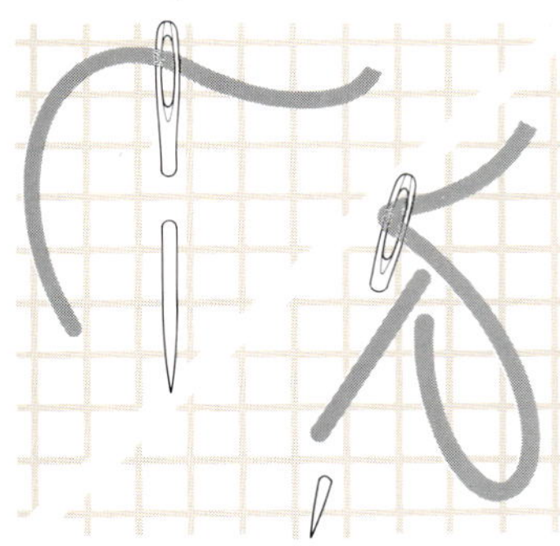

Fishbone 1. *This stitch is worked alternately down and then back up the canvas. Each row is made up of long diagonal stitches that span three horizontal canvas threads each.*

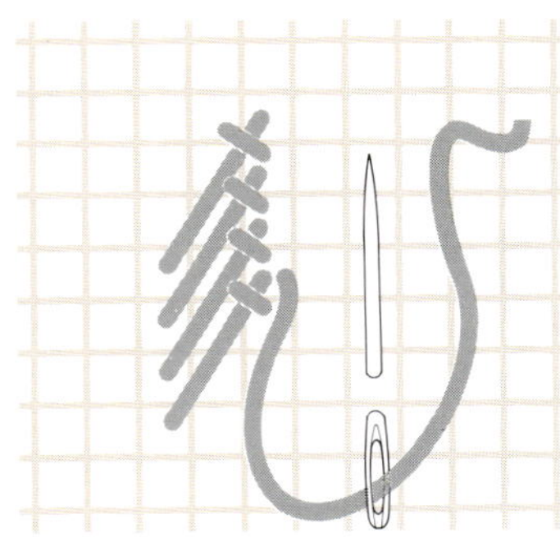

2. *Each long stitch is anchored by a short cross stitch over the mesh intersection at one end of the stitch. For rows worked downwards the small cross is at the top of the stitch.*

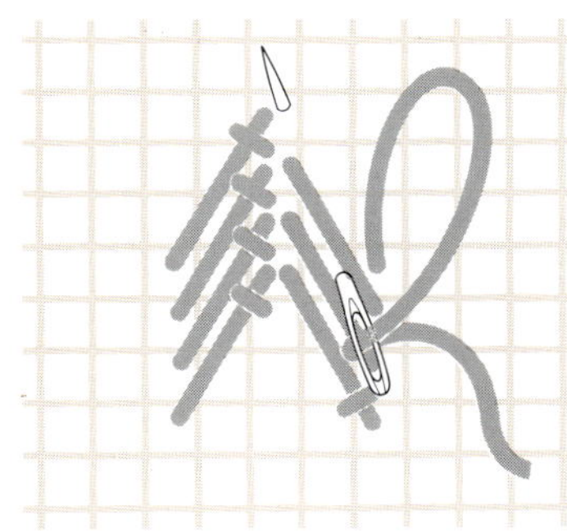

3. *For rows worked upwards, the small crosses anchor the bottom end of the long diagonal stitches. The final effect should be of a closely worked wavy surface.*

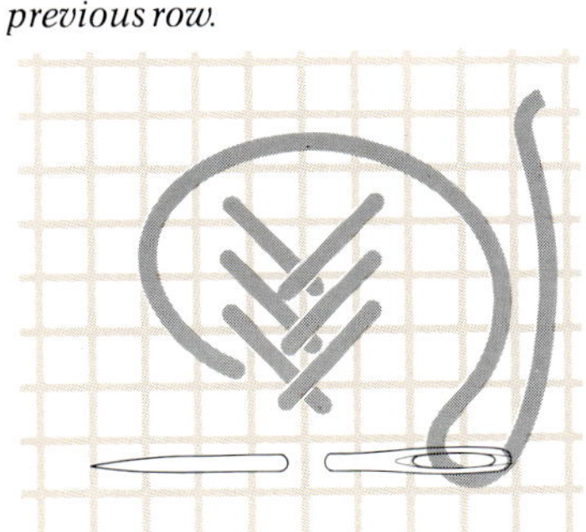

2. *Having completed a row, work the next row to the right of it making sure that the adjacent stitches are aligned and sharing common holes.*

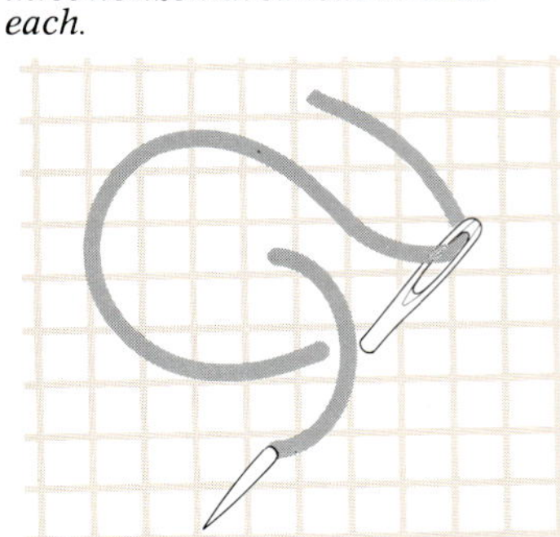

Rococo stitch 1. *When mastered, this stitch is highly impressive. Each globe-shaped unit is made up of four downward stitches spanning four horizontal canvas threads.*

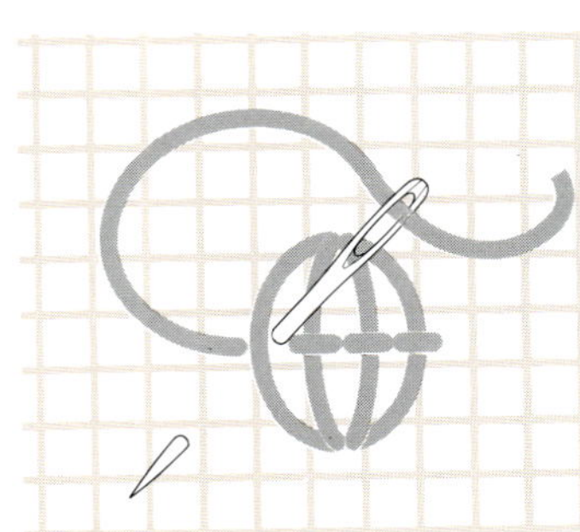

2. *Each downward stitch is anchored with a small crossways stitch spanning one vertical canvas thread. The curved effect is caused by the downward stitches.*

3. *The tips and bases of all four of these stitches share the same canvas holes. Work the rows in alternate directions interlocking the units as shown.*

Algerian eye stitch 1. *This attractive stitch is made up from rows of small star-shaped units. Work alternately from right to left and left to right.*

2. *Each star is made with eight stitches, sewn clockwise for the rows worked right to left and anticlockwise for the alternate ones. Align each star with the one above.*

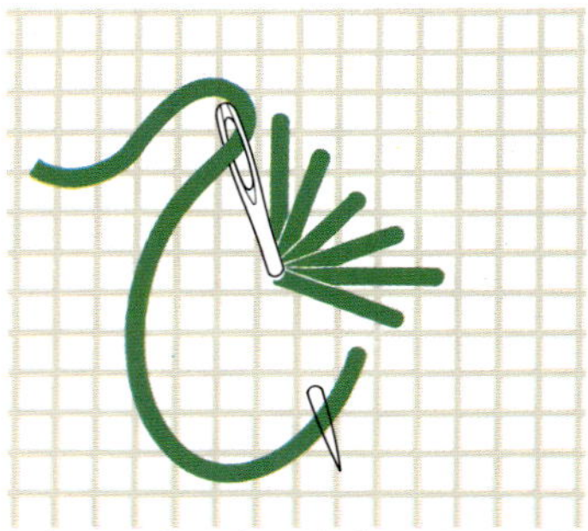

Diamond eyelet stitch 1. *This stitch is only suitable as a single detail or for covering a substantial area. Each diamond-shaped unit is made up from sixteen separate stitches.*

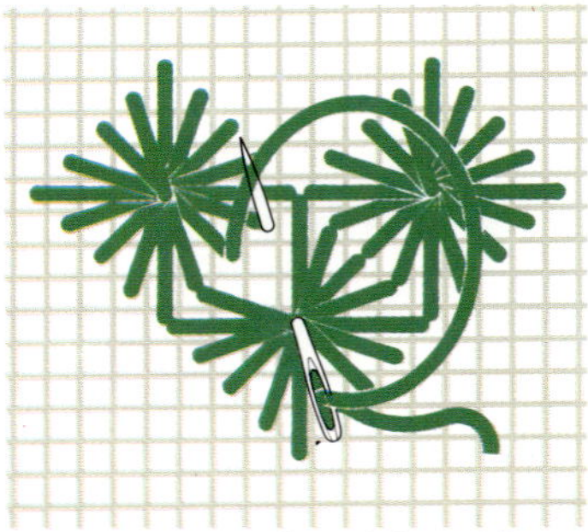

2. *Work one row from left to right and another from right to left. Make sure that each new diamond fits in between the two in the row above.*

result is highly textured. All these cross stitches need three plies for adequate coverage over 14 mesh canvas.

The completed Algerian Eye is a square unit, worked by passing eight stitches in a star formation through a central hole. Diamond eyelets are similarly worked but the four extreme top, bottom and side stitches are longer than the other twelve, so forming a diamond unit. Ray stitch is a square unit, with seven stitches worked into one corner. Leaf stitch is a large, particularly individual unit formed with eleven stitches in a fan shape. These stitches need only two or three plies of crewel wool on a 14 mesh canvas. All these stitches produce highly textured canvases; any of them could be used singly as a small feature within a whole work.

Making up

All canvaswork is freshened by stretching, even if it has been stitched on a frame and has very little distortion. For stretching, you will need a piece of unstained, unpainted wood, larger than the canvas and at least ½ inch (1 cm) thick; an old towel; rustproof tacks; a small hammer; and a steel rule. Place the towel on top of the board and put the canvaswork on top of this, face up. Pin the canvas out, using a steel rule as a guide for straight edges. Pull the canvas gently so that the original size and shape is restored. Dampen the canvas with a sponge, and leave it to dry naturally in a horizontal position.

Many people consider it best to have their work made up professionally; if a great deal of time has been spent on the stitching, it deserves the best finishing. However, if you wish to finish an item yourself, there is a simple method which is suitable for making up basic items such as cushions. For making up a cushion, buy a ready-made pad, slightly larger than your canvas, to support the canvas, especially at the corners. Machine or hand-stitch around the canvas and backing fabric with the right sides together, close to the canvaswork stitching. Leave a few inches along the bottom edge, turn the cover right side out, insert the pad and complete the stitching by hand. If the canvas pattern already has an interesting border, there is no need for the cushion to be piped. However, boxing, piping or mounting a smaller canvas on a larger cushion can give elegant effects. Tassels, fringes or cording made from matching wool can also be added.

__Right__ A Florentine sampler cushion designed to show a variety of patterns that are suitable for all-over designs on belts, bags or other small items. The borders between the different design have been worked in cross corner stitch.
__Far right__ A canvaswork cushion demonstrating a design known as Garden Path. It is worked in stranded cottons and rayons incorporating straight gobelin, Parisian, chequer and knitting stitches.

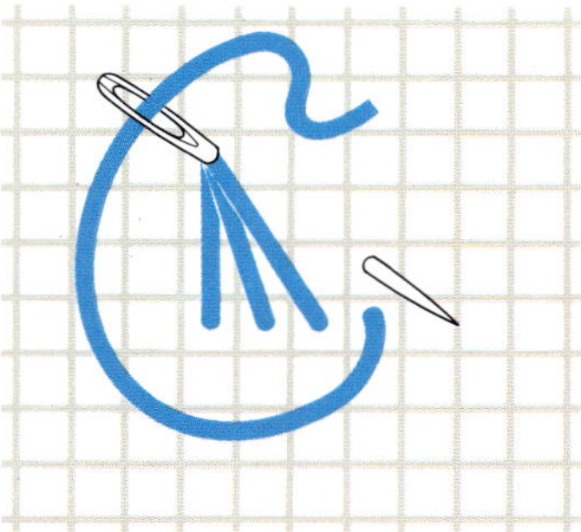

Ray stitch 1. *The unit for this stitch is a fan of seven stitches spread out from a single canvas hole. Each fan is confined by a straight vertical and straight horizontal stitch.*

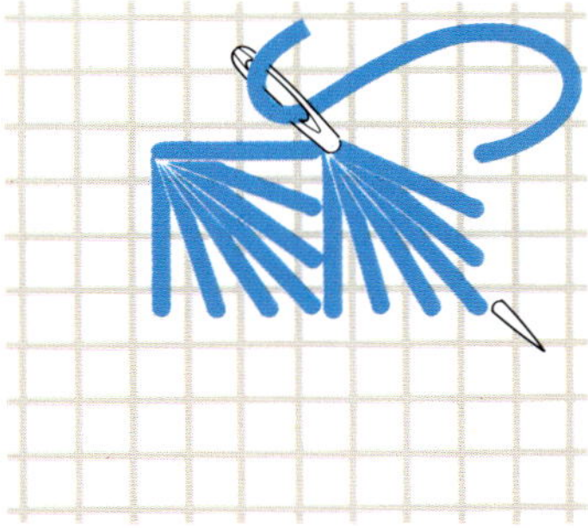

2. *Work one row from left to right and then one from right to left. Place the units next to each other as shown, and align each row with the one above.*

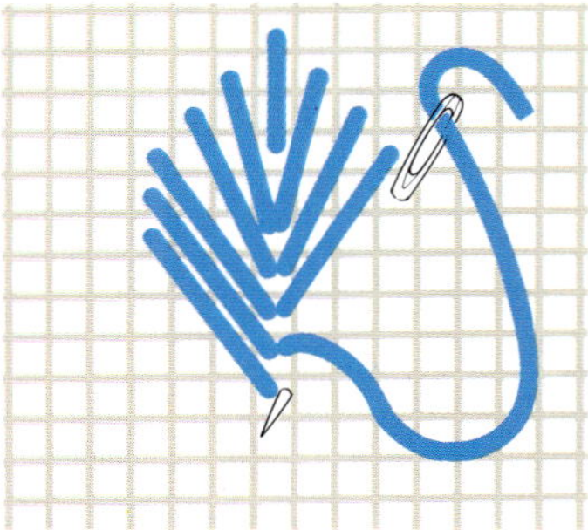

Leaf stitch 1. *Made up of interlocking rows of leaf-shaped units, this is another large stitch.*

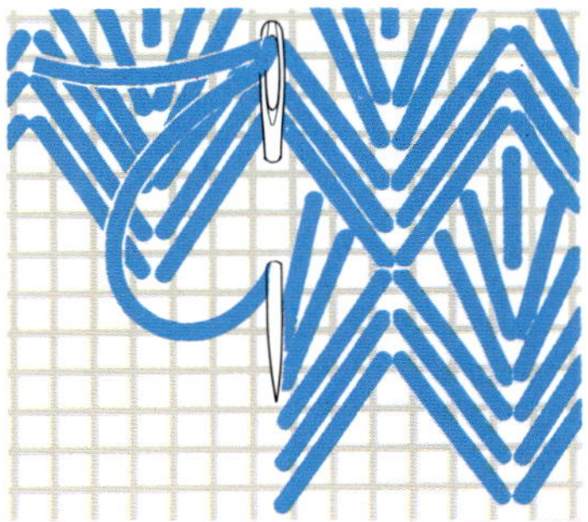

2. *The length of the leaf can be extended by adding more diagonal stitches. Work one row from left to right and then one from right to left.*

Left *A detail from a cushion worked entirely in a petit fleur design, of which there is a small section on the sampler cushion. Cushions can look extraordinarily effective in small repeating patterns, although large pictorial motifs tend to be more popular.*

Appliqué and Raised Work

Appliqué

One of the oldest known forms of needlework for the decoration of cloth or leather is the method of applying small pieces of material onto a background fabric with a needle and thread, creating a two-dimensional embroidery. Initially used to cover or strengthen worn cloth, appliqué developed into the practice of applying definite shapes and colours in individual designs for aesthetic reasons. Applying patterned fabric to a plain background takes less time than embroidery, and plain areas of fabric applied to a sumptuous brocade stand out in a bold design. It is an economic use of precious scraps of cloth, silks or velvets with either curved or rigid edges, and has proved to be a handsome and unusually decorative form of needlework. The stitches can be worked unobtrusively or more boldly.

History

Early appliqué work which still survives includes pieces of applied leather from Ankmim, dated between the third and seventh centuries B.C., which decorated Egyptian coiffure supports. Geometric shapes were stitched with thread onto crescent-shaped pads to attach to the head. Pieces remaining from the third and fourth centuries B.C. include part of a saddle cover found in Altai, South Siberia. Made of felt, it has a clearly designed griffin with raised paws and spreading wings. The appliqué design is emphasized with couched cords. Another piece, a large hanging made to adorn a burial chamber, is also in felt, with seated goddesses and horsemen. The colours – red, blue, yellow and black on a beige ground – remain clear. The horsemen have curly moustaches and purposeful expressions on large faces, and wear flowing capes. Details, stitched in simple linear embroidery, indicate the fashions of the time, and outline the shapes of the horses' manes and bridles.

Appliqué was used on the flags and banners of the Middle Ages which were carried into battle. Simple designs were applied to surcoats and jupons for the recognition of men wearing armour. At the start, only lords and knights carried devices, but later all their followers also wore heraldic symbols. It became a technical language of its own.

Crusaders returned to France and Britain from the Holy Wars with sumptuous silks, velvets and brocades which encouraged appliqué work. The reflective qualities of these different surfaces made these fabrics stimulating to look at.

An era of remarkable English embroidery, known as *opus anglicanum*, developed dur-

Left *A detail from the Earl of Westmoreland altar frontal. It is an early example of appliqué with additional embroidery. The Earl is depicted in armour, kneeling to the left of a crucifix, only a part of which is shown.*
Below *An appliquéd coverlet made in the 1850s and possibly intended as a marriage coverlet. The two female figures were probably inspired by Hiram Power's famous "Greek Slave" statue, shown in the Great Exhibition of 1851. The objects and animals, in wild profusion, have been cut from a variety of contemporary cotton prints.*
Above right *A hackney carriage canopy from Bombay worked in striking, blind appliqué. Cotton appliqué on tents and hangings was extremely popular in India during the nineteenth century.*
Right *A detail from an appliquéd chair at Hardwick Hall in Derbyshire. Chairs were upholstered from the middle of the sixteenth century onwards, and afforded endless opportunities for appliqué and needlework generally.*

ing the thirteenth and fourteenth centuries, when professional workshops became world-famous for their magnificent embroideries. Gold and silver threads with silk embroidery on linen were applied to velvet backgrounds during this time. The Westminster Chasuble, made a century later during the years 1475 and 1525, has finely embroidered emblems of rose, portcullis, pomegranate and fleur-de-lys, applied to velvet. Ceremonial occasions, such as the setting up of guilds and livery companies, led to the making of civic, as well as religious, embroideries, and also palls used for the funerals of guild members. Separate motifs were worked with precious metal threads, coloured silks and sequins on a linen ground, applied and then neatly finished off with a twisted metal thread cord couched around the edges. Some motifs have waxed edges to prevent fraying; some

are turned under; others have separate background threads unwoven and stitched through, to secure them firmly.

Sixteenth- and seventeenth-century appliqué was made for extensive use in the church and in great houses on bed valences and furniture coverings. As brocades and rich velvets became less costly and more plentiful, this type of embroidery declined.

The availability of cheap cottons in the late eighteenth and early nineteenth centuries did, however, boost the use of appliqué for decorating quilts and coverlets, both in Britain and the United States. A large and intricate English quilt made in the first decade of the nineteenth century has a central roundel scene showing George III reviewing red-coated soldiers on horseback. It is carried out in appliqué using plain and coloured printed cotton. Around the borders are pieced roundels depicting domestic and military scenes. Another coverlet from Britain, made around 1851, shows a great variety of patterns on a calico ground. Two female figures in the centre have clearly been copied from Hiram Power's celebrated *Greek Slave* statue, shown in the Great Exhibition in London in 1851. The coverlet is a riot of shapes cut from coloured and patterned cotton prints. There are jugs, scissors, houses, camels and a floral lozenge.

Appliqué techniques were taught in the nineteenth century at the Glasgow School by Jessie Newberry, Ann Macbeth and later Rebecca Crompton, who wrote the innovatory *Modern Design in Embroidery*. One of her most influential teachings was the importance of matching the designs and the materials of the embroidery to its subsequent use. One piece of her work, The Magic Garden (1937), is made of raw-edged appliqué pieces embroidered with coloured silks

Left *A detail from the beautifully worked New Forest Embroidery commissioned by the New Forest Association to commemorate 900 years of Forest life. It was designed and organized by Belinda Montague, and was intended to hang between the windows on a wall of the Verderers' Court at the Queen's House in Lyndhurst. The whole piece worked in three panels measures 25 x 2 feet (7.7 x .7m) and more than 60 volunteers helped with it. A variety of techniques have been employed in addition to appliqué, depicting birds, animals and flowers, and historical scenes such as the one shown.*

Far left *The lovely sixteenth-century Patience hanging from Hardwick Hall. She is one of the virtues on a series of large hangings, that may well have been worked by professionals, and could have been made out of cut up vestments.*
Left *A large and intricate English quilt made in about 1805, with plain and printed cotton appliqué. The central roundel probably represents George III reviewing volunteer troops in 1803.*
Above *A brightly coloured Hungarian leather jacket with red and brown leather appliqué. These jackets were warm and attractive, and very popular during the nineteenth century.*

using French knots, couching and honeycomb stitches. This panel has vitality, with contrasts of texture and line, and clever combinations of patterned and plain materials.

Appliqué is an international embroidery form. Nineteenth-century Iranians used felted woollen cloth as a form of inlay. Shapes were applied edge to edge, with outlines of couched cords. This is known as Persian Resht work, the designs often resembling cloisonné enamel work. An original feature is the incorporation of portraits enclosed within a frame of flowers.

Leather jackets with brightly coloured leather appliqué are a valued Hungarian tradition, as a protection against the cold. By contrast, in nineteenth-century India, tents and hangings were made from cotton appliqué in bold designs, to provide shade while travelling. North American Indians devised a striking method of design for blankets and dress still used to this day.

In the San Blas atolls of Panama, and in northeast Colombia, the Cuna Indians work a traditional style of reverse appliqué known as "molas". The design, created by cutting linear shapes in step formation through several layers of different coloured, plain cotton material, reveals the pattern in reverse. The edges of each step are neatly tucked under and stitched. Traditionally, molas incorporated pre-Christian mystical designs, including devils, spirits and monsters. Reverse appliqué panels are used now on the front and back of blouses, and increasingly on cushion covers and bags.

Aside from its widespread use to decorate clothing and accessories, appliqué is often used today to create large and striking murals. The wide range of fabrics now available and the development of protective fabric sprays offer many advantages to the designer of hangings and panels incorporating appliqué.

In 1968, Lord Dulverton commissioned the Overlord Embroidery, which took 20 people from the Royal School of Needlework five years to complete. It is made of 34 panels, each 8 x 3 feet (about 2.5 x 1 m). Appliqué designs portray the efforts made by the Allies to liberate Europe during the Second World War.

An outstanding appliqué embroidery, Monarchy 1000, was designed and worked by Audrey Walker in 1973. The panel, 9½ x 7½ feet (3 x 2.3 m), is worked in turquoise, blue, green, grey, white, cream and gold and shows a thousand years of monarchy with gold kid lettering depicting nine royal houses. The materials applied onto a cotton canvas include a range of furnishing fabrics, linens, chiffons and nets. Simple stitches of straight lines, seeding, knots, cretan and herringbone are used perfectly to blend the hard edges of the appliquéd shapes

A revival of decorative ecclesiastical embroidery has developed since the Second World War and the English embroiderer Beryl Dean has designed and produced many works, using hand- and machine-stitched appiiqué extensively in her designs, combined with rich metal thread and silk embroidery. The Silver Jubilee Cope (1976-77) was designed and worked by Beryl Dean, helped by other needleworkers. The design of St. Paul's Cathedral and 73 churches radiate to the base of the cope from a central point at the back of the neck. The buildings are named and the architecture has been faithfully recorded even down to the many types of weather vanes. Silk organza in warm stone colours and grey fabrics with subtle touches of green are applied to a fine cream wool.

__Right__ A detail from the extraordinary Silver Jubilee Cope (__far right__). Designed and worked by Beryl Dean, helped by members of the Stanhope Adult Education Institute, it is a remarkable piece of contemporary appliqué. The cope itself is made from a fine wool, and was worn for Queen Elizabeth's Silver Jubilee in 1977. It is now housed in the Treasury of St Paul's Cathedral.

__Right__ A detail from the Overlord Embroidery, designed as a tribute to the Allied Forces who took part in World War II. The 34 panels are predominantly appliquéd, but many of the outlines and details in the work have been enhanced with finely executed embroidery.
__Far right__ A cushion cover worked by Jessie Newberry in the early part of this century. Appliqué has been used in a typical art nouveau design, and the dominant colour throughout is a muted green.

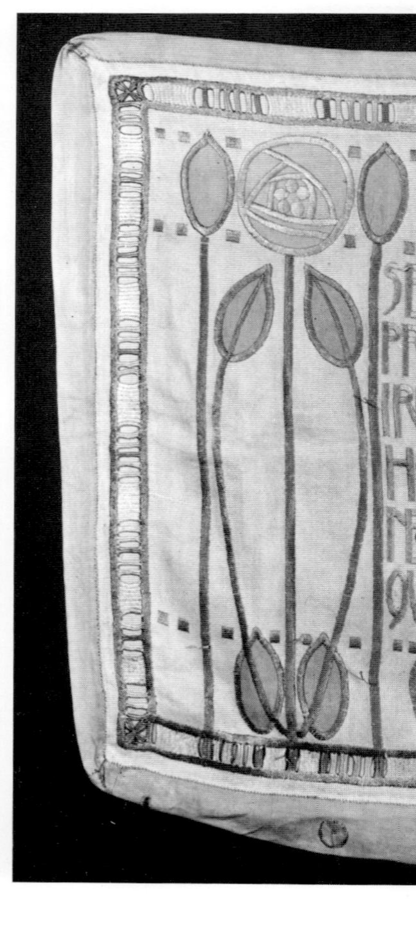

Materials

Fabric

A firm but pliable fabric is most suitable for the background. A collection of any plain, patterned or textured materials can be applied, but it is best, although not always practical, to be consistent in using cotton on cotton and wool on wool. Clear plastic bags keep selections of different coloured pieces separate and easy to view.

Appliqué on an article to be washed must be made from washable materials and it is sensible to pre-wash all materials before applying them. Leather and felt are easy to apply on decorative articles, and materials like Viyella and cotton make appliqué work more straightforward at the beginning. Many manmade textiles have a springy nature and are difficult to handle, as are loosely woven or bulky fabrics, although this may be overcome by experience. Materials such as Thai silk are exciting to use when placed to catch the light on reverse weaves. Shot silk can also be used to great effect; similarly, unusual visual results can be made from silk organzas and nets. Felt has an ancient history of use for appliqué in Middle Eastern countries and continues to be popular today. It is made by kneading or trampling moistened goat's or sheep's wool together, which is then flattened and laid out to dry. As it is a non-fraying fabric, felt lends itself well to appliqué work.

Materials which tend to fray or stretch can be held by applying fine iron-on interfacing to the back of the fabric, although this cannot be used on transparent materials.

Thread

As a general rule, the colour and character of the thread should be similar to the material used. For cottons and materials of a similar weight, use an all-purpose (size 50) sewing thread. Never force a thread through a fabric as immediate puckering and distortion occurs. Use coloured threads for particular effects, and silk or metal threads for further decoration when the basic appliqué is complete. Remember dark tacking or basting threads may leave marks on a pale material.

Equipment

Sharp scissors and fine sharp pins are essential. Crewel, sharps or between needles should be used. You may also need gloving needles for leather appliqué.

If complete accuracy is desired, then work should be performed using a frame. The background fabric mounted into the frame needs to be slightly slack while tacking the pieces into place, then tightened for final sewing to prevent puckering. (Some would argue that all rules are meant to be broken; even puckered shapes can be used to create part of the design.) The shape and size of the frame depend on the type of work: a square frame is needed for large work, a narrow, bordered, circular frame for machine work.

Techniques

Design

It is essential to consider the purpose for the completed appliqué, and plan the design before beginning. Pencil several ideas roughly on paper. Simple, bold shapes are necessary for this type of embroidery. Tribal art is often simplified and a useful source. Outline shapes of leaves, petals, fruit and letters will initiate a free design, which can be added to as the work progresses. Compositions are more complex, and need detailed planning.

Consider the juxtaposition of colours in the intended design. Using colours next to one another in the spectrum, with small areas of opposing colour, may be a guideline. Also, light against dark colours, and warm against cold, can create interesting contrasts. Particular care must be taken for work to be used in a church or on a dark wall.

To plan the design, coloured paper cut into shapes, or designs or shapes taken from magazines, wallpaper or photographs, can be moved around until a pleasing arrangement is achieved. These shapes can be fitted with glue, tape or pins to a background sheet. It may be easier to create the whole design from one piece of wallpaper or from a picture. Either way, these designs can be transferred to the background fabric by using tracing paper, or by copying, preferably in sections.

A more direct method of designing is to trace around templates onto the background fabric using a dressmaker's pencil or a hard lead pencil. Templates may be freely drawn, traced or copied onto a piece of stiff card and cut out, or they may be shapes cut straight from magazines or wallpaper.

If a shape is repeated in the whole design, it is sensible to have a paper shape cut from the template for each repeat, to maintain accuracy. Before cutting the pieces to be applied, it is important to match the grain of the background and the applied materials exactly, as the two materials then move together and will not pucker. (A pulled thread will define the directions of warp and weft threads in the fabric.) Some patterned materials, which demand a specific placement in the design, can be applied with iron-on interfacing. This can be used to prevent puckering, but will immediately change the character of the material. Test a scrap first, in case the iron-on interfacing alters the surface.

Felt and leather need no preparation before being applied but other appliqué fabrics may need to be backed with an interfacing to prevent fraying or to give extra body. Velvets and wools can also be backed with lightweight materials, and silks, cottons or linens with muslin.

Basic appliqué 1. *Mark the required shape on the fabric by drawing round a template. Remove the template and mark a second broken line 1/4 inch (5mm) out from the first.*

2. *Cut out the shape leaving another generous margin (about 1/2 inch/1cm). Only attempt simple shapes at first.*

3. *Work small running stitches by hand or machine just outside the innermost marked outline. These are stay stitches that will make the turning crisper.*

4. *Cut out the shape using the second marked line as the edge, and make cuts and notches along any curved sections to reduce bulkiness on turning under.*

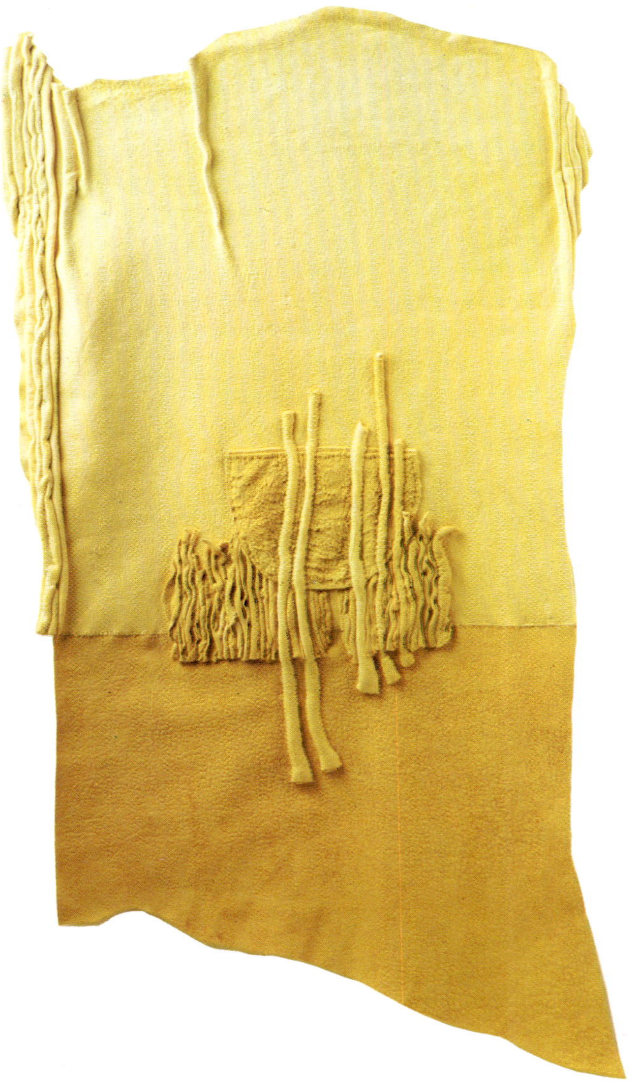

Far left The beautifully designed Monarchy embroidery worked by Audrey Walker in 1973, and displayed in the Pump Rooms at Bath. The piece is largely appliqué work, with additional embroidery for details and lettering. Most remarkable is the fashion in which the designer has contrived to make the different eras to flow into one another along the central pictorial section.
Left *A contemporary wall hanging in chamois leather. By using the same colour and fabric for both background and appliqué, attention is focused on the surface texture of the leather. It is an interesting and very tactile piece.*
Below *Neatening curves and corners. Clip inner curves, so the turning is not strained (1). Make notches along outer curves and take the points off corners to avoid bulkiness (2,3). Clip inside corners so the edges can overlap (4).*

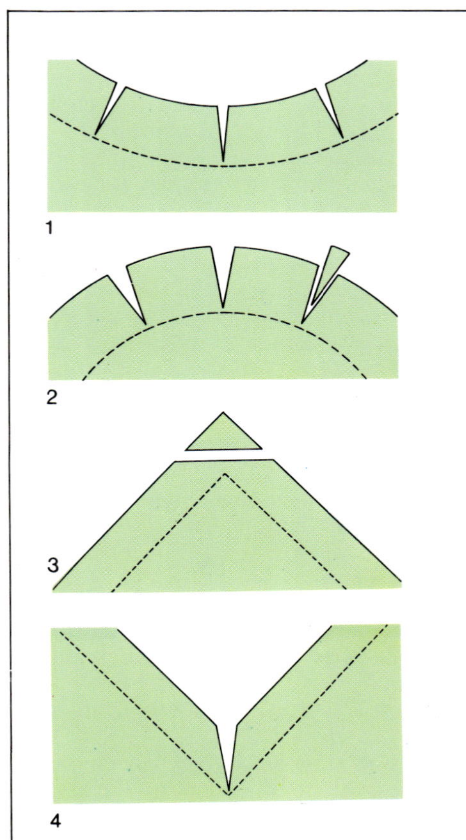

Fine or lightweight fabrics may not need backing, but their edges can be turned under, ready for hemming to the article. First, mark the motif on the appliqué fabric. Cut ¼ inch (6 mm) extra all round to allow for turning the edges under. Edges of curved outlines and corners may need to be clipped or notched so they can be turned under neatly. Finger-press the turned edges. It is best only to iron the edges if they are otherwise unmanageable, because this leaves a hem mark and destroys the slight puffiness of the two-dimensional edge.

For higher relief appliqué, the motif can be sewn down over varying thicknesses of interfacing templates, or can be stuffed with

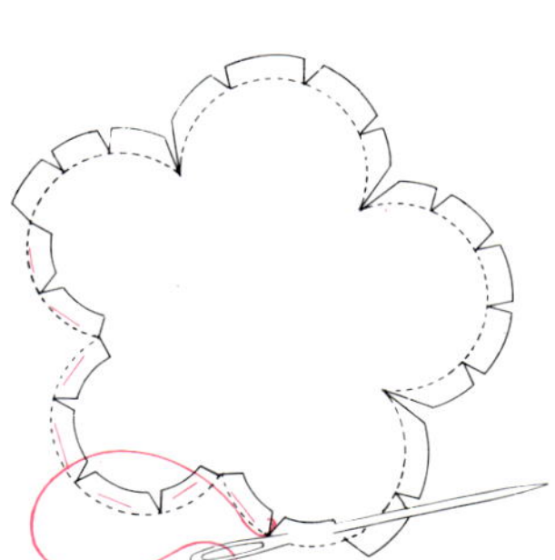

Sewing appliqué: First method 1. *Turn the edges under so that the stay stitching is just visible on the wrong side. Hold firmly and tack into place.*

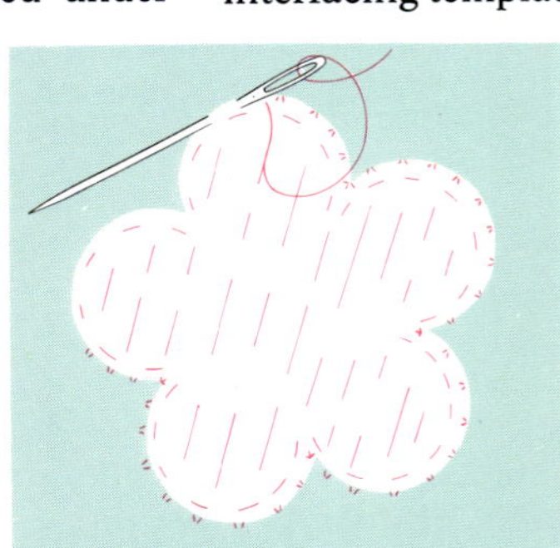

2. *Place the shape on the background fabric and tack it lightly into position. Attach round the edge with neat slip stitch and unpick the tacking.*

Sewing appliqué: Second method 1. *Place the shape on the background fabric without having turned in the notched border. Tack the central area into position.*

2. *Slip stitch the shape into position, carefully turning in the border at the same time with the point of the needle. Stay stitching should not be visible.*

either cotton or polyester wadding once it is in place.

Having transferred the whole design to the background fabric, lightly pin on the pieces using fine sharp pins horizontally and vertically, then tack them in the same way, never around the outside edge. If pin or needle holes mar the surface of the fabric, the woven threads can be gently coaxed back into line with a blunt-ended needle.

Leather must not be pinned, as the holes will always show. Work long stitches across the shape in both directions to hold it firmly in place.

Stitches

Many stitches may be used in appliqué, including running stitch, chain stitch, overcast and back stitch, depending on the desired effect. Buttonhole, herringbone, feather and cretan stitches are ideal for decorative edges, adding another dimension or colour to the shape. Stitches made to overlap outwards onto the background fabric lose the hard edge of the appliqué and are rewarding to use with freely designed work.

Slip stitch is useful for applying motifs invisibly, if they have a turning. If the turnings need to be tacked to hold them in place before stitching the motif to the background, there are two steps. The motif may be more quickly applied by tucking the seam allowance under at the same time as attaching the motif, leaving out the tacking stage. For slip stitch, bring the needle up through the background fabric directly under the folded edge and take a small stitch through and along the folded edge, then down through to the back, keeping the tension consistent.

Stab stitching may be used for leather and fabrics which do not fray. With this stitch, it is important to bring the needle up through the background fabric by the edge of the shape, and then stab vertically down into the shape. Continue the stitch around the edge of the shape.

Machine stitching Motifs can be attached by machine if the stitching does not need to be invisible. It is a faster, and probably more durable method of stitching. Straight stitching a motif to the background involves turning the edges of the mofit under and hemming them, before attaching it by stitching beside the folded edge. A zigzagging method involves tacking the appliqué material to the background in the shape of the desired motif, trimming the material to the tacking line in the precise shape of the mofit, and zigzagging over the raw edges.

Other types of appliqué

Reverse appliqué This method is the reverse of the usual appliqué method, involving the removal of fabric to form a design. Layers of different coloured lightweight cottons may be used; non-fraying materials are best because of the intricate cutting. All the layers should have a matched fabric grain.

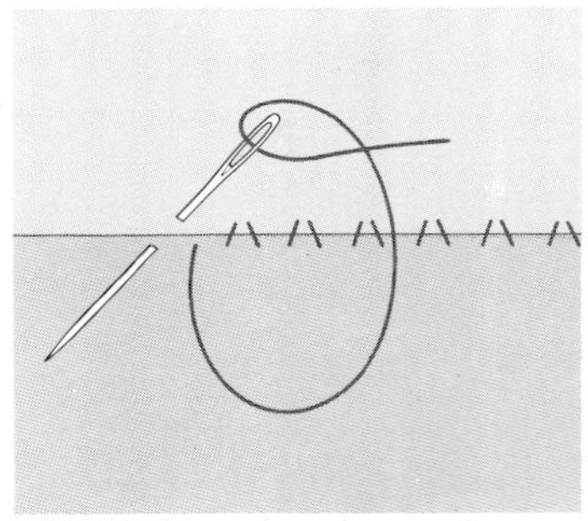

Slip stitch *Working from right to left, slant the needle through the folded edge then pick up a tiny amount of the ground fabric.*

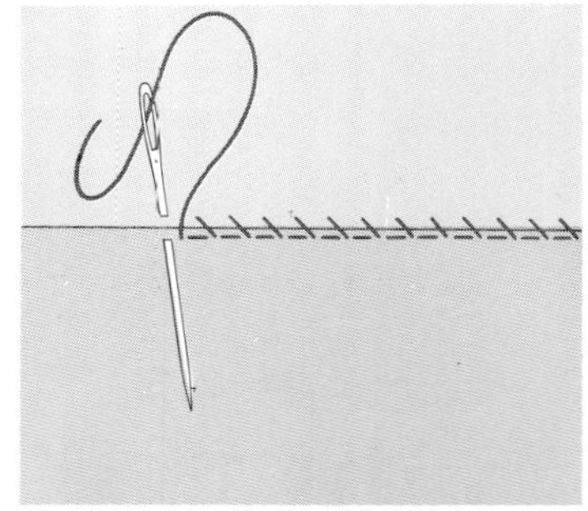

Stab stitch *Use this if the fabric is stiff or if there are many layers. Take the needle down through the fabric, then up in another movement.*

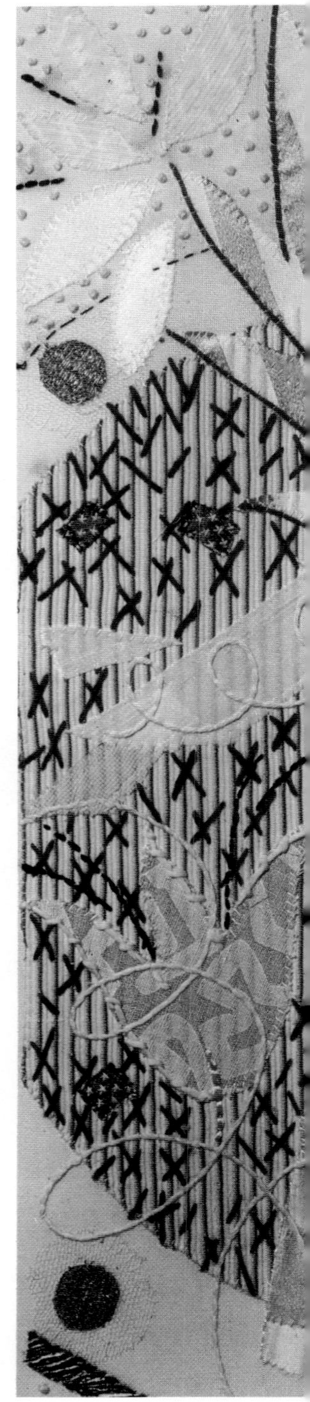

Above *A modern piece of appliqué featuring copper wire in a free-form landscape design. It is a fine example of how modern appliqué has moved away from the more traditional and stylized designs. This piece is full of movement, and traditional techniques such as machine embroidery have been used to very unconventional ends.*

There are two methods: the traditional San Blas method and the recently adapted cut-through method, the difference between them being the order in which the layers are cut and stitched. The more intricate results of the traditional method involve working from the bottom layer up, with more improvising, and the adding of patches and layers both inside and outside the motif.

Cut-through appliqué is achieved by stab-tacking up to five layers together, then cutting away shapes to expose the layers below. The first "hole" must be large enough to accommodate the whole motif. The bottom layer acts as a lining and is never cut. Having turned back the edges, and clipped or notched them if necessary, each layer is slip stitched to keep the area firm. Two layers cut at once can expose a colour out of sequence.

Designing reverse appliqué may seem puzzling, but experimental arrangements of

Above The Magic Garden designed and worked by the celebrated needlewoman Rebecca Crompton. It is an exuberant and original piece of work in which a variety of different techniques and stitches have been deployed. The Magic Garden was worked in 1937, and represented an exciting departure from existing designs and attitudes to needlework and appliqué.

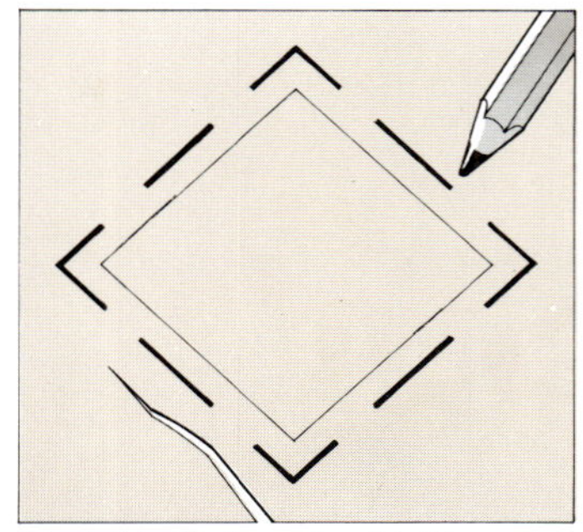

Straight stitch method 1. *Place the template on the fabric and draw round it. Remove and mark a second line ¼ inch (.6mm) outside the first. Cut out leaving a margin.*

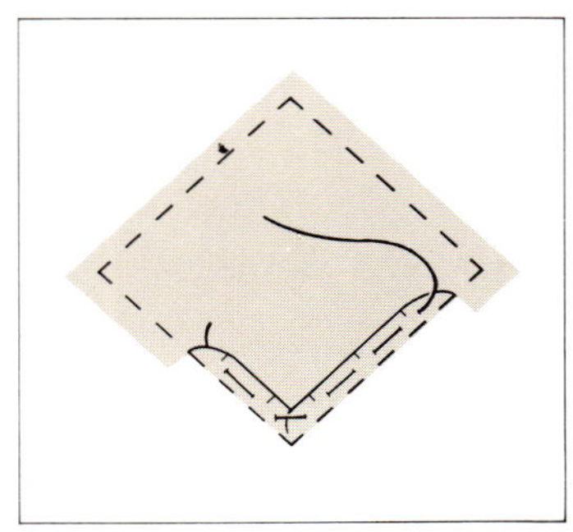

2. *Stay stitch round the outline of the shape, just outside the original line. Trim to second line, cut and notch the fabric at curved sections, fold over and tack as shown.*

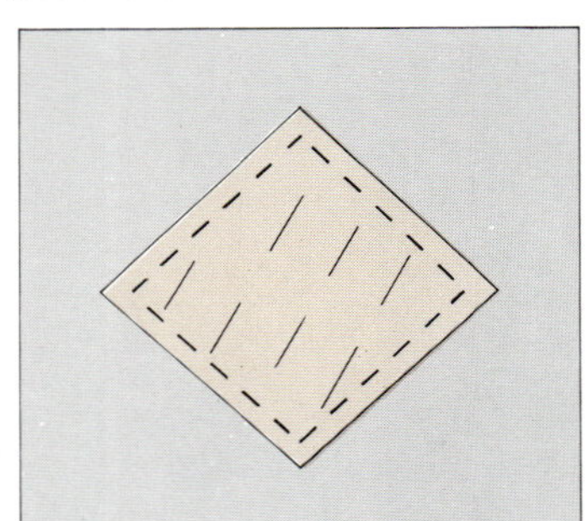

3. *Place the shape on the background fabric, and tack it lightly into position. Make sure that none of the stay stitching is visible before starting the machining.*

4. *Machine stitch the shape on round the edges using a medium stitch. End off the threads securely on the wrong side and remove all the tacking threads.*

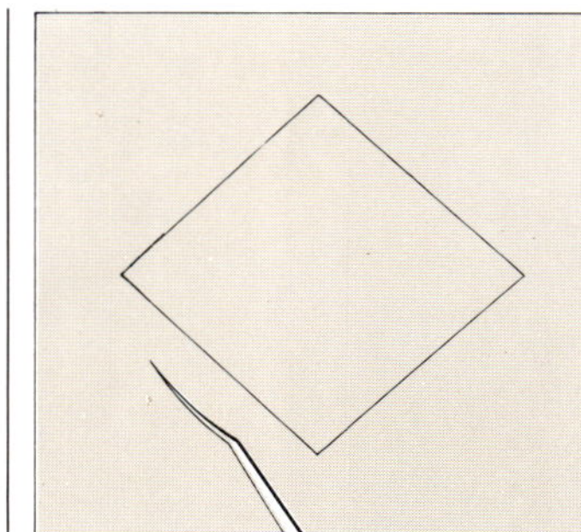

Zigzag method 1. *Place the template on the fabric and draw round it. Remove it and cut out the shape leaving a generous margin, about ¾ inch (1.6 cm) in width.*

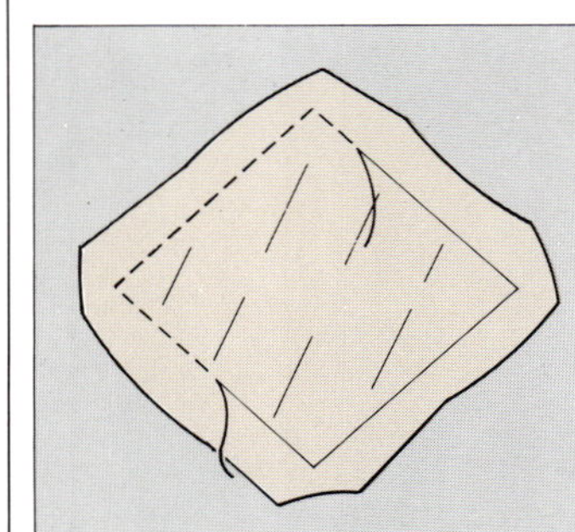

2. *Place the shape on the background fabric and tack it lightly into position. Machine stitch the shape on, placing the stitches exactly over the drawn outline.*

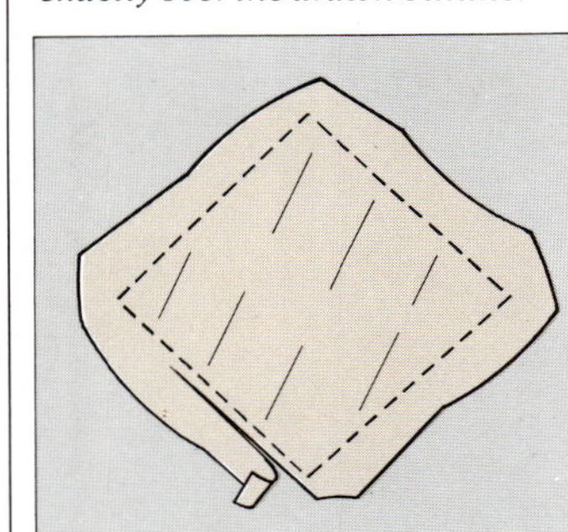

3. *Use a sharp pair of scissors to trim off the excess fabric. Cut as close to the machine stitches as possible without accidentally cutting them or the fabric.*

4. *Set the machine on a fairly close zigzag stitch, and sew round the outline over the straight stitches and the raw edge. End off securely and remove tacking.*

1

2

Examples of appliqué work 1. *A striking piece of appliqué work worked by Henri van de Velde and his Belgian aunt, Knokke. Each of the shapes is outlined in thread of three different colours. It was made between 1892–3 and seems very much ahead ot its time.*
2. *A brilliantly coloured hanging, worked in Indian reverse appliqué, from Panama. The technique is particularly suited to this type of tribal design.*
3. *Misfit is a piece of contemporary appliqué. After preliminary sketches were made of folded and draped material, the work evolved. A screenprinted background of dress patterns in sienna and orange complement the blue blouse with its foam-filled arm and leather hand. The latter holds a glass-headed pin.*
4. *Turkish lace oyahs. Oyahs are needlemade lace flowers, that were sewn to the edges of head scarves. The designs are charmingly abstracted from the natural forms of plant and flowers in subtle colours of fine twisted silk using minute stitches. Petals and leaves are made in flat shapes often with picot edges.*
5. *The Country Wife. a three-dimensional mural commissioned for the Festival of Britain, and designed by Constance Howard in 1951. The panel is worked to five-eighths life-size, and a wide variety of crafts and activities have been represented.*

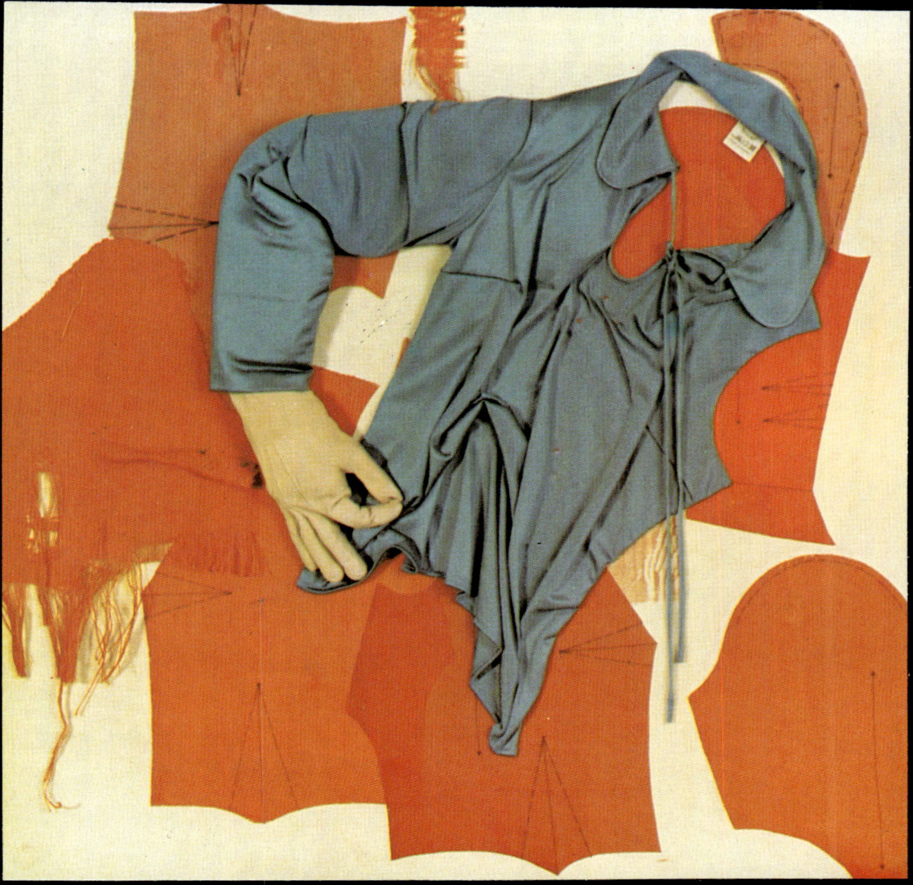
3

4

5

coloured paper or tracings on top of each other can help. Either use tissue paper for the pattern, and stab tack it onto the fabric with small stitches, starting from the centre to prevent puckering, or trace or copy the design onto the fabric layer by layer.

Appliqué decoupé This is similar to reverse appliqué, using just two layers. The top layer is cut away in a pattern to show a contrasting fabric underneath. Interesting patterns can be made by using embroidery in contrasting tones on both layers, to finish features in the design, or to decorate.

Inlay or Persian Resht appliqué This type of appliqué is almost impossible with materials which fray unless backed with iron-on interfacing, and for this reason is usually made of felt or leather.

Two different coloured fabrics are pinned to a board and with a sharp knife, the pattern is cut out through both layers around the design. The background can be attached to a supportive backing of paper or firm calico to prevent stretching while stitching. The contrasting colour or material is then inserted and stitched edge to edge keeping the surface flat. The join can be covered with a couched cord or decorative stitching.

Shadow appliqué Basic shadow appliqué is made with transparent fabric used as a background and a more densely woven fabric tacked to the wrong side. The design,

Above *An example of reverse appliqué. The piece shows four birds and the largest is depicted as the protector of the others. The eyes of the birds are the only embroidered details, the rest of the piece consisting of plain, bold outlines. It has a slightly disquieting effect, but is a striking demonstration of reverse appliqué.*

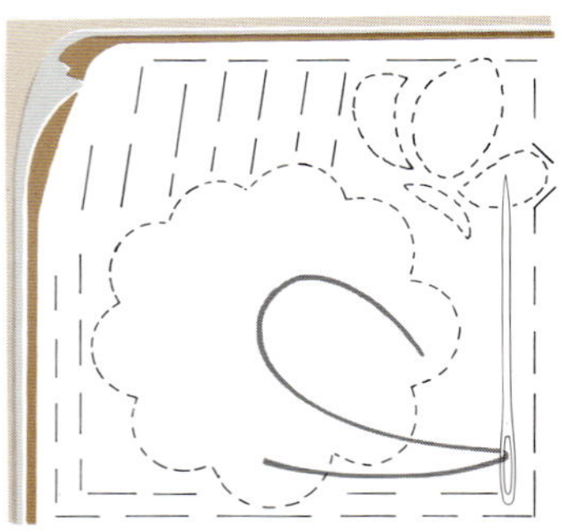

Reverse appliqué 1. *Place the selected fabrics on top of each other, align the edges if possible and tack them all together. Mark the design on the top layer.*

2. *Cut out the pattern from the top layer of fabric leaving a margin of 1/4 inch (6mm) beyond the marked line for turning under. Do not cut the second layer inadvertantly.*

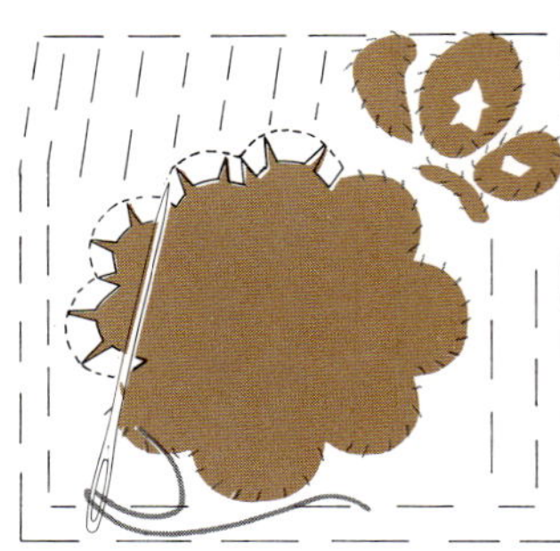

3. *Clip and notch the margin at curved sections and turn it under with the point of the needle back as far as the marked line. Sew edge to next layer neatly.*

4. *Continue to cut, tuck in and sew back each layer until the desired overall design has been realized. Work some stitches through all the layers if possible.*

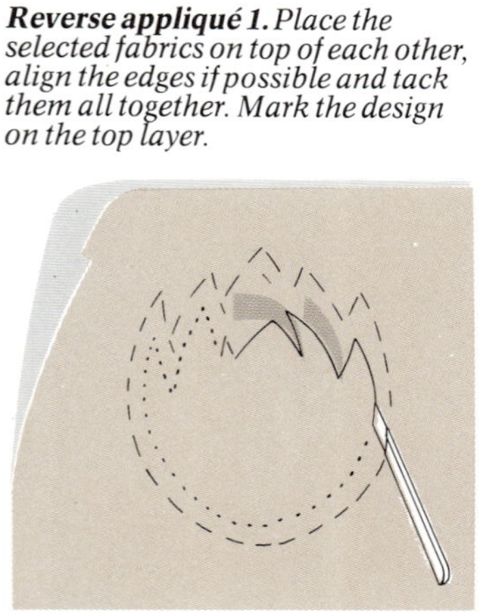

Inlaid 1. *Mark the design on one piece of fabric, lay it over another in a contrasting colour and tack the two together outside the marked line. Cut through along the line.*

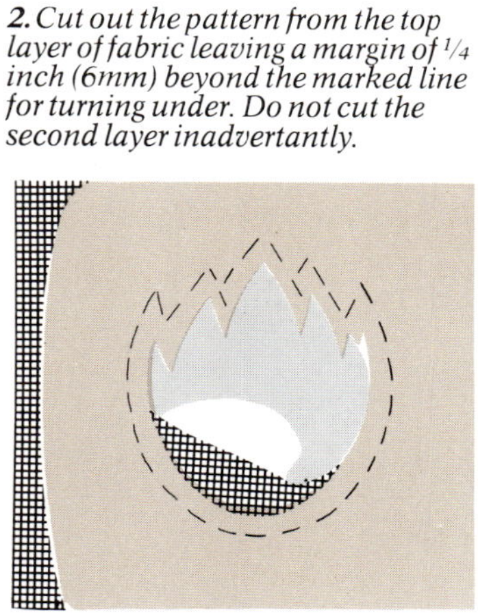

2. *Tack one of the pieces of fabric onto some backing material, and drop the shape or motif in the contrasting colour into the hole. It should fit exactly.*

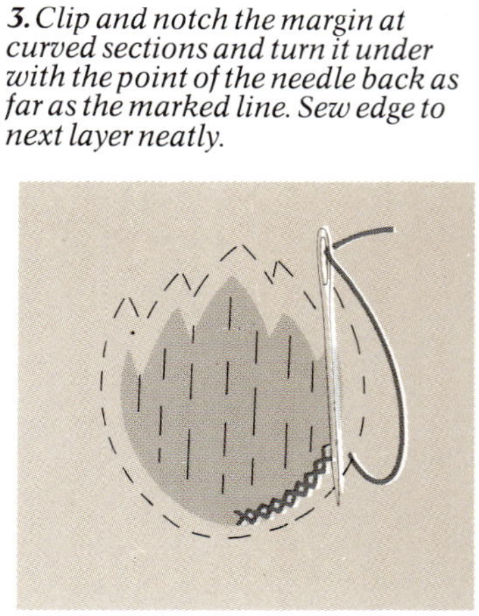

3. *Tack the motif lightly into place in its hole with vertical tacking stitches. Then sew the two edges neatly together with herringbone stitch. Remove tacking.*

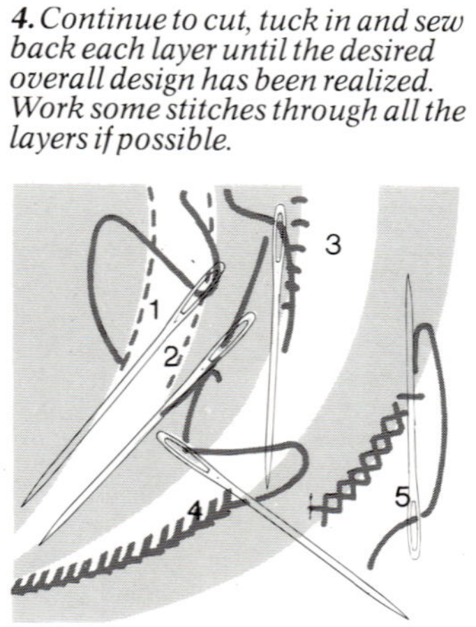

A variety of different stitches can be used for appliqué work: blind stitch (1), *running stitch* (2), *overcast stitch* (3), *blanket stitch* (4), *and cross stitch* (5).

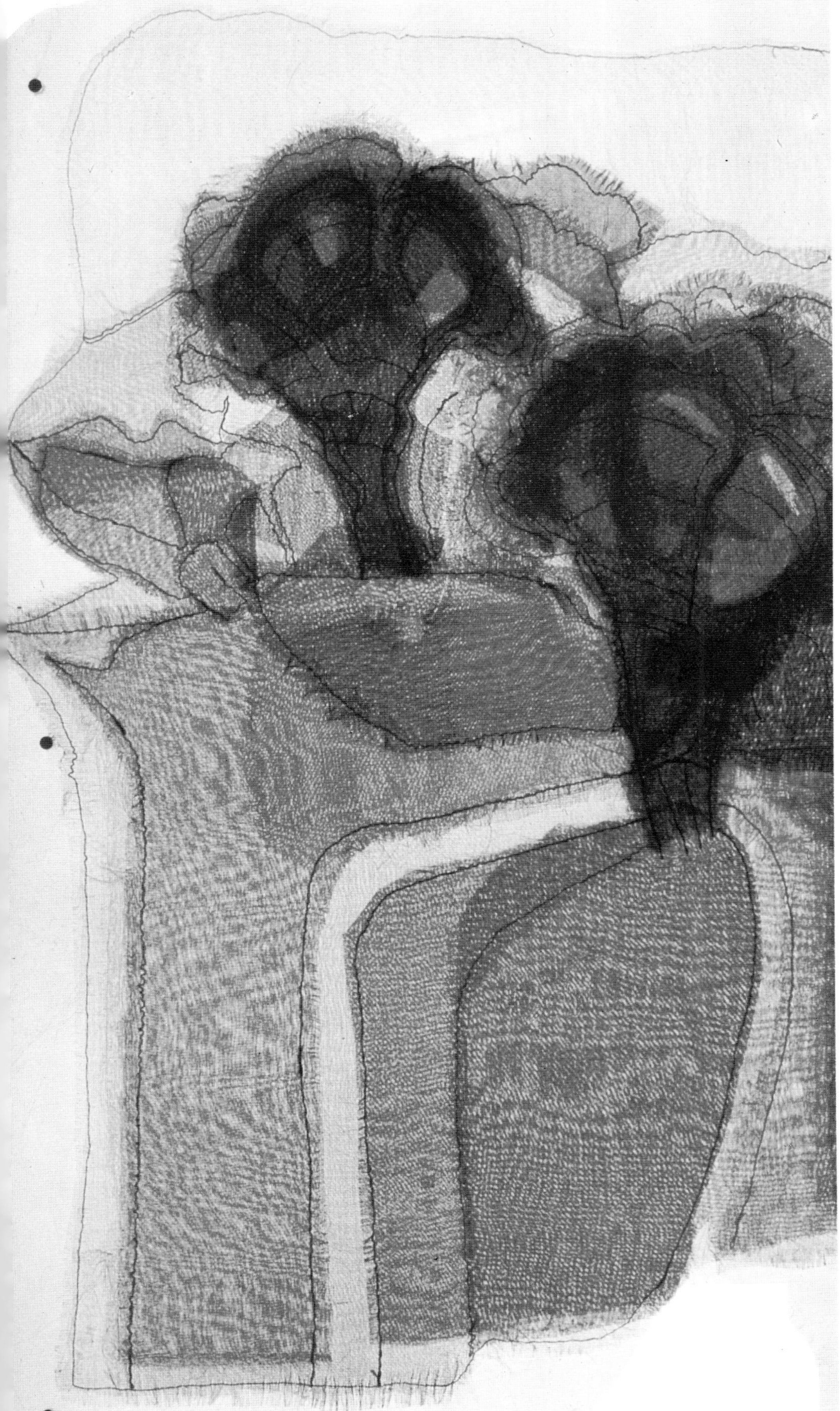

clearly marked on a piece of paper, is placed underneath both layers and worked lightly on the top. The design can be simply hand- or machine-stitched through both layers, then the excess of the denser fabric cut away with sharp pointed scissors. Several layers of colour and different coloured threads in overlapping designs can be used to give a bright, unusual, semi-transparent effect. Frayed edges can also be used to advantage as texture plays an important part in visual appreciation.

Appliqué perse This is a method using a motif from a printed fabric and applying it to a plain background. Iron-on interfacing helps with this method as difficulties may be found cutting out shapes which do not match the background fabric grain.

Ribbons and braids These can be applied in interlaced patterns or tucks, or can be ruched or reversed for a variety of textures, and stitched by machine or hand with exciting results. Victorians created flower motifs using a variety of narrow ribbons and interlaced them for basket patterns. Embroidery can also be used to enhance or decorate a work.

Raised Work

Any thread embroidered onto a material alters the texture of that fabric immediately; when single stitches are oversewn with other stitches, this texture becomes even more pronounced. Altering the type of thread used can also add to the textural effect. In these respects, almost any type of embroidery could be said to be raised, but true raised work came about when embroiderers began to exploit the textural characteristics of needlework further, producing designs in high relief. The great period of raised work occurred in the seventeenth century, when entire scenes were created in three dimensions, often with figures under a canopy in a stylized landscape. This work is often known by the colloquial term "stumpwork".

Left *A piece of shadow appliqué suggestive of trees in a country landscape. It has been worked in greys, mauves and olive greens with emphasis on the texture and weight of the layers of fabric that have been used.*

History

In the Middle Ages an early development of simple appliqué using shapes of material was the application of embroidered roundels or squares, worked separately and then sewn onto a background. This type of embroidery had more depth and dramatic effect than two-dimensional appliqué and first established its popularity in fourteenth-century Europe.

To produce the effect of raised embroidery, the pattern was first laid out on the ground material and then linen cords or coarse embroidery threads were couched down. Finer threads in silk or metal were couched over this raised surface. Other foundations of cord, parchment or felt were also used, often in graduated layers. This method was used to produce architectural designs in relief and to give contrasts of light and shade. Now in Vienna, the Burgundian Vestments mark the high point of pictorial work during this period.

By the end of the fifteenth century, ecclesiastical embroidery in Germany, Austria, Hungary and Italy had become so three-dimensional that it was more akin to sculpture or wood carving. With the use of paddings of wax, linen rags, or even carved wooden blocks over which the embroidery was worked, the effects of sculpture in high relief were reproduced. Examples include a magnificent cope, dated 1504, in Cracow, and a shield of a craft guild dated 1563-74, in Munich. The design on the shield shows three men in a boat, and is worked in metal threads which completely cover the ground fabric, a characteristic of much European embroidery of that time.

Raised embroidery developed later in England, during the reign of Elizabeth I. Design influences came from the East through the newly formed trading companies, and the immigration of skilled workers from Europe, as a result of religious persecution, led to improved methods and forms of expression. With sumptuous fabrics and threads from the East and the newly available steel needles, embroidery came into an era of great magnificence. Raised embroidery came to the fore; embroidered "slips" and "emblems" were worked on fine canvas and applied to cushions, gowns and curtains. Satin gauntlets worked with raised embroidery were often given as gifts. Book covers were also worked in this way. The Douce Bible, given to Elizabeth I as a New

Right *Sixteenth-century guild shield depicting three men in a skiff on the river Ilzstadt in Passau. It is signed by Wolfgang Popp.*

Left *A detail from an example of stumpwork depicting David and Bathsheba. This particular type of embroidery flourished towards the end of the seventeenth century, most themes being Biblical or historical. The disproportionately large and elaborate fruit in the background is very characteristic of stumpwork.*
Below *The ornate Bag of the Great Seal made originally for Sir Orlando Bridgeman in the late seventeenth century. The central panel with its coat of arms is an example of stumpwork at its most refined. The bag was worked in a professional workshop, rather than by enthusiastic gentlewomen.*

Year gift in 1583-4, was covered in red velvet, richly embroidered in gold and silver wire and decorated with seed pearls. Another curious embroidered binding covers a New Testament of 1625. The design, embroidered on a white satin ground, shows Abraham and Isaac on one side and King David on the other. The embroidery is thought to have been taken from a waistcoat belonging to Charles I.

A revival of English ecclesiastic embroidery in the 1630s led to the production of rich textiles for the church. A good example is a large, ornate, purple velvet pulpit hanging, dated 1633, which is embroidered with silver gilt metal threads and red silk cord. Arms of the Sandy family from the Vyne are worked in high relief embroidery in the centre and the background has many raised cherubs' faces, now black with age, with silver gilt hair and wings. Another interesting example is at Durham Cathedral, where there is a superb red silk cope with angels' faces in raised work.

Professional workshops produced a perfect specimen of secular raised work – the Earl of Bradford's Bag of the Great Seal, worked for Sir Orlando Bridgeman when he was Lord Keeper of the Seal in 1667-72.

Stumpwork

In the last three-quarters of the seventeenth century, a particular form of raised embroidery enjoyed a short period of prominence in England. This was commonly known by the descriptive term "stumpwork", probably derived from the French *estompé*, meaning "embossed". Stumpwork was characterized by three-dimensional doll-like figures, typically illustrating historical or Biblical themes. It was chiefly worked by the ladies of the great Stuart houses; often the finished embroideries were subsequently sent to be made up into cabinet or mirror frames by professional workmen. Some pieces were framed to stand as pictures on small portable easels. Others formed the panels on "caskets" or miniature chests.

A typical stumpwork piece of this period would include a king and queen (perhaps under a canopy and sometimes resembling Charles I and his queen), a castle or house, a stag, a unicorn, a lion, birds, butterflies, fruit and flowers, all set in a stylized rural setting. Religious themes – Esther and Ahasuerus or Solomon and Sheba – were also common, as were figures depicting the virtues or the seasons. Many of the scenes are alike enough to suggest designs might have been taken from drawings originating from professional workshops. Stumpwork was clearly a development of the high-relief ecclesiastical embroideries, but other influences are not hard to find. The excellent printed designs seen by travellers to Italy, Spain and Germany provided one source of material. Illustrated herbals, copies of needlework pictures and tapestries, bestiaries and pattern books were widely available from the beginning of the seventeenth century. *A Schole House for the Needle* by Richard Shorleyker was published at the same time, and this, too, had an influence on needlework methods.

During this period, white satin with a traditional blue-green selvedge, embroidery silks and gimp cord (a firm central core bound with fine silk) were imported from Italy. Milan and Venice produced metal threads and Florence specialized in plain woven silks.

The white satin, with a design sketched in ink, was backed with calico or linen and mounted on a large frame, ready for the high-relief pieces; these were worked separately on stretched linen held in a small hand frame. Figures and animals, usually 2½-3 inches (5.5-7.5 cm) high, were padded in life-like shapes and cut out, leaving surplus material to be tucked under and stuck onto a firm paper shape. The completed figure was then sewn onto the sketched satin ground. The attaching stitches were cleverly concealed by a couched fine gimp cord or linear stitches.

Faces were made of modelled wax, simple padded silk or embroidered satin stretched and glued over minute carved pieces of boxwood. Hands and legs were made in the same way, or formed of silk thread over twisted wire. The legs were often covered with tiny needlelace (fine buttonhole) stitches to suggest stockings. Shoes with red heels and bows or long boots with spurs were also added, all executed in immense detail. Hair and bunched ringlets were made from looped stitches, or real hair held in place with a lattice of threads. Embroidered fashionable gowns in bright coloured silk needlelace were neatly pleated and draped onto the figures; sometimes fine petticoats were also added. The draperies of the canopy could often be closed.

Above *A detail from a seventeenth-century scalloped mirror set in a stumpwork surround. Tent, satin and rococo stitches have been used in conjunction with buttonholing, darned silk pile and couched work. Some parts have been raised with padding. The gaps between the figures have been filled with animals, flowers and insects; the bee or fly on the left is the same size as the squirrels at the bottom; this disregard for proportion is highly characteristic of stumpwork.*
Left *An example of the primitive raised work of the Peruvian Chimu, on which small three-dimensional figures have been depicted. It is a detail from a royal tunic in the form of a short shirt made from cotton and wool.*

The background trees and sprigs of flowers were often worked in flat embroidery on the satin ground using floss silks. Leaves and petals were worked in frames of fine wire filled in with needlepoint lace stitches. These were attached only in one place, giving a three-dimensional look, sometimes with the addition of an embroidered shadow. Spring-like coiled purl was often used to give realistic foliage effects. Small pears and apples of carved wood, covered in minute lace stitches, were hung in clusters from the trees, often showing a childish lack of proportion. The landscape also included fountains, and rock gardens tufted with velvet stitch and coiled wire. Talc or mica

Right *This piece of stumpwork, of outstanding quality and beauty is a seventeenth-century Adam and Eve. The design is superior in both perspective and proportion to the majority of stumpwork.*

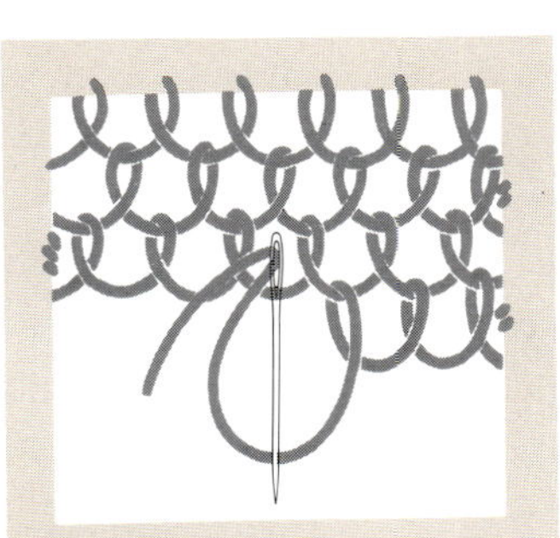

Detached open buttonhole *Work this simple filling stitch with evenly spaced loops, securing each row with tiny oversewing to the borders.*

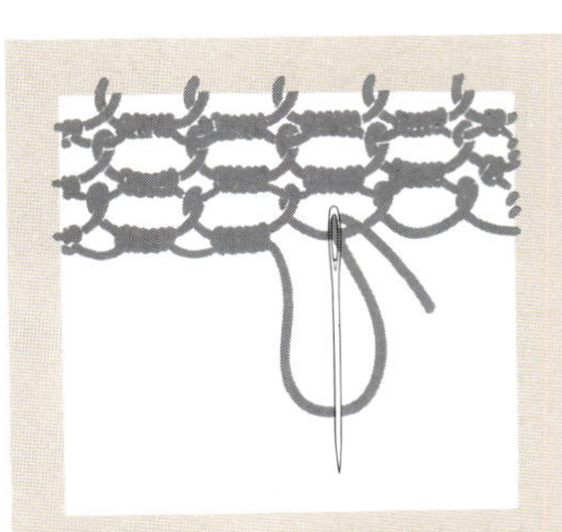

Detached space buttonhole *Work the first row of spaced loops from right to left and work back filling each loop with buttonhole stitches.*

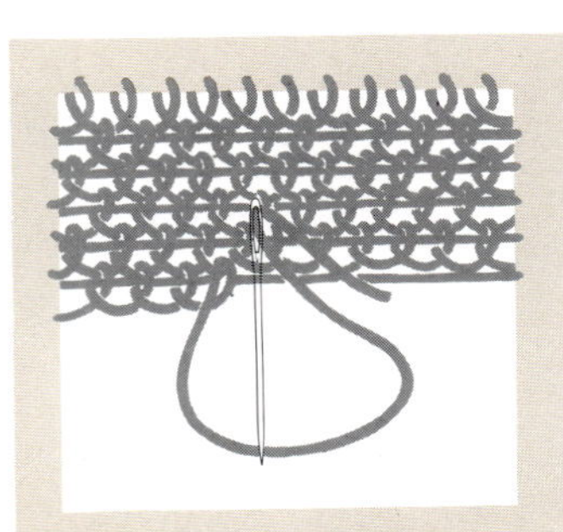

Detached buttonhole with a bar *Work loops across, then take the thread straight back. Work the next row through the loops above and over the bars.*

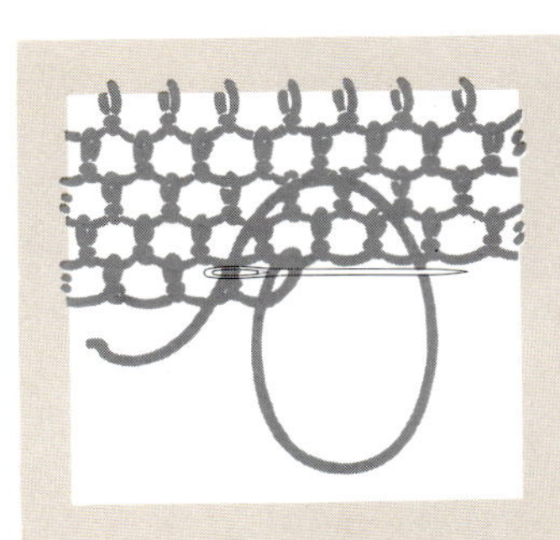

Detached knotted buttonhole *Make a loose buttonhole stitch and a second sideways around both threads of the first.*

was used for the windows of the house.

Plumules of peacock feathers were used to decorate birds, insects and sometimes the necklines of dresses. Seed pearls added touches of grandeur to necklaces and crowns. Spangles, small circles of silver wire beaten flat, were sewn on to suggest snowstorms in some earlier works. A good example of the use of spangles occurs in the earliest known piece of American stumpwork, dated 1644, by Rebeker Wheeler.

Although stumpwork travelled to the North American continent with the establishment of colonies there, this type of embroidery, together with raised embroidery generally, went into a decline by the end of the seventeenth century. Later examples show these techniques taken to excess, which may have contributed to their fall from favour. Another factor in the disappearance of raised work was the arrival of Indian and Chinese goods and the resultant fashion for Chinoiserie. Today, many surviving examples have lost the colourful character they once undoubtedly possessed, but the dexterity of the work is still impressive and can only be fully appreciated if one tries to copy a piece. Modern embroiderers have adapted and used many of the techniques of raised work in murals and needlework pictures, often to vivid and striking effect.

Materials

Fabric and thread

Traditionally, white satin has been employed as a background fabric, with linen or calico used for the raised work. Paddings for the raised figures of the past might have been

Below *The Paget family twentieth-century stumpwork worked between 1901 and 1927. The Paget family of Somerset, England own a stumpwork picture dated 1683, and worked by an ancestor Mary Ruddock who was married to John Paget. This inspired Sir Richard Paget to draw and design a picture of his family on the terrace at Cranmore Hall. The faces and hands were carved in wax from which plaster casts were made and later painted. Each lady of the family designed and embroidered her own costume and that of her husband, child or brother. The magnificient foliage and family arms were worked by Sir Richard's mother. Sir Richard Paget holds a stick of fused silica, a newly developed process on which he was working at the time.*

Left *Young Edwardian Lady a modern three-dimensional piece worked in 1974. This elegant piece demonstrates the adaptation of traditional raised work to contemporary designs. An almost ghostly effect has been achieved by working the figure's jacket in the same fabric as the picture's background.*

sheep's wool, hair or cotton tow. For modern three-dimensional work, stretching materials can be used because they mould easily around paddings, and other materials will stretch on the diagonal weave or slightly moistened. Modern paddings include cotton wool, terylene wadding for rounded shapes, and card or light wood for crisp shapes. Twisted, coloured silk threads are needed for working the raised motifs, and silks for flat embroidery. Figures and objects can be further decorated with metal threads, spangles, small glass beads and pearls. Small flakes of mica or talc can be incorporated for window glass; faces, hands and occasional bare limbs may be made from carved boxwood, shaped wire or plaster cast from wax moulds.

Needles

Pointed crewel needles of varying sizes are needed for laying foundation stitches and for embroidering. Tapestry needles with blunt points are useful for working needlelace stitches, which may be made to stand out from figures, so imitating clothes.

Techniques

It is important to plan raised work carefully, and it can be helpful to have drawings or photographs of the subjects from different angles. It is worth experimenting with paper to solve the problems of designing sizes and shapes before cutting into the material. Draw the outline of a motif on fine calico, and frame the calico to hold it taut. Place the shaped areas of padding on the fabric, and hold them in place with long retaining stitches.

Next, work needlelace stitches over the padding. The stitches depend for their size and type on the intended motif. If specifically made shapes are not used, a woman's face, neck and arms, for example, may be executed in split stitch and her hair in bullion stitches. Dress may be indicated by miniature embroidered garments. Strips of lace may be applied for collar and cuffs, and pearls may illustrate a necklace.

When the motif is complete, cut the fine calico about a quarter inch (6 mm) outside the edge of the motif, then cut small notches to accommodate the curves. Tuck the surplus under, stick onto the card shape and slip stitch to the background. It is possible to add stitches after the motif has been applied to the background, but this can stretch the fabric. Gimp cord may be used to outline the motifs when they are in place.

Left *This teapot sculpture made from quilted cotton and polyester filling and painted with acrylic shows the furthest limits of three-dimensional work: soft sculpture.*

Patchwork and Quilting

Patchwork

Patchwork, or pieced work as it is sometimes known, has been in existence for centuries but it is only within the last decade that this form of embroidery has caught the imagination and enthusiasm of needleworkers all over the world. Patchwork is an area of cloth made of small pieces of various materials sewn together, usually in a geometric pattern, and is often associated with bedcovers, commonly known as quilts.

History

The earliest known patchwork in existence today was found in a cave in Serindia on one of the old silk routes between China and India. A large collection of textiles was found in a walled-up chapel in the Caves of a Thousand Buddhas, and among them were several pieces of mosaic patchwork which were probably made prior to A.D. 900. The pieces from which the patchwork was made could have been votive offerings left by travellers on the old trade route.

Patchwork as we know it today was not made in England until textiles were easily available and cheap enough to allow materials to be spared before being completely worn out. Much early patchwork, from the Middle Ages, was really applied work. Textiles were scarce and the best pieces from such items as worn church vestments were cut away to be reused as a substitute for embroidery by applying them to another length of background cloth. By the time of the Stuarts, "India chinces", "glazed chinces" and "painted callicoes" were being imported into England by the East India Company, which was started in 1631.

Such materials were used to make one of the earliest known existing English patchwork bedcovers with matching bed hangings in about 1700; this can still be seen at Levens Hall in Cumbria. So far as is known it is the only patchwork in these materials which still survives. Also available from India were palampores (cotton bedspreads) many of which were printed with Tree of Life patterns as well as exotic flowers, birds and fruit. When the palampore was worn out the best pieces were cut away and applied to a cotton background in a new design to make another bedcover or perhaps a set of bed curtains.

Between about 1800 and 1815 cotton manufacturers were printing cotton panels with topical scenes often commemorating some notable happening: a royal occasion, a battle or perhaps a well-known political event. A panel such as this was often used to form the centre of a quilt top, borders being pieced and built up around it until the required size had been reached. These panels were again popular towards the end of the nineteenth century when many were printed to mark the centenary of the American Declaration of Independence (1876) and to honour Queen Victoria on her 1887 Jubilee. Today, quilts made in this way, with a central motif and a number of borders, are called Framed quilts or Medallion quilts.

In the United States, the women moving westwards with their families during the nineteenth century were often dependent on the contents of their scrap bags, for clothing and bedding. Every piece of material was hoarded, and it needed considerable skill to blend such pieces into a homogeneous patchwork pattern. Making one block of patches at a time was economical of time and storage space, and meant

Right *A Pennsylvania German quilt worked in a Tulips and Ribbons pattern. The tulips on this quilt are bright yellow with red centres, the leaves and ribbons are green and the background is white. It was made in the middle of the last century, when the tulip was a favourite motif with religious connotations. The sharp outline of the border contrasts dramatically with the more fluid lines of the ribbons, leaves and flowers. Both colour and design are very characteristic of Pennsylvania German quilts of the period.*

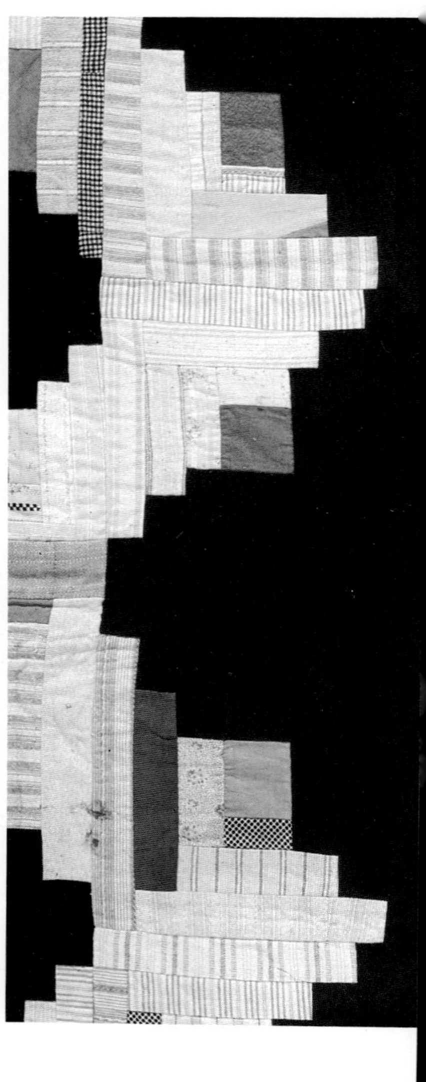

Above *A late nineteenth-century American quilt. Known as Double Irish Chain pattern, the chequerboard effect is achieved by alternating a five-patch block with a plain block. The latter has a small square appliquéd onto each corner. This quilt is creamy pink with red squares, and as the overall pattern is striking in itself, Double Irish Chain pattern is usually worked in plain fabrics. If patterned fabrics are used, the print should be a small one.*

Left *One example of the endless variations on the Log Cabin quilt pattern, arguably the best known of all the different patterns. Log Cabin quilts are always made up from strips of fabric placed round a central square, and divided diagonally into halves or quarters. The light and dark strips must be in sharp contrast; traditionally the light strips represent the firelight, and the dark ones, the shadows. Courthouse Steps, Barn Raising and Zig-Zag are all variations on the basic Log Cabin design. This particular one is a Dutch quilt.*

that the work was easier to handle. The patches themselves were an efficient way of using every corner or scrap of material, and were easy to cut out and sew. The whole family would assist in the making of patchwork.

It is not known exactly when the "block" method of constructing the tops of quilts began to take general precedence in North America over the whole cloth quilt. Certainly by about 1830, making quilts in blocks or squares of patchwork was the most favoured method, and designing patterns became a popular occupation, with various designs being published in magazines of the time.

There was a tradition in the United States at this time that a girl should have 12 patchwork quilts in her hope chest at the time of her marriage, possibly even 13, the thirteenth being the grandest – her Bride's quilt. Certainly in a country where winters were long and houses poorly heated it was sensible to have as many warm bedcovers as possible. Consequently girls were taught at an early age to piece simple blocks for quilt tops. As they were finished the tops were put away until the girl's engagement was announced, when they were made up into quilts.

In nineteenth-century America quilts were often made for a special purpose or occasion. A great number of Album quilts were made, although the practice was not so common in the British Isles. The quilt was a cooperative effort; each of the many blocks was made by a different person or group of people who usually signed and dated their work. Album quilts were made sometimes for presentation to the Minister or his wife, incorporating motifs relevant to the recipient's life or interests and often place of residence. Freedom quilts, another type of Album quilt, were made for young men on reaching the age of 21. Sisters and girl friends would piece a top ready for the young man's engagement when he would add this top to those of his future bride, helping to bring her total nearer to the dozen she hoped to acquire. Album quilts were often presented to a bride with hearts included in the design. Many fine examples of Album quilts were made in the Baltimore, Maryland area between about 1845 and 1852, the blocks often illustrating landmarks in the area or historical events which had some meaning for the residents. Two ladies, members of the Methodist church, Achsah Goodwin Wilkins and Mary Evans, were the foremost exponents of the intricate and beautiful work carried out on this type of quilt. Album quilts were also made for hospital use, usually of alternate squares of red and white material, the white squares having texts printed on them in indelible ink.

Many Friendship quilts were made by schoolgirls, each pupil in the class making a

Above *An Irish quilt, loosely based on the design known as Grandmother's Flower Garden. Each "flower bed" motif is surrounded with white hexagonals, and separated from its neighbours by interlocking red "paths". Patchwork made from different configurations of coloured hexagon pieces has always been popular, and designing such quilts is the way in which many people first become interested in patchwork.*

Right *An enchanting coverlet that represents hours of careful work. It was made for Mrs. Waterbury by her friends and presented to her on April Fool's day in 1853. Many of the blocks have been signed, and they range from the purely decorative to the religiously or historically significant.*

Top right *A Star of Bethlehem quilt of the type that was extremely popular in the last century and at the beginning of this century. The central star is mimicked by the four peripheral stars, with their identical red centres and tips. The border has a somewhat improvised feel to it, in contrast to the impeccably matched stars.*

Bottom right *A Feathered Star patterned quilt worked towards the end of the last century. Some of the triangular pieces are minute, and the quilt has been beautifully and very finely sewn throughout.*

***Right** An Amish quilt from Milton, Iowa, made in about 1920. It is worked in black, cinnamon and khaki shades, and is a variation on the Shoe Fly pattern. The Amish or Plain People belong to the Mennonite church. They do not believe in ornament or decoration and their patterns tend to be strong, geometrical shapes in solid colour.*

block which she signed. Modern Friendship quilts were made in 1976 to commemorate the Bicentennial of American Independence, the blocks usually incorporating events and personalities connected with the specific town in which the quilt was made.

During the latter part of the nineteenth century, much of the very ornate Crazy patchwork was made from silks, velvets, brocades and other such fabrics. These were heavily embroidered with a wide variety of stitches, many of which were original to the individual needlewoman, but the two stitches most often employed were herringbone and feather stitch. Much Crazy patchwork was decorated with flowers and birds painted on silk, sometimes photographs were included and ribbon embroidery often decorated the border. Most Crazy quilts were not bedcovers but decorative "throws" to put over the back of a sofa or perhaps a piano. Smaller items such as dressing-table mats and cushion covers as well as portieres were also made in Crazy patchwork.

The interesting names given to different patchwork patterns have varying origins – Dresden Plate and Churn Dash are taken from domestic objects; Whig Rose, Burgoyne Surrounded and Queen Charlotte's Crown (after George III's wife) from history;. Turkey Tracks, Pineapple, Rose, Lily and Dahlia have obvious domestic origins. Other designs are named after star patterns, and people and places from the Bible or Bunyan's *Pilgrim's Progress.* Some refer to the environment, such as Bear's Paw, Fence Rail, Windmill and The Rocky Road to California. Names for patterns vary considerably and change according to the part of the British Isles or American continent in which they are found. The pattern known as Orange Peel in America is known as Robbing Peter to Pay Paul in Somerset, and Pincushion in Northumberland. In the United States, Robbing Peter to Pay Paul is an entirely different pattern which is often known as Drunkard's Path or Country Husband elsewhere. It is wise not to be too dogmatic about patchwork quilt pattern names.

Perhaps one of the best-known patterns is Log Cabin. It is built up of strips of fabric representing the logs of the roof of a cabin round a central square representing the chimney, the strips on two sides being of dark colours and the strips on the other two sides of light colours. Traditionally, the central square of material should be red to denote the fire; the dark part of the square represents the shadow and the light part the firelight. If the square is yellow it represents the lantern put in the window to light the traveller on his way. Another version of this pattern,called Courthouse Steps, has a black central square, symbolizing the judge's robes. The name Log Cabin must have been given to this pattern once it reached the United States, as in the north of England it is called Log Wood, in the Isle of Man Roof pattern, and in Ireland a Folded quilt. It was at one time thought that the Log Cabin pattern had come to Ireland from America, but research has shown that it was used in Scotland during the eighteenth century and subsequently crossed the sea to Ireland. Because the narrow "logs" were often made from ribbon this is sometimes known as Ribbon patchwork.

Changing fashions and new inventions have brought changes in needlework techniques, and patchwork, which was for many years a country craft kept alive by women in the rural areas of Britain and North America, has once more become an art-form. Patchwork motifs are used today for decoration on aprons, skirts, curtains, table cloths, tote bags and many other items as well as quilts.

Materials

Making patchwork is very simple and no specialist equipment is required. There are, however, a few rules which should always be observed.

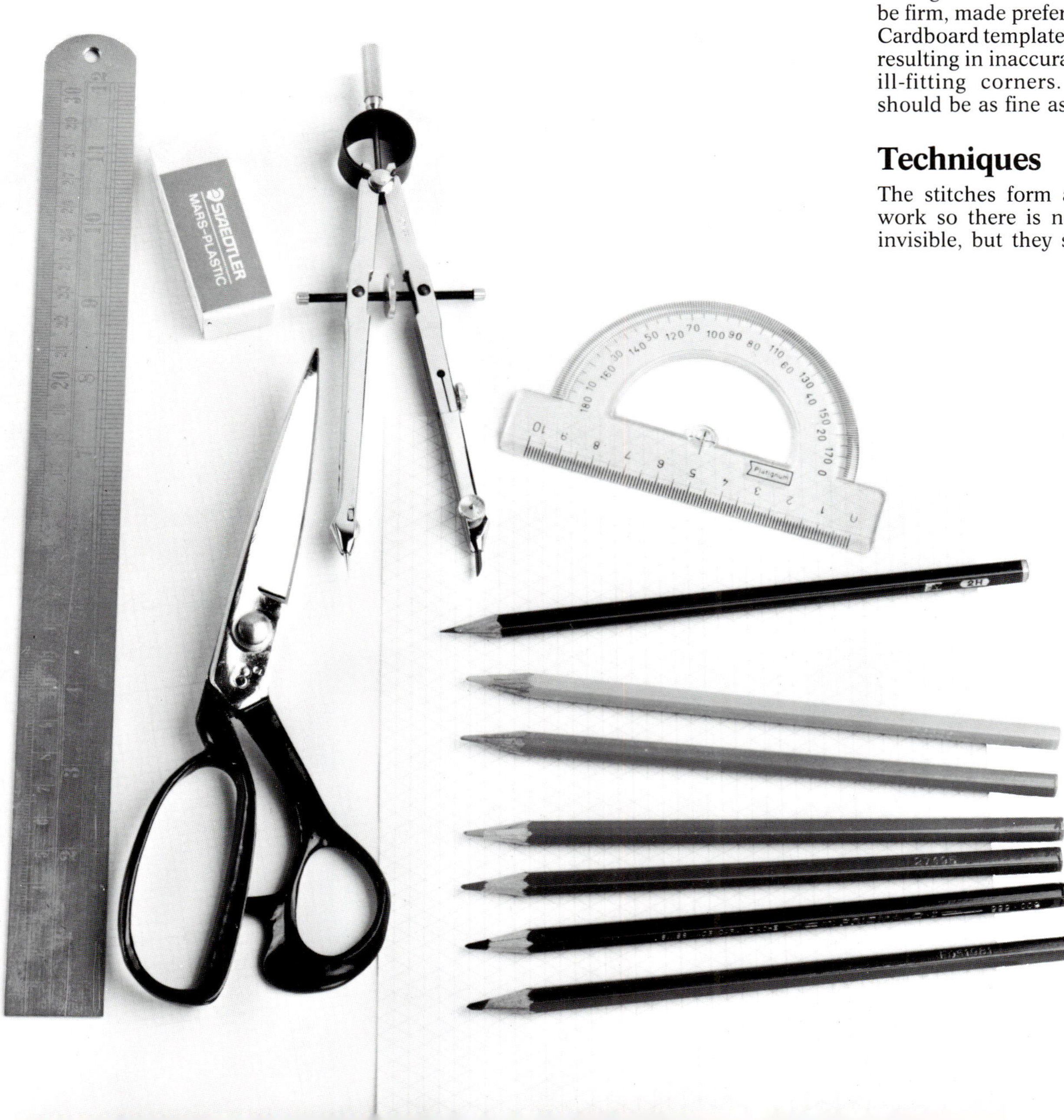

The fabrics should be firm and, if possible, fairly new. Brand-new fabrics should be laundered before use to prevent shrinkage of the work. It is inadvisable to mix fabrics of different types and weights in the same piece of work because different types of material may need different treatment and suit different purposes. Care should also be taken in choosing colours and prints, and solid colours should blend.

The purpose to which the patchwork will be put and the weight of the fabric should be considered before deciding on the size and shape of the individual pieces. If possible, all patches should be cut with the grain of the fabric running in the same direction. Before actually cutting the cloth, it is often helpful to draw out the design on squared paper and to colour the shapes in different combinations until a satisfactory arrangement has been achieved.

The template, which is the pattern for the basic geometric unit in a patchwork, should be firm, made preferably of metal or plastic. Cardboard templates easily fray at the edges, resulting in inaccurate shapes of fabric, and ill-fitting corners. Needles and cotton should be as fine as possible.

Techniques

The stitches form an integral part of the work so there is no need for them to be invisible, but they should not be obvious.

Left *Although patchwork can be worked with scraps of material and very little equipment, care must be taken when making the pieces. Use a proper template, and draw round it neatly with a sharp pencil. Cut out the pieces with a sharp pair of scissors to ensure clean edges, and try to align the templates with the grain of the fabric where possible. Proper attention at this stage will reduce the likelihood of a buckled and misshapen patchwork.*

Details of particular stitches are given with the different patchwork techniques. Many women prefer to use a sewing machine to piece the blocks. There is no rule about which method to use; it is a question of preference.

English method

In what is generally known as English patchwork, paper shapes are cut round the template from good quality paper or thin card – one shape for each patch. These must be very accurate or the patchwork will not lie flat and corners may not meet. The papers are placed on the reverse side of the material and cut round, leaving a turning of about ¼ inch (6 mm). The turning is folded over the paper and basted, taking care not to catch the paper. Two patches are placed right sides together and oversewn (whipped) along one side. Other patches are made in the same way until the required motif has been assembled. Once a patch has been completely surrounded on all facets, the papers can be carefully removed.

To achieve a neat outline and accurate angles, it is advisable to make hexagons and octagons by the English method. For the Grandmother's Flower Garden pattern, one hexagon is surrounded by six others and sometimes a further circle is added. When sufficient motifs have been made, they are joined together, with a band of neutral coloured hexagons between.

American method

Other geometric shapes are easy to piece using the American method. Here the template is placed on the wrong side of the fabric and a pencil line drawn round it. Each shape is cut out, leaving a suitable turning. The shapes are arranged with the right sides facing and sewn together along the pencil lines with a running stitch. The seams are then trimmed to about ⅛ inch (3 mm) and pressed to one side. If possible, press towards the darker material so that the seam will not show through. It is always helpful to build up the patches in such a way that they make larger blocks which can be joined with long straight seams rather than many short seams.

Above *Crazy quilts became increasingly popular during the latter half of the nineteenth century. Some of them were totally irregular in design, simply using any colour, size or shape of scrap that the maker could lay hands on. Others, such as this one, were worked in blocks with one recurrent motif like the fan. Crazy quilts were renowned for the richness and variety of their designs, and were often embellished with ribbons, appliqué and elaborate embroidery in addition to the patchwork. They were often too decorative to be confined to the bedroom, and were used as "throws" over sofas and mantlepieces.*

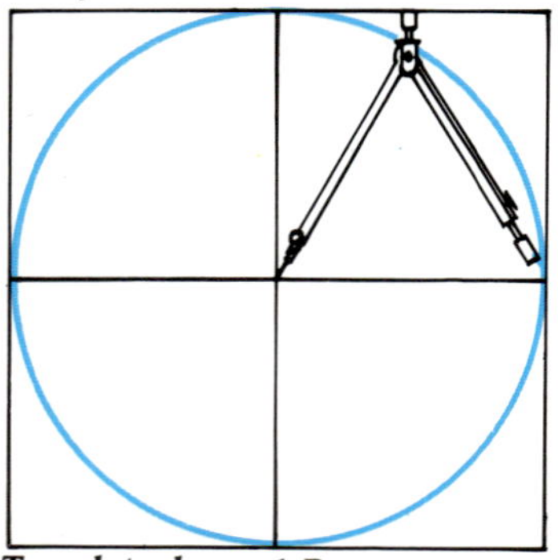

Template shapes 1. *Paper templates must be carefuly and accurately drawn. Use a sharp pencil, ruler and compass to draw the shapes.*

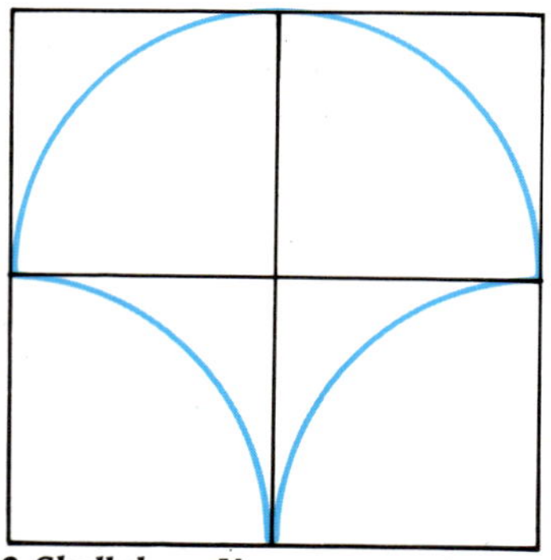

2. Shell shape *Use a compass to draw a semicircle. Lightly draw in two diameters, and keeping the same radius mark in the two quadrants.*

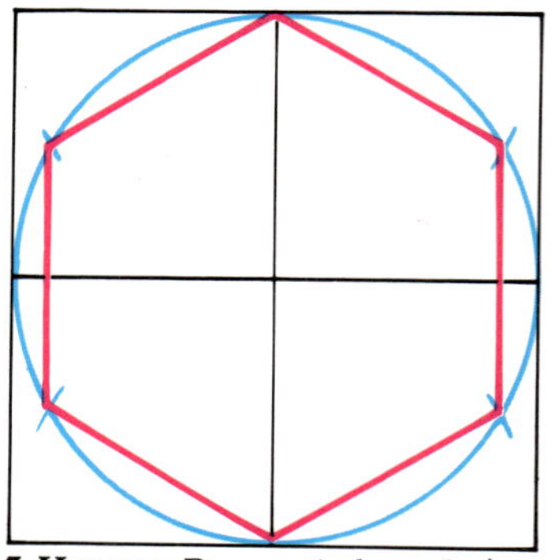

3. Hexagon *Draw a circle, and keeping the same radius, mark off six arcs on the circumference. Join up these dots to form the hexagon.*

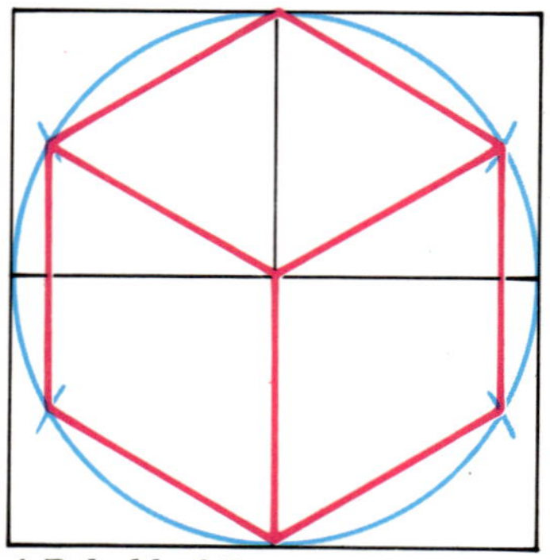

4. Baby block *Draw out the hexagon as described, and then draw in two radii from alternate corners into the centre as shown.*

Left A modern Bicentennial friendship quilt made by the staff of the American Museum in Britain in 1976. The crossed flags at the centre of the quilt stand for the friendship of England and America. Each participant chose the design for the block she was working, and some of these designs represent objects from the Museum's collection. The quilt has been backed with green and white printed cotton, the green matching the banding.

Above A patchwork quilt made in Maryland, U.S.A. in the 1840s to the well-known Grandmother's Flower Garden design. The border is made from chintz, manufactured in England in the early part of the century, and the hexagonal motifs are made from English furnishing fabrics. Some groups of three hexagons have been cut in one piece thus reducing the number of seams.

Squares are simple to sew. A four-patch block consists of four squares, two each of two contrasting materials, sewn together to make a larger square. A nine-patch block consists of five squares of one fabric alternating with four squares of a contrast. All block patterns can be made into many designs according to the way in which the blocks are joined together. Triangles and diamonds can be joined to make stars and flower shapes, and used in conjuction with squares to make up the block.

Crazy patchwork

Like Log Cabin patchwork, Crazy patchwork does not need a template: both patterns use what is known as a "foundation block". In Crazy patchwork, a square of cotton is cut to the size of the intended

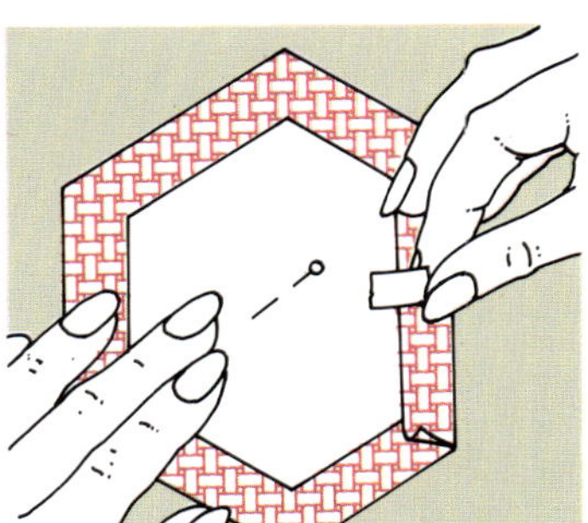

Patch backing 1. *Place paper template on fabric, wrong side up. Secure with a pin, and fold each edge tightly over. Anchor edges with adhesive tape.*

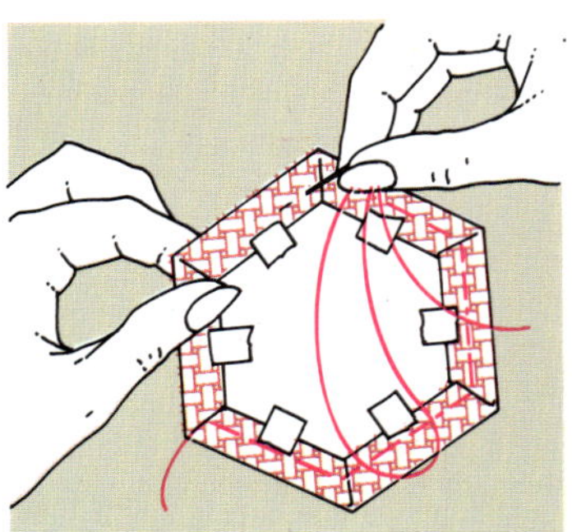

2. Tack round the edges of the fabric to hold it down over the paper, taking care not to penetrate the paper itself. Keep the fabric pulled taut throughout.

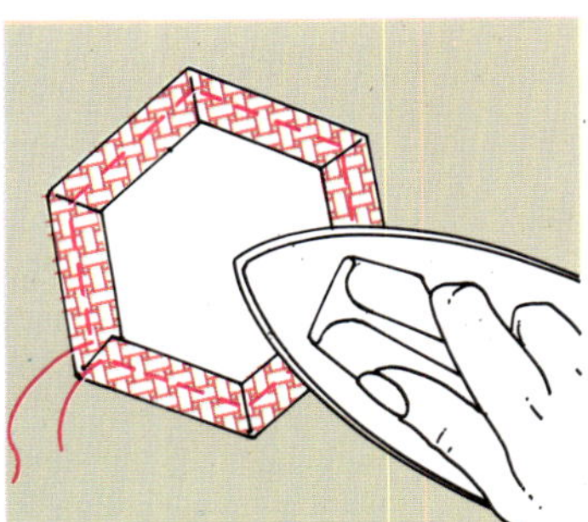

3. Remove the adhesive tape, and press each patch on the wrong side to ensure sharp clean folds. This stage is vital in achieving a well-finished item.

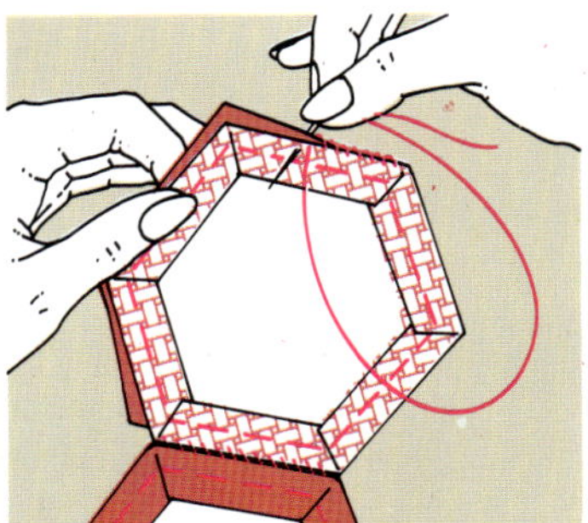

4. Lay two patches together, right sides inwards, and overstitch them neatly together along one edge. Do not remove tacking until hexagon is completely surrounded.

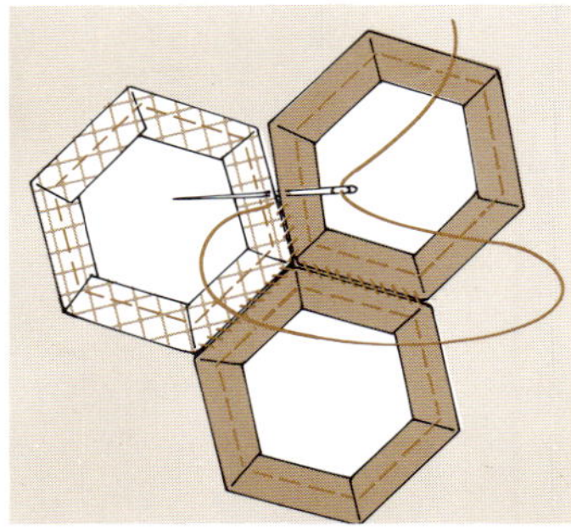

Hexagons into rosettes 1. *Join two hexagons together with neat overstitching. Then join a third hexagon to both of the original ones as shown.*

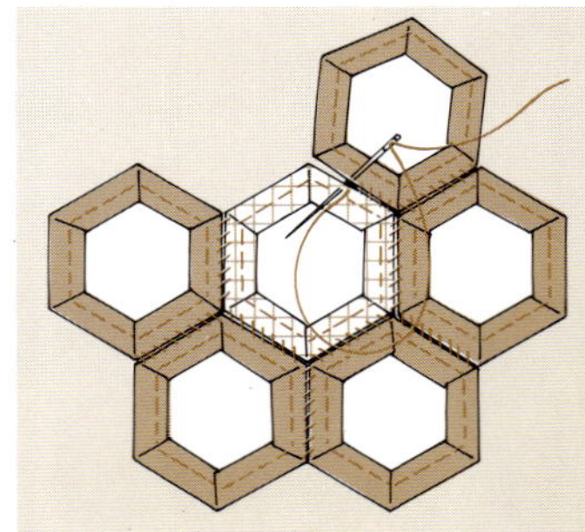

2. *One of the first hexagons must be considered the centre of the rosette, and six others sewn round its sides. This rosette is the basis for many designs.*

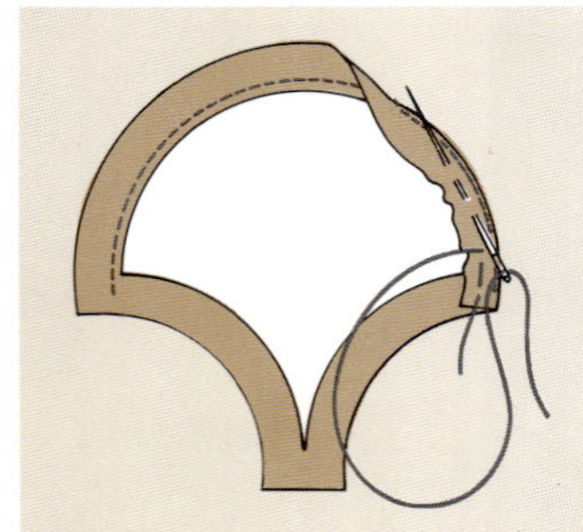

Shell patchwork 1. *Stay stitch round the top curve, turn the seam allowance down onto the template, and tack it carefully into position.*

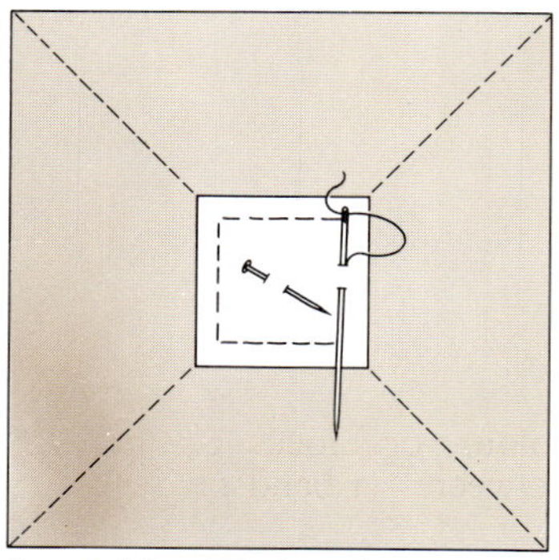

Log Cabin 1. *The foundation block should be creased diagonally. Pin the central square where the creases cross.*

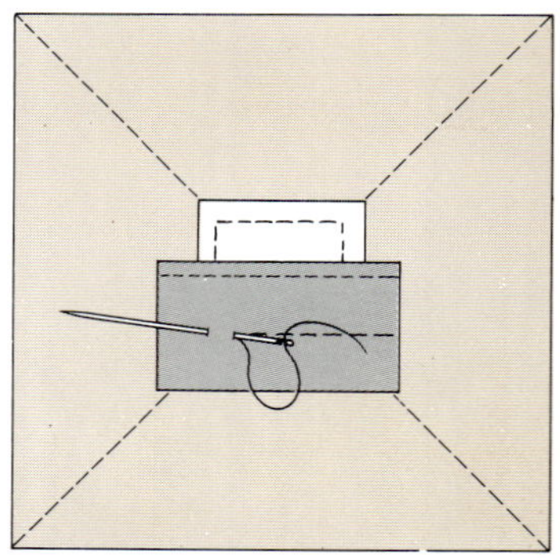

2. *Sew a strip of light fabric to the central square with running stitch, right sides facing. Press away.*

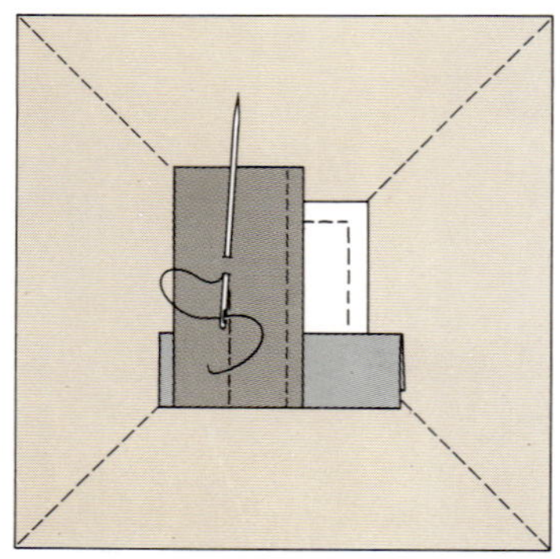

3. *Sew a second strip of light material to the second side.*

Left *Remember that the border of a quilt must be an integral part of the design as a whole. Borders can be plain, picking out colours in the quilt, they can contrast with the patchwork, or simply add to the overall area.*
A selection of popular borders for quilts:
1. *Check border;*
2. *Target border;*
3. *Victory border;*
4. *Navajo border;*
5. *Paris border;*
6. *Arrow border;*
7. *Sawtooth border;*
8. *Zigzag border;*
9. *Cascade border;*
10. *Plains border;*
11. *Hourglass border;*
12. *Scallop border;*
13. *Diamond border;*
14. *Brick border;*
15. *Rosette border.*

Traditionally certain borders have become associated with particular designs, but each individual must select the appropriate colour, design and weight of fabric to border the quilt in question.

finished block, with ½ inch (1 cm) turnings on all sides, and fabrics such as silks, velvets and brocades of random shapes and sizes are sewn on. It is usual to start in one corner and baste down each patch slightly overlapping the preceding one. It is only necessary to turn in a hem on edges which will not be covered by other patches. When the foundation has been completely covered, the edges of all patches should be embroidered with a feather stitch, herringbone or another fancy stitch in a variety of colours. The blocks are then joined together and the joins also embroidered over. Crazy patchwork is backed but not usually quilted. Instead the top and backing are "tied". This involves taking two small back stitches over each other at unobtrusive places, and tying off the ends on the back of the work.

Log Cabin patchwork

In Log Cabin patchwork, templates can sometimes be used but they are not essential. The foundation block of the required size, with ½ inch (1 cm) all round for seams, should be creased diagonally in both directions, the resulting creases being the lines at which the rows of "logs" cross. Pin the central square, representing the chimney, to the centre of the foundation, then assemble five different fabrics in light shades and five in dark shades, and decide how wide the strips of fabric for the logs should be. Cut two strips of light material and two of dark

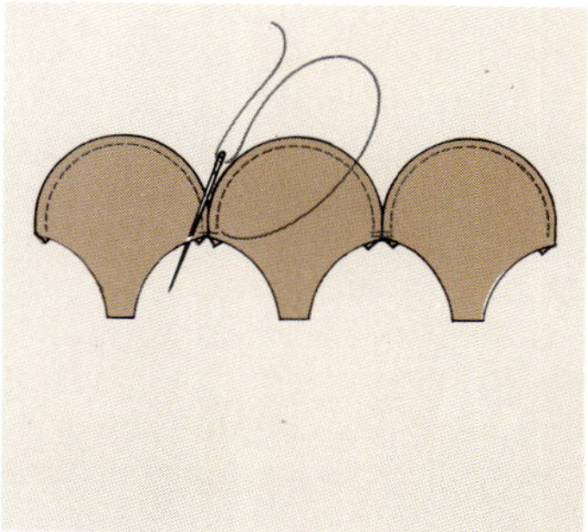

2. Place prepared shells in rows, right side up, and tack them together at the lower seam as shown. Make sure they are properly aligned and lying flat.

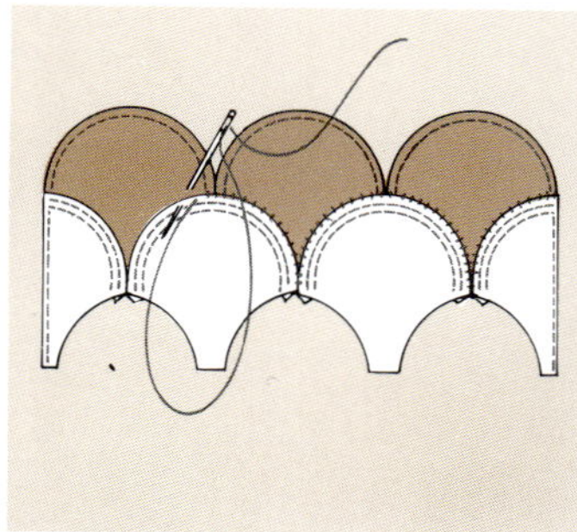

3. Place the second rows over the first, covering the stalks, and pin and tack it into position. Then carefully overstitch the rows together following the curves.

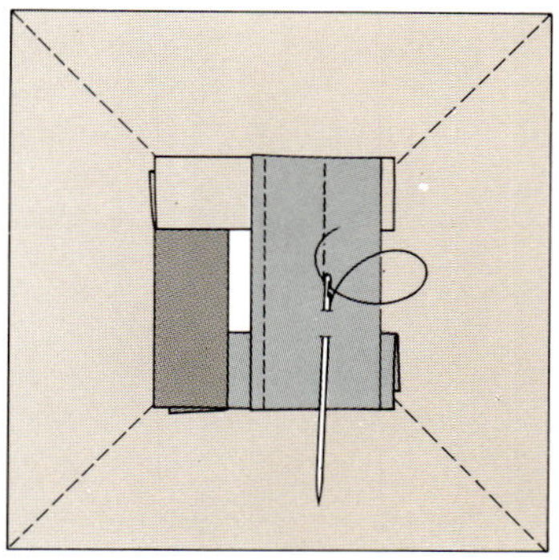

4. Sew dark strips to the other two sides of the square in the same way.

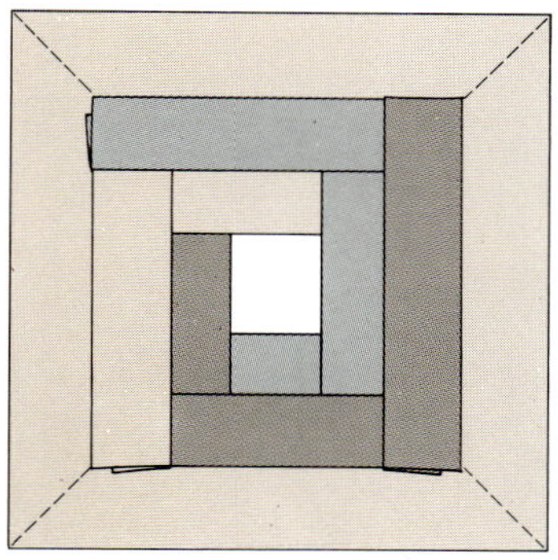

5. The strips should be longer in each succeeding row. Keep light and dark strips on the same sides and continue until the foundation is covered.

about two inches (5 cm) longer than the central square. With right sides facing and using a running stitch, sew the first light strip to the central square ¼ inch (6 mm) in from the edge, taking the stitches through the foundation block. Press the strip away from the centre. Sew the second light strip to the second side of the square in the same way, followed by dark strips to the remaining two sides. Continue in this way with the other fabrics, making the strips longer on each row and keeping light and dark fabrics always at the same side until the foundation has been covered. When the required number of blocks have been made they can be sewn together in many different ways. Lay out the blocks and move them around to see which pattern is the most effective.

Assembling blocks

When the geometric shapes have been assembled into squares or other shapes known as "blocks", according to the pattern, they can be joined together in a number of different ways to make a "top", which is then treated as one piece of cloth. Pieced blocks can alternate with blocks of solid colour, or blocks can have a "sashing" between – a band of neutral fabric which frames the blocks. Sometimes pieced blocks are set with other pieced blocks, which results in a secondary pattern being formed. It is advisable to have an odd number of

Far left *A nineteenth-century quilt designed in the Straight Furrow pattern, a commonplace variation of the Log Cabin design. The blocks are very large in this particular quilt, and the stripes or furrows are worked in a fiery combination of yellow and earthy browns and reds.*
Left *This top was never actually made up into a quilt, but was worked in beautiful pastel English chintzes at the beginning of this century. These chintzes were largely made in the middle part of the last century, but include a roller print of around 1800, and an exquisite copper plate print manufactured in the 1770s. This top is in perfect condition and has been very carefully worked.*

blocks across the width of a quilt and down the length, so that there is no centre seam.

Some pieced blocks which have been assembled into a quilt top do not need an added border because the design makes its own border, as in the case of the Double Wedding Ring pattern. However, some patterns are enhanced by the addition of a border, which can also be added to produce a top of a larger size. Usually, border patterns are of appliqué, perhaps with bundles and bowknots, or a trailing vine with rosebuds and foliage.

When the top is complete, it is ready to have a padding and backing attached, and may then be quilted. However, when using patchwork motifs as a decoration on clothing or household articles, they are pieced in the usual way, then simply sewn in place. Making patchwork for these small-scale objects provides good practice for larger projects like quilt tops or throws.

Preparing the fabric 1. *Care should be taken to prepare the fabric properly, particularly if a frame is not being used. Arrange the layers on a flat surface.*

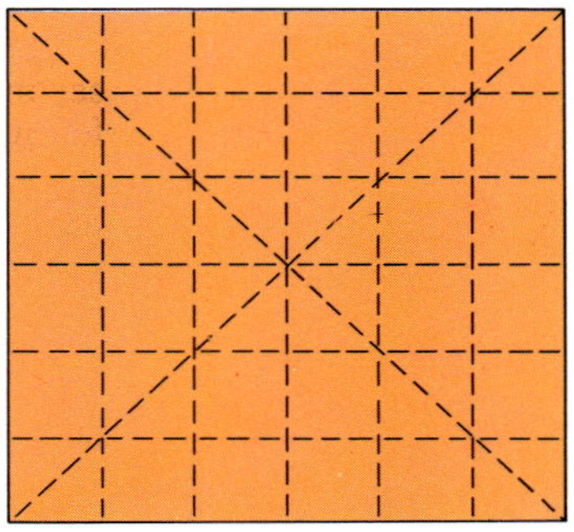

2. *Place the padding on top of the backing fabric and cover both with the top fabric. Tack them down with horizontal, vertical and lastly diagonal lines.*

Above *This quilt was worked by Mrs. Isabella Woodwright and her daughters in the early 1850s. It is currently housed in the Cheltenham City Museum, England and is a fine example of chintz appliquéd onto a quilt.*

Right *A detail from a beautiful eighteenth-century quilt. The quilting has been emphasized, and plays a prominent part in the design as a whole, and the pink embroidery of the central motif has been worked to create a very subtle shading effect.*

Quilting

The true quilt is a textile sandwich with a top layer, a bottom layer and a filling which may be added for warmth. A quilt top may be made of patchwork or appliqué or a whole piece of cloth. Quilting is the pattern in running stitch which holds the three layers together. It is the last process in the making of a quilt.

History

The earliest quiltings seem to have been made in the East, but there is very little documentary evidence of this. A jacket worn by a carved ivory figurine of about 3,400 B.C. which was found in Egypt, appears quilted in a pattern of straight lines which is sometimes used today. The technique was known throughout Asia and spread to the Middle East. By way of the trade routes, it then spread through North Africa to Europe and across to the British Isles where it can be traced back to the thirteenth century. In the seventeenth century, quilting skills were taken to North America by the early colonists.

References to English domestic quilting are very rare, but there are records of quilted armour from the time of William the Conqueror (*c.*1028-87), through to the thirteenth century. During the Crusades, men wore quilted jackets under their heavy metal armour to prevent chafing, and the only protection for light troops was a thickly padded jacket. The surcoat of Edward, the Black Prince (1330-1376) is in the possession of Canterbury Cathedral; made of red and blue velvet and embroidered with gold, it is quilted lengthways. Soldiers wore quilted clothing for protection even in the seventeenth century. When the English first landed at Jamestown, Virginia in 1607, many soldiers wore padded jackets in place of armour.

Early bed quilts were purely utilitarian – thick, warm bedcovers and bed hangings were essential in the cold houses of the Middle Ages. By 1540, however, when Katherine Howard received 23 quilts of sarsenet (a soft silk) as a sign of favour before her marriage to Heny VIII, bedcovers were being made from fine fabrics, often beautifully embroided as well as quilted.

Quilting was freely used on the splendid costumes of succeeding reigns and by the eighteenth century quilted clothing was high fashion for both men and women. Men wore quilted breeches, often of silk satin, and quilted waistcoats, while women wore quilted bodices, capes and beautiful petticoats or underskirts. The skirt of the fashionable dresses of the time were open from the waist to the hem to show the elaborately quilted petticoat underneath. Many of these underskirts were made of silk with a homespun linen backing and a padding of carded sheep's wool which made them very light and warm. Others were made of calamanco, a fine worsted woven in East Anglia. When fashions changed, quilted petticoats and underskirts were still worn in the country districts of South Wales and in the north of England. Quilted and corded underskirts were worn by many fisherwomen on the northeast coast until the beginning of this century.

The main quilting areas in Britain were the northeast of England (Northumberland and Durham) and the valleys of south Wales, although a certain amount of quilting was carried on in the West Country from Cornwall as far north as Hereford, and in Cumberland and Westmorland. Patterns in Britain were regional, but once they had crossed the ocean they spread throughout the whole of North America, and are now used by quilters everywhere.

The traditional British quilt was made from whole cloth and quilted in running stitich. Often both top and backing were white, at other times contrasting colours were used. Reversible quilts had tops and backings of similar quality. By working in running stitch, the pattern is identical on both sides.

The tops of eighteenth-century quilts were of satin, silk (perhaps lutestring or sarsenet) or linen, with a backing of linsey-woolsey, a mixture of linen and wool. Towards the end of this century, block printed and copper-plate printed fabrics were used. The origins of block printing in Europe are difficult to discover, but by the 1760s calico printing was started in Lancashire, and it is thought that the technique of copper-plate printing first came to England a few years earlier. In 1783 the first roller printing machine was patented by a Scotsman, Thomas Bell, and for many years block printed

Left *A plain quilt with a chintz border that was worked in the north of England. A variety of motifs have been incorporated, with particularly attractive designs built up at the corners.*

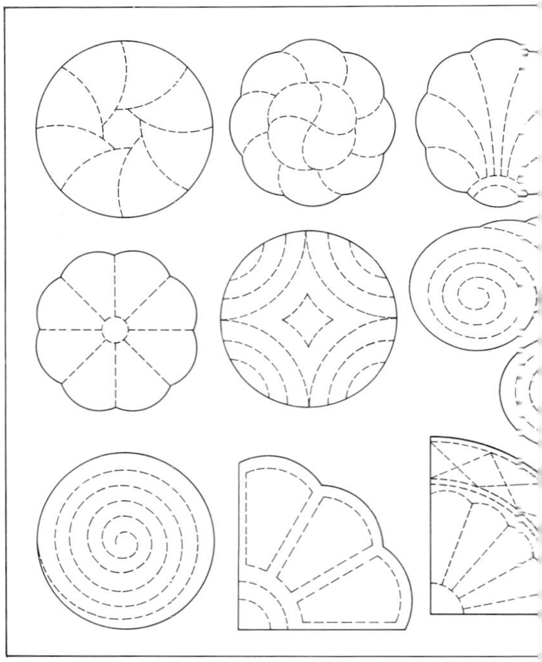

fabrics and roller printed fabrics were both available. However, the cottage or farmhouse quilts of the 1700s would have been made of homespun or linsey-woolsey until the imported calicoes and printed cottons became cheap enough to buy in quantity. By the mid-nineteenth century cottons of many types were in use, and until the early twentieth century, sateen and cotton poplin were used for quilt tops.

In England, wool from local flocks of sheep was used for padding before cotton was imported. Both were utilized until the late nineteenth century when cotton-wool became the favourite and now most women seem to prefer a padding of manmade fibres. In South Wales, wool was too valuable to be used for padding so old blankets, pieces of old clothes, even woollen stockings were used for filling.

Quilts made in Ireland and the Isle of Man often had no padding at all. They consisted of only two layers of fabric quilted in what is known as "waves" – a chevron pattern which covers the entire surface of the work. English and Welsh quilts were, however, usually thickly padded. Most of them were made at home by the mother and her daughters, and in Wales, during the nineteenth and early twentieth centuries, at least six were considered necessary for a girl's dowry.

Before the American War of Independence, American best quilts were very similar to those in England: whole cloth in solid colours enlivened with graceful patterns in running stitch. The making of a bedcover of this type, where its beauty depended solely on the design and stitchery, presented a challenge to the needlewoman. The tops were made from linsey-woolsey, or from glazed calamanco. Soon after 1700, the East India Company was exporting Indian chintzes and calicoes to the colonies, but cotton tops were not widely used until the end of the eighteenth century or the beginning of the nineteenth. The calamanco was exported from Norwich, as were quantities of sheep's wool for the padding. Sheep are not indigenous to the American continent and the first were taken there by the early colonists, so it was many years after colonization before there was sufficient wool even for clothing.

After cotton became a staple crop, quilts were padded with cotton straight from the cotton boll. Often the seeds were not completely removed and can still be seen in many American quilts.

A quilting frame was part of the furniture in many homes and quilting was a relaxation. Women would quilt between other household tasks and in the evening. In some areas quilting "bees" or parties were held. American quilting bees have been well publicized in literature and song and similar social events took place in Ulster and the Isle of Man. The programme for the bee was much the same wherever it was held. The hostess, who had a bedcover to be quilted, issued invitations to all the experienced needlewomen in the neighbourhood who arrived during the afternoon and sewed in relays until supper. By then the men had arrived from work and the quilting frame was put away. The hostess provided as grand a supper as she could afford, and after all had eaten a social evening was held.

Quilting patterns were taken from many objects such as shells, seaweed, flowers, foliage and feathers, and cups were used for circles. Many of the patterns have some significance: pineapples, for example, were the sign of hospitality, and pomegranates the sign of fruitfulness. The Rose of Sharon used on marriage quilts came from the Song of Solomon, "I am the Rose of Sharon and the Lily of the Valley." It was always considered unlucky to sew a heart on any but a Bride's quilt.

In England and Wales, there were at one time professional quilters, often village dressmakers, who would make quilts for those who could not sew. In parts of Wales, itinerant quilters would travel the countryside carrying a portable quilting frame to make new quilts and repair old ones. There were also professional quilt markers, known as "stampers", who would mark out the design on the quilt top in blue pencil for the customer to sew. The most famous of the quilt markers was George Gardner, who died just before 1900. With his successor, Elizabeth Sanderson (1861-1934), he was responsible for marking many fine north country quilts.

Quilt clubs originated in the mining villages of the north of England and South Wales in the early years of the twentieth century, and chapel quilt clubs often took the place of whist drives as a way of raising money for chapel funds. In North America and Canada there has always been a community tradition of quilting to raise funds for the church, and today churches of every religious denomination have active quilting groups.

There are few countries in the world where some form of quilting is not worked. Much of it is primarily utilitarian but often decorative at the same time. Although the word "quilt" brings to mind a bedcover, the technique of quilting can be used on many other items and is particularly suited to

Left *A selection of popular quilting motifs. They can be reproduced to any size, and used to enrich the pattern of the quilt as a whole or repeated along the borders. There are endless variations of the standard shell, heart, leaf and feather shapes.*

clothing. Many decorative wall hangings have also been made incorporating forms of quilting.

Materials

Quilting – the last step in the making of a quilt, joining the top, the filling and the backing with a pattern sewn in running stitch – is possible on a great variety of materials, as has been illustrated in its history. Fabrics should be firm and closely woven, and soft enough to sew through with ease. Preferably they should have a slight sheen to give highlights to the pattern but should not be shiny. The most popular materials today are pure cotton or a polyester/cotton blend. Silk can look beautiful, but it is expensive, difficult to care for, and does not wear well. The backing should be of a similar or complementing fabric. Several types of manmade fibres are available for padding, making the quilt easy to wash and hardwearing. Some quilters still prefer to use carded sheep's wool.

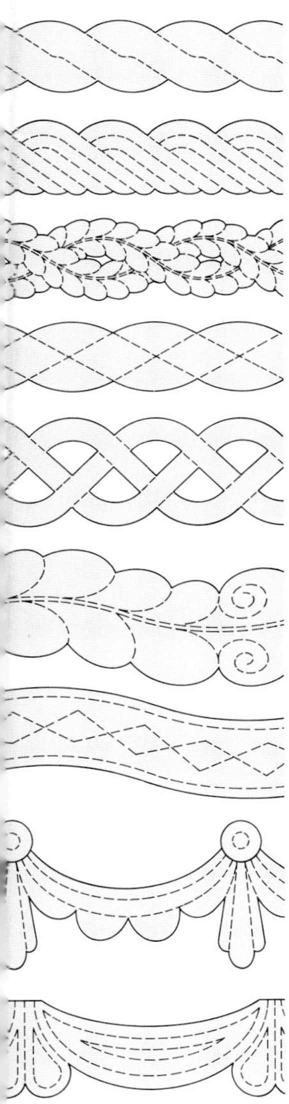

Right *Some of the materials used for quilting. Manmade fibres can be machine washed and tend therefore to be more popular for padding than the traditional sheeps' wool. Fabric can be obtained with the filling material already attached. Use strong thread as it will have to penetrate and hold together the different layers.*

Left *Borders vary from the straightforward to the highly elaborate. Select one that is appropriate to the design of the quilt as a whole, and do not attempt the more complicated twisted designs until competent in the art of quilting. Sections of these borders can also be used as single motifs, or worked into designs for corners and centrepieces.*

Above This charming Album quilt was made for Mrs. Fauset by friends as well as the staff of Warrington College of Art, England where she was a tutor for 20 years. It was to mark her retirement, and the family depicted in the panel at the centre of the quilt are Mrs. Fauset with her husband and children. **Right** November Morning, an attractive modern quilt that could be used as a wall hanging. It was made by Francesca Kemble and measures 56 inches square (14 3cm sq). Traditional quilting and patchwork was the inspiration for this piece, but the maker has broken up the design in some sections to achieve a smashed window effect. **Far right** Loon and Rattails quilt worked by Helen Kelly and measuring 81½×94 inches (206×239 cm). The very brilliant green quilted background, subtle bullrushes and simple well-placed ducks all combine to create an unusual and striking quilt.

Techniques

Design

Care should be taken in planning the design, which should be suitable in every way for the article which it is to decorate. For instance, if making a bed quilt, the central pattern should fit the top of the bed, and when quilting clothing, the patterns should be central to the figure. When making quilted clothing, the garment should not be cut out until the quilting has been completed, as the quilting pulls in the work slightly making it a little smaller. The designs for quilting patchwork should follow the pattern of the patchwork itself.

While planning the design it is worth remembering that when natural fibres such as sheep's wool or cotton are used for the filling the lines of quilting should be no more than 2 inches (5 cm) apart, in order to prevent shifting, but with manmade fibres, which are usually sold in sheets, the spaces between the lines of stitching can be wider.

Quilting patterns should be cut out from such materials as thick cardboard, plastic or metal. The pattern is placed on the quilt top and a yarn needle or bodkin used to trace round it, leaving a mark on the fabric which is the sewing line. Traditionally, only the outline of the quilting pattern is marked, and the remainder sewn in freehand. On dark materials, very finely sharpened tailor's chalk may be used for marking. It is possible to buy marking pens, the colour of which will wash out; lead pencils should never be used for marking as they leave a muddy line which never completely disappears.

Setting up the frame

Although patchwork can be worked in the hand, a frame must be used for best results in quilting. Some quilters find that a large embroidery hoop is adequate but its use does mean that the work must be very well basted so that the three layers do not shift when the position of the work on the hoop is changed.

The simplest quilting frame is made from two long pieces of wood known as rails, and two shorter, flat pieces of wood which are

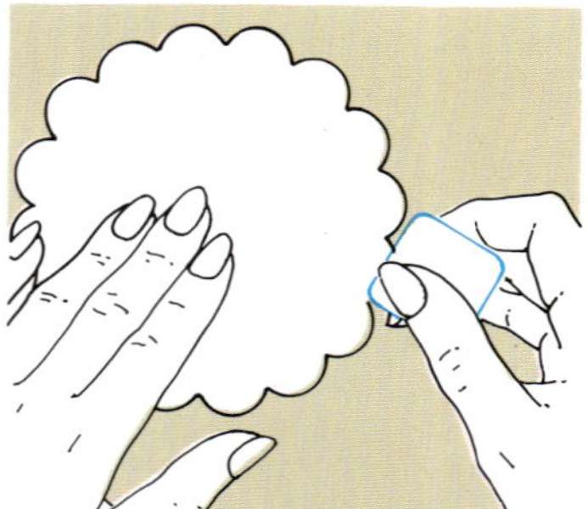

Marking designs 1. *Place the template on the selected top fabric, and either draw round it with tailor's chalk, or make a crease with a needle held flat.*

2. *Remove the template and mark in any additional lines or details within the basic outline. Use a ruler for lines.*

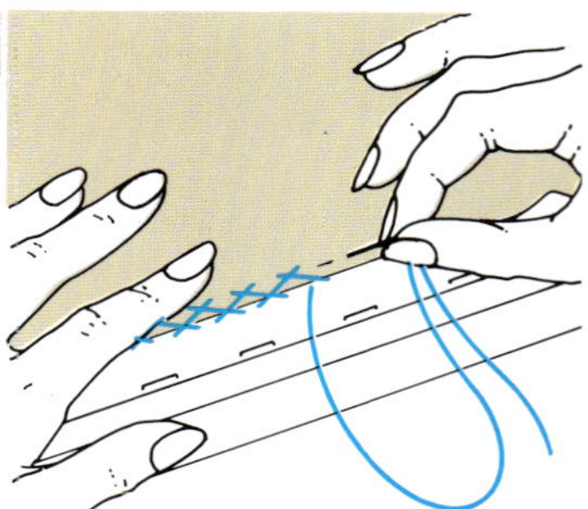

Quilting on a frame 1. *Attach backing fabric to runner webbing, wrapping excess round one runner to obtain a convenient size. Secure in frame.*

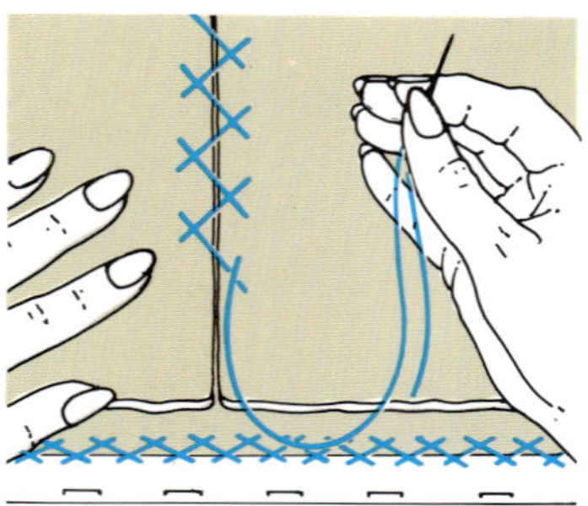

2. *Lay padding on top of the backing fabric having trimmed it to the appropriate size. Tack pieces together if necessary, and arrange evenly.*

known as stretchers. The stretchers fit into slots in the rails and are held in place by pegs. Both rails have a strip of strong material such as braid or upholsterer's webbing nailed to the inner edge. Each end of this type of frame can then rest on the back of a chair and can easily be put away when quilting has finished for the day.

The top, padding and backing are placed together and basted across one end. This is then sewn to the webbing on one of the rails and wound round until approximately 24 inches (61 cm) remain free and can be basted to the webbing on the other rail. The stretchers are then attached and pegged to keep the work taut. After each breadth has been quilted, it is wound on to the front rail and another breadth is unwound from the back.

Stitches

Although small quilting stitches are commendable, the regularity and evenness of the

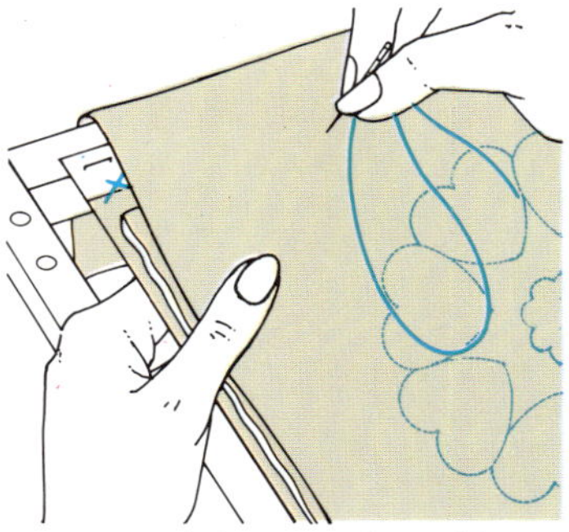

3. Place top fabric over the padding, allowing it to hang over unwrapped runner. Tack three layers together at that end and pin them at other end.

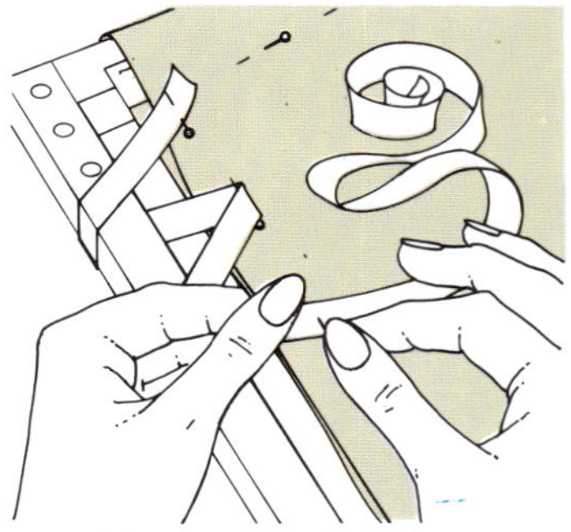

4. Use fabric tape to wind zigzag fashion around the side stretchers, and pin these tapes into position on either side through all layers.

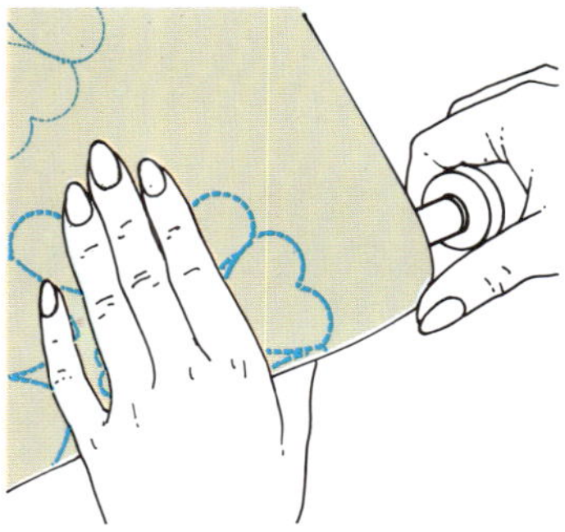

5. Quilt stretched area, and then unroll the next section rearranging pinned tapes and securing runner accordingly. Repeat until complete.

***Cord quilting 1.** Trace the required pattern with a double outline onto the selected fabric, and place it on top of the backing fabric.*

***2.** Pin or tack these two layers of fabric together, and then stitch carefully along both outlines. If fabric is stretched, loosen it.*

***3.** Thread a wide-eyed needle with cord of a suitable width, push it between the two layers of fabric in between the two stitched outlines.*

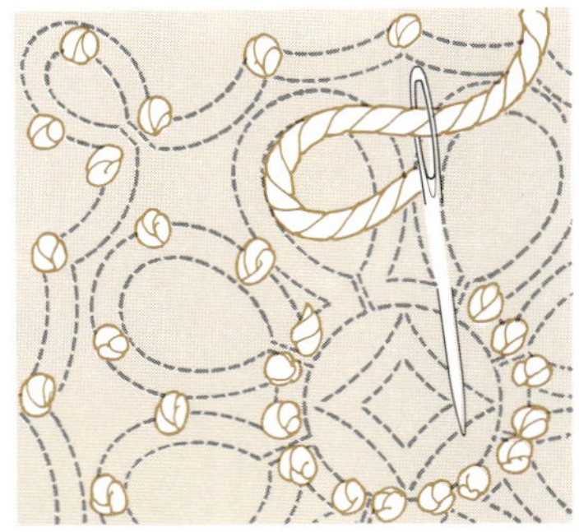

***4.** Push the cord along the outline to fill out the design. At sharp corners, bring the cord out at the back and form a small loop to prevent buckling.*

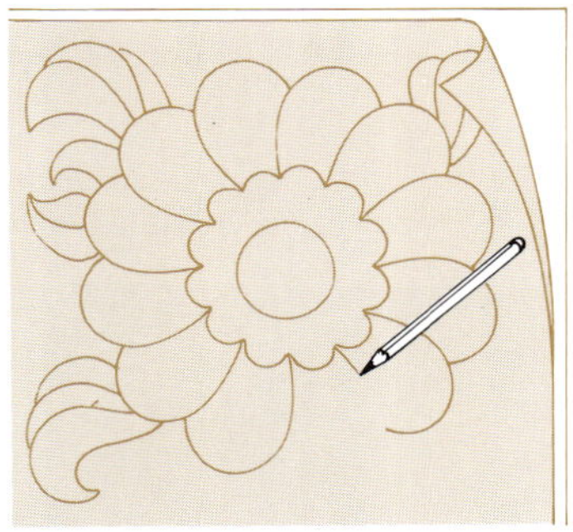

***Trapunto quilting 1.** Trace the required design onto the selected fabric. Each area to be worked in trapunto quilting must be enclosed.*

***2.** Tack the fabric onto a backing fabric with the wrong sides facing inwards. If possible, mount it on a frame for the next stage.*

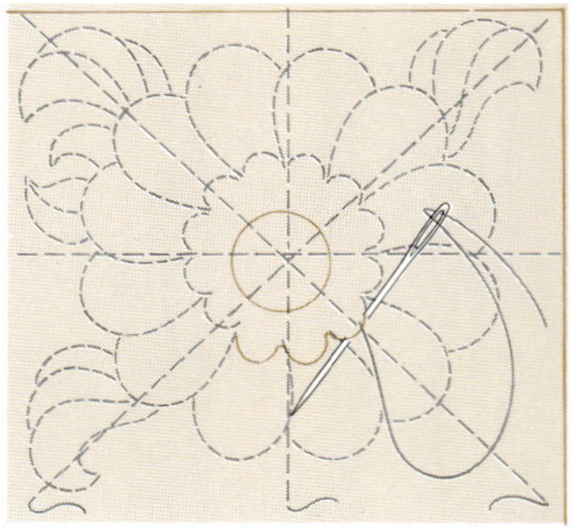

***3.** Sew along the outline with small neat running stitches taking care to penetrate both layers. Work from the centre of the design outwards.*

***4.** Remove tacking, and make small slits in each enclosed area on the wrong side of the piece of work. Do not make more slits than necessary.*

***Right** A coverlet with a pattern of red baskets, worked in New Jersey during the nineteenth century. It is a perfect example of quilting, patchwork and appliqué worked into a single and very pleasing bedcover. The white background is made from diamond-shaped blocks quilted with a pineapple design, and the red baskets are formed from small red and white triangles of quilted patchwork with appliqué handles. The coverlet is wider than it is long, and would hang down to the floor on either side of the bed.*

Tied quilting 1. *Mark generously spaced dots onto the fabric as if for smocking, in the required pattern. Tack all the layers together.*

2. *Sew the thread or threads through all the layers at each dot. Leave one long end, work a back stitch with the other and tie off with knot or bow.*

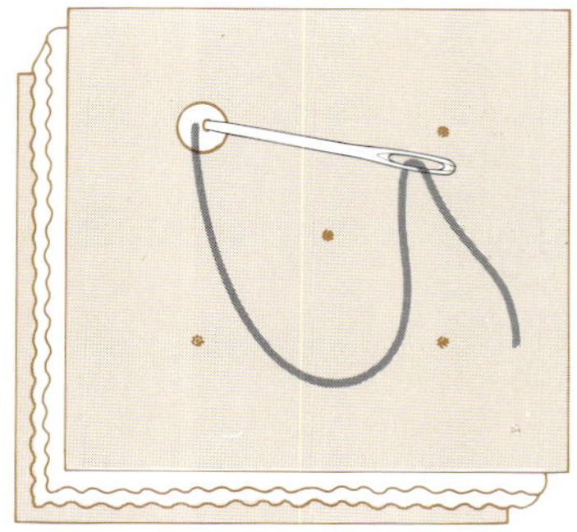

Button quilting 1. *Proceed initially as for tied quilting, but sew a button over each dot, with another placed precisely underneath it on the backing.*

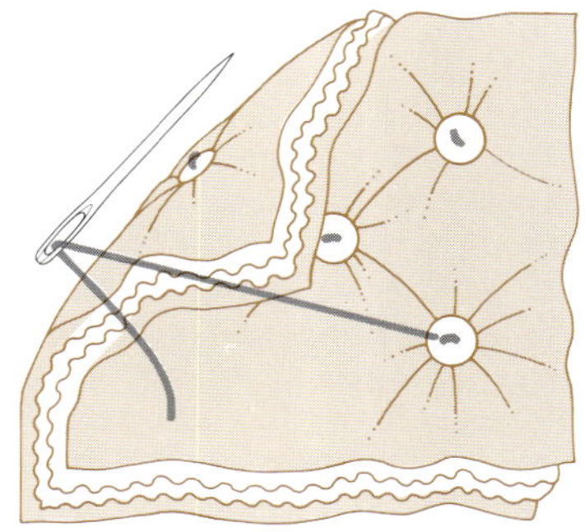

2. *Secure the buttons firmly. They should sink down into the fabric. End off the thread amongst the central padding after every few buttons.*

5. *Gently push padding into each enclosed area through the slits. Use cottonwool or kapok, and insert it with a crochet hook or blunt needle.*

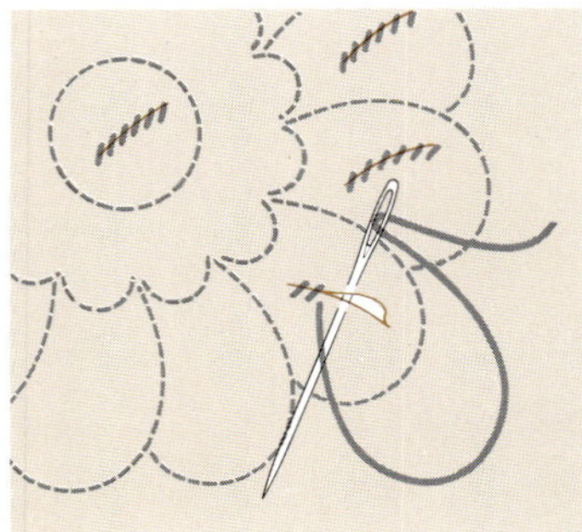

6. *Stuff the quilt as evenly as possible, and slip stitch the small slits back together. Stitch on a lining if wrong side is to be exposed.*

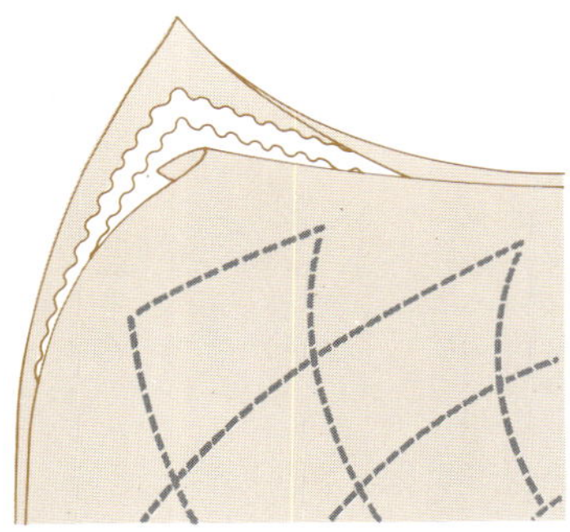

Finishing off 1. *Trim both edges to within a 1 inch (2.5 cm). Turn the bottom layer under the padding, and the top layer over it neatly.*

2. *Press these two edges together, and work both layers at once in running stitch as close to the edge as possible. Repeat closer in.*

Left *A remarkable American quilt where the appliquéd thistle design has been made from a single piece of fabric. The motif is white and the background, a crimson red. The leaves resemble the feathers and ferns worked into other American appliqué quilts.*

stitches are more important than the actual size. It is the pattern contained within the stitches in a low relief, rather than the stitches themselves, which is important. Size 9 needles and a strong cotton of a colour which tones with the top of the quilt should be used. To give ease of handling and to prevent tangles the thread can be passed over a cake of beeswax.

The traditional quilting stitch is not a stab stitch where the needle goes down then up again in two separate movements, but a running stitch where several stitches are taken up on the needle before it is pulled through. One hand should be held underneath the work to guide the needle back to the top. At first it may be possible only to take one stitch on the needle at a time, but it is advisable to practise until five or six stitches can be made before drawing through the needle and cotton. The use of a running stitch means that the quilt will be completely reversible.

If the top of the piece of work to be quilted is made up of multicoloured geometric shapes, the usual method of quilting is to outline each shape with running stitch. The back of the work would then show the same pattern in outline.

Finishing

After the quilt has been removed from the frame there is a choice of ways to finish the edge. Traditionally in Britain, the back and the top are turned in and sewn together with two rows of running stitch, $\frac{1}{8}$ inch (3 mm) apart. Some early American quilts were finished in this way, but in others the backing, cut a little bigger than the top, was taken over to the right side, turned under and neatly hemmed down. As fabrics became more plentiful it became customary to bind the edge either with a self colour or a contrast, and in some cases a piping cord was inserted.

When the quilt is complete, it is a good idea to add one's signature and the date of completion on the back. This can be done by embroidery or in marking ink.

Smocking

Smocking is a method of decoration that forms an integral part of the design of a garment and also has a practical purpose. It is a method of gathering a width of material into regular folds, giving elasticity to the gathers, which fit snugly around the chest and forearm of the wearer. Without drawing elaborate designs on the fabric beforehand, the grouping and variation of a few simple stitches will give a whole series of different rectilinear patterns and textures. Thread of the same colour as the fabric (self-coloured) is traditionally employed for all the decorative work.

The technique gained its name from the "smock", the protective outer clothing of rustics in Western Europe. The word "smock" is derived from the Anglo-Saxon verb *smoce*, meaning "to creep into".

History

The methods of pleating or organizing folds of fabric that preceded smocking are evident in the portraits painted during the Renaissance. These paintings were generally executed in great detail, but unfortunately the method of stitchery used on the extravagant garments of the sitters was not sufficiently well defined to establish how the gathers were secured. It is most likely that simple retaining stitches were worked on the underside, being entirely functional rather than decorative.

Once the effect of organized folds of fabric had become an established fashion, the next development was the decoration of the "reeds" or "tubes". The decorative, surface stitching provided a unique resilience that ordinary tucks or pleats could not give. This quality made smocking suitable for decorating garments for children and active adults.

Derived from the Saxon tunic, the smock comprised two rectangles joined at the shoulders and sides, with two smaller rectangles folded lengthwise and joined at the shoulder level to make sleeves. Shepherds, carters and waggoners in the late eighteenth century wore undecorated smocks and other basic clothing, but the traditional "smock-frock", now recognized for the beauty of its hand embroidery and its simple construction, is a remnant of mid-nineteenth-century rural England and Wales. The makers and wearers of smocks belonged to an undocumented society and there are few recorded details of how and why smocks were made and worn.

The word "frock" had long been associated with an upper garment worn by men; the composite term "smock-frock" describes the voluminous garment very well. In *Under the Greenwood Tree*, the Victorian novelist Thomas Hardy describes the garment as "a long white smock of pillow case cut". It was constructed from a series of rectangles of tough homespun and hand-

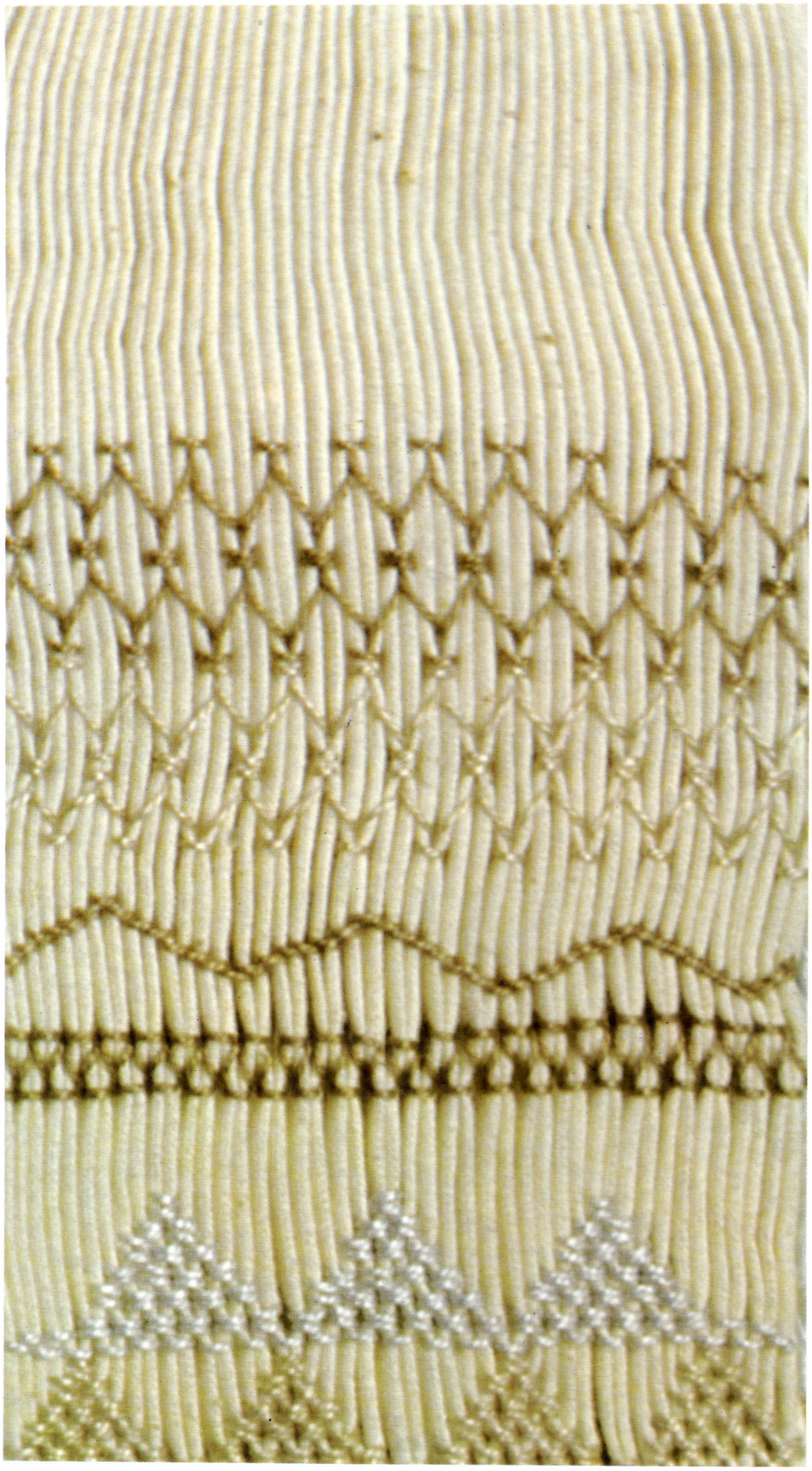

Left *A hand-smocked sampler worked in linen thread on a calico ground. It is a modern piece that has been sewn at Goldsmiths' College, London, using traditional materials and techniques.*

Right *George Morland's* The Reckoning *or* Outside the Alehouse Door. *Moreland lived from 1763–1804, and smocks featured in paintings of country scenes during this period demonstrate the characteristic fullness and gathered shoulders that we associate with smocks, though they have not yet begun to feature lavish embroidery or decoration.*

woven linen, providing excellent protection against the climate in the days before synthetic fabrics.

The smock-frock varied in style according district, occupation and occasion. Worn by many rural labourers and tradesmen to protect their everyday clothes, or perhaps to hide their shabbiness, it was the shepherd's smock that blossomed into a highly decorative style. The shepherd wore his splendid protection well into the twentieth century, as shepherding was little affected by the industrial changes of the nineteenth century.

The smock was also worn by the "lower orders" of the countryside on important days and holidays. The Victorian Statute Fair or Hiring served as the annual employment exchange, when a large crowd of workers congregated in anticipation of future work. A clean smock presented the labourer to his best advantage – he was hired on face value. It was important to him as well as to the employer that his trade could be easily identified by what he wore or carried.

Gabriel Oak in Thomas Hardy's *Far from the Madding Crowd,* exchanged his overcoat for a "shepherd's regulation smock-frock" at a Hiring in Dorset. This was probably a reference to the manufactured smock, the product of an industry which enjoyed a short but prosperous trade, producing garments that were essentially functional.

Left *A shepherd's smock made from blue linen with smocked cuffs, shoulders and front panel. The wavy pattern on the shoulders and collar is formed by working smocking on the underside of the material.*

These smocks passed from the various manufacturers to the draper's store or the "slop vendor's stall" at markets and fairs. Such a garment could cost a week's wage; this was expensive, as smocks were worn by the lowest paid.

The most celebrated festive occasion to fall during the heyday of the smock was the Great Exhibition of 1851, when smock-frocked labourers journeyed on foot to see the products of the age. Such public fairs and festivals promoted and inspired the enhancing of the practical smock; fired by competitive spirit, rural women produced handiwork of unique skill. The smocking and other embroidery were carried out before any part of the garment was assembled. No curves meant no difficult shaping or construction, and the smock would be cut by eye. The incidental passing of knowledge and skills from mother to daughter and from neighbour to neighbour led to the merging of styles and types of decoration.

Many of the smocks that were made for celebrations or festivals have survived and are those white linen garments found in our museums today. These would be documented as "best" or "Sunday" smocks, and often "wedding" smocks. There is evidence that the best smocks of one generation were repaired and handed down to become the working garments of following generations. To possess two smocks was quite usual.

Holland or linen drill was originally used for smock making; this was an unbleached cloth with a twill weave, imported from The Netherlands. Eventually a heavy cotton twill know as "drabbett" became the fabric used most by the smock-making industry. The "Newark Frock" is now the best-known example of the factory-made smock; the linen and the garment were made at Newark-on-Trent by a Victorian family firm. Other manufacturers arose in the areas where the drabbet was produced. Often the smocking and the embroidery was a cottager's occupation, but the garments were subsequently sewn up by machine in the warehouse. Some smocks were entirely handmade by cottagers for local drapers.

Many coloured smocks were worn by farm labourers, yet very few have found their way into our museums. Some dark brown smocks are documented from the Surrey and Sussex areas. Made of fine linen, they were steeped in boiled linseed oil to improve their protective qualities. A rather stiff garment, waterproof and very warm, this smock required no laundering other than wiping down. The smocking on these garments was greatly enhanced by the dark background; the linen embroidery thread was tightly spun and waxed so it did not absorb the oil and darken.

Few smocks were exactly alike, but a similarity of style and decoration is usually apparent in a collection of smocks housed in a provincial museum. Often the garment can be seen to belong to one of three main types: the round smock, the shirt smock or the coat smock.

The round or "true" smock is the most widely recognized type. It is a reversible garment with the minimum of opening at the front and back neck. The generous cut prevented excessive wear in any one area, and, when signs of time did appear, the garment was reversed, distributing the wear

evenly. Only when the dirty front had been relegated to the back, and that too had become soiled, did the smock need to be washed.

The decoration that complemented the smocking was the round smock's most characteristic feature. This surface embroidery appeared in the "boxes", on the collar, cuffs and shoulder yokes. The box was the area either side of the front and back panels of smocking. The wealth of surface stitchery worked on the smocks between 1830 and 1850 was far in excess of what was needed for a durable outdoor garment. Early on, the decoration satisfied the humble needs of the wearer and the whim of the maker. The search for employment at a Hiring Fair was sufficient reason to suppose that the ornate scroll, the leaves, cones and geometric shapes were sympathetic with the wearer's trade, but similar designs later evolved regardless of the labourer's occupation. Although an affinity of embroidered designs was apparent in one area, it cannot be claimed with authority that a particular pattern was peculiar to a county.

Left *A smock made for, and exhibited at the 1851 Great Exhibition at the Crystal Palace. The embroidery is densely worked, with feather stitch running down either side of the central panel and leaf motifs worked into the collar and shoulders. Other smocks of the time featured wheat sheaves, hearts and flowers.*

Left *This short "shirt" smock was made in Lincolnshire in the early part of the nineteenth century. The material used is blue linen, and the sleeves have been carefully mended in the same fabric at some later date. The embroidery is very restrained.*

Right *A detail from the Great Exhibition smock above. Not only were smocks exhibited, but a vast number of country people dressed largely in smocks travelled to see the Exhibition. As* The Times *reported: "A remarkable feature of yesterday's experience in the interior of the Exhibition was the appearance there, at an early hour, of nearly 800 agricultural labourers and countryfolk from the neighbourhood of Godstone in Surrey, headed by the clergymen of the parishes to which they respectively belonged . . . the men wore their smartest smock-frocks and the women their best Sunday dresses . . ."*

The effect of the densely embroidered panels may appear awesome, but on closer examination it is clear that only three or four simple stiches were employed. They were single feather stitch (similar to blanket stitch), double, and treble feather stitch, known in the nineteenth century as coral stitch. All these stitches were closely related to one another and once the parent stitch had been mastered the others were natural developments. The threads used for the surface embroidery would be the same as those used in the smocking. This self-coloured textural effect was the essence of the traditional round smock of the Midlands and the southern counties of England.

Smocks of the southern counties near London, Surrey and Sussex were more sophisticated in style, being made of fine linen, which in turn produced fine, lace-like smocking. Very small areas of smocking either side of the neck opening back and front resulted in a garment not unlike the Elizabethan nobleman's shirt. Known also as Surrey smocks, these shirt smocks were identical back and front and had the advantages of being reversible.

William Cobbett, in *Rural Rides*, recalls Surrey children clad in smocks as early as 1770. The Surrey smock could still be seen worn by coffin bearers of the villages in Sussex and Hampshire as recently as 1930. Its influence of style spread widely to areas north and west of the home counties. Many smocks in the West Country had characteristics related to the Surrey smock, like the neat double backstitch and herringbone stitch. Generally, these smocks displayed very little surface embroidery. The stitches that were employed were of a functional quality, to attach the yoke strap to the garment, or to strengthen the edge of the collar and cuffs.

The coat smock, as its name implies, was a button-through garment. It was mainly worn by shepherds from Wales and the Welsh border counties and was made of very heavy linen for protection from the mountain rains and mist. The predominating feature of many of these smocks was the enormous embellished collar, often tucked on the outer edge to give it weight. These collars extended to become cape-like epaulettes of double-thickness fabric, adding to the smock's value as a weather-defying garment.

The embroidery designs had a strong Celtic ingredient. Whorls, swags, trees and heart-shapes were worked in a mirror-image pattern on the collar and epaulettes. Unlike the round smock, the "box" area was undecorated apart from single rows of feather stitch which flanked the large smocked panels back and front. A bold, open chain was peculiar to these smocks, worked so closely that little of the background fabric was seen.

Unfortunately, more evidence exists concerning the decline in popularity of the agricultural smock, than the rise. A daily paper for the eastern counties in 1914 commented on the decline in demand for smocks and the fact that they were naturally no longer available in the shops and gave a brief account on how to cut a smock from drabbet.

The smock had seen a century of change; the machine age had introduced farm implements that endangered the lives of the smock-frocked labour force, the unconfined looseness of the garment being a positive hazard. The indifference and change of attitude towards the smock was partly due to a fear of ridicule. Rural simplicity in clothing had become unpopular, especially as cheap machine-made clothes were easily available.

However, among the proponents of the Aesthetic Movement of the late nineteenth century, smocks and smocking became popular again. This influential group of artisans promoted new concepts in the design of everyday articles and advocated a simple, more healthy way of life, adopting the smock as a symbol of their protest against the opulence of the machine age. The simple, agrarian over-garment gained a new role and "revival" smocks became fashionable. "No artistic dresser would be without a smock, cut exactly like the farm labourer's" claimed the *Ladies' World* magazine of 1880.

Smocking enjoyed a renaissance during this period, and it was practised and perfected on different styles of clothing. Smocking was also adapted for the embellishment of such household trivia as handkerchief sachets and bedroom tidies, but it was for children's clothing that smocking proved invaluable, attractively combining utility with comfort.

Middle- and upper-class children throughout history have been dressed like their parents. Fashion decreed such cumbersome styles during the late nineteenth century that reformers in the Aesthetic Movement and many of their contemporaries were strongly opposed to such clothes for children. Their privileged offspring were clad in practical smock-type garments similar to those which had been worn for centuries previously by children from more humble origins. The theories and designs of the Aesthetic Movement had a permanent influence on children's wear, and, by the turn of the century, the manufacture of children's clothes was a separate industry.

Country smocks were the uniform for boys in the numerous village schools and were also worn in charitable institutions for

the poor. When the smock had become respectable and fashionable, a feminine version was worn by girls to protect their everyday clothes in and out of school. Infants and toddlers wore a fine homemade white linen garment with ample fullness in the body and sleeves, beautifully smocked at the neck and with lengthening tucks at the hem. Such was the quality of both linen and workmanship that these whitework smocks were repaired, lengthened and handed down, and still worn decades after their original vogue. These smocks have since become collector's pieces; they are exquisite reminders of the Edwardian nanny.

Influential illustrators of childrens books helped to promote the garments that were designed with childrens' activities in mind. Kate Greenaway portrayed small boys clad in either traditional round smocks or the skeleton suit of a much earlier period. Her dateless high-waisted chemise dress has

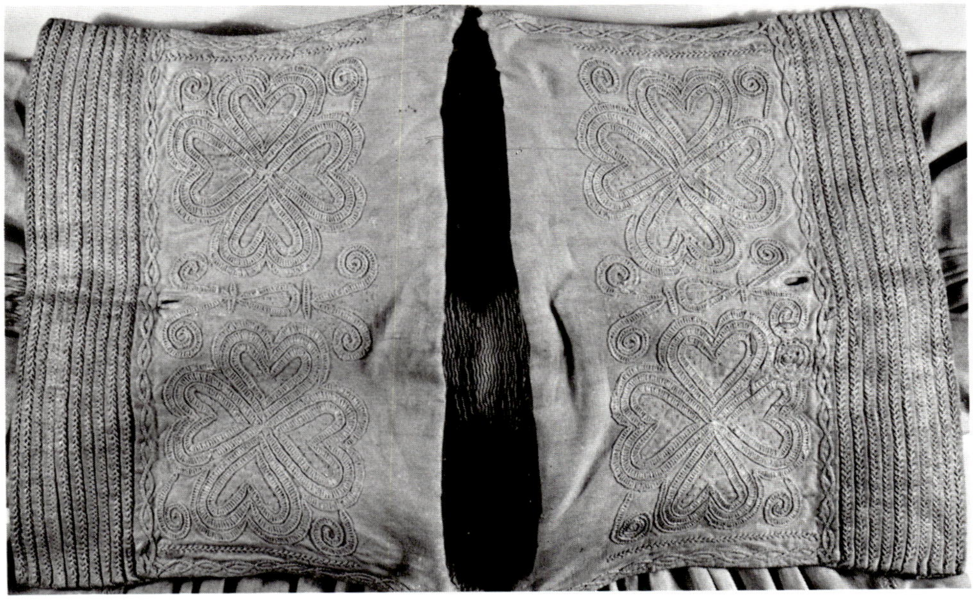

Far left *In the latter half of the nineteenth century, farmers would go into town on market days wearing top hats and smocks as in this early photograph of Samuel Sinfield of Moulsoe. They could be made from a variety of different fabrics; in "Under the Greenwood Tree" Thomas Hardy wrote in 1871, "Some were as usual in snow white smocks of Russian duck and some in whitey brown ones of drabbet."*

Left *Child's coat smock from Hereford. The embroidery is beautifully worked in feather stitch. Originally, extended epaulettes were added to labourers' smocks as extra protection against the weather. On this smock however, they simply provide additional room for the embroidery.*

Top *Squire Vaughan's smock from the Welsh Folk Museum at St Fagan's Castle in Cardiff. Coat smocks were usually made of heavy linen, with large flat collars and flapped pockets. The buttons only went down as far as the waist, and the ease of movement afforded by this style made them very popular among shepherds during the nineteenth century.*

Above *A detail of the collar of Squire Vaughan's smock. The tucks along the outer edges give the collar extra weight, and they are decorated here with single lines of feather stitch. The buttonholes on either side are used for attaching the collar to the body of the smock to prevent it from blowing up round the wearer's face.*

been worn by generations of children, imitating the charming, well-known illustrations.

The *Ladies' World* magazine of 1887 featured the celebrated Mab smock available from Liberty's of Regent Street. Made of light blue cashmere and smocked in silk, it was the perfect garment for the fashionable game of lawn tennis. Liberty's did not make clothes at that time, but their fabrics had a strong influence in the art world because of their quality and colours. Umritzar cashmere was an early success and was used for the Mab smock; in common with silk fabrics, it was ideally suited to fine hand-smocking.

Cotton blouse-smocks were advertised in the quality newspapers in 1916, "for house and country wear". In the early 1920s, classic blouses were hand-smocked, and in some instances called a smock, although their appearance was nothing like that of the agricultural garment of 50 years before.

Mass-market magazines instructed the growing home dressmaking industry in every aspect of needlecraft. *Weldon's Practical Smocking* detailed such items as a "plough boy's blouse", described as "exceptionally pretty for boys in petticoats". The publications that followed the example of these initiators of the "do-it-yourself" trade at the turn of the century, regularly published designs and instructions for making baby's and toddler's smocked clothing.

The styles of the 1920s were typically straight, often with the smocking contained in a hip yoke. For girls, a dress with a band of smocking set into a high yoke, puffed sleeves and a flat Peter Pan collar, was a popular style from the 1930s. The smocking was often shaped and a similar garment was designed for boys, with the top buttoned onto matching pants to form a romper suit.

Soft colours and many new inventive stitches featured in the smocking of this period. During the 1920s and 1930s, silk crepe-de-chine and shantung were suggested as suitable choices of fabric, but cotton gingham has been a more practical favourite since the prewar years.

Attempts to standardize clothing for economical or political reasons have often resulted in a fashion for simple garments elaborately embroidered: in these instances, smocking is an obvious choice of technique. In 1944, the Board of Trade in Britain limited the amount of fabric used per garment as part of wartime rationing; this restriction unwittingly created a vogue for homemade embroidered clothing. In the United States, designers have always aimed to achieve the maximum effect using a minimum of material. Many home dressmaking journals and commercial patterns include clear instructions for smocked garments.

Traditional American smocking does not

Above *A smock made for a child in heavy cotton drill, and sold in Pulloxhill, England at the beginning of this century. The sale tag is still tacked onto the bottom of the garment. (17nls indicates the size; one nl or nail equalling 2¼ inches (16 cm)).*

require preliminary gathers to form the familiar reeds or tubes of English smocking. Instead, simple ruching is worked across the fabric in a regular pattern based on a grid of dots. This technique uses less fabric than the English method, but does not have the same resilient character.

Colour has always played an important role in the designs of American smocking, which rely on colour and shape rather than texture for their appeal. Pictorial motifs feature widely and even complete scenes are worked on children's clothes. Borders of snowmen, strawberries, animals and teddy-bears in bright colours enhance the bodices of girls' dresses. Smocking is worked on a wide variety of items, from men's shirts to sunbonnets, and even Christmas tree decorations. Kits are available with detailed instructions for the enthusiast.

Today, the smock is again enjoying a period of popularity as part of the vogue for richly decorated traditional garments. With present-day interest in rural crafts, smocks and smocking are very much alive.

Left A copy of an illustration from Ladies' World *of 1880, entitled Afternoon Tennis. The older girls are wearing the dresses that came to be known as Mab smocks, where the tucks in the yoke were gathered into a sash at the waist. The younger girl's dress is lower-waisted, but both types of smock were easy to move in as well as being attractive.*

Above The popular Mab smock for young ladies that was featured in the Liberty's Catalogue of 1886, shown here in an illustration from Ladies' World *of the following year. Liberty's was famous for the quality of its fabrics. Floppy soft-brimmed hats, often decorated with large bows, were worn with the Mab smock.*

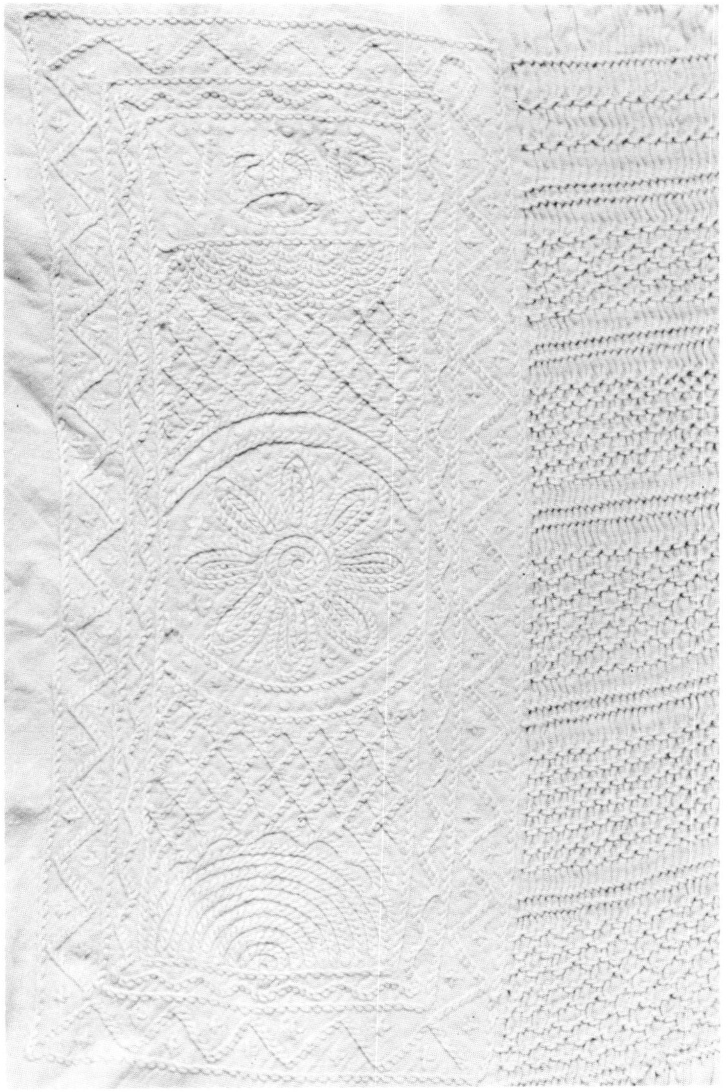

Above *A beautifully embroidered round smock from the Hereford and Worcester county Museum at Hartlebury Castle, England.*
Left *A detail from this smock, taken from the box panel to the right of the central smocking. All the embroidery is worked in single feather stitch, including the royal commemorative initials and crown at the top. There were combinations of stitches to represent different counties, as well as certain motifs for particular trades.*

Left A selection of threads that can be used for smocking. It is important to remember weight as well as colour when deciding which silk to choose. Avoid using elaborate threads and stitches on highly patterned fabric. Linen thread is traditionally used for smocking, but a lot of people find it too hard to work. Steer clear of the very expensive silks when learning to smock.

Materials

Fabric

Smocking can be worked on almost any fabric, but some fabrics lend themselves to the technique more than others, as they provide a natural grid for the gathering threads. These include ginghams, and spotted and regularly striped fabrics, which also give an interesting visual effect when finished.

Floral viyella, Liberty lawn or any small patterned fabric make attractive dresses for children, or over-blouses for adults. The smocking on a patterned fabric needs to be simple and textural to complement rather than distract from the fabric design. Tussore and other wild silks are naturally textured and will smock successfully. Other fabrics like silk or polyester satins and velvet are difficult to prepare for smocking, but worth experimenting with to achieve a deep luxurious texture with only a few simple retaining stitches.

If a fabric is sufficiently firm to hold the preparatory gathering threads, then it can be smocked. Smocking on a very stiff fabric will result in work that will not stretch. On a limp or floppy fabric, the smocking will not be resilient and the fabric will return to its original shape having been stretched. Traditional fabrics such as linen and cotton drill, with their firmness of weave and creasing properties, will form neat "tubes" more readily than a loosely woven fabric.

Smocking need not be confined to clothing; many embroiderers have adapted the technique to textiles generally. Hessian, P.V.C. and other unconventional fabrics are used for wall hangings and collages, and smocking has been combined with screen-printed and painted fabrics for the same purpose.

Thread

Twisted threads are the best to use for smocking as they are strong and are less likely to shred than a stranded variety. D.M.C. and coton-à-broder are available in a wide range of colours; these are versatile threads suitable for many fabrics, used singly or doubled in the needle, and are particularly good for beginners and children. Cotton perle is also an attractive twisted thread with a high lustre and can be combined with other threads. Hard twisted linen threads are ideal for traditional smocking, but are difficult to use. Softly twisted embroidery silks are rare and expensive, but a good alternative is firmly twisted buttonhole silks which are usually available in a variety of colours.

Crochet threads are effective for experimental work, but the very shiny ones are not easy to use. Gold and silver threads look attractive in small areas even though they are stiff to work.

Right *Smocking can look effective on a variety of different fabrics.* ***1.*** *Silk georgette is a luxurious diaphanous fabric which will gather up very tightly.*
2. *Viyella is popular, particularly for children's clothes.*
3. *Hessian is an ideal fabric to experiment with. Use in conjunction with appliqué for cushions, bags and wall-hangings.*
4. *Tussore silk is a gorgeous fabric that can be smocked on luxury garments such as evening dresses or jackets.*
5. *Polyester satin is both floppy and slippery. Only the most experienced smocker should attempt to work it.*
6. *Cotton drill is tough, inexpensive and will pleat up firmly.*

Left *A variety of techniques have been used to decorate this exotic silk jacket. Mock smocking on the wrong side has caused the attractive free-form ruched effect round the collar and at the top of the yoke. Appliquéd leaf shapes, couched on gold thread, delicate embroidery and sewn on beads all contribute to the overall texture. It is a perfect example of adapting traditional techniques to modern and original ends.*

1

2

3

4

5
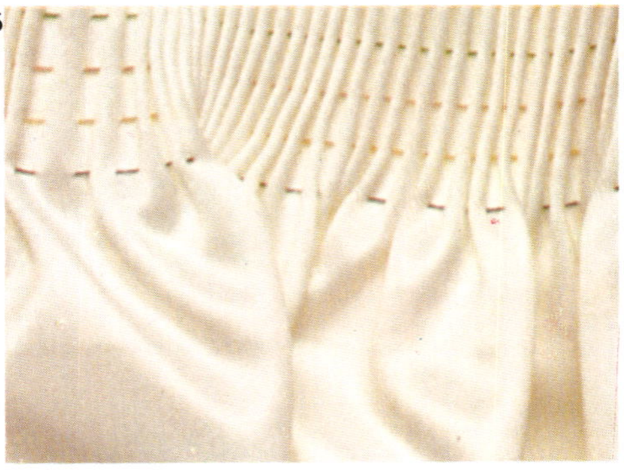

6

Techniques

Preparing the fabric

Counting and picking up the linen threads of the fabric at regular intervals was the method of gathering the tubes in the nineteenth century: a tedious, eye-straining occupation. The "iron-on" transfer used today marks the fabric with parallel rows of dots which are then gathered, but this is still a labour-intensive task. The smock gathering machine was designed to eliminate this task for the embroiderer. Although it gathers up small areas for smocking very efficiently, it cannot always cope with heavy cottons.

Smocking dot transfers are available in many different spacing sizes, the most commonly used for garments being sizes K and O. The wider the spaces between the dots, the more fabric will be taken into the gathers. Commonly available transfers are intended to produce gathers which reduce the width of the fabric to approximately one-third of its original size. However, the reduction of fabric width is not only affected by the spacing of dots, but also by the type of stitches employed and the thickness of the fabric. It is often worth experimenting with fabric and dots to establish exactly how much fabric will be taken up.

The paper transfer should be one row of dots deeper than the intended depth of smocking. Cut the transfer to size and place it face down on the wrong side of the fabric. If the uncut edge of the transfer is placed along the straight edge of the material, this will ensure that the rows of dots are parallel with the grain or weave of the fabric. Avoid joining two transfers together, as this often leads to misplaced dots and difficulty later on. Transfer the dots to the fabric with a warm, not hot, iron. Excessive heat may prevent the dots from washing out when the work is completed. Rip the paper transfer away when it has changed colour slightly, which indicates that it has made good contact with the fabric beneath.

If a curved yoke of smocking is required, it is more practical to make a perforated stencil for marking the dots. Starting at the top with holes close together, increase the measurement between each hole by a fraction in each subsequent row. This only works successfully on a depth of approximately 2½ inches (6 cm) or less. Commercial paper patterns can be adapted for smocking in this way where they feature normal gathers.

Creating folds in the fabric resembling tubes or reeds may be tedious, but care taken at this stage will ensure a well-embroidered item. Use a polyester thread which is strong; cut a thread for each line to be gathered approximately 6 inches (15 cm) longer than necessary and make a large knot in the end. Start gathering by stitching in at one dot and out at the next, making stitches of equal size either side of the fabric. Leave the ends of the cotton free. Make the required number of rows.

To pull up the work, flatten it on a surface with one hand while gently pulling pairs of threads with the other. Work the fabric up the threads a uniform amount on each. Stretching the fabric in the direction of the tubes and stroking them with the eye of a needle, will help them to lie parallel. Allow the tubes to distribute themselves evenly to a

Right *This child's coat smock is made from natural coloured linen, and smocked with coton a broder used in double thickness. The buttons are horn, and the garment is based on smocks worn by children working in the fields at the end of the last century.*

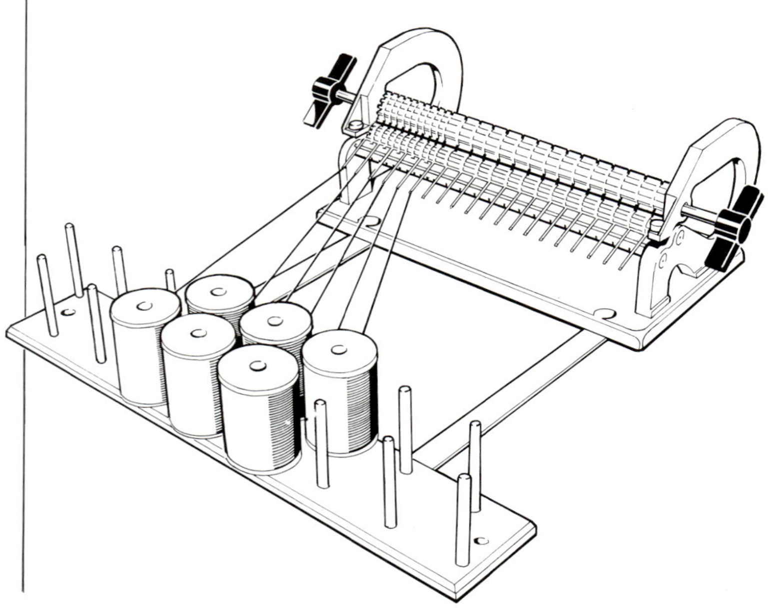

Below *A small smocking machine can be used to pleat up the tubes evenly.*

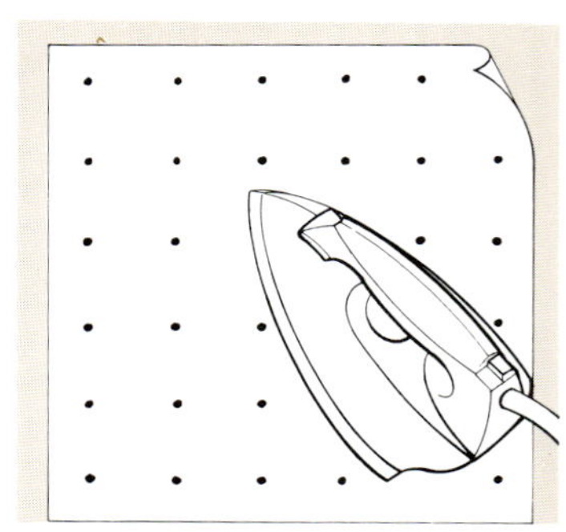

Using transfers *Cut the transfer paper to the size required and place it ink side down on the wrong side of the fabric. Press with a warm iron and peel off paper.*

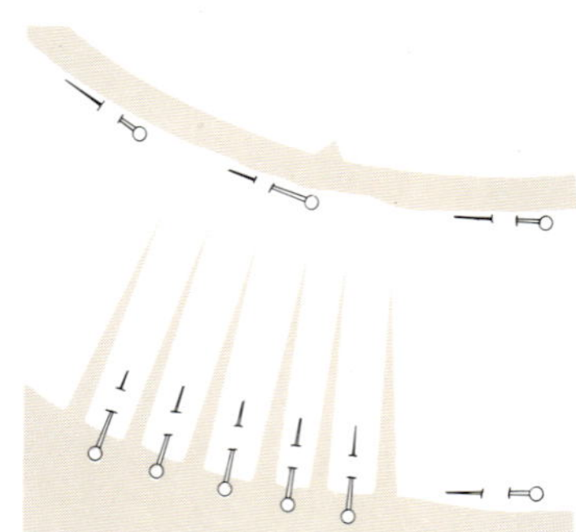

Marking curved area *Use the same procedure, but slit the paper between the vertical rows up to the top horizontal row for the curved section.*

measurement slightly narrower than the finished work. This will allow for the expansion of the embroidery once the retaining gathers have been removed. Secure the tubes by inserting a pin at the end of every two rows and twist the threads round a pin in a figure-of-eight movement.

Stitches

The traditional nineteenth-century smocking stitches are strong and firm, being variations of the simple outline stitch. Chevron and honeycomb stitches are the techniques used on the luxury fabrics of the twentieth century; these stitches are more resilient than the first group and take up less fabric. These differences should be taken into consideration when combining the two types of stitches in one piece of work. The greater elasticity of the chevron group is ideally suited to the lower edge of the smocking on a curved yoke or child's garment.

The traditional stitches worked in broad bands of texture divided by single rows of outline stitch still give a satisfying result. Do not overcrowd the rows of smocking, as well-formed tubes have a pleasing effect unadorned. It is a good general rule to start the work with a row of outline stitch to organize or "set" the tubes to lie parallel. Endeavour to work at an even tension, bearing in mind that the natural tendency is to pull the stitches too tight, thus reducing the elasticity of the finished article. The retaining threads of the gathers are visible between the tubes and provide a guide for keeping the smocked lines straight.

Most stitches are worked from left to right. Start with a small knot carefully concealed in the first tube, then pick up each tube in turn at a regular depth. Avoid finishing off threads within the line of smocking, particularly on fine fabrics where the finishing stitches will be visible from the right side. At the same time it is important that the initial length of thread should not be so long that it becomes woolly in appearance towards the end of the row. Finish off the line of smocking with three or four overstitches securely worked into the last tube.

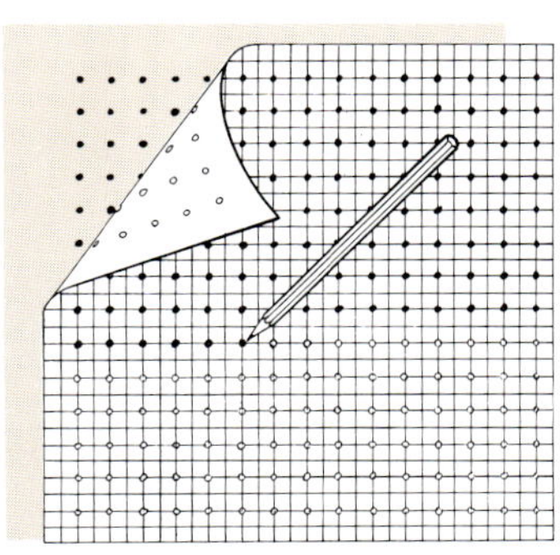

Marking with graph paper *Cut graph paper to the size required, and pierce small holes at intersections with a sharp point. Lay on fabric and mark carefully through holes.*

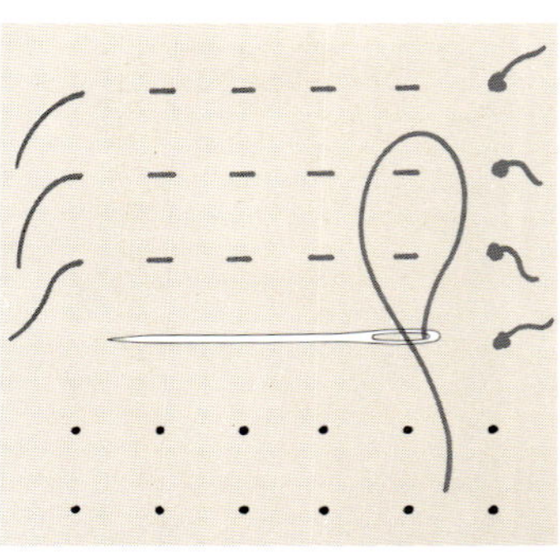

Gathering 1. *Work rows of running stitch over each line of dots, covering each dot with a small stitch as shown. Allow plenty of thread for each row.*

2. *Pull the threads in pairs to gather the fabric into tubes ready for smocking. Space them as evenly as possible. Secure the thread ends round pins as shown.*

Below *A beautiful jacket made from tussore silk, with rouleau loop buttons. The little pink birds are appliquéd on, with embroidered feathers, and the russet leaves are also appliqué work. The scattered flowers have been tatted on. The smocking is randomly worked, providing on this particular garment a discreet textural background for the embroidery and appliqué.*
Bottom *The smocking on this jacket has also been worked at random, but can be seen to be much tighter. In comparison with the jacket above, the smocking becomes a much more dominant feature of the design as a whole. The miniature stars of seeding stitch have been very finely worked indeed.*
Below right *This jacket has an almost ecclesiastical feel to it, with its stand-up collar. The smocking is regular and closely worked, and the gathers extend downwards to frame the lively leaf design.*
Right *An Agra silk jacket in deep gold, with couched threads, appliqué and beads sewn into the tiny pockets formed by the smocking stitch, giving it a rich and subtle texture.*

Above *A gorgeous evening jacket with an inspired use of colour. The smocking is worked at random, and very loosely, in pink as well as cream to pick out the colours in the embroidery and appliqué overall. The stitching extends either side of the tubes at intervals, causing the areas of smocking to be incorporated very successfully into the overall design. The long thin appliqué leaves echo the shape of the smocked areas on either side of the revers.*

Outline stitch is a simple interpretation of stem stitch, which can either be worked with the thread above the needle, or below the needle for a neater rope-like effect.
Cable stitch is similar to outline stitch except that the needle is inserted at right-angles to the tubes and the thread is held alternatively above and below the needle.
Wave or trellis stitch is a combination of the previous ones. Using the visible gathering threads to determine the size of the wave or trellis, keep the thread below the needle on the upward movement. On the downward movement keep the thread above the needle.
Vandyke stitch is worked from right to left. Each tube is backstitched to its neighbour making a very strong resilient stitch, but it is slow to execute.
Honeycomb stitch is the quickest method of smocking as two rows are worked simultaneously. It needs some care in execution. As the majority of the thread is on the underside, it is ideal for patterned or piled fabrics. Beads or sequins can be applied to the work with chevron or honeycomb stitch.
Chevron stitch is the most versatile of smocking stitches; it can be varied in depth and width and combined with other stitches. It can be worked in a single row or reversed upon itself to form diamonds.
Surface honeycomb stitch is a minor variation of chevron stitch. Each tube is over-

Right *This mandarin-style jacket is made from rough cream coloured silk with pink and burgundy appliqué and embroidery. The loose random smocking is worked in the same colours, picked up again in the bands of stitching round the sleeves and the collar. The smocking is taken quite low so that the gathers fall almost to the hem.*

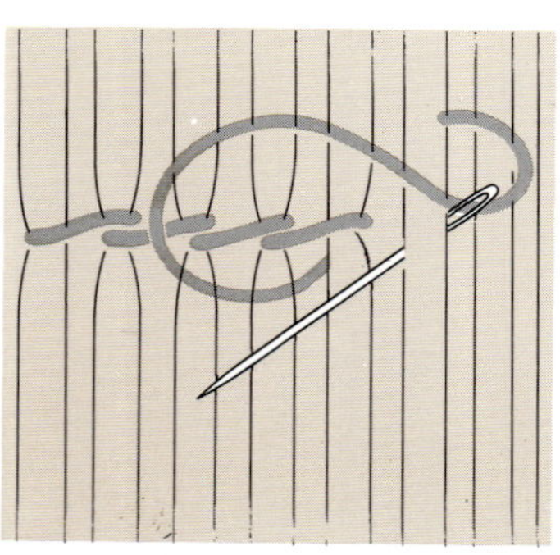

Outline stitch *Work this stitch from left to right making a small diagonal stitch in each tube. The thread can be kept consistently under or over the needle thoughout.*

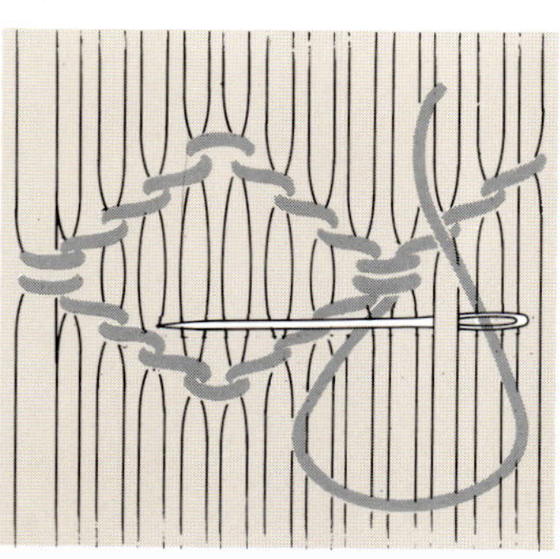

Wave and trellis stitch *When working these diamond shapes, keep the thread above the needle when stitching downwards and below for stitching upwards.*

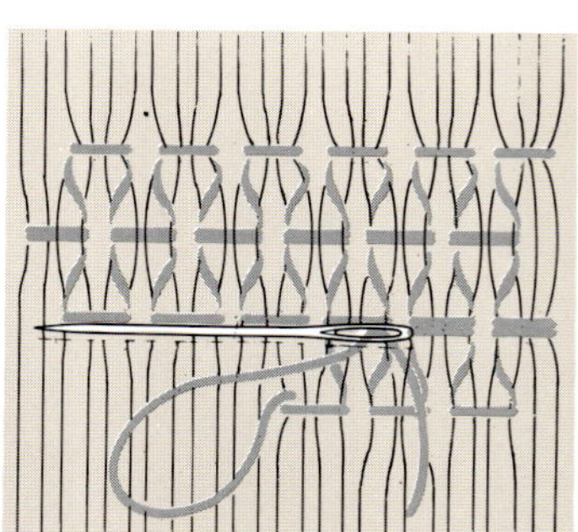

Vandyke stitch *Anchor the tubes with small horizontal stitches on alternate levels as shown, worked as a continuous back stitch from right to left.*

Honeycomb stitch *Stitch two rows at once, working backwards and forwards and catching up two tubes with each horizontal stitch that is made.*

Left *A detail from a green silk housecoat with gold revers, cuffs and hem. The same gold has been used for the appliqué and smocking. There are also several lines of silvery blue smocking. Lines of seeding stitch mingle with loose random smocking and couched threads to create a very interesting and unrestrained overall texture that extends down the yoke and up over the shoulder of this garment.*

sewn to its neighbour, first above and then below. It is a very stretchy stitch.

Feather stitch is very attractive on children's clothes.

Variations

Most smocking stitches can be worked on a grid of dots applied to the right side of the fabric to give a technique called "mock smocking". This method really has very little in common with smocking: mock smocking does not stretch, it does not require preliminary gathers and it takes up less fabric. Vandyke stitch is possibly the most successful stitch for mock smocking. Although this is difficult to master, an attractive ruched effect is achieved if it is worked neatly.

Once the basic principle of smocking is understood, there are many opportunities for creative experiment. Smocking can be worked in a figurative way to portray leaves and flowers, as on the Great Exhibition Smock of 1851, merging smocking with other methods of embroidery. It can also be worked in a random way, using stitches not normally associated with smocking, such as cretan stitch. Breaking the rules by varying the size of this stitch within each row, and by not keeping the row at right-angles to the tubes, gives the designer the freedom to mix colours and thicknesses of threads for a rich textural surface. Interesting clothes can be made with small areas of experimental smocking combined with other embroidery methods such as quilting, appliqué, couching, beadwork and machine embroidery.

Finishing

When the smocking is complete, the pins holding the retaining threads can be removed. Flatten the work on a surface with the palm of one hand and withdraw the retaining threads by firmly pulling each knot with the other hand. Excessive handling while working smocking and embroidery will fray some fabrics. Stay stitching across the top of the fabric will help to prevent this. Stretch the smocking gently and steam press on the underside to improve its appearance. Use small sharp scissors to "layer" the tops of the tubes, reducing the bulkiness where they are to be set into a yoke or cuff.

Always smock and embroider each piece of fabric before making up a garment. Laundering is no problem; cotton and linen garments can be machine-washed and even boiled, but subsequent steam or damp pressing will be necessary.

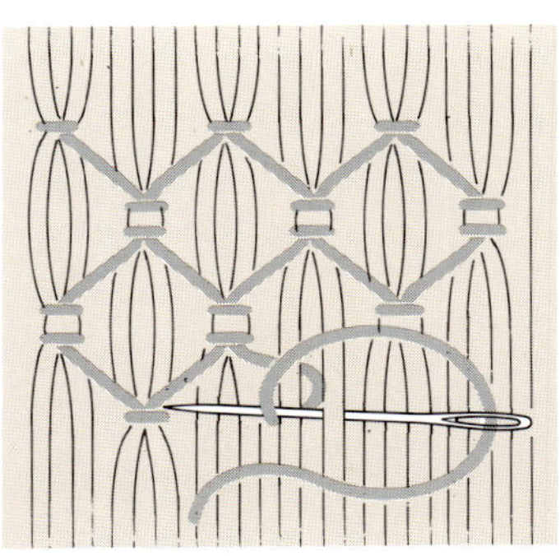

Chevron stitch *Work the horizontal stitches across two tube widths each, positioning the ends of the diagonal linking stitches between the joined tubes.*

Cretan stitch *To achieve this diamond effect, work alternate rows upside down and aligned as shown. Try to work an even number of rows.*

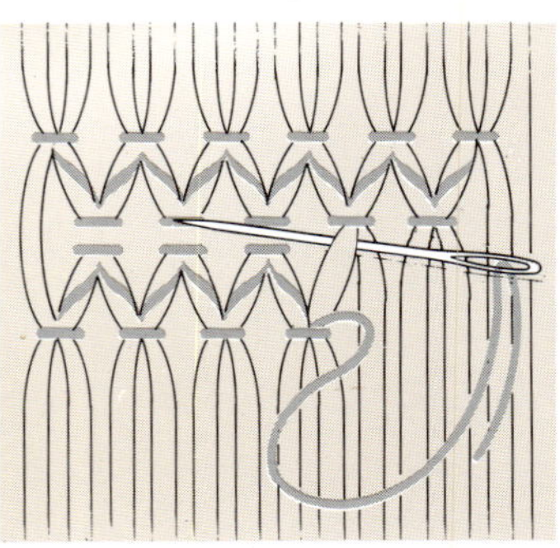

Surface honeycomb stitch *Sew each tube to its neighbour above and below, working from right to left. On subsequent rows, only work full back stitches along the bottom.*

Feather stitch *Work from right to left, making two feather stitches upwards followed by two downwards and linking them together in the formation shown.*

Silk, Metal Thread and Bead Embroidery

Silk and Metal Thread Embroidery

Silks and metallic yarns both have the effect of giving embroideries an unusual richness, but they require different application techniques. As well as being used as an embroidery thread to construct complete works, silk can enrich and embellish other pieces of embroidery. Metallic yarn embroidery, however, is a surface embroidery, the yarns being laid on the fabric, or over other stitches, and couched into place. Used together, the metallic gleam complements silk's brilliant colours and rich texture, to create the most luxurious type of embroidery.

Silk has a great affinity to dye so its colours are often bright and intense and can be exaggerated by the way in which the silk is spun. Floss silk has little twist and this results in a smooth, reflective surface, making the colours more vivid than those of the textured surface of heavier spun yarns.

Metallic yarn embroidery is often called gold embroidery, yet there is little or no gold content except in some pieces of work several hundred years old, when gold leaf was incorporated. Much of the gold-coloured yarn used since then has been, in fact, silver gilt. These have different qualities: where gold leaf stays bright, silver gilt can tarnish, which is sometimes considered an attractive effect.

History

Silk was discovered by the Chinese over 2,000 years ago and its secret was kept until about A.D. 600. Many stories are written as to how the bombyx mori moth was smuggled from its country of origin, but nothing of the history is sure until A.D. 909-916 when it was used for the red couched threads of the maniple and stole found in the tomb of St. Cuthbert. This is almost certainly the earliest existing set of silk and gold embroidery. Worked in the Anglo-Saxon period, the gold is exceptionally thin and appears to have been hammered flat after couching. The maniple and stole are embroidered with figures of saints, with their names beside them, down the lengths of the articles. They are not as clearly visible as those in work of less than two centuries later, much of which survives in near perfect condition.

The Sicilian Coronation Mantle of the Holy Roman Empire, embroidered during the years 1133 and 1134, is also worked in thin gold strips, but in this work the main stitch is underside couching. It is a fine piece of Islamic embroidery, dramatic both in subject matter and workmanship. The designs of lions and camels show careful observation, and interesting textures result from the combination of gold strips couched

Above *This is a beautiful example of* opus anglicanum, *worked between 1315 and 1335 in silk and metal threads. It is part of the Marnhull orphrey – a band of gold embroidery – and the design is similar to religious paintings of the time. There is some use of shading in the figures and their clothing, but no indication of perspective. The silver gilt and silver threads were couched to outline the robes and Christ's halo.*

with coloured silk threads, with rows of pearls, and the addition of skilfully made ornaments set with precious stones. The Kufic inscription round the edge tells of its being made in Palermo; its design indicates the uniting in one country of Mohammedans and Christians.

In England at this time the *opus anglicanum* era was just beginning. Some of the most beautiful and delicate embroidery in the world was to be worked during this period; many of the finest pieces are dated around 1300. An early example of the style is the mitre portraying the martyrdom of St. Thomas of Canterbury, dated 1180-1210. It is worked in silver gilt with underside couching, and lettered in a similar style to the St. Cuthbert set, but the figures are stylized and the form of the bodies badly observed, unlike the finest of the later works.

Underside couching was used for most of the couching in *opus anglicanum* work. The advantage of this stitch, and one of the

Left *A gold thread and sequin embroidery from the nineteenth century, this is a detail of an Indian cover. It is carefully worked with the threads couched to emphasize the textures and directions of growth of the leaves and petals. Despite the difficulty of working solely in metal, the detail is remarkable.*

Below *This section is only a small part of an 18 foot (6m) hanging depicting scenes from Chinese court life. It was made with coloured silks and metal threads on silk in the late nineteenth century. Detailed observation and rich embroidery make it a remarkable piece.*

Left *A pair of mittens from the seventeenth century show fine decorative work in silver, silver gilt and silk threads on satin. Because they have remained in good condition, the long-and-short and satin stitches with couching are easily visible.*

reasons why the work is so well preserved, is that the couching thread is often on the wrong, lined side of the work. The stitch was achieved by bringing the needle through the fabric and over the thread to be couched, then returning the needle through the same hole and pulling it sharply, so that the thread being couched made a loop through the fabric. Patterns such as herringbone were thus achieved, imitating a decorative weave.

The figures featured in the ecclesiastical embroidery, such as the Syon cope, consist of saints and apostles in scenes from the Bible. They are often clothed with drapes to the ground, which are beautifully arranged to show careful drawing of the subject and are enhanced by the use of silk yarns. Silk was used extensively, for faces and figures as well as backgrounds. There is careful shading in clothing, and where a figure shows bare limbs, attention to the anatomy is very

marked on the finest pieces of work. An example of this on the Syon cope is the quatrefoil with Doubting Thomas thrusting his hand into Christ's side. The rib structure, ankles and feet of the Christ figure show great realism. The chain or split stitch was worked to emphasize the shape and movement of the body. In contrast, the hair is an unrealistic, striped green, and the background, carrying the main figures, is of a faded red alternating with green.

One of the most beautiful examples of shading in the clothing, using split stitch and underside couching, is in the figures of the Pienza cope. The subtlety of some of the colours is attractive to the modern observer who is used to the vivacity of chemical dyes on silk. The faces are beautifully sculptured using split or chain stitch so intensely worked that often the spiral of the cheek rises in relief.

According to the manuscripts, inventories and wills of this period, bed hangings and dress were elaborately embroidered but no pieces remain. Similarly, only very few heraldic articles have survived. Embroidery owned by a religious community, which had been made there or received as a gift, had a better chance of survival, partly because it had limited use. (Some of the finest pieces can now be seen in Europe where they were sent to be safe from Henry VIII's later purge of the monasteries in the 1530s.)

After the peak of *opus anglicanum* at the beginning of the fourteenth century, embroidery became less skilled, and figures were not so well observed. This decline is often attributed to the Black Death of the 1350s. Silk continued to be used, but quicker methods were employed, such as laid work. Threads were laid parallel, solidly covering the background fabric. A second layer of threads was placed over the first creating a lattice pattern, and at each point of crossing, this layer was stitched holding the first in place. Underside couching was still used, but often the length of the stitches and the thickness of the threads were badly proportioned, leading to a heavier effect.

Some work survives from the sixteenth and seventeenth centuries, despite Henry VIII's disbanding of the monastries. Most of this is secular, but there are several prayer book and Bible bindings, now kept in museums. A book entitled *Horae Successivae* (1632) by Henshaw, is bound in white satin, and has a cover embroidered with sprigs of flowers including a pansy, a pink, a rose, and strawberries. Butterflies, a snail and a caterpillar fill the spaces between the leaves and stems of the sprigs. The whole cover is beautifully adorned, and the stems and outlines of the flowers are embroidered with couched metal cords. As they are raised, this helps to protect the long-and-short shading stitches. Spangles are sprinkled over the background.

Other articles, such as dress accessories and soft furnishings, were embroidered in a similar manner. Metal purls were sometimes used to enhance the seeding blackwork patterns on coifs. Nightcaps, gloves, sleeves and sweetbags sport beautiful flowers in floss silks. Flowers and animals of both this and the Stuart period that followed were popular because of the preoccupation at this time with natural products for both medicinal and cosmetic reasons.

Picture frames, mirror surrounds, caskets and pictures themselves were commonly worked in the seventeenth century. Once again, metal threads were used to surround and enhance the silk which was often worked with the beautiful needlepoint lace stitches of the raised or stumpwork.

Outside the home, embroidery decorated ceremonial and heraldic garments, such as the tabard and other garments worn by civic dignitaries and soldiers. Some of the work was not just raised but heavily padded, for example the Chancellor's bags of this period which carried the Great Seal of England. A new one was made for each new reign, often bearing the Royal Coat of Arms. Above and below the coat of arms on one of these bags is a curly-haired cherub with a carefully moulded face flanked by wings. Much of this is worked in a type of metal yarn called plate, with the hair worked in purls. The lion and the unicorn bodies are embroidered in silk, the moulding of each shape indicating a highly professional piece of work.

In the courts of the eighteenth century, silk was not used just to decorate accessories. Women's dresses and men's coats and waistcoats, elaborately embroidered with delicate silk and metal threads, were a manifestation of wealth. Professional work of an exceptionally high standard shows

Left *This detail of a seventeenth-century stumpwork depicts the story of Judith and Holofernes. Odd details, like antlers and pears, are raised, and Judith's dress decorated with needlelace and pearls.*

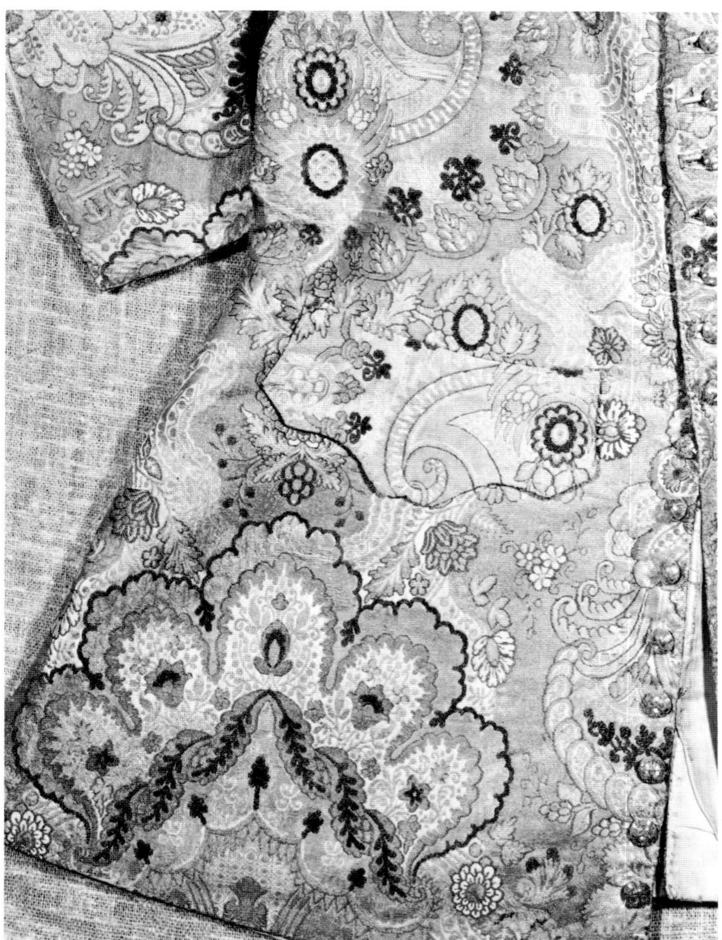

Above *The detail of this stylized sleeved waistcoat made* c. *1728, was brocaded in coloured silks, chenille and silver threads.*

Above *This detail of an eighteenth-century quilted bedcover is filled with the attractive, pastel shades of silks which were by then generally available. Delicately worked in a naturalistic design, the suggested light texture of the petals and leaves contrast with the texture of the basket which is more dense and tightly stitched.*
Right *This elaborate cap was worked for a grenadier of the 43rd Foot, c.1745. The gold thread, some of which is raised, was stitched to delineate George II's initials and his crown, with thistles and roses interwoven around the edge.*

beautiful floral forms in long-and-short stitch, split, brick, rococo and tent stitch on silk satin with metal work and chenille. Many of the examples found are from Lyons, France, which was one of the great silk weaving and embroidery centres at this time. English work is similar but perhaps not so fine. One coat typifies the style of this period, with a silk brocade pile background and heavy metal thread embroidery, predominantly worked in plate. Other examples show exquisite long-and-short stitch silk flowers, with buds and leaves, sometimes naturalistic, sometimes stylized. The skirts, bodices and stomachers of the ladies' dresses were similar in design.

This expansive work was carried through to bed covers and their accompanying three pillows and bolster. Longleat House, Avon has a magnificent set with metallic yarns couched using stringing methods and vivid and delicate long-and-short stitch, stem and satin stitch flowers.

A tradition of naval and military uniform using metal threads was becoming established during the eighteenth century; by the end of the century, they were no longer being used for ordinary dress. To find metal and silk embroidery during the nineteenth century, one turns once more to the church. Altar frontals and banners became a feature in many churches; some are still being used and can be found in both city and country churches throughout England. Banners were also used by other organizations such as trade unions. They are not all enhanced with metal couching; much depended on the skill of the maker and the wealth of the donor. The madonnas in some of the Mother's Union banners were masterpieces of needlework. Long-and-short stitch in floss silk created beautiful shading and the gold couched lettering infilled with blue satin stitch was popular.

William Morris (1834-1896) designed much embroidery, and directed his skilled needlewomen to unpick old embroideries to discover the old techniques. He created kits for people to work and had specific ideas for design: "roses, however unmistakeably, roses, shall be quaint and naive to the last degree, and also since we are using especially beautiful materials, that we shall make the most of them and not forget that we are gardening with silk and gold thread."

Two women from the late nineteenth century, Jessie Newberry and Ann Macbeth, believed that embroidery, as a creative skill, was within everybody's scope. Jessie, who was the wife of the Director of the Glasgow School of Art, started classes there in 1894. Her idea was to use materials which anyone could afford, so she embroidered with wool and silk on such everyday fabrics as flannel, linen and hessian. Her designs, colours and simple stitchery were new and very simple. Clear lettering and simple rose shapes in

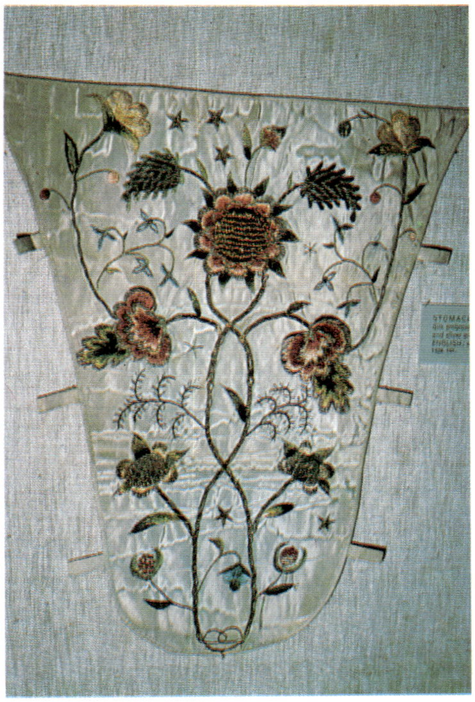

Left *Probably made in the 1920s specifically for the European market, this Chinese shawl shows an almost exclusive use of satin stitch in the decorative embroidery. The pinks, blues and yellows of varying shades enliven the black silk background.*

Above *Worked in coloured silk and silver threads, this luxurious English stomacher from the eighteenth century has a graceful floral design. Stomachers for women were often boned or stiffened in some way.*

pastel shades typify her work.

The quality and quantity of work produced in the twentieth century competes with some of the best of previous centuries. Much has been contributed by embroiderers devoted to metal thread embroidery for ecclesiastical purposes, particularly Beryl Dean, who has worked a great number of copes, banners and altar frontals for churches throughout the world. To celebrate the Queen's Silver Jubilee in 1977, the Jubilee cope, worn by the Bishop of London, was finely embroidered, with the outlines of the applied cloth which illustrate the spires, towers and doors of the featured London churches, emphasized by couched synthetic thread. This gold colour creates a richness against the varied stone-coloured pieces of applied cloth, and brings out the names of the churches embroidered beside them.

Another embroiderer, Barbara Dawson, has made an impression on the work of this century by freeing gold work of its traditional stiffness of design. She has encouraged more random experimentation with yarns, placing purls across threads with little regard for their uniformity of size, or even spacing.

Silk and metal threads have been used to decorate cloth in many countries of the world; the beautiful Indian work with beetle wings, and Spanish dress and horse trappings associated with bullfighting are good examples. Some metal thread work from China is of an exceptionally high standard. The subject matter is different, featuring either flowering peonies, chrysanthemums, plum blossom and butterflies or dragons. In Japan, they use heavily embroidered *kimonos* and *fukusas* in traditional ceremonies. The decoration on Greek waistcoats and similar garments from the Middle East, and on Russian peasant costumes, are further examples of the worldwide popularity of this medium.

Materials

Fabric

Before choosing a fabric on which to construct a silk or metal thread embroidery, the weight and colour should be considered. The fabric should be suitable for the purpose to which the embroidery is to be put. Many furnishing and dress fabrics are suitable, but, for example, a fine dress material would not be strong enough to make a large banner. Although a small piece of work could be executed on a heavy furnishing fabric, this would also be suitable for an altar frontal. Linen can be used if the fabric is to be covered in stitches.

Left *The selection of silk threads shown here includes* (top to bottom): *two hanks of coarse embroidery or knitting silk; a skein of 7-stranded d'Alger silk; oval silk – a flat silk thread sometimes known a French floss; gobelin silk; perle silk – a tightly twisted single strand silk.*
Below *This selection shows some gold and silver-coloured threads with some other metallic-looking threads ranged between. Most of the threads are in fact made from lurex. Normally only the finest can be stitched through fabrics.*

For metal thread work, colours need not be pale, but, as a general rule, gold looks better on hot colours such as orange, red and brown; and silver suits blues and greens. The fabric colour for silk work depends on the colours of the silks to be used; often both depend on the design or the use of the object to be embroidered. It is usually best to use natural colours for flowers if they are set in a naturalistic design, but if the embroidery is for a cushion, for example, to suit a particular decor, then the colours will be dictated by the colours in the room.

Silk thread

Several ranges of silk threads are available in different colours and weights in skeins. Silk floss is loosely spun, and when it is used in silk embroidery, it lies smoothly on the fabric reflecting the light, creating a glossier effect than the more tightly twisted yarns.

Fine silks are sometimes sold as stranded silk, enabling the worker to use one strand for very fine work, or the full quantity, which can be doubled, for a heavier thread. The sheen of the silk is less apparent in this form. It is suitable for freehand stitches such as chain or stem stitch. The heavily twisted yarn, called perle, is suitable for such stitches as raised chain band, coral stitch or couching, achieving a less reflective but more textured effect.

Rayon imitations of silk are fairly readily available. Originally they were manufactured for machine decorations on lingerie, and known as "trimming embroidery floss". Some are imported from India. They have a brilliance of colour, and do not catch on rough fingers like real silk, but need skilled and firm handling because they tend to untwist.

Traditionally, metal yarns have been couched with Maltese thread or a silk called "horsetail". Recently the Maltese thread has become too fine and it is preferable on occasions to use ordinary dressmakers' silk. Both these threads need waxing, to prevent knotting, for protection and to darken the colour. The stronger synthetic threads are also used for couching, as silk does not wear well against metal threads.

Metal thread

Traditional yarns made and used for metal thread embroidery fall into four main categories. The first of the four categories includes the two main types of "wrapped" yarn. The first type, "Japanese gold substitute", is an updated version of what was known as "Japanese gold," which was gold leaf backed on paper, cut into thin strips and wrapped round a silk core. The second type has a silk core with very fine wire wrapped round it. This is called "passing thread". Both are available in gold and silver, and have at various times been made in other materials such as copper, or coloured bronze. Despite its name, passing thread can usually only be couched to the fabric.

Left *The cream silk embroidery on cream silk was carefully worked to produce a reversible pattern on this Chinese shawl. The intricately twisted border of fine silk threads, heavy silk fringe and the precise geometric floral pattern on the shawl itself, which includes peonies and chrysanthemums in satin stitch, combine to create a beautiful and decorative garment.*

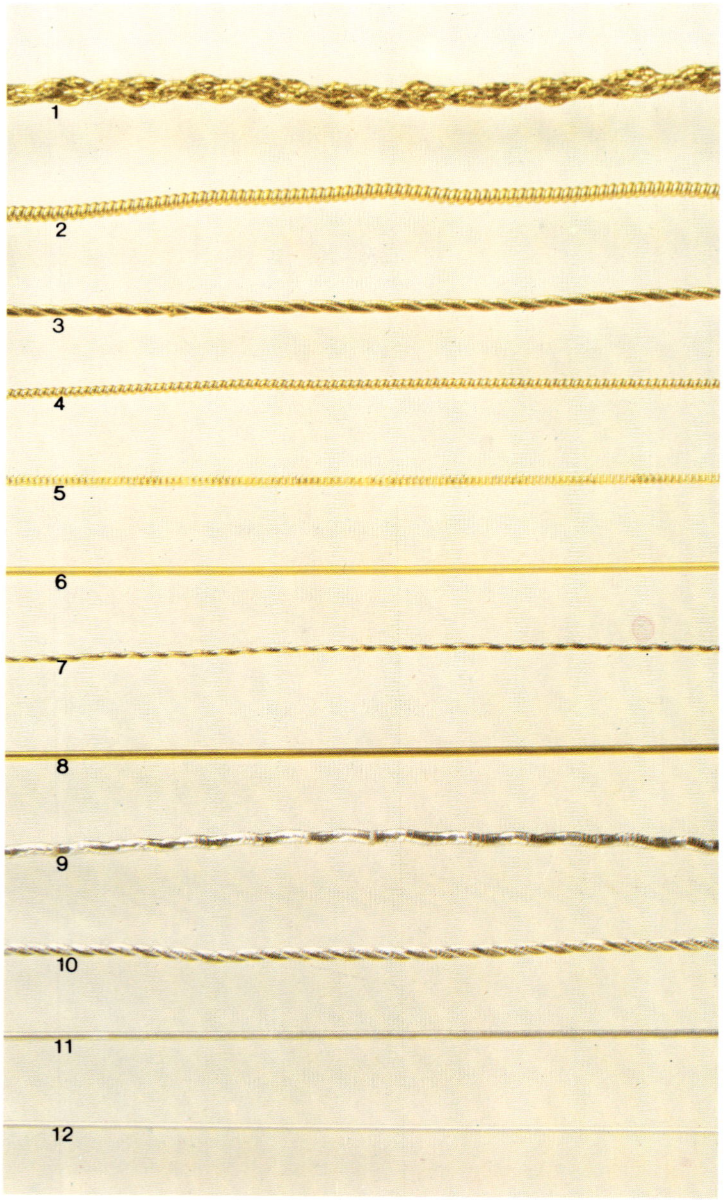

Left *From top to bottom these metal threads are: an 8-ply gold lurex* (1); *a no 3 gold pearl purl* (2); *a no 10 twist gold* (3); *a no 1 gold pearl purl* (4); *a gold check purl* (5); *a smooth gold purl* (6); *a thin gold rococo* (7); *a rough silver purl* (8); *a thick silver rococo* (9); *a no 10 twist silver* (10); *a smooth silver purl* (11); *a silver passing thread* (12).
Right *A sumptuous piece from a much longer hanging, this is a Chinese silk and metal thread embroidery. The couched gold threads are laid to follow designs on the robes or on the canopy, and to indicate the way the robes fall, so giving them a three-dimensional appearance. The silk threads are worked in satin stitch, some of which has been padded so giving the faces of the courtiers an almost sculptured look, with shadows where the padding falls away slightly. The embroidery is intricately and ingeniously worked.*

The second category, of plied yarn, includes both the wrapped yarns, which can be plied like fine wire. Several singles create a heavy plied yarn resulting in a cord, which is capable of retaining the shape it has been given.

Thirdly, a strip of metal, beaten flat, is called "plate" and is available in gold and silver. The advantage of these strips is that they crease and can be applied easily by catching down the creases with couching thread. They can also be crimped along the thread of a screw or the teeth of a metal comb.

The fourth category consists of "purls" or "bullion". These come in several forms, made in gold, silver and copper. In manufacture, a metal wire is wrapped around a rod, and the resulting form depends on the size and shape of the rod. Check purl, of a facetted appearance, is wrapped round a three-sided rod. It unwraps slightly after manufacture, giving it its characteristic light-catching appearance. Rough and smooth purls are serpent-like before use, rough being less shiny and whiter in appearance than the richer colour of smooth. These three are cut into varying lengths and stitched like single beads. They can be clustered together, covering the background, or spaced out; they can be stitched randomly using random sizes, or they can be cut into similar sized lengths and stitched in a chequer-board pattern.

Pearl purl is manufactured in the same way as the other purls, but it is stretched before use, so it looks like a spring, and stitched down like a cord. All these purls are made in about seven sizes, but are not always readily available as they are expensive stock items.

Many of the metallic yarns tarnish, particularly silver, if they come into contact with wood or cigarette smoke, damp or acid. They can be coated with shellac or clear nail varnish, or rubbed with a chamois. The Lurex yarns have yet to show how they will last.

Lurex yarns, metallic in appearance, and cheaper than other metallic yarns, are made of a plastic laminate with a metallic pigment between. They are often of a looped construction, similar to a crochet chain, made of continuous filament yarn with little or no metal content. Some are made to resemble the traditional metallic yarns. Their disadvantages are that they are difficult to couch, as they spring from position during folding and stitching, and must be handled with great firmness; also they do not retain

crimps, which makes designs less durable.

Frames

It is essential to use a frame for both metal and silk embroidery. A round frame should only be used for practising, or for working a very small embroidery, as it always causes fabric distortion and can soil the background. If the fabric is not held with the warp and weft at right-angles, the couching may buckle and straight lines be crooked, on removal from the frame.

Techniques

Design

The use of silk and metal thread embroidery has usually been limited to decorative work due to its fragility. Silk embroidery can be used to enrich other types of embroidery by filling in various shapes within the design.

Right *Apart from its aesthetic content, this bird is also valuable as an illustration of a variety of metal threads in use. Couched Jap gold fills the upper body, and passing thread the under body. Silver-coloured rough and smooth purls fill the chest, and cut check purls and bullion speckle the wing and head. Pearl purl outlines these areas, and a synthetic cord outlines the whole bird and delineates the legs. The beak is in plate and the eye a bead on a sequin.*

Designs for floral patterns in silk, to be embroidered on mirror surrounds or purses, for example, can be naturalistic or stylized. The growth lines of the flowers, having been drawn onto the fabric, must be carefully followed, particularly when using long-and-short stitch. The leaves can be worked in seeding stitch, and the stems in raised chain band.

Metal threads are used to outline shapes in other works, emphasizing particular details and brightening the whole effect. Using the small purl chips, or pieces, backgrounds can be made to glitter. Small articles, like pincushions or small pictures, can be delicately worked with metal thread hearts, for example. Starting from the outside shape, the threads to be couched, perhaps passing thread, pearl purl and rows of Japanese gold substitute, can be alternated, then the centre filled with a mixture of check and rough purl chips. If initials or other lettering are required, they can be traced or copied, then couched from the outside to the centre, perhaps filling the central space with seed beads or imitation seed pearls. There is great scope for experimentation with different combinations for different effects.

Stitches for silk embroidery

Long-and-short stitch is most commonly used by silk embroiderers, but it is one of the most difficult stitches to perfect. If a shape such as a petal is to be worked, a split or stem stitch should be stitched around the outline. Then, the first row of alternate long and short stitches is sewn, bringing the needle up over the split stitch, thereby creating a neat edge. The length of the short stitches in the first row should be two-thirds the length of the long stitches. In the second row, all the stitches should be the length of the longer stitches, with the needle coming up a third of the way up the length of the previous long stitches, and halfway up the length of the short stitches. The result of the second row looks similar to the first row. The rest should be completed in the same way as the second row. All the stitches must pierce the embroidery silk of the previous row, thereby merging completely. Gradual colour changes can thus be effected, with the colours of different rows blending into each other, and the possibility of a shaded effect if so desired. This is a characteristic of this type of stitching. The needle should not come up beside the previous yarn, as this gives a pitted appearance.

French knots can be used to give a textured effect. Pull the thread through the background fabric, and hold it taut with the left hand. Place the point of the needle under the thread and over, then take the needle down to the right of where it came through the fabric. Pull the thread loosely or tightly depending on the kind of knot required, before taking the needle through. Clusters of knots are very effective with different weights of yarns.

Stitches for metal thread embroidery

Couching is usually used to fix metal threads to the background fabric. The colour of the thread used for couching is unimportant unless it is in deliberate contrast to the background fabric. Wrapped threads, which are usually laid in pairs, should have the couching thread lying at right-angles to them. Twists and plied yarns such as cords, should have the couching thread placed at an angle across the yarn so that the couching thread lies in the twist. These are usually stitched singly, not in pairs. Pearl purl is also attached in this manner. All other purls are

Left *This is a small section of a Chinese embroidery depicting a vase of flowers. The bright blue colour of the woven background fabric sets off the gold and white silk embroidery of the vase; above the section shown, the flowers and leaves are stitched in suble shades of pink and green, which also stand out well against the background. Some of the petals are outlined with gold thread. The effect is colourful and rich. In this detail the vase is filled with hundreds of white silk French knots, and surrounded with gold silk satin stitches. The vase motif is also in gold silk.*

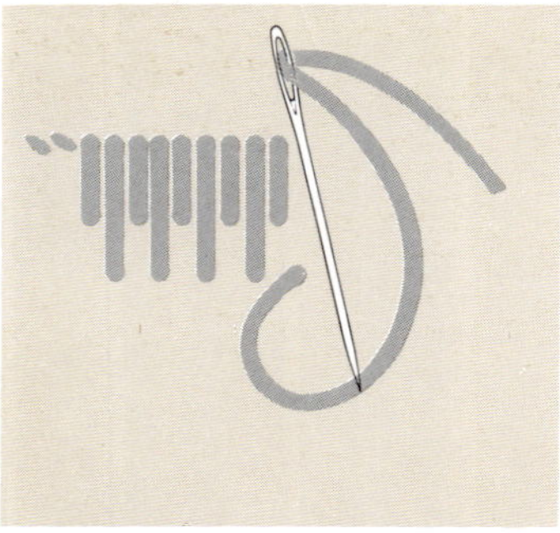

Long-and-short stitch 1. *Care must be taken to achieve an effect of even shading. The first row is worked from left to right following the brick stitch pattern.*

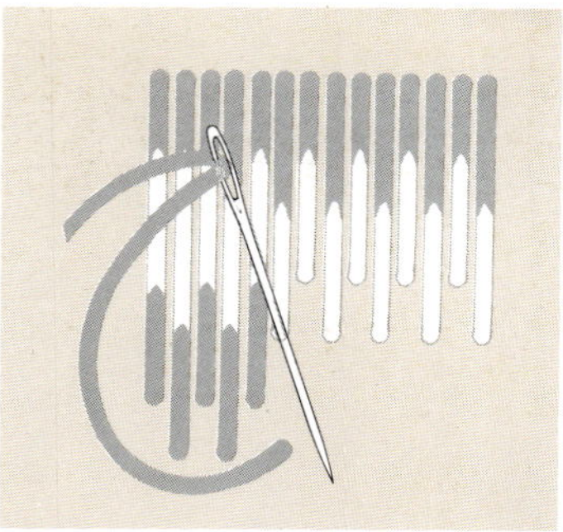

2. *In subsequent rows all stitches are the same length as the longer stitches in the first row. It is essential that each new stitch pierces the stitch above.*

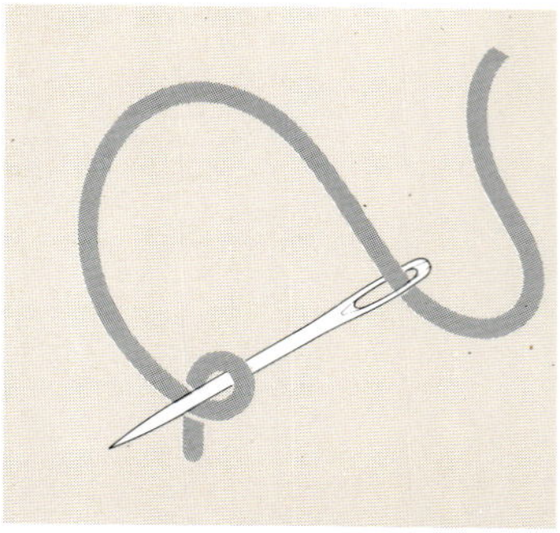

French knot 1. *The thread must be wound firmly round the needle to ensure a neat result. It is advisable to secure the twists with one hand while tightening the thread.*

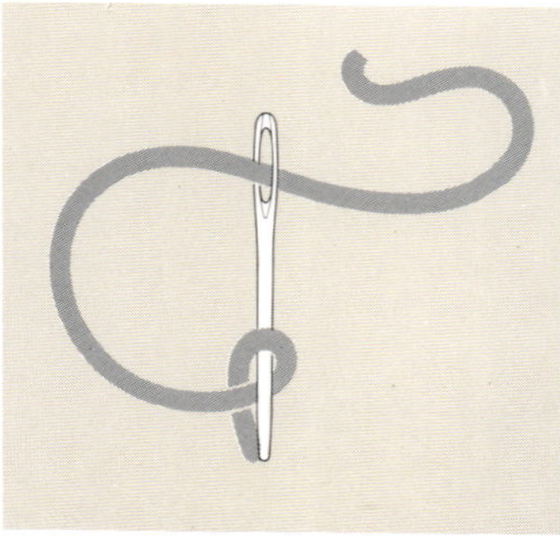

2. *Continue to keep the spare thread taut and insert the point of the needle very close to the original starting point. It must be pulled through carefully.*

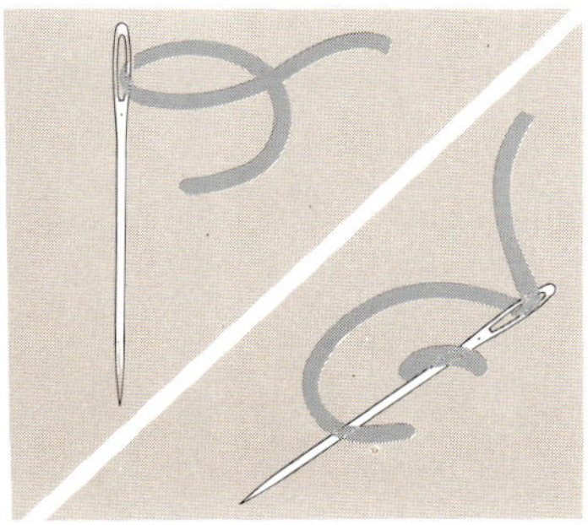

Pearl stitch 1, 2. *Work a small vertical stitch at the back of the fabric, pull it through and leave a small loop. Insert the needle back through this loop and pull tight.*

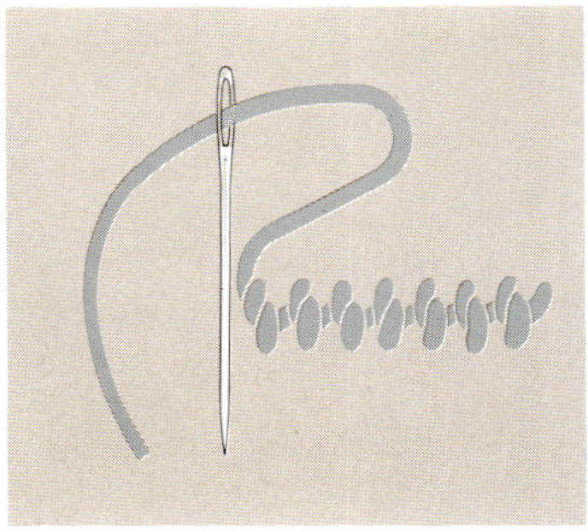

3. Repeat stitches close together for a neat rope-like effect, and further apart for the more ragged edge shown above. Keep the stitches a consistant height.

cut into short lengths of about 1/16 to 1/4 inch (about 2mm to 6mm), depending on the effect required, and stitched singly like beads.

Raised work can be created using couching. The gold raised areas of the bed covers at Longleat were created by attaching card shapes and string in place on the background, before couching the metal thread at right-angles over them. The effect of this type of padding is quite angular.

Felt paddings can also be used, which raise an area in an undulating way. A piece of felt is cut to the size of the area, then a second piece is cut and trimmed slightly smaller, and possibly a third piece. The smallest piece is attached in position, and the largest piece of felt placed over the others and stitched neatly with the needle coming up in the background and back through the felt and background. The metal thread is then stitched over the top. Sometimes, the metal thread does not need to be couched if the padding is loose and it is easy to pull the thread through.

Right *This piece is a detail from a beautiful Chinese embroidery depicting birds of all colours in graceful positions. Made to decorate a cuff for a robe, the embroidery is rich and unusual. The blue background fabric sets off the white silk of this crane, which has a bright red patch at the top of its head and yellow shades worked into the wings in satin stitch. The surrounding gold threads in bold designs are laid in pairs, which is a typical Chinese embroidery technique. The crane itself was a symbol of the first order within the Chinese social hierarchy.*

Bead Embroidery

Throughout history, beads have been made from a great variety of materials, including simple seeds and shells and other natural materials such as porcupine and feather quills, moulded clay, stones and crystals.

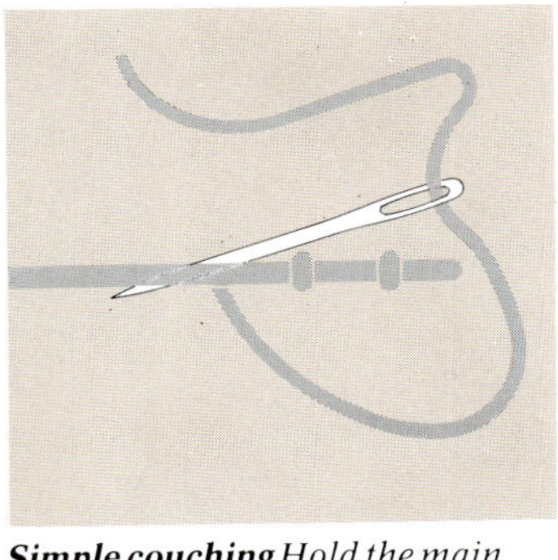

Simple couching *Hold the main thread firm and attach it to the fabric with the couching stitch shown. The visible stitches should be at equal distances.*

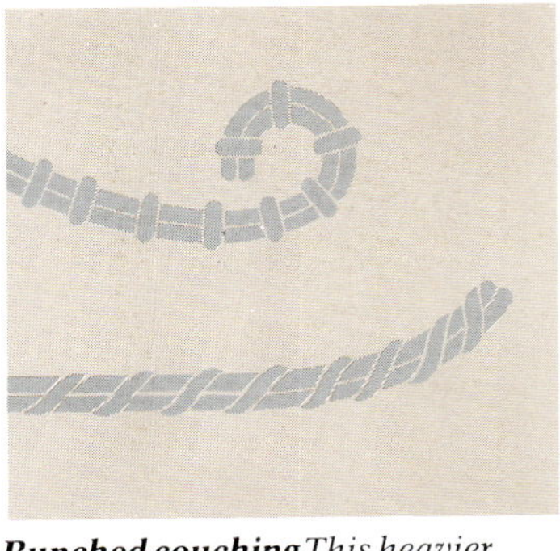

Bunched couching *This heavier effect can be achieved by using more than one laid thread. Pull the overcast stitches tight and the laid threads will bunch up.*

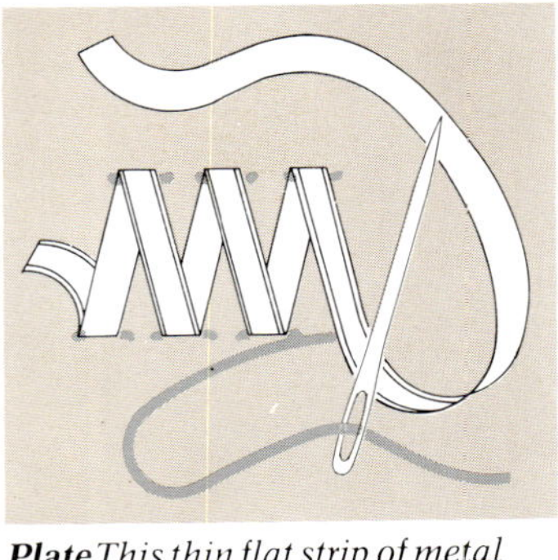

Plate *This thin flat strip of metal catches the light. It can be bent into a zigzag shape and sewn down with loops at each bend as shown.*

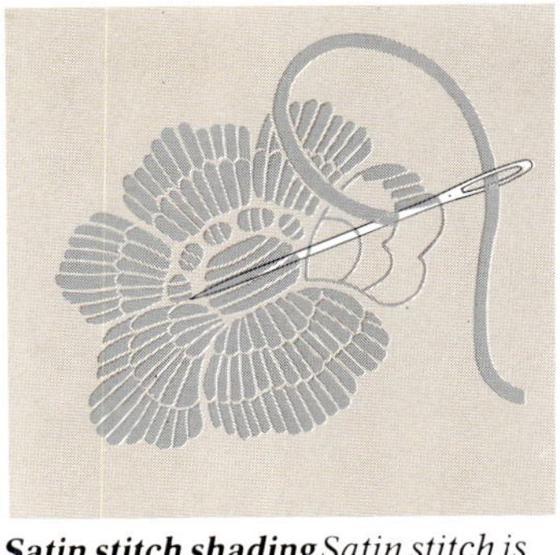

Satin stitch shading *Satin stitch is an extraordinarily versatile stitch, and can be used for delicate shading both of layers and small contained areas.*

Above *From the late eighteenth century, this charming picture shows an intensive and successful exploitation of the tambour hook. It was embroidered with silk and metal threads on satin.*

Right *An exquisite piece of nineteenth-century Chinese embroidery, made to decorate a sleeveband, silk and gold threads were applied with satin stitches, seeding, Peking knots, laid work and couching. Fearsome dragons have been worked with particularly intricacy, and the voiding between the petals and within the leaves is a typical Chinese technique.*

Far right *This Japanese* fukusa *from the nineteenth century was stitched with gold and silk threads on a beautiful piece of bright silk. It was carefully worked, in preparation for presenting a gift with the* fukusa *as its covering.*

Left *From the late nineteenth century, this section of a Chinese sleeveband shows some delicate work in silks and metal threads on a gold silk background. The design is imaginative and colourful. The rough texture of Peking knots in shades of green, grey, blue and red in the mythological butterfly shape, contrasts with the smoother, more reflective surface of the flowers and leaves in satin stitch and laid work which indicate the velvety textures of petals. Couched metal threads add glitter to the butterfly outline.* ***Top*** *The beads in this picture were stitched to the canvas in the late nineteenth century in a Berlin woolwork design. White highlighting on the tips of the petals gives depth and life to the flowers, which must have taken some time to work, considering the size of the beads. To give some indication of their size, the centre of each flower contains at least ten. Some of the beads at the centre of the righthand flower have fallen off, revealing the canvas beneath. This emphasizes the importance of firmly securing beads to their ground: if this is not done, the friction between the beads and by the beads to the thread causes rapid wear.* ***Above*** *This bead flower motif was worked on velvet by Canadian Indians in the late nineteenth century. Using contrasting colours for a simple, bright result, the Indians threaded then stitched the beads in leaf and flower shapes around the previously stitched stems and veins.*

The use of beads has been similarly varied: they have been used for decorating the body, clothing and household articles; for counting and as currency; and for sacred rites, including counting prayers.

Beads have limited use in embroidery. They either constitute an entire piece of work, as in North American bead work, or the beads are stitched to enhance other types of embroidery, such as metal thread and silk work. They can be used as an edging, or threaded as tassels or fringes. They add colour to an article, provide an extra dimension and give interesting textural or reflective effects.

There are many types of beads, not all of which are suitable for embroidery – some have difficult shapes. Suitable beads are mainly made of porcelain, glass or plastic. Antique beads made of amber, rock crystal, jasper, jade or jet can also be used.

History

Seed pearls, found in freshwater mollusc shells in most parts of the world, have been used to enrich embroidery for centuries. These pearls, usually small and not uniform in shape, were very popular in the embroidery of the *opus anglicanum* era in the thirteenth century.

Naturally shaped or handmade beads were variously employed in embroideries until the Middle Ages, when the making of glass beads developed in Venice and Murano which became the world centre of the glassmaking industry. Manufacturing secrets were jealously guarded, but when Venetians emigrated and set up factories in other parts of the world, the process was no longer a mystery. The great advantage glass beads offered for embroidery work was that they could be manufactured with a hole, whereas pearls needed to have holes bored and beads made from precious materials such as jade and amber had to be both shaped and bored.

Fifteenth- and sixteenth-century explorers from Europe took cheap beads around the world to exchange for the riches of conquered lands. Similar types of beads still feature in the traditions of tribes from Borneo and North America, and also in Eskimo and Zulu decoration. These primitive peoples used beads to adorn their bodies, for making skirts and head-dresses and to decorate shoes. The North American Indians developed a highly sophisticated type of work; their designs were simple, but often dramatic and colourful. The Zulus of Natal made friendship necklaces for gifts, with messages spelt out in specific colours – white was used to express love, for example.

Beadwork was very evident during the middle decades of the seventeenth century in Europe. Purses were sewn with coloured beads with such inscriptions as "The gift of a friend" and "Remember the poor". Mirror frames, baskets, pictures, caskets and book-covers were commonly decorated in this way. The designs were similar to those used

Right *Beadwork of extreme delicacy and intricacy decorates this base of a late seventeenth-century basket. The work depicts the Biblical story of Susannah and the Elders in raised motifs of many different colours. Fruit, leaves, intertwined branches, a wall and the robes of the woman and two men are all made of tiny, secured beads. The positions of the hands and the expressions on their faces are surprisingly expressive considering the difficulty of working to such a small scale.*
Above right *This beadwork firescreen is a typical piece of Victorian grisaille work. The beads, in various shades of grey with white and black highlighting and shading depict an angel and her cherub. Strung tassels and twisted beads in three shades, surround the screen.*
Below right *These two bead embroidered purses were made in 1634, in England. The fabric, the tassles and drawstrings have deteriorated badly, but the beadwork remains in good condition, with neat, geometric designs and the lettering still clearly visible.*

for stumpwork and silk pictures of the same period. Subject matter included Biblical or mythological characters in contemporary dress, flowers and herbs found in the gardens of the time, butterflies, squirrels and fountains, none of which were drawn in proportion.

Beads were used with great enthusiasm again during the nineteenth century. Bags were made by knitting and passing beads up the yarn, one bead per stitch. Cushions, hand screens and footstools, all in Berlin woolwork, were enhanced with beads. A particular type of beadwork of about 1860 was called "grisaille" beadwork, using only grey, white and black beads. The contrast

between the transparent and opaque beads often added an interesting quality, despite the lack of bright colours in this type of work.

In Victorian times, beads were fastened to fabric by tambouring. This was ordinarily worked by placing the background fabric into a round tambour frame with the right side uppermost. The right hand wielded the tambour hook – a type of crochet hook used to pierce the fabric – and the left hand guided the yarn to the hook. The result was a chain stitch. When used for attaching beads, however, the fabric was laid into the frame wrong side uppermost and the design was marked. Beads were threaded onto the yarn in the order they were required, with the left hand feeding beads up towards the hook.

Tambouring was a hand method which preceded the invention of the Cornely sewing machine. This was an industrial machine invented and patented by Bonnaz, a French engineer, in 1865, and manufactured by Ercole Cornely. It developed from a single needle machine using only one reel of thread, to a more complex machine with an eye-pointed needle, two threads and a bobbin. It was used to attach pre-strung sequins to fabrics, which were to be made into garments and other accessories.

In the early twentieth century, beads were a popular decoration on fashionable clothes and became widely available in all shapes and sizes. The beaded bodices and skirts of the 1920s demanded large orders from bead manufacturers. Unfortunately, the weight of the beads and the thin fabrics on which they were mounted resulted in very few pieces surviving.

The English designer Norman Hartnell was a great supporter of beadwork, favoured again by some haute couture designers of the 1950s. His designs for Princess Elizabeth's wedding dress, then her coronation dress, and some of the royal family's evening dresses of the time, are fine illustrations of this. The Emmanuels' design for Lady Diana Spencer's wedding dress, for the

Left *All the beads shown here have specific names, which indicate their shape. In the boxes are rocailles - little rounded beads. On the right there are round multicoloured rocailles with round interiors; the other two boxes contain gold and silver square rocailles with square interiors. The rows of strung cylindrical beads, available in a variety of colours and sizes, are bugles. The smallest are on the right, medium in the middle and the largest on the left. These can be bought separately or on strings. On the left is a pile of paillettes, and below it a pile of the smaller curved couvettes.*

Above *This waistcoat, decorated with beadwork floral motifs, was embroidered by North American Indians in the nineteenth century. The colourful design was influenced by European floral prints from French Canadian convents.*
Above left *These three cone-shaped crowns of the African Yoruba tribe, show a bold and colourful use of beadwork in effective designs. Rows of strung beads combine in blocks of colour to form simplified designs and geometric patterns. The weight of the crowns must have prohibited their being worn for long periods.*
Below left *This beadwork from the seventeenth century, depicting Abraham about to slay Isaac, shows a direct technique of bead application. The figures and animals are crudely portrayed.*

occasion of her marriage to Prince Charles in the summer of 1981, made extensive use of beadwork to decorate and enrich the ivory taffeta and the silk tulle veil. They used mother-of-pearl sequins and pearls. Once again now, beads are regaining a more popular usage, with other designers incorporating them into knitted garments and on suede.

Materials

Beads

Many kinds of beads are available today, including Venetian and Japanese millifiori beads, cloisonné, Chinese porcelain, Indian glass and German wood beads, as well as those made of papier maché and plastic. Glass beads with facetted surfaces can be lined with foil and are available pierced and ready for stitching. They can also be mounted on metal claws for attaching to the fabric.

It is difficult to be precise about terminology for different beads, but retailers will probably stock a good selection. Round rocailles or seed beads have round holes and are round inside and out. Toscas or square rocailles have square holes and are round on the outside. Charlottes are facetted beads. Bugles are long and cylindrical. Paillettes are what are commonly known as sequins with a hole in the middle; sequins, in fact, have a hole to one side. Couvettes are concave sequins. It is best to keep the different types of beads in containers, as they are fragile and break easily.

Fabric and thread

Background fabric can be of almost any type: plain, patterned, or embroidered. Beads can be attached singly to enhance the pattern on the outlines or ranged at different points on the pattern to complement it. Naturalistic touches can also be added – for example, eyes to an embroidered animal motif. Beads can be bought and attached in rows, but the fabric and the string should be strong. A calico backing fabric helps to support the fabric shape and add strength.

Stitching yarn should be strong. Often a synthetic stitching yarn, as used in dressmaking, is best.

Needles

Beading needles are fine long needles, which are available in sizes between 10 and 15. They are useful when the hole is too small for embroidery needles or when a long needle is required to pick up several beads at once.

Techniques

A slate frame is essential. The fabric grain must be straight on the frame, to avoid distortion. If a finished piece such as the top of a box or a garment is to be shaped, it should be cut out after working.

Design

Small objects lend themselves to bead decoration. Discs encrusted with beads in spirals can be strung together as a necklace or hung as a pendant. Initials on a small bag or on a pocket could be filled in with beads. A sequin in the centre of a box lid with a row of beads surrounding it could be the foundation for further decoration: beads radiating from the centre or stitched in concentric circles. Always design the work with the shape of the article or garment in mind.

Floral motifs can be shaped with single lines of beads or sequins used to illustrate petals, or with smaller beads in rows filling the petal shape. Rows of beads used to illustrate stems or veins should be stitched to the fabric in the direction of growth. What

Above *Paillettes and beads have been sewn to this piece of net with a tambour hook. Transparent yet reflective paillettes were applied in rows to outline the shapes of petals; small paillettes of different colours and rocailles were stitched to delineate stems and small leaves. Silk and gold threads combine to give a rich and fine result.*

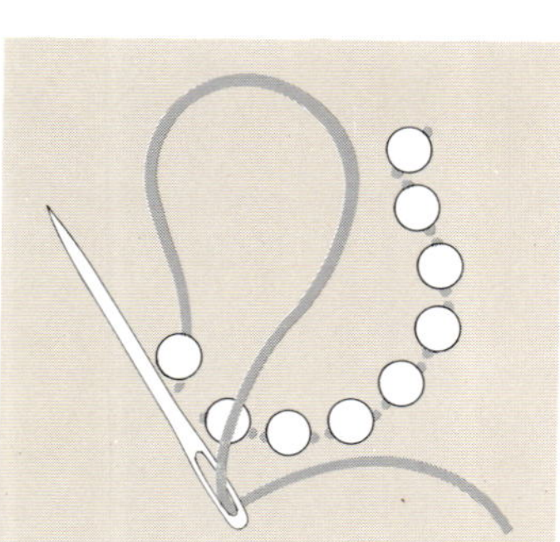

Applying beads individually *Beads can be attached to fabric with a single stitch. Thread the bead and take the needle back close to the beginning of the stitch.*

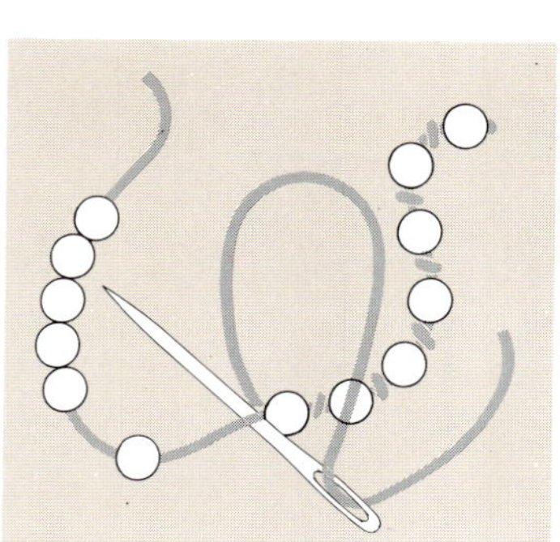

Couched beads *A popular way to attach beads is to couch them onto the fabric. Strung beads are sewn on in lines with small overcast stitches between each bead.*

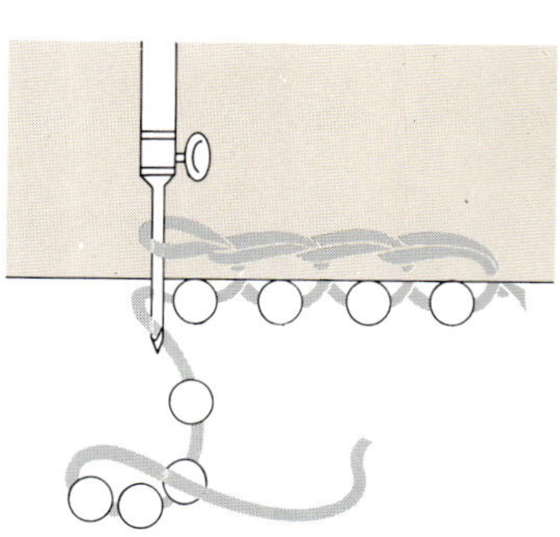

Applying beads with a tambour hook *Having placed the fabric with the right side down in the frame, take the threaded hook down, push a bead into position, and loop up.*

Looped bead hem *An article decorated with beads can be further enhanced by a loosely buttonhole stitched hem into which beads are incorporated.*

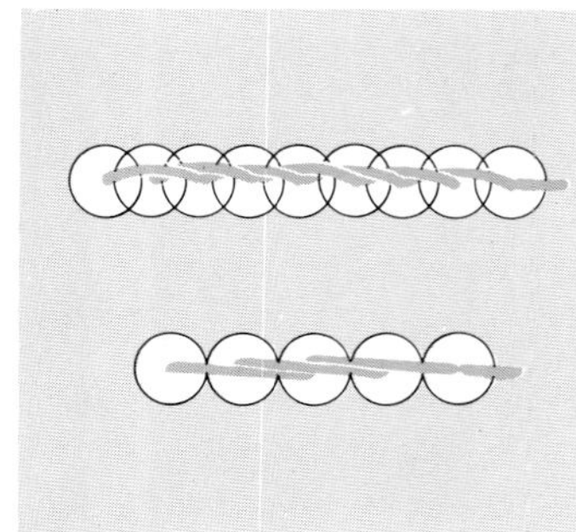

Sequins 1. *They can be attached in different ways depending on the kind of decorative effect required.*

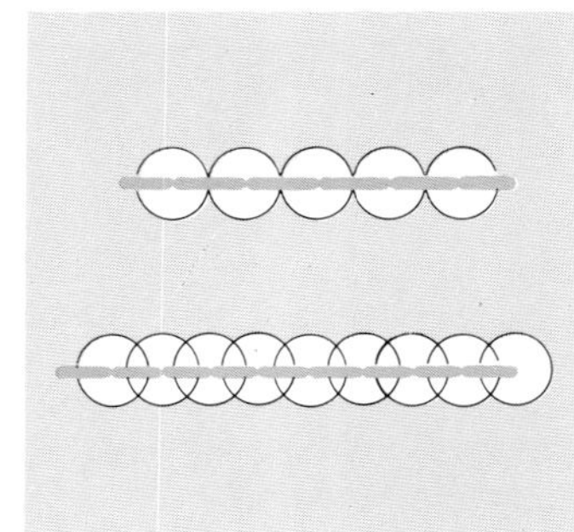

2.Back stitch them on in a line side by side or overlapping slightly.

shape the beads or sequins are should be taken into consideration as they may be used to emphasize the shape of the motif – for example, round beads or sequins could be used for rounded petals, smaller beads for the tips of stamens.

The colour of threads may well be visible, so they should either match or contrast, whichever is desired. A particularly rich effect may be achieved by stitching with metal thread, especially if the background is silk or velvet. The qualities of the beads themselves are enhanced by using dramatic or unusual colour combinations. Three shades of the same colour could be used for a subtle effect. Exploit the glinting quality of facetted surfaces, the rich effects of mother-of-pearl, or the depth of colour offered by pieces of glass in the light.

Stitches

Stitch the beads singly or in rows to the fabric. To couch beads, first string them loosely, then overcast the string after each bead with a strong thread. Looped or hanging fringes must be attached to the edges of fabric with firm stitches and strong thread, as they may be heavy. The type of stitch depends on the desired effect. Sequins can be attached with invisible stitches when overlapping, or visibly with a back stitch for further decoration, if the thread is to be displayed.

Above left *This photograph showing a section from the lower part of a 1920s Parisian dress illustrates intricate decorative beadwork. Tiny beads of different shapes, sizes and colours have been threaded and attached to create an eye-catching fringe below an orange ribbon on the net surface. Paillettes, bugles and rocailles have been stitched with threads of contrasting colours in dainty floral patterns on the net and in more solid designs underneath.*

Above *A hand-size clasp purse, probably made and decorated for evening wear. The bold floral design in beads of multiple hues, including pink, blue, orange and yellow, are stitched to a luxurious green velvet background.*

Machine Embroidery

Machine embroidery has today acquired the status of a creative form. With patience and practice, the machine can quickly produce original embroidery that has great individuality. Machine embroidery on its own offers tremendous scope, together with speed of working, which is much appreciated by busy designer embroiderers. Used in conjunction with hand embroidery, which it can complement and in some cases imitate, it provides many creative possibilities.

Contrary to popular belief, even straight stitch machines can be used for many decorative techniques; zigzag models offer limitless possibilities. With the continual updating of sewing technology, intricate designs can be carried out rapidly with minimum effort.

Successful machine embroidery depends largely on practice, enthusiasm, and a thorough knowledge of the working of the machine, especially the different settings for each technique. The machine handbook will supply the answers to most problems; if not, the manufacturer or a local sewing machine dealer may be approached to give advice. By experimenting with settings, machine embroidery's potential can be explored.

History

The first industrial embroidery machines were developed in Switzerland in about the 1840s, and were used for embroidering designs on natural fabrics. By the middle of the nineteenth century, this had become a prosperous industry. The embroidery produced in this way compared favourably with that carried out by hand; as decoration on all types of clothes became fashionable towards the end of the century, industrial embroidery machines were in great demand.

By 1900, the Cornely machine was manu-

Above *This fan was embroidered on a domestic sewing machine in about 1900. The silk thread on painted bolting cloth was worked in running and satin stitches with lace-work fillings and picot edges. The result is delicate and elegant.*
Right *Designed and stitched by Rebecca Crompton in the late 1930s, this machine embroidery was created in free running stitch.*
Far right *These four brightly coloured postcards were worked during the First World War in Switzerland. The flag decoration was stitched on a hand machine; the other three on a schiffli machine. Both of these types of machines are multi-needled, capable of reproducing many copies of a design at one time.*

factured in France; it could produce multi-directional moss and chain stitching, and was able to braid, cord and carry out double zigzagging. The Cornely and the "Irish" machine by Singer, which produced a wide zigzag, have been in common use since then.

In the 1930s, art students were encouraged to explore the use of domestic sewing machines for creative purposes. The innovative embroiderer Rebecca Crompton, and Dorothy Benson, another embroidery instructor, were leading figures in the promotion of machine embroidery at this time. Despite their encouragement, however, this type of needlework continued to provoke a negative response from many embroiderers. Decoration by machine was considered to lack character and to reveal little skill on the part of the operator. This criticism was partly due to the fact that most early machine embroidery tended to be composed of instantly recognizable rows of automatic patterns with little variation. Specialist embroiderers consequently felt that it was only suitable for children's clothing or small domestic items. Had more sewing machine manufacturers promoted the wider application of automatic techniques, it would have taken less time for the free and creative use of the machine to be accepted.

Equipment and Materials

Sewing machines

It is best to learn on an electric zigzag model so that both hands are free to guide the embroidery. Progress will be quicker because these models offer more techniques.

When buying a machine, the most important thing to remember is that the machine must suit you and be able to fulfil your requirements. There are many different

models on the market; thorough research will enable you to come to a better decision. Try out various techniques on the machine before making a final purchase.

All machines should satisfy some basic requirements. The controls should be easy to identify, reach and manipulate; the speed control should be efficient and easy to use. Tensions must be easy to control and change. Since machine embroidery demands frequent bobbin changes, the bobbin should be readily accessible and easy to remove. If you will have to move your machine frequently, consider the weight.

Another important consideration is the service provided by the manufacturer. In addition to a clear instruction book, manufacturers should offer a guarantee, accessories if required and an after-sales service. Some companies provide tuition in techniques.

After purchase, follow the instructions in the handbook regarding maintenance. Clean and oil the machine frequently.

Thread and yarn

It may take some time to build up a good collection. Most embroiderers have an enormous variety of threads, to which they continually add. To carry out the full range of techniques, a basic range of threads and yarns will be needed.

Machine embroidery thread is available in two thicknesses – 30 and 50. The higher the number, the finer the thread. This is a cotton thread, noted for its lustrous appearance. It can be purchased in both plain and shaded colours.

Mercerized cotton thread is usually used for garment construction. It is available in two thicknesses – 40 and 50. The higher the number, the finer the thread. This thread has less lustre than machine embroidery thread but is considerably stronger and has the added advantage of being widely available, whereas machine embroidery thread is

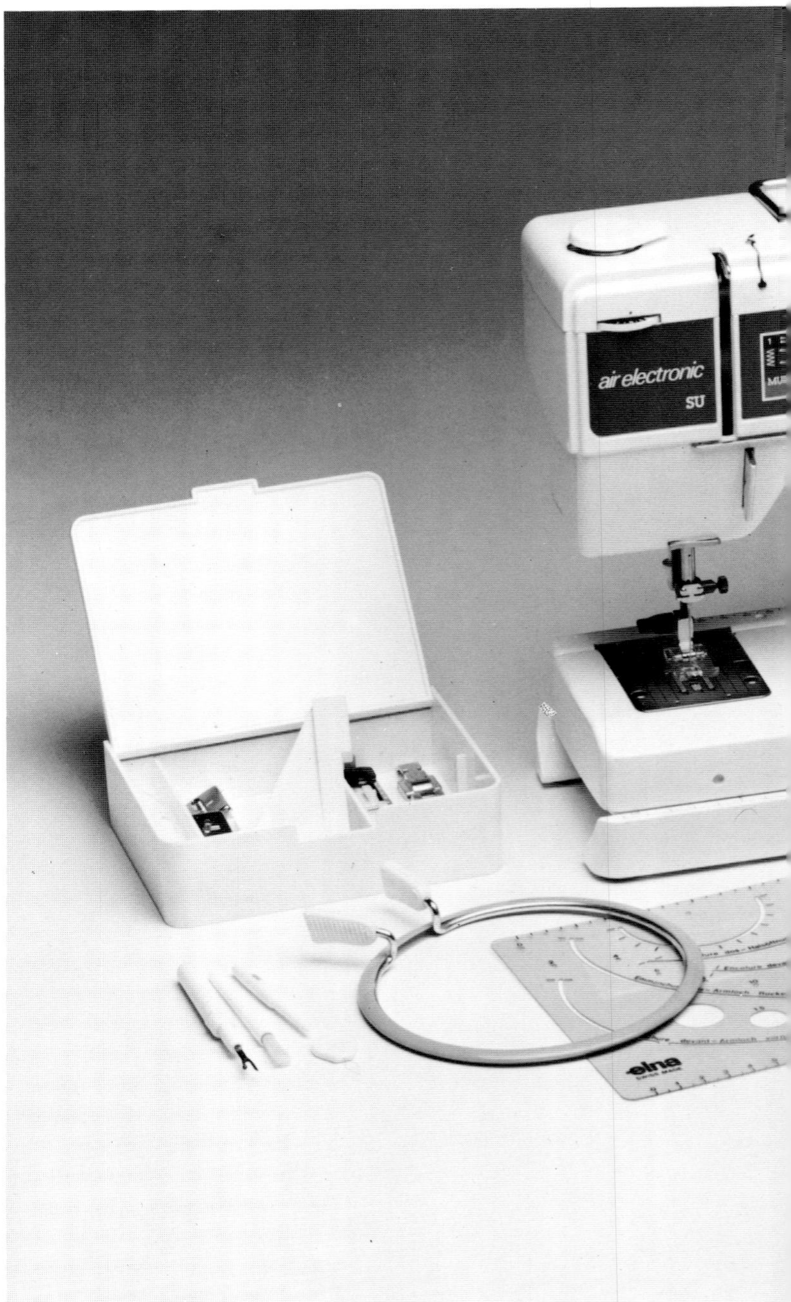

Above *This photograph shows some of the equipment that is necessary for creative machine embroidery. The domestic Elna machine is light, and has straightforward controls at the same time as being capable of a range of complicated manoeuvres. The selection shows* (***left to right***)*: a plastic box for storing equipment including a choice of feet; a stitch ripper; a cleaning brush; a stiletto; a needle threader; a plastic hoop frame; templates for stitching accurate curves and letters; aids for holding the templates in place while stitching; a selection of threads; some stitch or pattern programmers which fit into the machine.*

Below *The domestic Bernina sewing machine is suitable for free running and zigzag stitches. It is a light, modern machine with the dials, controlling tension, stitch length and stitch width, easy to manipulate and readily to hand on a panel together. The bobbin is also readily accessible in a front-opening partition. The space under the arm of the machine has been made as high as possible so allowing the embroiderer to handle fabrics and frames without too much restriction.*

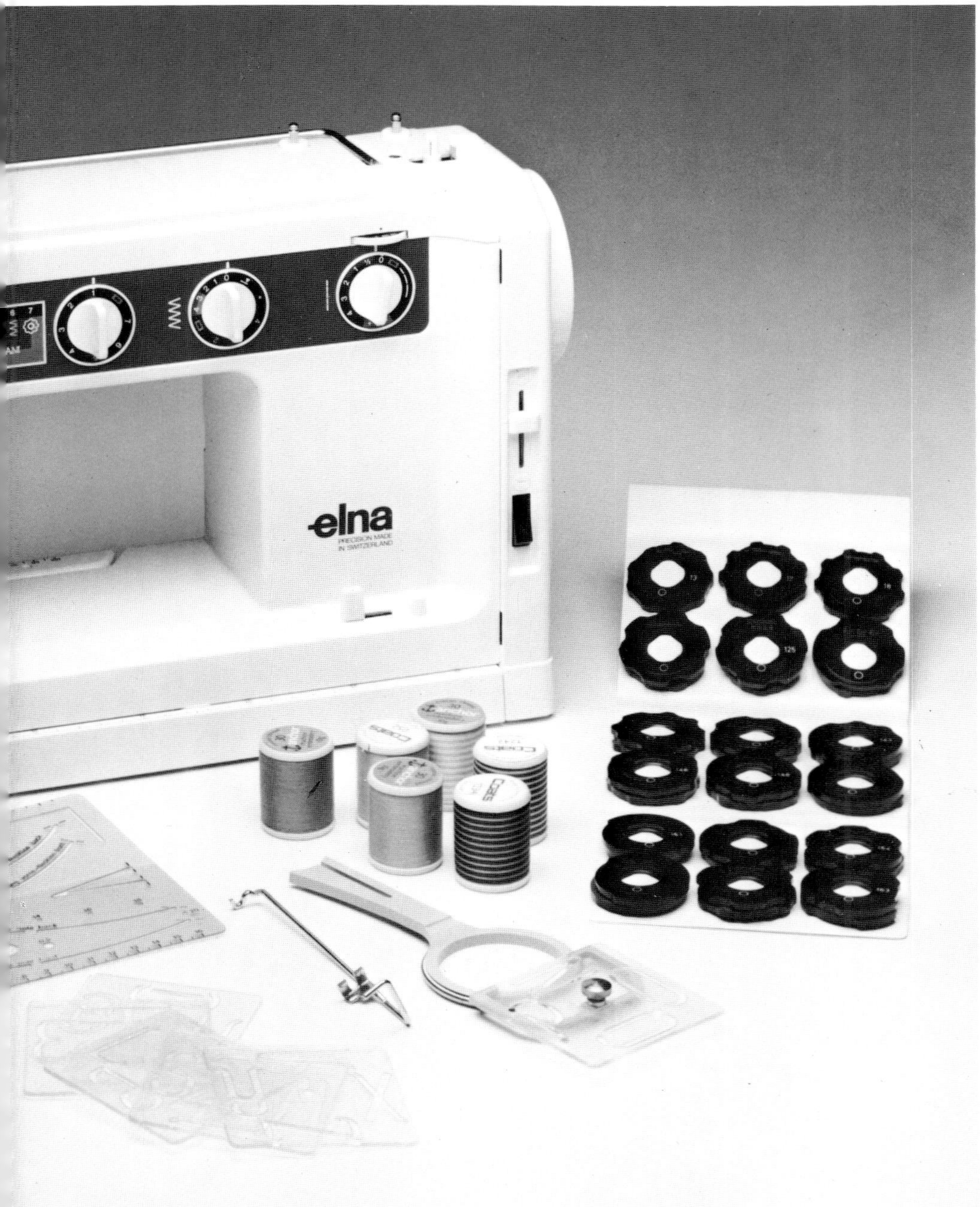

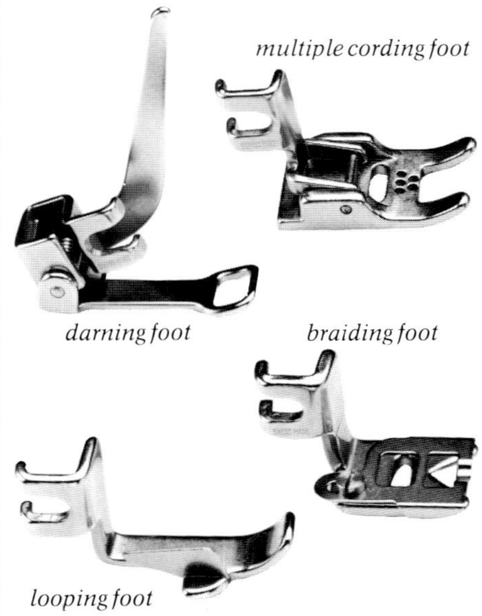

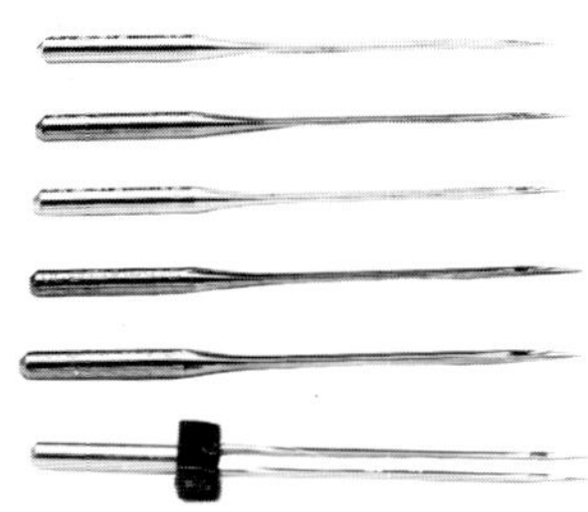

Different machine feet are used for different types of stitching, including the possible attachment of cords to fabric, five at a time. The needles are of different sizes; the last is a twin needle for producing two rows of stitching. Needles for triple stitching, for tacking and for stitching leather are also available.

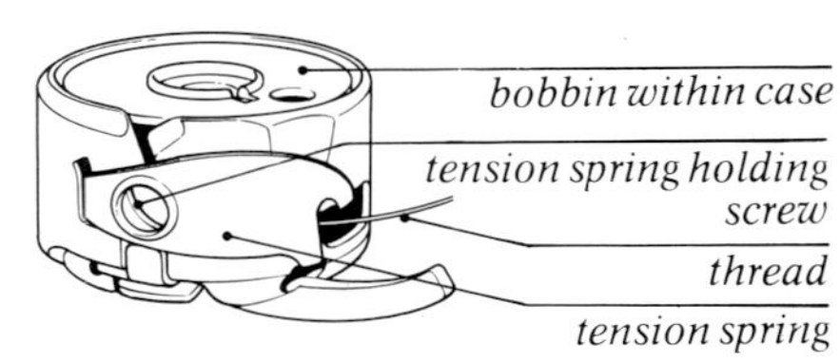

sometimes hard to find. (Sylko no. 50 and Sylko Supreme are good substitutes for no. 30 machine embroidery thread and are stronger.)

All cotton threads need a certain moisture content to function efficiently. Central heating can cause this moisture to be driven off, with the result that threads may break. This essential moisture can be restored by leaving the threads by an open window overnight.

Invisible thread is wiry and springy but useful for achieving a glittering effect. Used to create areas of light-reflecting texture, it will tend to take on the colour of the fabric.

Nylon and polyester threads can be used as long as certain factors are remembered. Owing to their extendable nature, they will "relax" after the fabric has been removed from the frame and puckering may occur on fine to medium-weight fabrics. At very high speeds, they sometimes shred and will melt under a hot iron. If tensions are slackened, this will help to alleviate the puckering problem.

Metallic threads and yarns that can only be used on the bobbin are in plentiful supply, and produce a gleaming cable stitch, which must be carried out with the wrong side of the fabric uppermost. Select these from the fine yarns sold for crochet and knitting. Others, made for use through the needle, can also be used on the bobbin.

Yarns Use fine to medium weight yarns that, when wound onto the bobbin, will run off easily with the bobbin tension loosened or with the tension spring and screw removed. Heavy or slubbed yarns, either matt or shiny, are used for couching.

Fabric

Most plain woven fabrics can be used for machine embroidery, particularly furnishing fabrics. Collect dull and shiny fabrics both in bright colours and subtle neutral shades. Calico, which can be laundered to remove dressing and then vat- or spray-dyed, is a versatile, inexpensive fabric. Collect an assortment of satins, velvets and metallic fabrics or anything that appeals to you. Scrim is ideal for pulled fabric or drawn thread work and organdie, nets or organza for fine embroidery.

Needles

As for normal sewing operations, choose needles with both the fabric weight and thread thickness in mind. Carry out preliminary practice sessions using a heavier needle than usual for the fabric on which you are stitching as it will give a little leeway when handling the frame. Heavy handedness will then be less likely to result in broken needles. At first, breaking a few needles is quite usual and part of the learning process, although too many breakages can be expensive and may indicate that something is wrong with your technique or your machine. Manmade fabrics blunt needles quickly and a "plonking" noise indicates that the needle needs changing.

***Above left** The fan, of which this is a detail, is of a patchwork design, with pieces of lace, voile with a woven spot and silk joined together by machine and hand. The embroiderer found the machine stitching preferable for this piece as the result was flatter. Despite the fact that they are modern, the fan, and its matching dress and gloves have a distinctively Victorian look, the fabrics having been stained and antiqued and messages sewn in.*

***Above** Landscape with an Otter is a modern embroidery picture of a fantasy landscape which was worked on a domestic Bernina. Tiny pieces of print and plain fabrics were attached to the quilted calico ground with free zigzag stitching. The "drawing" is a combination of machine and hand stitching.*

Left *Some of the lines in the grid are raffia and piping cord trapped under a layer of fine silk organza and secured to the calico ground with a twin needle. The rest are couched lengths, stitched to the calico on a Bernina. The repeated rose motif is free machine zigzag, done on a Singer Irish machine.*

Frames

The best ones are the narrow wooden ring frames with a screw adjustment that can be tightened. For practice purposes or when using fine to medium-weight fabrics, small frames with an outer ring of plastic and a sprung metal inner ring are ideal. Bind the inner ring of wooden frames with bias binding. This keeps the fabric tight and clean and helps to keep the weave even.

Techniques

Preparing the machine

The machine handbook will usually list this under "free darning". On some machines, the feed can be lowered, and, on others, it is covered with a plate. Others have an extra needle plate or incorporate a device to raise the needle plate. In each instance, the feed is put out of action.

Free embroidery is a development of free darning. All domestic machines are capable of being used for this purpose. On old machines when there is no apparent way to put the feed out of action, small washers can be placed around the screw holes under the needle plate to raise it above the level of the feed. Failing that, tape can be placed over the feed, leaving the space through which the needle passes exposed.

Remove the sewing foot and holding screw and put them in a safe place. Thread the machine with the same thread top and bottom, setting tensions to normal and other controls to nought.

Framing the fabric

Test the ease with which the two rings of the frame will push together, with no fabric inserted. Adjust the screw so that this can be done with a little effort. Place the outer ring on the table with the fabric over it. Push the inner ring into the outer, using a firm, even pressure. The fabric must be drum tight with no weave distortion and should produce an audible note when tapped. One of the main causes of unsatisfactory results is fabric being slack in the frame. Check this regularly, as stitching causes the fabric to slacken gradually. Instead of a frame, a darning foot may be used, especially when the fabric is too bulky to insert in the frame, or when a very firm, crisp fabric is used.

How to begin stitching

Place the framed fabric under the needle with the fabric flat against the working surface, opposite to the way in which hand embroidery is worked. Lower the presser foot take-up lever, even if there is no foot to place on the fabric. This lever also tensions the top thread and if left up, causes loose stitches or jammed threads. Bring the bottom thread up through the fabric by turning the wheel towards you while holding the top thread. This is the starting procedure for all free embroidery. Stick self-adhesive labels, on which you have written brief reminders of instructions, to the front of the machine where they will be in constant view.

Holding both top and bottom threads under your left index finger, and the frame on the rim at either side, with fingers just over the edge, start to run the machine. After making a few stitches, cut away the ends of the threads to avoid their becoming entangled with the stitching. With the feed out of action, stitching will only show when you move the frame. Run the machine fairly fast and move the frame smoothly and control will become progressively easier. It helps to practise with the machine unthreaded. Move the frame from side to side, back and forth, in circles and ovals, and both clockwise and anticlockwise. Practise writing your name and drawing. Move the frame to describe oblongs, squares and triangles in the same manner.

The slower the frame is moved, the shorter the stitch length, and vice versa. With the feed out of action, the stitch length is entirely dependent on the operator.

It takes time to become accustomed to running the machine for prolonged periods. Always work with the table and chair at a comfortable height, making sure that your back is well supported and it is wise to stop when you feel tired. It is a good idea to keep some framed fabric ready for practising whenever possible.

Stitches

Free machine embroidery is based on two stitching sequences – free running and free zigzag. Variations are brought about by altering tensions, using threads of different textures and thicknesses, varying stitch widths and settings, and by subtle frame movements.

Free running stitch is the straight stitch used to form lines of stitching. You can experiment with the speed at which you move the frame, in conjunction with the speed at which you run the machine. Run the machine slowly, and move the frame around, and back and forth to produce more angular effects. Develop a rhythm so as not to bend or break the needle.

Free zigzag stitch is carried out using any of the stitch widths and the same frame movements as free running stitch. Move the frame smoothly and slowly, and satin stitch will result. Hold the frame still and a satin stitch bead will form. Groups of these worked close together will produce beautiful textures and if the stitches are cut, tufting will result. Small flowers can be worked by radiating zigzag stitches from one central point. If, when one flower is complete, the needle is left in the fabric on the outside of a petal, another flower can be started beside the first, and so on, without fastening off each time.

Zigzag textures If zigzag stitches are worked side by side, encroaching on each other, around in circles or squarely or diagonally on top of one another, an infinite variety of textures can be achieved. These are ideal as filling stitches, to offset bolder hand techniques, to produce repeat patterns or foliage or grasslike textures.

Automatic stitches In similar manner, intricate patterned textures, unrecognizable as automatic stitches, can be produced effortlessly by selecting from the numbers of preset sequences offered by automatic machines. Experiment with threads, speed and frame movements.

Drawn thread and pulled fabric work Wide zigzag, when used on loosely woven fabric, such as scrim or muslin, can produce counterparts to hand techniques. Threads

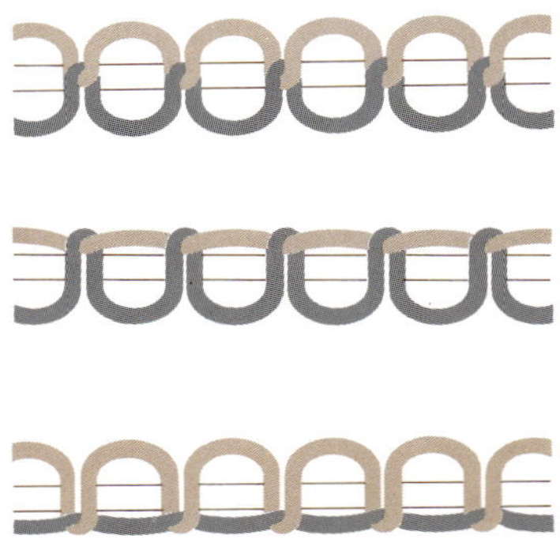

Left *The first line of stitching shows a correct tension for free running and free zigzag stitch. The second shows a tight upper thread, which is a suitable tension for whip and feather stitches. The third shows the upper thread too loose, or perhaps the bottom thread too tight, which would suit cable stitching.*

Above and right *These pictures show the results of different types of machine stitching in varying patterns. All but the tree design illustrate free zigzag stitching; in the picture below there are also tufting and French knots in high relief, the tufting raised above the level of the zigzag. The tree is in free running stitch; it is a simple design in dark red on white.*

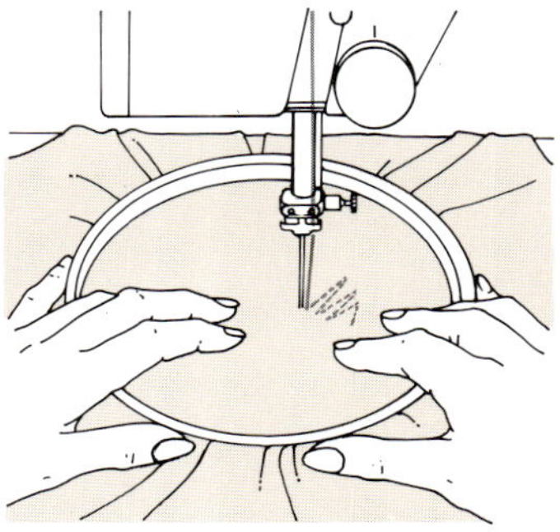

This diagram illustrates the correct position for controlling a frame when machining. The hands should be well in front of the needle.

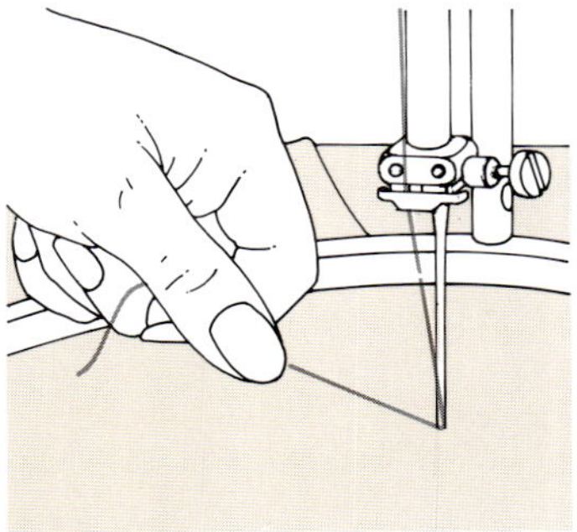

Drawing up the bobbin thread
1. *Holding the upper thread firmly in the left hand, place the needle in the desired position and make a stitch.*

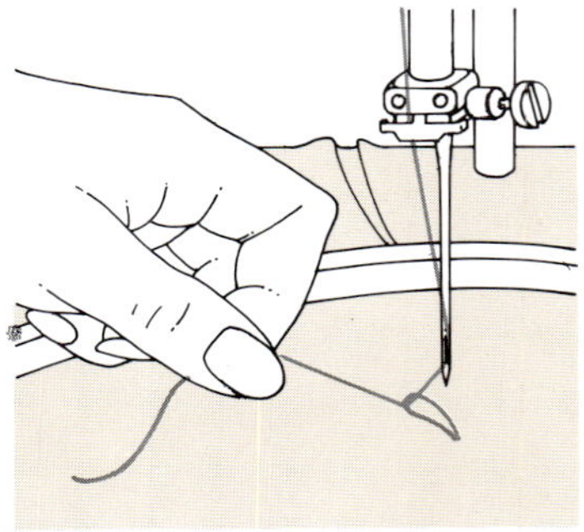

2. *When the needle passes back through the fabric, it will have looped the lower thread beneath the fabric. Pull at the taut upper thread to bring it through.*

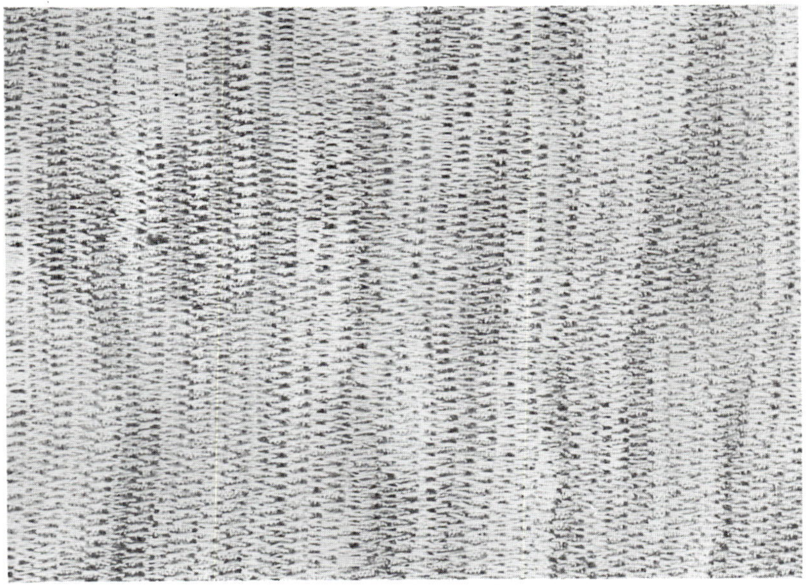

Examples of machine embroidery
Machine embroidery need not be the restricted medium that is commonly imagined. It can be used in conjunction with other techniques to produce a variety of subtle and three-dimensional effects as these examples demonstrate.
1. *This vivid and intensely worked piece was embroidered on the Singer Irish industrial machine in straight stitch set on free machining. It could also have been done on a domestic model set on free machining. The dyed cotton fabric was worked with a mixture of D.M.C. machine cotton and Indian rayon Natesh machine thread. Each very stiff emblem or motif was cut out as close to the stitched outline as possible, and the piece built up as a sculpture by mounting them on top of each other.*
2. *Japanese Lady in Grey is a free interpretation of a Japanese print. It was embroidered using straight stitch on the domestic Bernina sewing machine with D.M.C. machine cotton and Natesh Indian rayon. The picture has been worked with great delicacy, and is beautifully mounted.*
3. *Smorrebrod is an extraordinarily lifelike series of pieces worked by Beryl Greves in 1972. Embroidered on a domestic machine with straight and zigzag stitches set on free embroidery, some stitches have been added later by hand. It demonstrates very humourously that there are no limits to what machine embroidery can be used for.*
4. *This wall sculpture was made in white silk by Sally Freshwater. The horizontal support is made from dowel rod, and the pleats have been machined into the fabric. It measures about $3^1/_2 \times 1^1/_2$ feet (1 × .5 m), and is a striking modern piece that can be displayed in several different ways. It*

1

2

3

4

5

required only the most straightforward machine stitching to make.

***5.** A very original technique was pioneered by Denziel Grant for this piece. Thin strands of wire have been machined into tightly fitting pleats in satin finished cotton. The method is akin to Italian cord quilting but wire replaced the cord giving a material that could be shaped or moulded into the faces shown. The shadow profile is an integral part of the design, and the lighting has been arranged to this end.*

can be removed from the fabric at random, or in definite patterns, and those left can be drawn together in clumps, moving the frame slowly when blocks of satin stitch are wanted. Working into the same fabric with narrow or wide zigzag, or any of the satin stitch-based automatic patterns, will form open lace-like textures.

Open work and eyelets Cutwork is an extension of the way the machine can be used to mend a hole. First, practise mending a hole, following the instructions in the machine handbook.

First attempts are easier when medium-sized circular or oval shapes are used. The neatest effects can be achieved on closely woven natural fabric, like organdie. Matching the thread colour to the fabric, stitch circles of small free running stitches. Run over these three or four times, superimposing one row upon the other. With the fabric still framed, cut away the centres of each circle taking care not to cut the stitching.

Using the same or a different coloured thread, and making sure that the fabric is tight, start the stitching on the edge of one hole. After making a few stitches to fasten on, cut away the thread ends to prevent them becoming entangled. Stitch across the hole to the opposite side, catching the threads to the fabric. Cross the circle again and continue until a trellis of threads has been formed. This can be in a spider's web or a random design. On this mesh, further stitching can be worked. The edges of the circles can be neatened with any neat finishing technique.

Eyelets can be made by punching out small circles with a stiletto, and with no. 50 machine embroidery thread radiating fine lines of free running stitch to and fro around the hole. Accessories for making eyelets are available for some machines.

Lacework (dissolved fabric work) Acetate fabric is used for this technique which is based on the way guipure lace is made. When the embroidery is complete, it is cut out and the background dissolved by immersing it in a pan of acetone. Test the fabric first to make sure that it dissolves completely. Diacetate and triacetate will not dissolve completely and cuproacetate will leave fine cupro filaments in the embroidery. Use machine embroidery thread or Sylko, as cotton will not dissolve in acetone. Some glossy threads do dissolve, so make careful tests before stitching. Whatever technique is used, make sure that each stitch sequence is linked on all sides or the embroidery will disintegrate when the fabric is dissolved. If zigzag stitches are used, they will need free running stitches on or under them for support. Dissolve the fabric in the open air or by an open window, away from naked flames. Protect clothing and surfaces, and wear rubber gloves. When the acetone is supersaturated and will no longer dissolve fabric, pour it away down an outside drain.

Cable stitch Threads and fine yarns that cannot pass through the needle can be wound on the bobbin and the embroidery worked with the wrong side of the fabric uppermost. When using a machine with a removable bobbin case, the tension spring and holding screw will often need to be removed to allow for the passage of the yarn. Stick these to tape to keep them safe. Take note of how they come apart so that reassembly is easy. It is a good idea to have extra bobbin cases so that one can be kept for

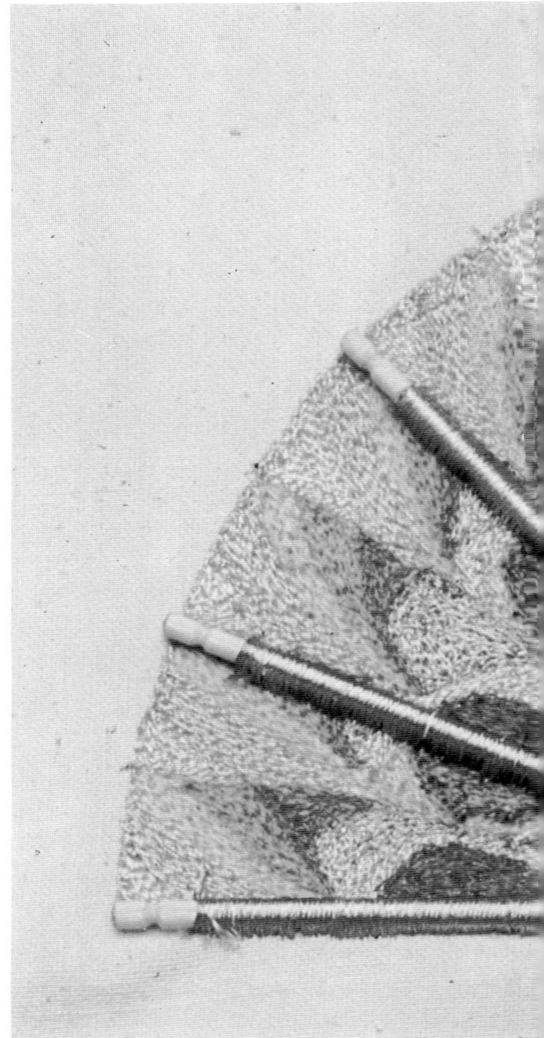

Right *With one colour of D.M.C. machine embroidery cotton at the top of the Bernina domestic machine, and another colour at the bottom, straight stitching was worked up and down a piece of vanishing muslin. The muslin was ironed and so crumbled away, leaving a delicate lace grid.*

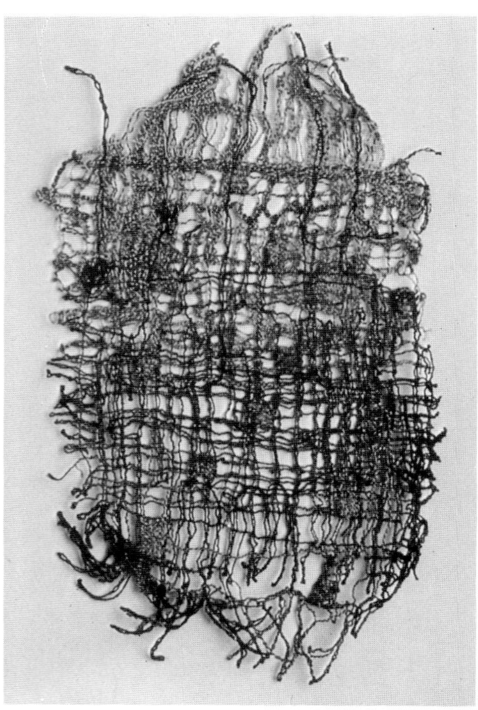

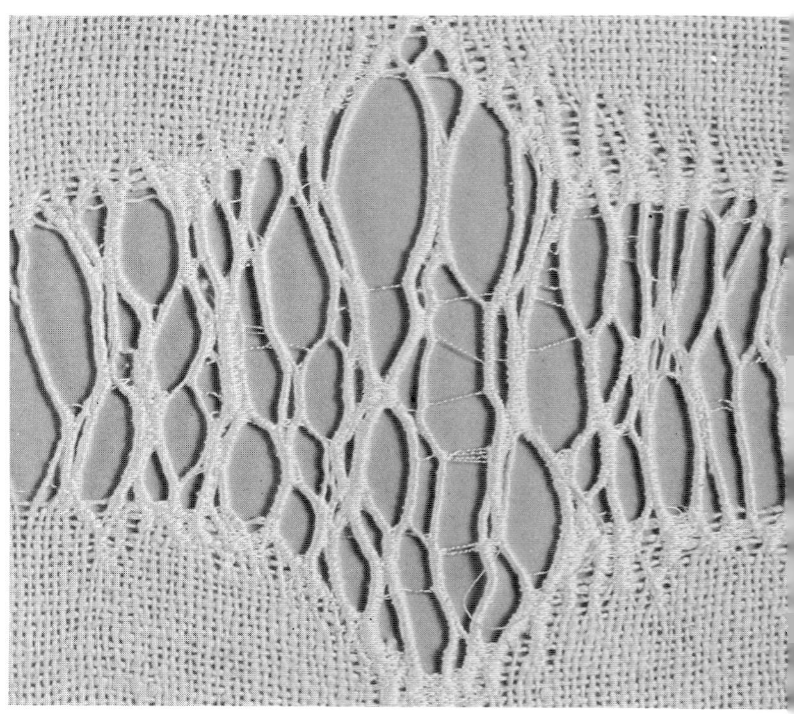

Left *This intensely worked and patterned piece in the shape of a fan was straight stitched using an industrial machine set on free machining. The stitches are close together, worked in bright pink, yellow and blue D.M.C. machine cotton and rayon machine thread on a cotton ground. Cocktail sticks have been attached to the resulting strong, almost structurable textile.* ***Below*** *These three pieces of creative embroidery show the potential of the sewing machine in adapting traditional hand embroidery techniques. The drawn thread work, cutwork and lacework illustrated (**left to right**) have been stitched with great attention to detail and with interesting results.*

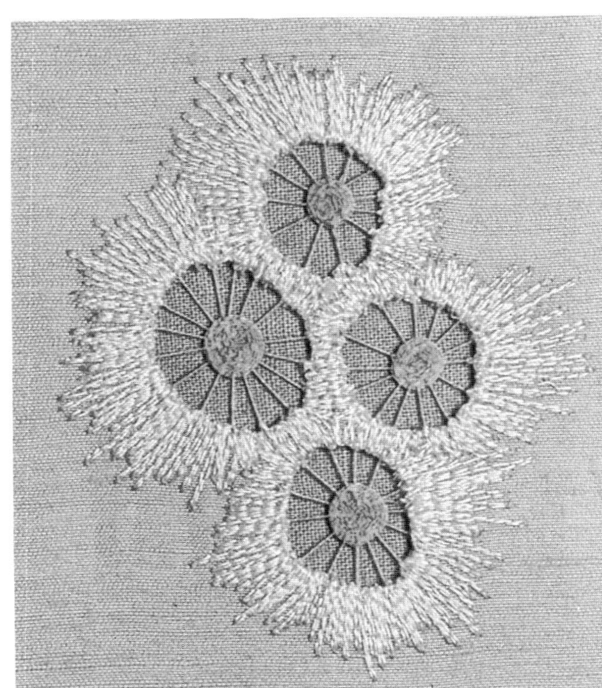

normal stitching, and the others kept with the tensions set, or removed for threads of various thicknesses.

Before starting to embroider, bring the heavy bobbin thread up through the fabric. Use a stiletto or bodkin to make a hole large enough to ease the yarn through. Use free running stitch and vary the movements of the frame. Experiment with tension changes to the top thread – many interesting textures can be discovered by accident. Try using a zigzag setting and matching colours, or contrast the top thread and the bobbin yarn. When finishing off, bring the bobbin yarn through the fabric in the same manner as for beginning stitching.

Quilting Careful preparation is the main requirement for success with free machine quilting. Top fabric, padding, and a backing fabric, such as muslin, must be sandwiched and carefully pinned all around the edges. Then, starting from the centre, make parallel lines of tacking up to the fabric edges to form a grid, and then sew more lines radiating from the centre point in star fashion.

Any form of free stitching may be used, but simple lines of free running stitch produce good results rapidly. The fabrics may be too thick to frame, in which case the darning foot must be used. During quilting, fabrics tend to "shrink", so allow extra fabric on all dimensions.

Using two layers of fabric, parallel lines of stitching, between which thick, soft yarn can be threaded, will produce Italian quilting. On many zigzag machines, twin needles can be used to do this quickly and efficiently. Follow handbook instructions when using these – if handled improperly, they will break easily and are expensive to replace.

Whip and feather stitch Free running stitch is used for these stitches, which rely on imbalance of tension, or thread thickness, or both, depending on the machine. On many machines, whatever the thread used, merely increasing the top tension can produce the right results, but on others a thicker top thread is needed, sometimes with the top tension increased and the bottom tension decreased.

The bottom thread, due to the extra pulling power of the top thread, comes up through the fabric and whips round the top thread lying on the surface. If the frame is moved slowly, the top thread is obscured, but when moved quickly the individual stitches become obvious. If contrasting threads are used, variety in tone will result when the movements of the frame are altered. By moving the frame quickly and then pausing, the bottom thread will build up at the pauses and barely cover the top thread. By moving the frame in small arcs or spirals, in widening sweeps, you can produce feather stitch.

Couching Yarns can be applied to the surface of the fabric to build up areas of very heavy texture. Rug wool, heavy slubbed yarns, thick chenille, tape, braid, ribbons or cut or torn strips of fabric can all be stitched down to make exciting surfaces.

Heavy slubbed yarns are best to use at first as these are easier to apply than fine ones. Use a fine thread that matches the yarn, and slightly loosen the top tension so that the bobbin thread will pull it down well into the fabric for discreet stitching, which will show very little under close scrutiny. The yarn may

Far left *Tucks were sewn into a piece of beige calico using D.M.C. thread on a Bernina machine, and cotton piping cord was threaded through the pipes. The calico was cut into strips and the edges turned, and these were interwoven and secured by hand. The resulting corded quilting is of an unusual raised texture.*

Left *To achieve this quilting effect on a piece of pure silk satin, lines were straight stitched on a machine in contrasting black D.M.C. cotton. The trapunto quilting technique was used, stuffing cotton waste wadding through the calico backing by pulling the threads apart.*

Above *This charming seaside scene was created by combining machine and hand embroidery with fabric painting. Free running and zigzag stitches were used, with cable stitch, and whip and feather stitches giving different textures to the surfaces of the waves, clothes, hats and rooftops.*

be pinned into position to form the design and the pins removed during stitching, or it can be applied freely while guiding the frame with one hand. Using free running stitch, and, running the machine fairly fast, stitch along the yarn and across it in the indentations made by the twist. Aim to make the stitches as small as possible.

Zigzag stitch may flatten attractive yarns but it is useful for applying flat ribbons, braids and tapes. Looped couching is formed by holding down loops of yarn, ribbon or braid on the fabric and running a few stitches across the base of each loop. Flat coils of yarn can be made and pressed into position with bonding web before securing them with stitching worked in spirals.

Braiding, looping and multiple cording Used with the feed in contact with the fabric, the braiding, looping and multiple cording feet produce most attractive results. If these accessories are not supplied for your machine, those produced for other models may fit. Narrow braids, ribbons and thick yarns are passed through the opening on the braiding foot, which can be adjusted according to width or thickness. The design can be drawn on the fabric, or on paper pinned to it, in which case the design is followed by stitching through paper and fabric. The paper will easily tear away afterwards. It is advisable to sew slowly and carefully. Straight or automatic stitches may be used.

By using a narrow zigzag stitch and a short stitch length, the looping foot will make upstanding loops as the needle swings over a vertical flange on the foot. If two threads are used as one through an adequate needle, the loops will form more profusely. These may be left, or cut to form tufting. Reinforce the fabric with paper on the wrong side and tear this away afterwards. Sew at a regular speed.

The multiple cording foot makes it possible to couch up to five fine yarns in parallel lines onto the fabric simultaneously. If unnoticeable stitching is required, match no. 50 machine embroidery thread to the yarns or use invisible thread. The step stitch, which makes small stitches left and right to form a running zigzag, is the most discreet stitch to use.

Whipped cords If a yarn is run under the cording foot while the machine is set for satin stitch, with the feed in contact with the fabric, whipped cords can be made. A wide zigzag should be used, as the whipping will adjust itself naturally to the thickness of the yarn. Hold the yarn firmly both behind and in front of the foot, but do not pull it faster than the machine feeds it. To make a tapered cord, start by feeding three or four yarns under the foot together and cut them away one by one as the whipping progresses. Join two whipped cords together with more stitching to make branched effects.

Below *This is a detail from a shaped mound made of various pieces of machine embroidery and other thread work which was designed to decorate the centre of a table. Representing a grassy bank, it has been worked in various shades of green wools, with purple and pink flowers in French knots and tiny metal stemmed and coloured plastic flowers placed randomly over the surface. The tufting in this detail resembles a mossy patch of grass with surprising realism.*

These illustrations show three uses of the zigzag stitch. The first shows plain zigzag; the second shows the couching of a single cord, keeping the cord centred with a special foot. The third shows multiple cord couching, using a foot capable of guiding up to five cords at a time. Each cord is secured singly under large zigzag stitches.

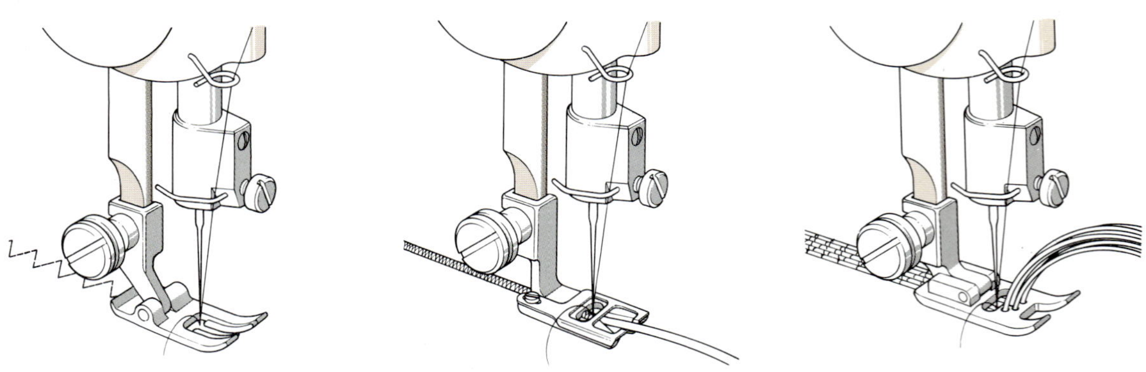

1

2

3
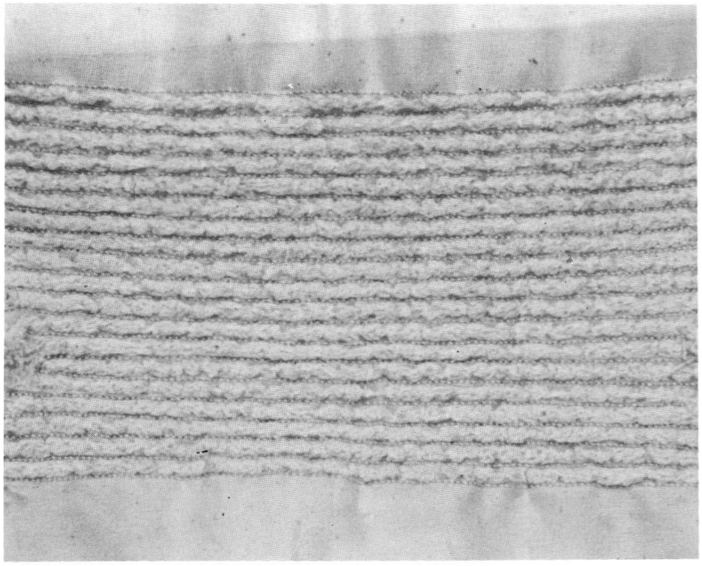

4

5

Left *Many different results are possible when creatively machine embroidering, often depending on the length and width of stitches, their tension, the texture and colour of fabrics and materials combined or used singly, and whether they are cut or otherwise changed after stitching. A selected range of results is visible in this panel of five examples.*
1. *Satin stitch was zigzagged over a cotton piping cord, with the stitch lengths close together and the bottom tension slightly loose so the bottom thread colour was pulled to the top.*
2. *Using a tacking foot on a Bernina machine and stitching close, the tufting was created by cutting.*
3. *Corded quilting was made by straight stitching with a twin needle on calico topped by a piece of silk organza. The resulting channels were threaded with a cotton snarl weaving thread.*
4. *Mixed threads were wound tightly over a U-shaped piece of metal, then a line of machining stitched down the centre of the U. The tufting was achieved by cutting, and pulling out the metal.*
5. *Using different colours, this typical piece of tufting was created on the cut pile tufting machine.*

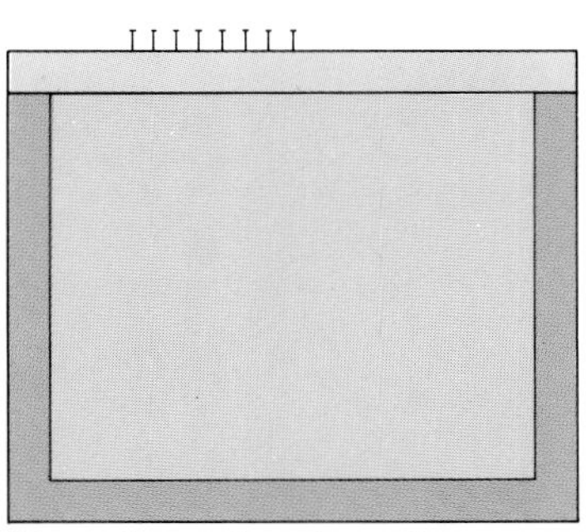

Mounting 1. *Place the embroidered fabric over the board right side up. Turn back two opposite edges, and pin them into place working from the centre of each side outwards.*

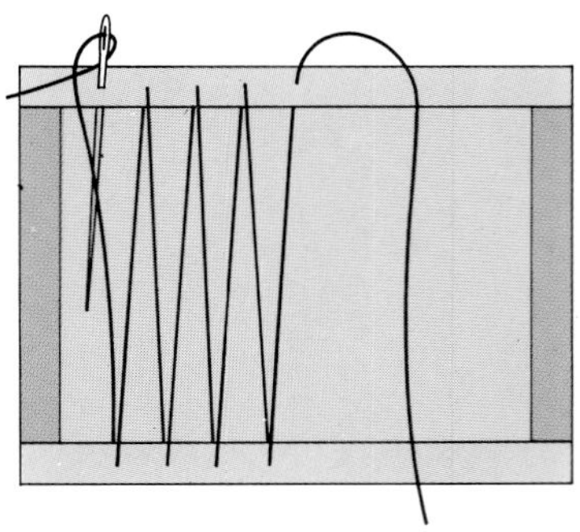

2. *Sew these two sides together with a lacing stitch across the back of the board, again working from the centre outwards to the sides. Keep lace taut.*

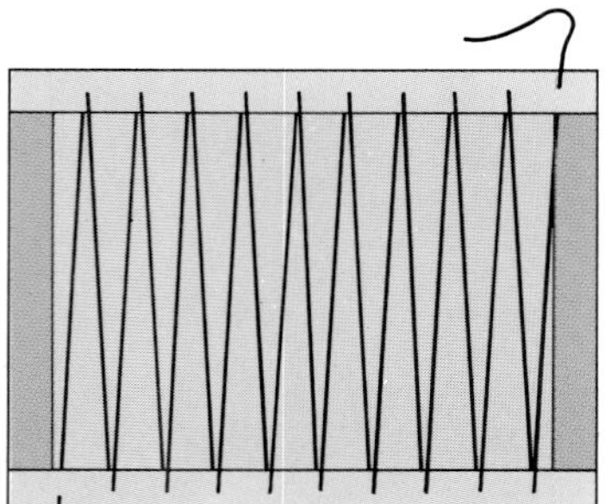

3. *Having completed the lacing as shown, end off the thread and take out the pins. Check that the fabric has been firmly and evenly stretched across the board.*

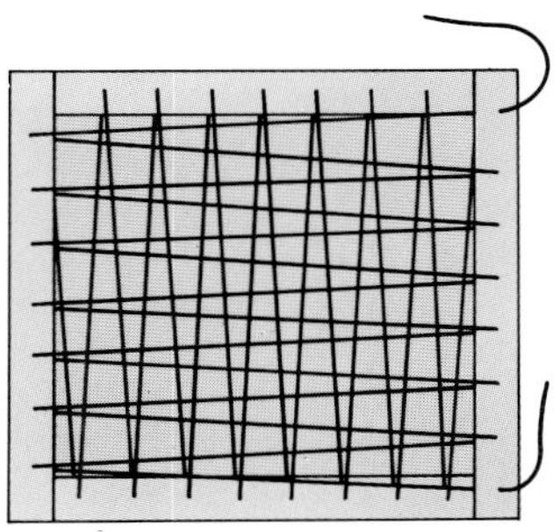

4. *Turn the two remaining edges over and lace them in the same fashion, making sure that the corners have been neatly secured and there are no wrinkles.*

Counted Thread

Counted thread is any method of stitching where stitches are worked over a counted number of warp and weft threads, although it is associated primarily with cross stitch work. It is generally executed on linen, or any other fabric with easily seen warp and weft threads, ideally of the same thickness. Such fabric is often called "evenweave".

Designs are usually copied from a graph or chart, but designs already printed or stamped on the fabric cannot be termed counted thread work, because as it is impossible to print an exactly aligned design on natural fibres the stitcher tends to follow the printing rather than counting the threads. Counted thread can, however, be worked by carefully copying a motif which has already been finished. A pattern on a family sampler, for instance, can be the inspiration for a tablecloth border.

As well as being the main counted thread technique, cross stitch is also a universal needlework form, worked in more countries and for more varied purposes than even tent stitch. Other techniques in which threads must be counted – canvaswork (needlepoint) and pulled thread, for instance – warrant their own coverage, but blackwork, counted thread stitching worked in black on white or natural fabric, is included in this chapter.

History

As early as the seventh century, the Copts were known to have used cross stitch techniques, but the earliest surviving pieces date from medieval Germany. It was not until the Tudor period in England, however, that cross stitch first rose to prominence, when gentlewomen began to stitch domestic needleworks in addition to the professionally worked ecclesiastical pieces.

By the sixteenth century, the lady of the house was producing pillow and cushion covers, coverlets, carpets and other pieces with the aid of her staff and friends. Counted thread purses were popular products. Stitching was done with wool thread, which could have been produced locally, and silks imported from the Middle East. A soft linen fabric, known as "canvas", was used and designs were copied from a number of sources which included the many herbals and gardening books then available. Jacques le Moyne's *La clef des champs*, published in 1586, is often quoted as a design source.

One surviving example of early counted thread work is a nearly square cushion cover filled with a stylized floral design. The stunted foliage is a forerunner of the many floral motifs known as "slips" that were later worked in the seventeenth century, typically with this type foliage and gently curving stems, such as the celebrated Traquair House panels.

Another example of counted thread work from this period is a lady's purse, decorated with a geometric pattern of pyramids. Excellent eyesight and good light must have been needed to produce this intricate piece, as it measures only 4½ square inches (11 sq cm).

Other embroiderers preferred emblematic designs. Motifs had a great symbolic importance. Queen Elizabeth I, for instance, was described as Mercilla in Edmund Spenser's *Faerie Queene* (1590), wearing skirts:

> Bordered with bright sunny beams
> Glistering like gold among the plants enrolled
> And here and there shooting forth silver beams.

As contemporary poets sometimes compared the queen with Virgil's Astraea, the virgin whose return brought eternal springtime, spring flowers were popular motifs associated with the queen. A portrait of the queen at Hatfield House shows part of

Above *This sixteenth-century octagonal panel, is one of the panels worked in cross stitch and applied to a screen. The initials stitched in the corner stand for Elizabeth, Countess of Shrewsbury, more commonly known as Bess of Hardwick.*

Left *Reworking some typical seventeenth-century designs for the textile study room at the Victoria and Albert Museum, London, Louisa Pesel (1870-1947) embroidered this sampler in cross stitch with the horizontal bands in back stitch. The figures in pink at the top are known as "boxers" or "amorini", and are often found on cross stitch samplers.*
Far left *A counted thread cushion cover from the late sixteenth or early seventeenth century. The design features rose "bosses" and flower designs between trellises. The background is worked in a single dark colour.*

her dress embroidered with eyes and ears, symbolizing vigilance, and a serpent of wisdom. She holds a rainbow, a symbol of peace after storms. Another device encountered in sixteenth-century needlework was a sieve, referring to the legend of the Vestal Virgin who filled a sieve with water from the Tiber, without spilling a drop. This was intended to convey the sovereign's chastity and discernment. A pelican was used to represent the fact that, as the bird feeds its young with its own blood, so was the queen mother of her people. Such emblematic motifs were copied from continental publications and from such English works as *Heroicall devises of M. Claudius Paradin,* and G. Whitney's *A choice of emblemes and other devises, for the most parte gathered out of sundrie writers, English and moralized, and newly devised,* published in 1586 and dedicated to the queen's favourite, Robert Dudley, Earl of Leicester.

Mary, Queen of Scots, was a sixteenth-century embroiderer who incorporated emblems into some of her pieces. The Oxburgh Hall hangings show allegorical patterns associated with the Scottish queen and with Bess of Hardwick. Under the care of Bess' husband, the Earl of Shrewsbury, Mary spent much of her long imprisonment, from 1569 until her death 18 years later.

Another panel almost certainly worked by the Scottish queen and now at Hardwick Hall, Derbyshire, includes applied pieces of fine tent stitch (forming half-crosses) on coarser canvas. There are scrolled designs of thistles of the queen's native Scotland, white lilies as reminders that she was, briefly, queen of France and roses, symbols of the third crown she claimed – that of England – and for which she eventually lost her head.

The applied medallions are similarly meaningful. The most famous representation shows two frogs standing on a well, wondering whether or not to jump in in case the well is dry. This illustrates *Negotiorum jubeo spectare exitium eos, qui inchoare quid volunt* ("I bid those who want to begin anything to look what the end of the matter will be"), from Gabriel Faerno's version of *Aesop's Fables,* published in Antwerp in 1573. Mary, Queen of Scots, used this as illumination of her own predicament, wondering whether or not to try to escape.

In 1586, an inventory was made of the imprisoned queen's possessions. This "Chartley Hall Inventory" includes four small panels of human figures worked in cross stitch and another panel showing a peacock's tail.

Cross stitch was also extensively used for working "Renaissance twist", a long braid of canvas with a central strip carrying twisting shapes at regular intervals. Such decoration was probably the work of professional embroiderers and it was subsequently applied to bed hangings such as those at Hardwick Hall.

In general, by the beginning of the seventeenth century, the cross stitch variant, tent stitch, was becoming the most popular form of the technique. Basic cross stitch was temporarily dormant, emerging, as far as furnishings were concerned, in the marvellous floor carpets of the eighteenth century. Some of these reached gigantic

Right *These magnificent cross stitch and long-armed cross stitch patterns were worked on a carpet made* c. *1600 in England. Stitched in coloured wools on a linen canvas over 9 feet (2.7m) long, the border patterns are thought to have been influenced by the patterns on sixteenth-century Caucasian knotted carpets. The naturalistic floral sprigs include the emblematic rose and thistle motifs of England and Scotland.*

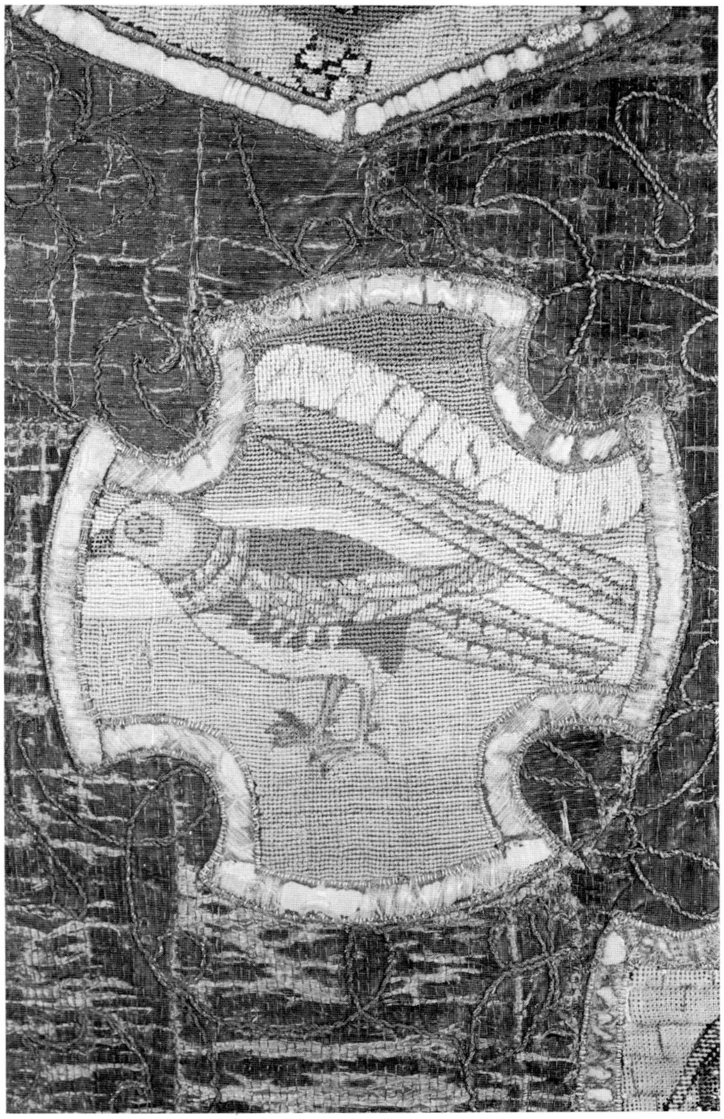

Above left *A lady's blackwork hood from the sixteenth century. This was worked in stem stitch, double coral stitch and speckling with a pattern of honeysuckle, lilies and canterbury bells. It has an outer border of bobbin lace. The style was long for the modest, elderly ladies of the time.*

Above *A detail from one of the Oxburgh hangings at Oxburgh Hall, Norfolk. The applied motifs are in cruciform shape, worked in coloured cross stitches. This one illustrates "a phesant", the lettering still legible despite the age of the hanging. It is often associated with Mary, Queen of Scots, but in fact unlikely to have been worked by her.*

Above *An attractive piece of Levantine counted thread, its irregular shape is accounted for by the fact it was worked on a non-evenweave fabric. The uneven stitchery was sited and sized by eye; patterns were handed down from generation to generation. Such work is timeless in technique and design.*

Left *This is a section from the Dowell-Simpson sampler, patches of which were worked by the family and friends of Mrs Edward Dowell in the second half of the nineteenth century. Because it was worked over several decades, ending at a length of 41 feet (12m), it illustrates the progress of Berlin woolwork, the designs of which changed from simple, coloured patterns to garish and extravagant. The patches were pieced facing different ways. It is thought to be the world's largest sampler.*

Below *This shows a detail from the Dowell-Simpson sampler. Domestic scenes, animal and bird motifs and geometric patterns are cross stitched on several different pieces of soft canvas, in a bright variety of colours.*

proportions, as is evident from an advertisement in the *Daily Post*, May 1728, for sale of stock of Thomas Phill, "Upholsterer to her late Majesty Queen Anne" which included, "above 100 Carpets of all Sizes, particularly a most curious Needle-work Carpet, four Yards long and three Yards wide, which was intended for a Foreign Prince."

Samplers

Samplers, or needlework test-pieces, are particularly important in the history of cross stitch. The earliest dated English sampler was probably worked by Jane Bostocke in 1598 to commemorate the birth of Alice Lee, perhaps her sister, two years earlier. This piece, measuring 18 x 16 inches (46 x 41 cm), worked mostly in silks on linen, includes cross stitching, along with back, buttonhole, chain and satin stitches, bullion and French knots and many other techniques.

Cross stitch was only one of the stitches worked in samplers until the eighteenth century. By then some pieces, perhaps worked by girls only six years old, were exclusively cross stitched.

Traditionally, sampler patterns are copied from a chart, a worked example, or counted by the embroiderer. Many samplers have an outer border enclosing at least one alphabet and a set of digits, an inscription, the name and age of the embroiderer and the date. Other popular motifs include a range of crowns, recognizable houses and other sites, and a wide variety of flowers.

If there is not a stitched date, a sampler can sometimes be identified by its size: mid-eighteenth century pieces, for instance, are often height to width in a proportion of three to two, say 13 x 9 inches (33 x 23cm). Other identifying factors include the appearance of such motifs as "boxers" – pairs of figures, often nude cherubs flanking ceremonial urns – that sometimes appear on samplers worked in the seventeenth and early eighteenth centuries. Particular forms of samplers include map samplers, worked during the last decades of the eighteenth and the first decade of the nineteenth centuries, and family tree and "record" samplers, both of which were particularly popular American designs.

All the way through the nineteenth century, the working of Berlin woolwork samplers was a favoured pastime for needleworkers, exclusively adults. In about 1804 or 1805, a Berlin printseller, Herr Philippson, first produced hand-coloured graphed patterns, a vast improvement over the all-black charts previously available. Other print publishers were quick to follow his example, and it is estimated that by 1840 there were some 14,000 different patterns being circulated from needleworker to needleworker.

Although some Berlin woolwork pieces were later made up into firescreen panels,

Above A visit to the Boarding School *was painted by George Morland during 1788 and 1789. In this detail, mothers are looking at samplers in progress. A finished sampler hangs above the fireplace with its pair.*
Left *This is a large Berlin woolwork sampler, embroidered during the nineteenth century using counted thread techniques. Nearly all the counted patterns were adapted from seventeenth-century pieces of embroidery, and stitched in bright wools.*

prie-dieux, or gentlemen's slippers, most of them were worked as decorative exercises. Small areas of brightly coloured patterns – even brighter after the patenting of aniline dyes in 1856 – were often stitched on satin ribbon-bound samplers several feet long, and as narrow as 4 inches (10cm).

Berlin woolwork disappeared as abruptly as it had begun, towards the end of the third quarter of the nineteenth century. Its full progression from rather cautiously bright to garish, and perhaps outrageous, patterns, can best be seen on one of the world's longest samplers, the Dowell-Simpson sampler, 41 feet (12m) long. Formed of small patches of different soft canvases, most of them elaborately stitched with brightly coloured motifs, the project was organized by Mrs Edward Dowell, wife of a Norfolk vicar. From about 1848 onwards, she asked family and friends to stitch patches, which she patiently pieced together over the years.

Samplers in the usual sense – that is to say, a small wall-hanging picture no more than

15 inches (38cm) high – are enjoying a great revival today. Old pieces, particularly if provenance is well documented, are realizing good sums in the salerooms. In fact, all forms of counted thread are increasingly popular with a large number of enthusiastic needleworkers, particularly in Denmark and the United States.

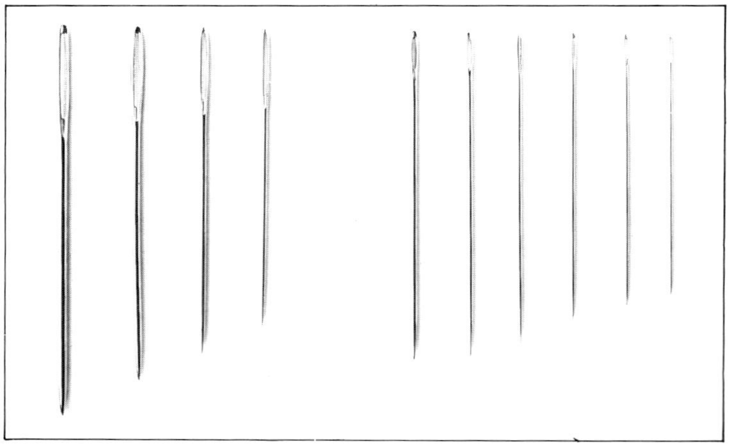

Left *This photograph shows four tapestry needles: sizes 18, 20, 22 and 24 (**left**); crewel needles sizes 5, 6, 7, 8, 9 and 10 (**right**). The blunter tapestry needles are useful when working on large meshes; the finer crewel needles should be used on close-meshed linens and cottons.*

Materials

Fabric

The best fabric for counted thread work is one which has easily seen warp and weft threads. These should be the same thickness, or a distorted pattern will result. One of the most popular fabrics is Glenshee, an evenweave with 29 threads per inch. Counted stitches can be worked best over two threads (resulting in 14½ stitches per inch) or three threads (resulting in just under 10 stitches per inch).

As well as other linens, hardanger and aida can also be used for counted thread work. Hardanger fabric has pairs of threads woven together. Aida has four threads woven to form blocks over which stitches can be formed.

Thread

A single strand of six-stranded cotton can be used for counted work, as can threads such as Danish flower thread (an all-linen thread that is always stitched single thickness), perle cottons and pure silks.

Needles

It is essential to work with a blunt-ended (tapestry) needle so you do not split fabric threads. Tapestry 22 or 24 work best on Glenshee.

Techniques

Design

Since counted cross stitch generally relies on stitches of the same size covering the same number of warp and weft threads of the ground fabric, the easiest way to design is to use graph paper. If you can block your design straight on to the graph paper, so much the better. If you would rather draw your design in linear form and then transfer it, you can use the graph tracing paper method.

Inspiration for general cross stitch patterns can come from a variety of sources. The cross stitched yoke of an embroidered robe would lend itself to a border design for a tablecloth and a set of napkins. Brickwork patterns can also be inspirational, particularly for designing colour stitches.

If you are designing samplers it is particularly important that you centre your designs vertically, with the left of the piece as equal

Alternate cross stitch *If the rows are being worked as half crosses initially, these diagonals in turn can be worked alternately as shown.*

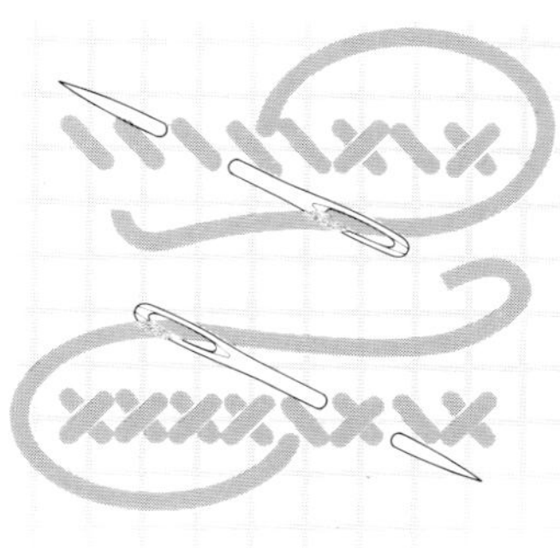

Having completed all the half crosses, fill in the whole crosses alternately as well. Working cross stitch in this fashion ensures an even tension and finish.

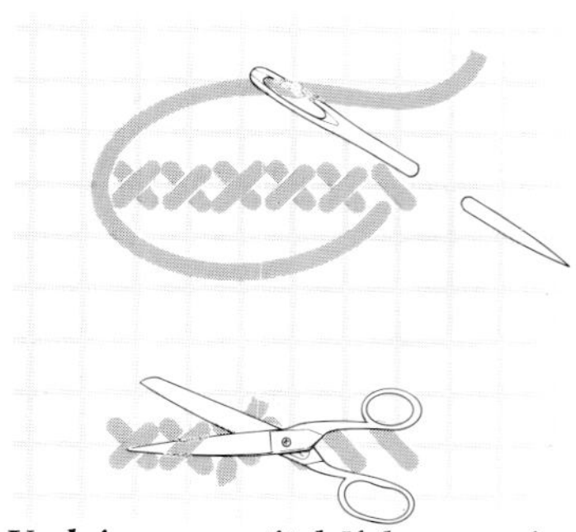

Undoing cross stitch *If the rows of cross stitch have been worked cross by cross, they will be relatively easy to undo individually.*

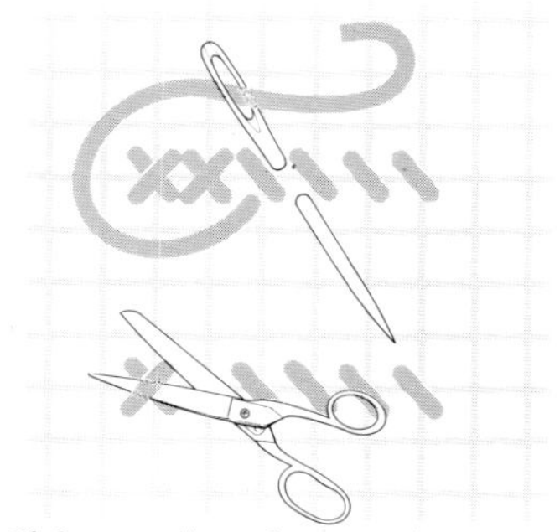

If the rows have been worked as two superimposed rows of half cross stitches, all the diagonal stitches must be removed to undo one cross.

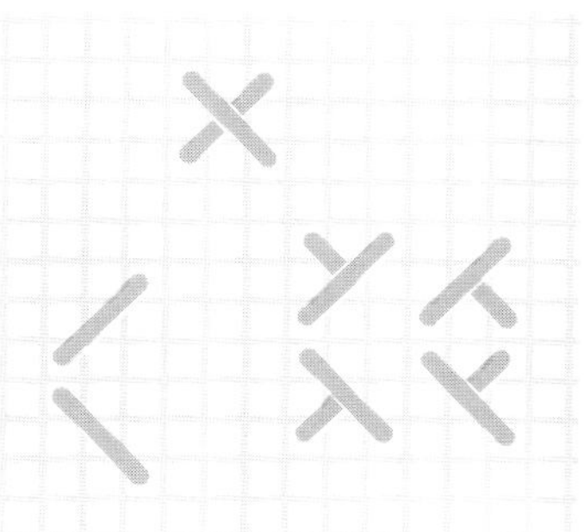

Variations *Cross stitch is a surprisingly versatile stitch, and can be worked in different combinations of halves and three-quarters as shown.*

The stitches can vary in size. These span from one to four canvas threads in both directions. Measure the threads between the tips of the diagonal stitches.

Waste canvas *To work closely woven fabric, tack canvas over it as a space guide, and work both layers together. Then remove the canvas thread by thread.*

Below *Geometric patterns lend themselves well to counted thread work, precision being relatively easy to achieve on a canvas. This modern sampler shows how architectural forms can similarly be simply transferred to a canvas, which is the reason many samplers illustrate churches, houses or homes, as well as the alphabet, numbers and mathematical designs.*

Left *This selection of evenweave fabrics includes (**top left to bottom right):** white, cream and tan scrims of jute or linen; a linen huck; an 18 mesh cotton; 4 evenweave linens of 20, 25, 30 and 35 meshes; and a linen cotton crash.*

to the right as possible. Make sure to centre your name or whatever other inscription you choose. To centre the design, mark the vertical centre of the graph paper with a clear line from top to bottom. When blocking out the design, equalize blockings in both halves as much as possible. To centre your name and inscriptions, first block each line out on another piece of graph paper. Count how many squares across you have used. Mark the vertical halfway point. This will be the vertical centre of your design and you can now block out the inscription again, this time correctly centred on to your main graph paper.

If you have uneven numbers of squares as you count across your draft wording, there are two remedies. If you have more than one word in the line, adjust the number of squares left between the two words by adding or subtracting one square. This will give you an even number of total squares. Alternatively, if you only have one word on the line, "centre" the word so that the extra square lies on the right of the central line.

Stitches

Counted thread consists of two diagonal stitches which bisect each other. It does not matter if the upper diagonal goes up to the right or to the left as long as all stitches are consistent. Neighbouring stitches share common holes. Rows share holes with those above and below. It is important to maintain an even tension throughout to avoid "dropped" stitches. The work can be handheld, but it is often preferable to have the fabric held taut in a frame or hoop.

Cross stitches can be worked over one, two, three, four, or as many fabric threads as you like – the main consideration is consistency. When working stitches over one fabric thread, it is important to avoid every alternate stitch "slipping through" to the back of the work. Form each row in four stages. First, work the first diagonals of alternate stitches. On the return journey, fill in the first diagonals of the other stitches. Then work alternate upper diagonals and fill in the other upper diagonals on the return.

Regardless of how large your stitches are, an alternative way of working stitches is to make them in two stages, with all the first diagonals stitched first and all the upper diagonals worked on the return. It is also possible to work a row by forming one complete cross stitch at a time. The main advantage of the latter method is that if you have to undo work – as even the best needleworkers must from time to time – you can take out complete stitches simply by snipping through each upper diagonal.

Begin cross stitching with a waste knot, coming in from the area of the fabric that you are next going to cover with stitches. Finish a thread in the same way, with a waste tail going to an area to be stitched over.

Cross stitch can be worked as an edge binding. It can also be worked on a closely woven or matter ground by using "waste canvas" temporarily tacked onto the main fabric. (If you do not have any waste canvas, soak an area of single-thread, mono canvas to remove the stiff sizing and, when it is dry,

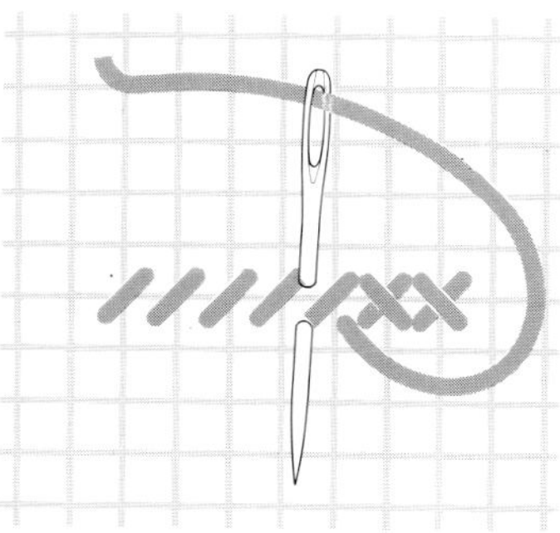

Directions *Rows of cross stitch can be worked cross by cross.*

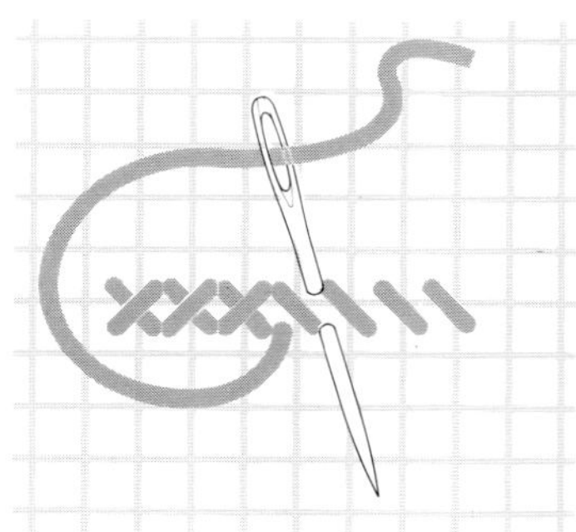

Alternatively a row of diagonal half cross stitches can be made into whole cross stitches.

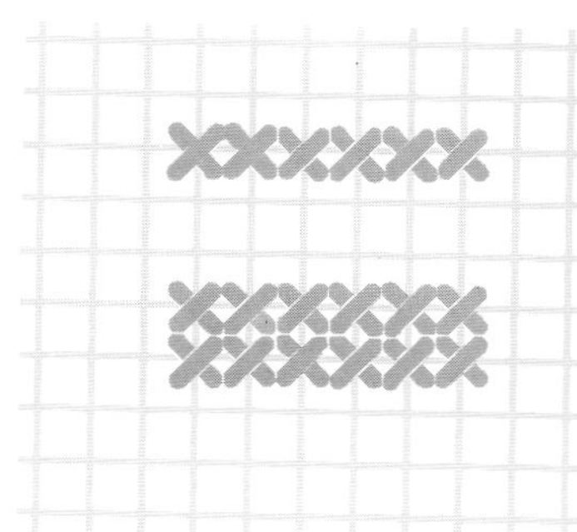

This can either be done from right to left and back again, or left to right and back again, depending on personal preference.

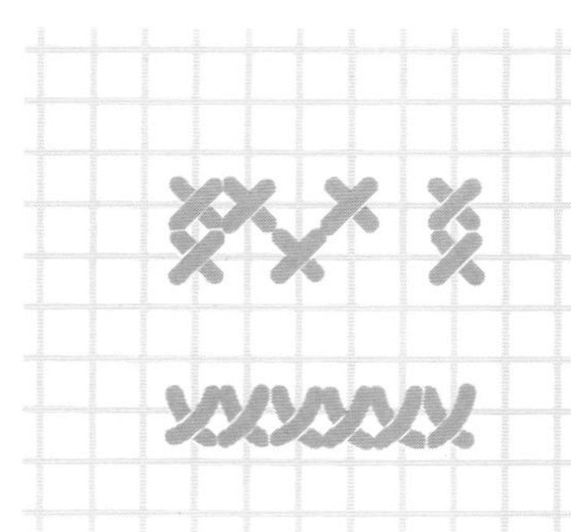

Uneven cross stitch *It is essential to work cross stitch firmly and evenly, otherwise stitches sag as shown, exposing the intersections.*

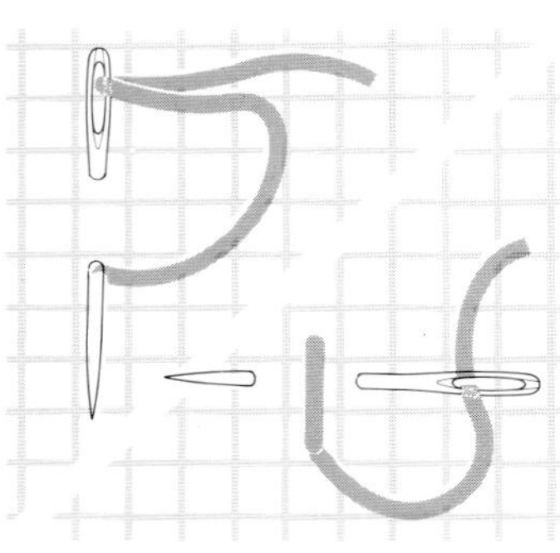

Diagonal cross stitch 1, 2. *Initially tricky to work, this stitch is like a compressed version of Montenegrin stitch arranged diagonally.*

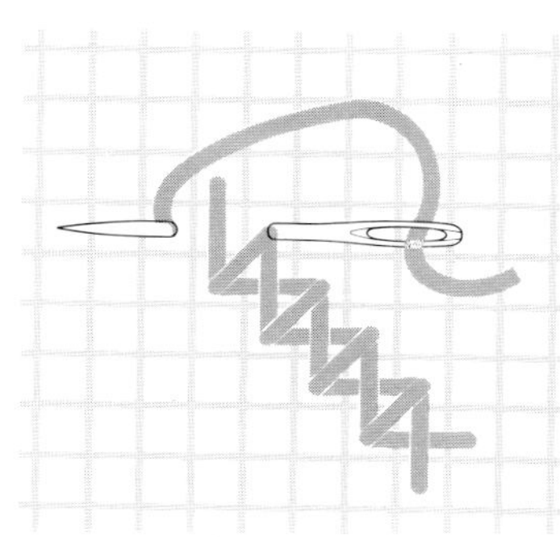

3. *The diagonals intersect over a hole, and the plain bars must be positioned over the adjacent cross stitch, stitch tips.*

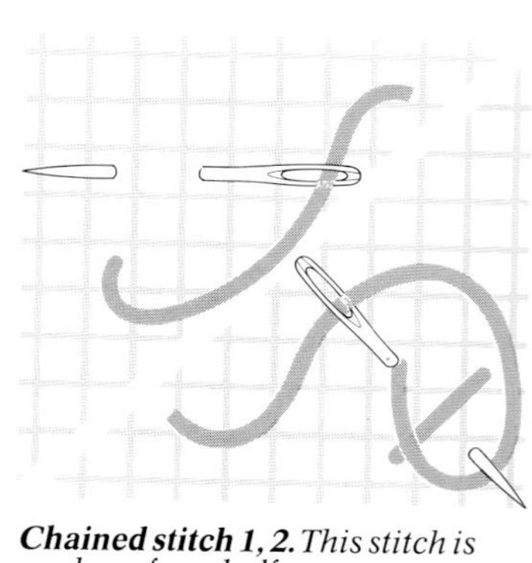

Chained stitch 1, 2. *This stitch is made up from half crosses intersecting with loops that span two intersections each.*

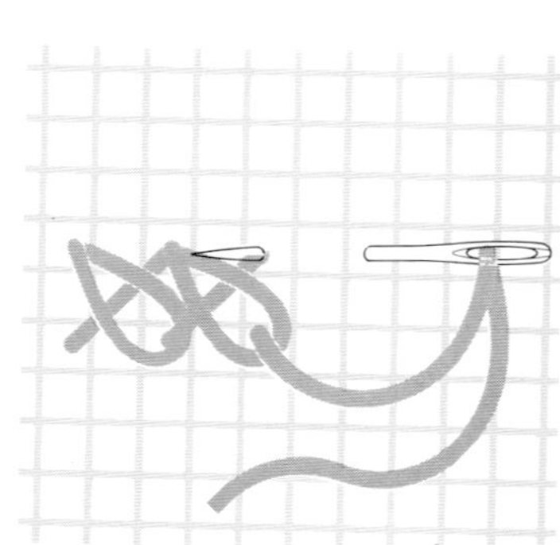

3. *Position the needle as if to work the second diagonal, but form a loop and work the stitch on the back of the canvas bringing it up to start the next stitch.*

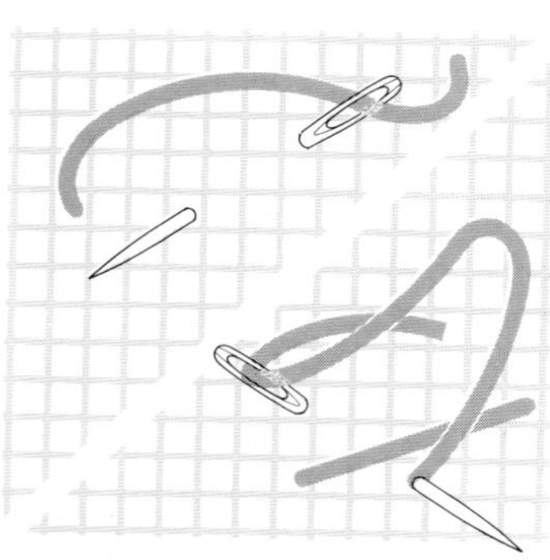

Montenegrin stitch 1, 2. *A form of cross stitch made up of wide flattened out crosses and vertical bars. The crosses are two intersections high by three wide.*

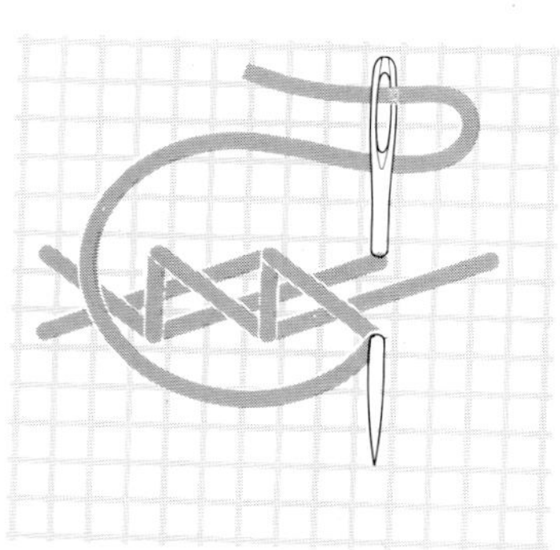

3. *Work a cross with a low intersection as shown, but bring the needle point back up to make the vertical stitch before embarking on the next cross.*

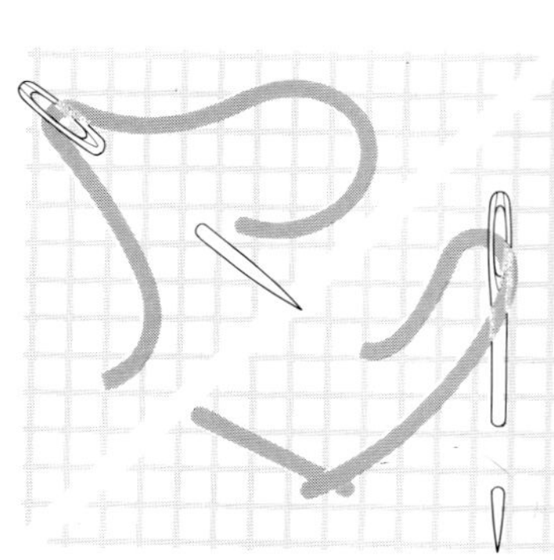

Basket stitch 1, 2. *This version of cross stitch is made up of crosses that are two threads high by four wide, overlapping to form diamonds.*

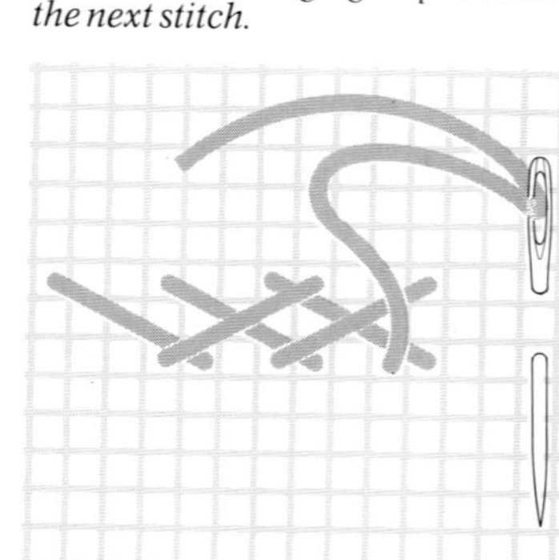

3. *The two diagonals of the cross intersect over a hole rather than a thread or intersection. Work first row from left to right.*

use this instead.) Stitches are formed over the waste canvas and, when the pattern is worked, threads of that canvas are removed one by one. This does result in looser stitching, but it allows the counted thread technique to be used with a great number of fabrics.

Variations

Half cross stitch, in which only one diagonal is worked, is one form of the needlepoint tent stitch. The needle goes into the fabric at the top of a diagonal stitch and emerges again immediately beneath to form the bottom of the next diagonal. Although this gives, from the front, the same effect as other forms of tent stitch, on the back it is recognizable by short vertical stitches. This method of tent stitch uses less yarn than other forms but stitches are inclined to distort canvas or fabric. Technically, however, all forms of tent stitch viewed from the front are half cross stitches.

Three-quarters cross stitch is sometimes necessary, especially when stitching diagonal ends of roofs on house motifs, for instance. This consists of one diagonal of usual length and the other only half-length, terminating at the junction with the main diagonal.

Long-armed cross stitch, sometimes known as long-legged cross stitch, has one diagonal much longer than the other.

Montenegrin cross stitch also has one diagonal longer than the other, though in this variation there is also a vertical stitch.

Herringbone and basket stitches are both forms of cross stitch. Herringbone is opened out. Paradoxically, basket stitch is both opened out and worked so close together that it looks like a closely woven basket.

Rice, also known as crossed-corners stitch, is an embellishment of the basic cross. Each arm of the cross is itself crossed with a diagonal, this subsequent crossing bisecting the distance from the extremity of the arm to its crossing with the other main diagonal.

Double cross stitch is another embellishment of the basic cross. A simple diagonal cross is

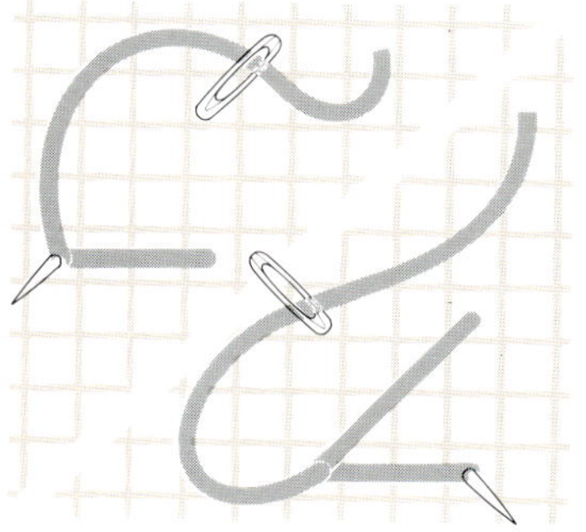

Italian stitch 1, 2. *This is made up of large basic cross stitches worked here across three canvas threads, surrounded by a box of plain stitches each.*

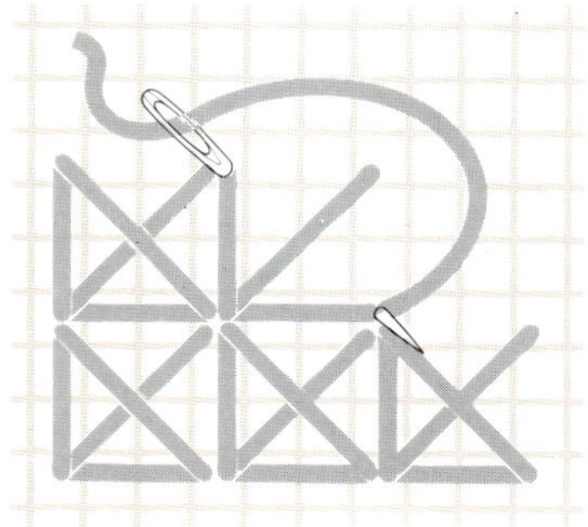

3. *Arrange the second row underneath the first so that there are six stitch tips disappearing into a single canvas hole.*

Double herringbone stitch 1. *This stitch is made up from rows of alternately facing diagonals, interlocking at top and bottom.*

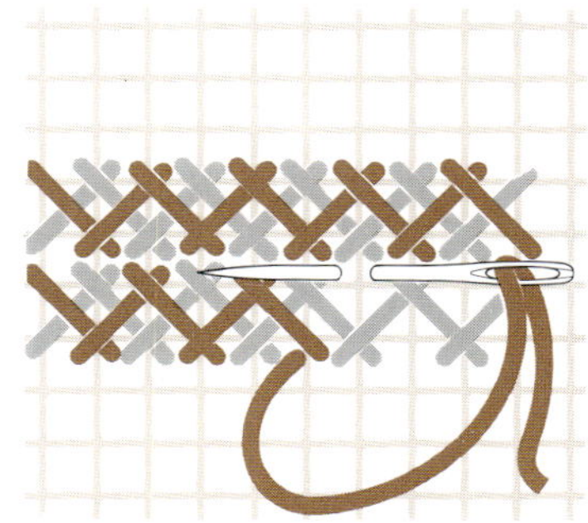

2. *Work the diagonals over two canvas threads each, and then repeat the stitch in the gaps left, possibly in a different colour.*

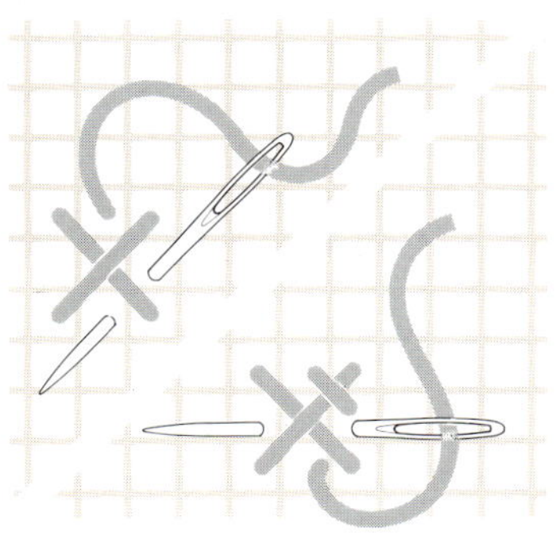

Rice stitch 1, 2. *Begin by working a basic cross stitch over two canvas intersections. Each stitch tip is then anchored with a small diagonal.*

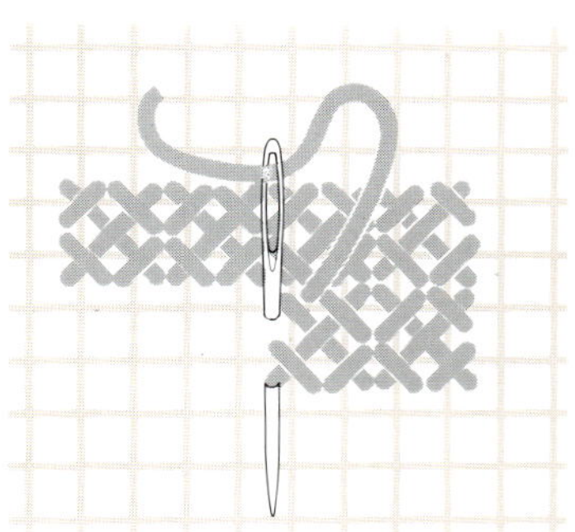

3, 4. *The extra diagonals should form broken diamonds. Work rows alternately from right to left and then back underneath in the opposite direction.*

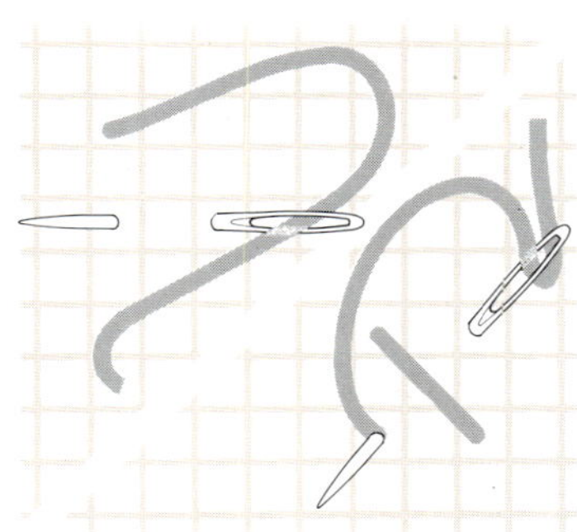

Underlined stitch 1, 2. *Work a row of basic cross stitch, two thread intersections by two thread intersections.*

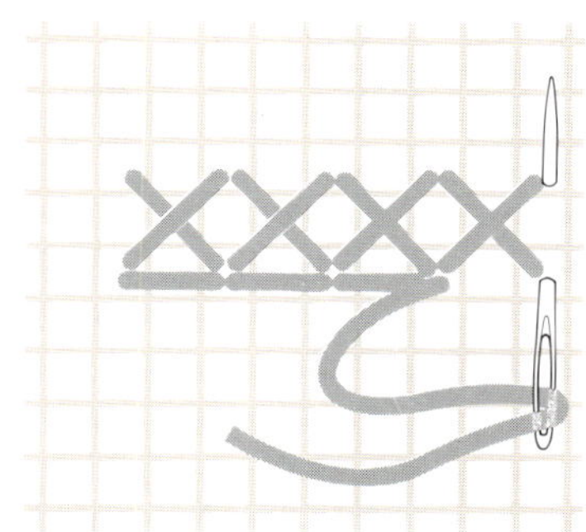

3. *Underline each cross with a horizontal.*

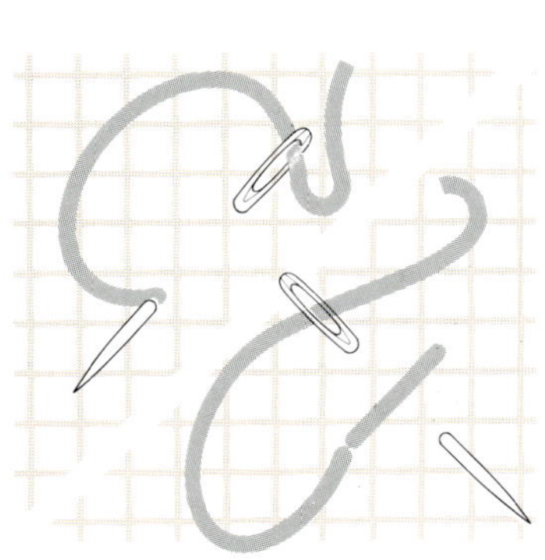

Two-sided cross stitch 1, 2. *A type of marking stitch. Work the crosses as shown, so that equal-sized crosses form on the back of the fabric.*

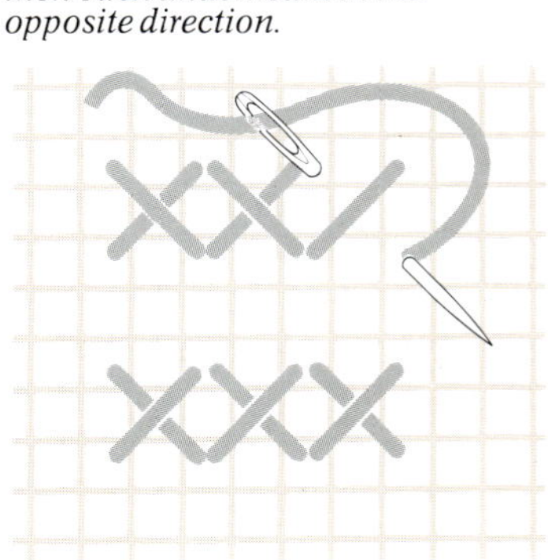

3. *Work all the diagonals in one direction before forming the crosses. Suitable for table napkins where the wrong side will often be visible.*

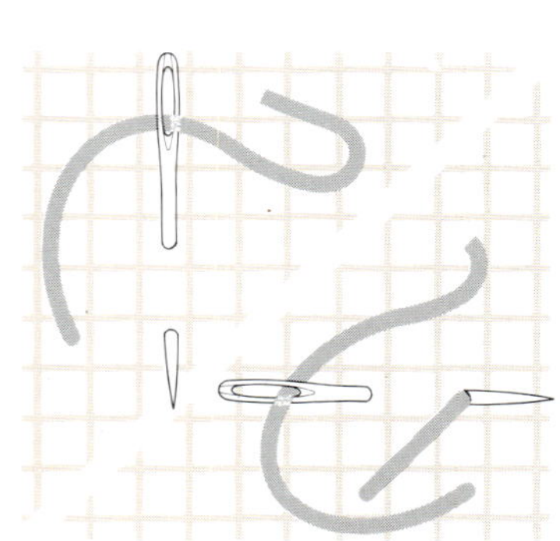

Marking 1, 2. *If the back of the fabric is to be regularly visible, cross stitch should be sewn differently to achieve a series of regular squares.*

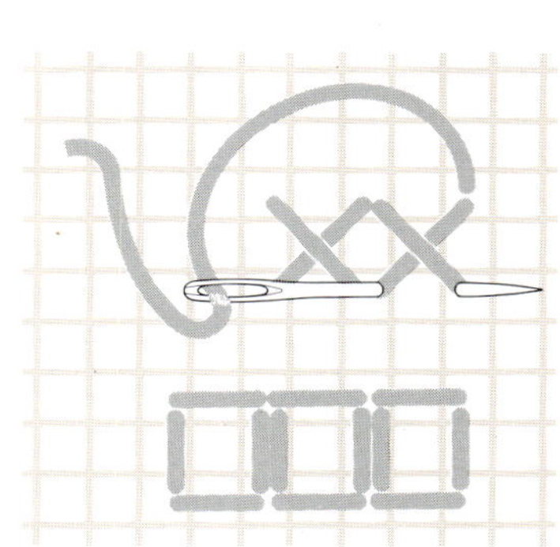

3, 4. *By going over some of the stitches twice on the front, these small squares will be formed on the back of the fabric as shown.*

subsequently covered by a horizontal and a vertical stitch to form an upper upright, St. George's cross. This looks particularly effective if the second cross is worked in a different colour from the basic stitch.

Diagonal cross stitch, another St. George's cross, has vertical and horizontal arms bisecting each other. There is one bordering stitch, joining the bottom and righthand of the cross, and rows are formed diagonally down to the right.

Marking cross stitch takes its name because it was often used for monogramming household linens and clothing. It produces a neat reverse, sometimes a mirror-image of the obverse design. The easiest way of making this stitch is to work first diagonals of alternate stitches of a row. On the return journey, work the upper diagonals of those same alternate stitches. (If you turn your work over, at this stage, you will see that you also have alternate whole-crosses on the reverse.) Your next outward journey fills in the first diagonals of the interstices and, on the return, you work the upper diagonals of those stitches. You will now have complete crosses both on the front and the back.

Italian cross stitch is sometimes known as arrowhead cross stitch or two-sided Italian cross stitch. In this stitch, each cross stitch has one vertical and one horizontal bordering stitch, making each stitch look like an arrowhead. When two or more rows of stitches are put together, stitches look as if they are "boxed". If individual stitches each have a lefthand vertical stitch and a lower horizontal stitch, then in order to "box" an area of stitches, you will have to work extra vertical stitches to the right of the right stitches of each row and extra horizontal stitches along the top of each stitch in the uppermost row.

Blackwork

Blackwork is usually described as counted thread stitching worked in black thread on a white or natural fabric. It can, however, be worked in monochrome colouring – traditionally dark green, brown or blue – and it can also be worked in freeform designs rather than as counted thread.

History

Blackwork was mainly known as "Spanish work" until about 1530, and is still sometimes referred to by this name. It was known before the end of the fourteenth century in England – Chaucer mentions:

Hir coler aboute
Of cole-blak silk, withinne and eeke withoute

in *The Millers Tale,* written in the last decade of that century, but the technique was popularized in Britain after the marriage of Catherine of Aragon and Henry VII's son, Arthur, in 1501. Whether or not Catherine of Aragon worked any blackwork herself is not known, although it is thought that she learned to embroider from her mother, Queen Isabella. She is certainly known, however, to have had clothing embellished with blackwork in her trousseau.

Throughout the sixteenth and seventeenth centuries, blackwork was used by both professional and amateur needleworkers, especially to decorate cushion covers and other fine household furnishings. Most of the surviving examples from this period,

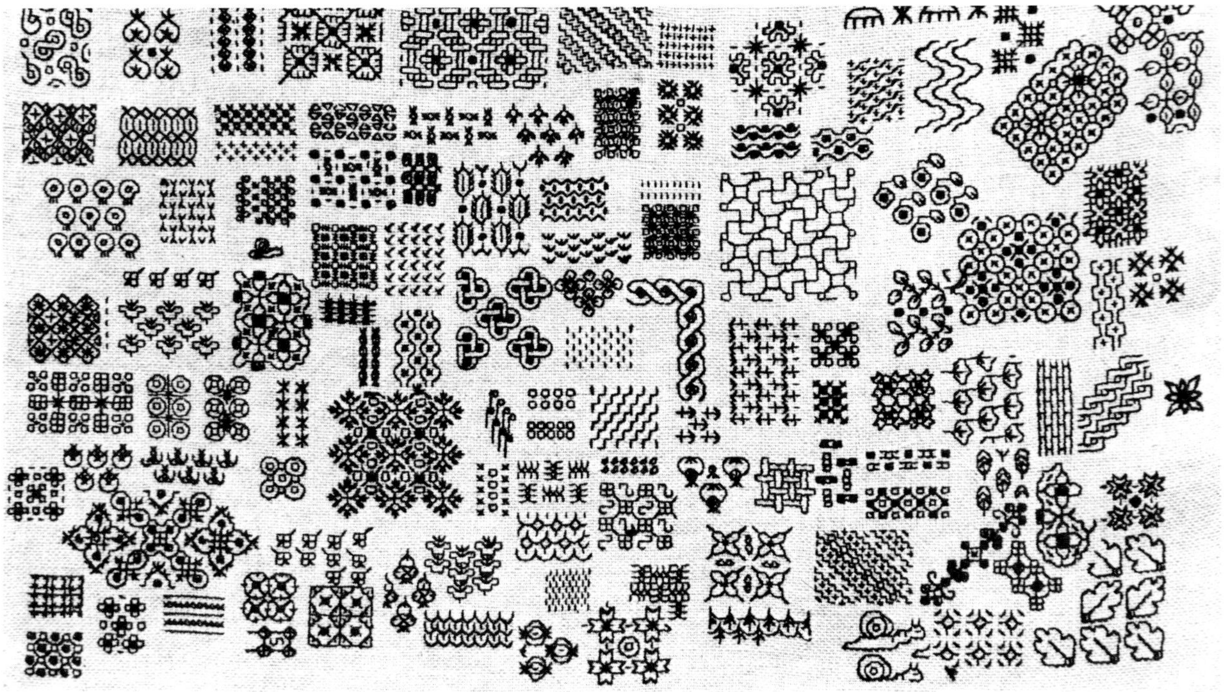

Left *This is a modern blackwork sampler, which was embroidered with many of the most popular filling patterns from historical pieces. It measures 13 x 8¼ inches (33 x 21 cm), which gives some indication of the size of the detail.*

Left *This detail of seventeenth-century blackwork embroidery is part of a sleeve panel, where geometric patterns were used to fill the floral and leaf motifs. Sometimes pieces were further embroidered with gold and other metal threads skilfully woven or threaded on the right side of the fabric, so as little as possible was wasted on the back.*

Below *Seventeenth-century "band" samplers were often three times as long as they were wide. This one measures 28 x 8 inches (71 x 21 cm) and was worked with complicated designs, some of which are raised.*

however, are costume pieces, with decoration on neckbands and cuffs, on entire areas of ladies' chemises, jackets and hoods, and also on men's shirts, nightshirts and caps. As well as these examples, blackwork can also be studied by examining portraits that show the subjects wearing finery with blackwork embellishment. So many portraits by Holbein show people wearing clothing decorated in this way that double-running stitch, one of the main blackwork techniques of that period, is still sometimes called Holbein stitch.

Designs were sometimes copied from the title pages of books, and from other engravings. These frequently consisted of small floral motifs, or geometric patterns that bore resemblance to Moorish themes, perhaps carried from North Africa to the Iberian Peninsula over the preceding centuries. As with other forms of counted thread, Levantine silk thread was used, invariably on silk or linen fabric.

At the beginning of the eighteenth century, blackwork was superseded by polychrome stitching. During the last few decades, however, it has enjoyed something of a revival, especially in North America, South Africa and New Zealand – and not only among counted thread enthusiasts.

Materials

Blackwork is generally worked on Glenshee or another evenweave linen. This technique is best executed with a single thickness of thread, for example, one strand of stranded cotton or a thickness of perle cotton. Since clearly defined junctions of stitches help to give the overall effect, it is better not to use a napped or furry thread such as wool. As with other counted thread forms, a blunt tapestry needle is required and the work can be handheld, if desired.

Techniques

Design

Part of the fascination of blackwork is forming repeating patterns with varying density. Before beginning stitching it is a good idea to sketch out various patterns on graph paper, filling some of them in. You might prefer to have greater density of stitches at the bottom, in the middle, or around the edges of an area of pattern. Colour in some of the motifs to see if you would rather work in strict blackwork or use a colour.

Apart from copying old blackwork pieces and perhaps gleaning ideas from books – title pages of old manuscripts, for example – ideas for blackwork design can also be taken from tiles, wrought-iron gates, railings and other architectural features, and even from nature, such as bare winter branches.

Stitches

The main stitches used in counted thread blackwork are: back stitch; buttonhole stitch; chain stitch; coral stitch; double-running or Holbein stitch; Pekinese stitch; and seeding or speckling.

If you have a large area of fabric to cover it is advisable to start a repeating motif pattern in one corner of that area and count the motifs both vertically and horizontally. Wherever possible, try to bring the thread out of an empty (unstitched) hole of fabric and down into a filled hole into which a stitch has already been worked. This should prevent the embroidery threads splitting, which tends to result in messy definition between one stitch and another.

In the past, some blackwork pieces were further embellished with spangles, flat metal discs with central holes, held in place with radial stitches. This technique can be used for extra decorative effect.

Above *This detail shows part of an unfinished nightcap, worked in a curling feathered design on a fine linen ground. The bottom line of design is worked in reverse, ready to be turned up into a brim. The blackwork stitches have been embroidered in green silks in this case, and decorated with metal threads and spangles in part.*
Above right *This is a detail from a linen panel c. 1600. The scrolled pattern was marked in blue pencil and the embroidery partially enhanced with straight stitches along the design outlines. Silver-gilt thread was woven through the straight stitches.*
Far right *This linen shirt, attributed to Dorothy Wadham, wife of the founder of Wadham College, Oxford, was embroidered in blackwork designs in pale purple silk. Early seventeenth-century blackwork was often worked in colours other than black.*
Right *The design ideas of Middle Eastern mashrabiya, or fretted wooden screens, can easily be adapted to blackwork.*

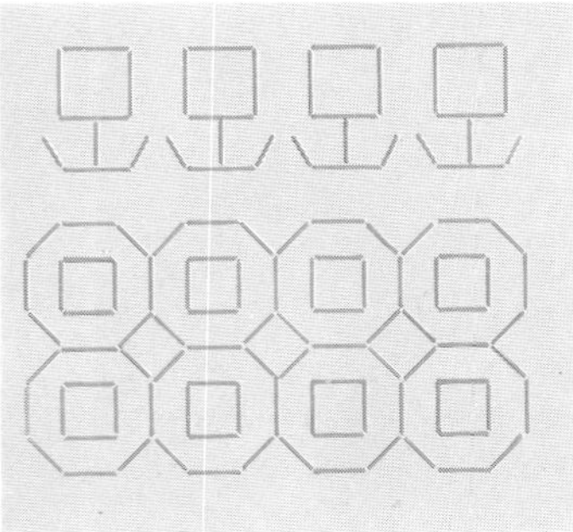

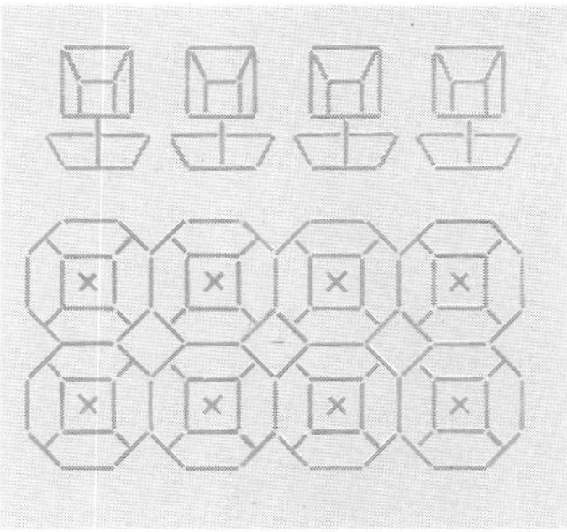

Spangle embellishment *A traditional way of decorating blackwork was to sew on small spangles, with radial stitches, at focal points in the design.*

Blackwork 1. *Aim for variety in the density of blackwork, to achieve diverse effects. Both patterns above are of a light overall density.*

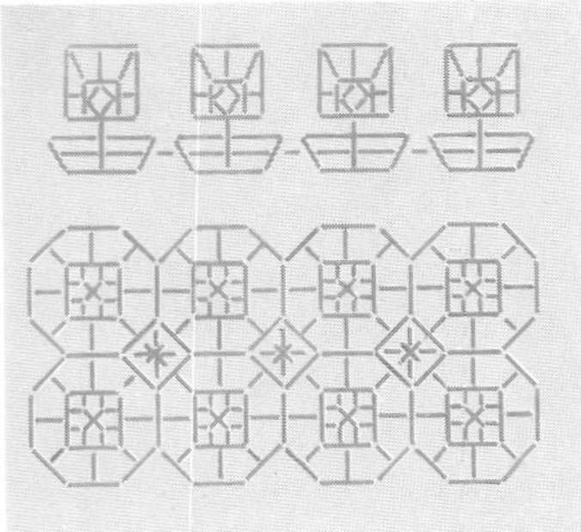

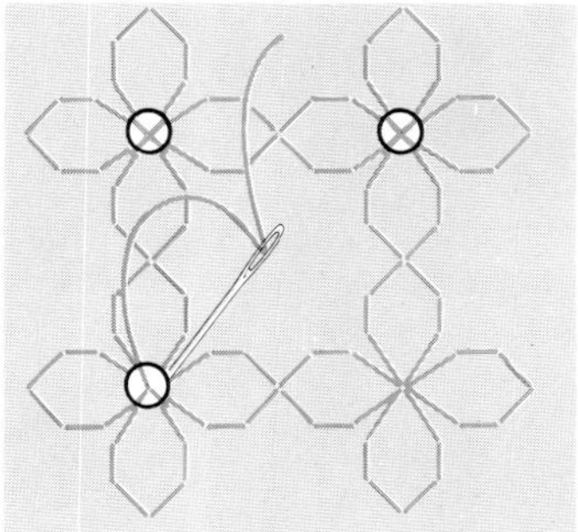

2. By adding slightly more detail to these basic designs, a denser effect can be achieved as shown in the two repeating patterns above.

3. Add in still more details to darken the design further. Although the scale of the outlines have remained the same throughout, the overall effect has altered radically.

Crewel

Crewel embroidery is generally defined as a variety of different surface or above-surface stitches worked in coloured two-ply woollen yarn on closely woven linen fabric, the threads of which are not counted. The word crewel is believed to have come from the Anglo-Saxon word *cleow* meaning a ball of thread. There is evidence that embroidery using a wool thread has a history going back thousands of years, particularly in Britain, where it has always been a notable embroidery medium.

History

Little is known to us today of the early wool embroideries, but one piece of work which has survived is the famous Bayeux Tapestry. This is not a tapestry at all, but an embroidery worked in a worsted thread on linen, which tells the story of the Battle of Hastings and the events leading up to it. It was thought to have been commissioned by Odo (*c.* 1036-1097), the Bishop of Bayeux and half-brother of William the Conqueror, for his cathedral which was dedicated in 1077.

The embroidery is over 230 yards (210 m) long and 20 inches (50 cm) wide, but it was worked on several pieces of linen, probably to enable many people to work on it at one time. The pieces were joined together after the embroidery was finished. The main story is told in the centre band, while in the narrow borders at the top and bottom, there are heraldic beasts. Where the battle is shown at its height, the story overlaps onto the borders and many decapitated bodies are depicted in the lower border. There is no perspective in the embroidery – men, horses, trees, buildings and ships are all roughly the same size.

The embroidery was worked in laid work, which are long stitches taken across an area on the surface and caught down with small stitches, and couching. Only eight colours were used – terracotta, buff, yellow, two blues and three greens. These appear to have been used entirely at the discretion of the embroiderer: there are green and buff horses and rust and buff trees, the latter often used to separate one event from another.

After the Bayeux Tapestry, there are few surviving examples of crewel work for 600 years, although embroiderers did not waste their time in the intervening centuries. In an early medieval manuscript, a lady wrote, "I do no other work but read my psalter, work in gold, silk or cruells, play a tune on my harp, checkmate someone at chess or feed the hawk on my wrist."

With the beginnings of overseas trade, and the formation of the East India Company by London merchants in the early 1600s, many exotic goods from India and China became available. These included silks, embroideries, spices, jewels and pearls, as well as the painted cotton hangings called palampores. The Indian designs on these hangings, however, were not wholly pleasing to the English. The first palampores had white designs on a coloured background, and did not sell well. The process was reversed – coloured designs on a white background – with little more success. By 1670, European merchants had provided patterns which were beginning to influence the Indians in their designs. The resulting bed curtains were extremely popular and were bought by all but the poorest people. The designs on these palampores had a great influence on English embroiderers and initiated the golden age of crewel work.

Early seventeenth-century embroiderers tended to use monochromatic colours for crewel work curtains worked in the coiling patterns and flowers associated with Elizabethan blackwork designs. Palampore design gave embroiderers a new challenge and they set about working the designs with enthusiasm on twill weave fabrics.

Below *Part of the celebrated Bayeux Tapestry, this is a detail of Norman sailors and soldiers making the voyage to England to confront Harold at the Battle of Hastings. The scene depicted is lively and attractive, with the figures in a variety of positions, talking in anticipation of the coming event. There is also a strong sense of movement, of the wind in the sails and the forward motion of the boats. These were worked in laid and couched wools, and other details in stem and outline stitches.*

Right *This bold design of crewel work from the mid-seventeenth century is part of a bed hanging. The repeated leaf and flower motifs have mixed origins in Eastern and European design ideas.*

If some of the motifs on the palampores appear slightly strange, this is not surprising. The original patterns sent out from England would undoubtedly have been adjusted to fit standard sizes for bed furnishings; the Indians would also have been quite unfamiliar with the English flora and fauna. As the designs progressed, it became obvious that there was a mixture of patterns with an Eastern influence, combined with those of a European interpretation. This is particularly apparent in the portrayal of the oak leaves that were such a feature of crewel work. This Eastern influence, combined with the Tudor fascination with floral shapes, became known as Jacobean work, the name being applied to the design rather than a particular working method or stitches. Even today, crewel work is often rather mistakenly called Jacobean work.

It was Indian craftsmen who also discovered that if certain natural substances were added to their dyes, it made the dyes completely colour-fast. The introduction of these mordants or fixatives did a great deal to promote the popularity of the cotton hangings. It was a considerable time before the nature of these mordants was investigated.

Probably not all crewel work made around this time was executed by women. Owing to the coarseness of the crewel wools and fabrics, and the size of some of the hangings, it is quite possible that men may have contributed. It is also quite unlikely that the seventeenth- or eighteenth-century embroiderer would have been able to design her own work, except the simpler pieces, and instead pattern drawers would have been employed when embarking on larger pieces of crewel work. Towards the end of the seventeenth century, designs for crewel work were first published in London.

The legend of the Tree of Life also played a great part in influencing crewel designs and motifs derived from the story were used enthusiastically by English embroiderers. This legend probably arose in the Middle Ages when people believed in a paradise located beyond India. This fantasy probably inspired the exotic flowers portrayed by contemporary artists. The Tree of Life design consists chiefly of unnatural-looking leaves and floral forms on a central tree-like growth rising from rounded hillocks. Quaint, almost grotesque, animals and birds, such as rabbits, deer, squirrels, peacocks and birds of paradise, were introduced, as well as English flowers such as the rose, the national emblem, the carnation, which was a symbol of the Stuart family, honeysuckle, marigolds, irises and the potato flower, together with other exotic many-petalled flowers. Not only

Left** It was fashionable during the seventeenth century to embroider bedcovers, hangings and window curtains with crewel work. The leaf patterns on this hanging, made* ***c. *1696, are flamboyant and unrealistic, but distinctive.*

***Above** This is a section of a bed hanging made by Abigail Pett. It illustrates the extraordinary range and scope of her vision, and of her creative powers. Every motif is slightly different, and the patterns unusually striking. In this hanging, she has included dragons, reindeer, lions and leopards, camels, monkeys, squirrels and multicoloured birds. It is hardly possible that she would actually have seen many of these species, yet they are all recognizable.*

did the Indians produce these designs for the English merchants, but they were also exported to China.

The most famous of all the seventeenth-century crewel work must be the bed hangings made by a certain Abigail Pett in 1675. Her identity still remains a mystery, despite many attempts to find out who she was. The scale of the work she undertook was vast by any standards, and on the bed curtains and valances there are no two motifs exactly alike in stitch or colour. Here, again, the effects of trade with the Far East are apparent in some of the exotic birds that are portrayed. It is difficult to imagine anyone today embarking on such a large project – and completing it.

In the eighteenth century, during the reign

Right *A detail of the hanging opposite, this photograph does some justice to the precision of the work Abigail Pett executed. The exaggerated tree motif shows a fine and consistent quality of stitching, in blocks of colour and in tiny geometric patterns which add interest to the texture of the work. The tree trunk has notches down the sides, giving a rough, bark-like impression. The shaded colours and the voiding must have been carefully designed before each motif was worked; these complement the more realistic appearance of the animals, so the work gains unity.*

of Queen Anne, large ornate furniture was superseded by elegant rococo. The embroiderers' crewel work patterns changed too, becoming romantic and prettier. Instead of the thick trunks and heavy leaves, there were nosegays of flowers and delicate stems. The work became smaller and the motifs more delicate, although the Tree of Life continued being the basis for many designs well into the century. The use of silk increased around this time and a great deal of the embroidery was used for furnishings; everything from backs of chairs and upholstery panels to curtains and carpets. Gradually women learned the art of shading with crewel wools and silks, and this was done to perfection.

It was also about this time that women in

America began working with crewel wools, embroidering their "quilts, coverlids, counterpins and bedticks", but wools were very expensive there and, as time went by, they developed their own styles and techniques, which were more delicate in approach and therefore more economical. They also became very expert at spinning their own yarn and dyeing it.

With the profit from the Great Exhibition of 1851, the Victoria and Albert Museum was founded in London with the aim of showing the best decorative arts from all over the world. Some of the first exhibits were examples of crewel work. The museum was responsible for encouraging individuals to think about design, but it was William Morris (1834-1896) who finally changed the face of English design. Morris did not like Berlin woolwork, a type of embroidery worked on canvas with soft, bright wools and very popular with women in the early nineteenth century. After his marriage in 1859, he began designing embroideries for his own home, The Red House in Bexleyheath, Kent. He taught himself, and later his wife and friends, embroidery stitches, by carefully unravelling the crewel embroideries of the late seventeenth century, and by studying examples in the Victoria and Albert Museum. Crewel work seemed to him the ideal medium; he liked the large, flowing patterns and the muted colours that he had seen on pieces of crewel work in the museum.

William Morris was a keen supporter of all crafts, and, in 1861, together with some fellow craftsmen, he formed a company, initially designing mainly for the church. Morris went on to design many large-scale embroideries, such as hangings and coverlets with pictorial or bold flower and leaf designs, which were executed by skilled needlewomen. His second company, Morris & Co., was formed in 1875 with embroidery one of the most popular aspects of their commercial production. The company's work had the most far-reaching effects on embroidery in general.

Morris dyed his own wool, using natural dyes which faded to even more attractive tones, as he so disliked the garish colours of the aniline dyes used in Berlin woolwork. This preference for natural vegetable dyes has lasted to the present day. A friend of Morris, Thomas Wardle, was a fabric printer and Morris spent many hours in Wardle's dye shop to perfect the soft, luminous colours he wanted for his art needlework.

In 1885, William Morris's daughter, May, took over the management of the embroidery workshops. She was a very accomplished embroiderer and teacher, and in 1893 wrote a book on embroidery design called *Decorative Needlework* to encourage embroiderers to make their own designs. By the end of the nineteenth century Morris & Co. were selling embroidery kits with the designs already drawn on the linen background, together with specially dyed silks or wools and often with a corner already worked, to guide the amateur embroiderer.

Art needlework became as popular at the end of the nineteenth century as Berlin woolwork had been earlier on. There was a return of naturalistic designs and flowing lines, instigated by Morris. Unfortunately, as so often happens, the increasing popularity brought about a drop in quality and the standard of workmanship became deplorably low.

In 1872, the Royal School of Needlework was founded in London. The establishment of this institution was yet another turning point for crewel work. The women admitted

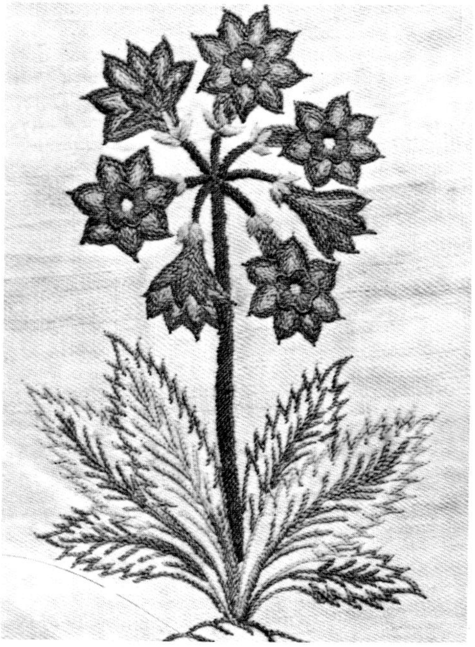

Right *From an eighteenth-century bed hanging, this primula was embroidered in coloured wools. The seven separate flowers on the single plant have been stitched in different positions, giving a three-dimensional impression. Stem, satin and long-and-short stitches have been used in the hanging, among others.*

Left *This bed hanging was made in the early eighteenth century. It shows a patient attention to detail – the exotic flowers, butterflies and intricately feathered and coloured birds are set in a close design. Again, the tree, this time a palm, looks unrealistic, although the monkeys and elephants help to place it in its tropical setting. The stitches used on this piece are many and various.*

Below *This is a delicate piece of crewel embroidery from the early eighteenth century illustrating a wide selection of flowers, many of which have long been connected with English history and folk lore. Amongst the selection are roses, honeysuckle, May blossom, daffodils, snowdrops, tulips, carnations and lilies, all embroidered on linen in bright wools.*

to the training school were taught to think of embroidery as art. When non-vocational classes were started, the basic teaching was crewel work which was thought to be the best training in surface stitchery. Even in the School's workrooms a tremendous amount of crewel work was done. Curtains, screens and other domestic furnishings were available for sale, enabling the School to become self-supporting by 1884. A shop was also opened where crewel wools and prepared designs could be bought. In 1899, the Royal School moved to its own premises in South Kensington. Its influence can be gauged by the fact that even in the United States crewel work became known as South Kensington embroidery.

At the turn of the century at the Glasgow School of Art, Jessie Newberry started an embroidery class, teaching crewel work in the style of William Morris, using long-and-short stitch on linen. However, she soon developed her own style and incorporated linen appliqué with crewel work, in a style we know today as Art Nouveau. Along with her colleagues, she became a pioneer of the modern approach to needlework as it is taught today in schools and colleges. New ideas and fresh approaches to design meant that embroiderers started experimenting with different techniques and combinations of techniques.

In the 1920s and 1930s countless crewel

work patterns were published in needlework magazines and there were innumerable kits on the market for making up cushions, firescreens and other projects. But the beauty and colour balance of the original work was lost and this "Jacobean style" work was far removed from the seventeenth-century masterpieces.

In the 1930s and 1940s, embroidery standards were low. Crewel work consisted mainly of tablecloths and traycloths bought ready printed with repeated motifs in each corner. Although crewel work on its own has never regained its earlier popularity as a means of decorating household furnishings, a great number of embroiderers, particularly in North America, have taken the art to an

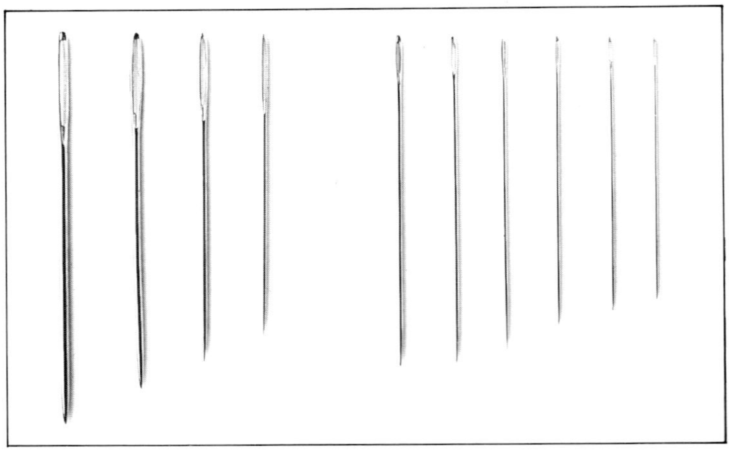

Right *This selection of needles shows the variety generally used in crewel work. On the left are chenille needles, sizes 18, 20, 22 and 24, with large eyes and relatively sharp points. On the right are crewel needles of sizes 5, 6, 7, 8, 9 and 10. These are used for stitching fine strands of crewel wools.*

A piece of cotton twill ready for embroidering in a round, wooden frame. Beside the frame is a selection of crewel wools.

Left *This seventeenth-century hanging was worked mostly in chain stitches, which accounts for the specks of background fabric showing through the embroidery. The wools are in strong shades of a blue green, with yellow highlighting the upper edges, giving the stems a three-dimensional appearance. Voiding was also used to separate some of the petals.*

advanced level. Others experiment, combining crewel with canvaswork, appliqué, beadwork or machine embroidery.

Materials

Fabric
With the wide range of fabrics available today, choosing an appropriate material can be difficult, but there are a few guidelines to remember. It is always best to use as good quality a fabric as you can afford. The weave should be firm and close, but avoid a very tightly woven fabric, as this will make stitching difficult.

Traditionally, linen is the best material for crewel work. In the eighteenth century, a linen and cotton twill weave fabric was used. Many furnishing fabrics can be suitable, but ensure that the material is firm enough to bear the weight of the embroidered wool. Denim and ticking can be used to good effect. Beware of using lightweight fabrics, such as cotton or lawn, as these materials will pucker under the weight of the crewel wools.

If you have a piece of fabric that you particularly want to use, but think it might be too fine, you can mount it on a backing material like calico or old sheeting before starting the stitchery. This also applies to loosely woven fabrics. Fabrics should be chosen carefully when you are embarking on a project that is to receive any amount of wear and tear such as chair seats or cushions.

Thread
Crewel wools are the most suitable and can be bought by the skein, or in hanks if a quantity of one colour is needed. These are available in a large range of colours, and are generally colour-fast and moth-proofed. Crewel wool is a fine two-ply yarn but can be used singly, or with several strands together.

Three-stranded Persian wools can be separated to suit your needs and to give contrast of texture. When working on very coarse materials, it is also possible to use rug wools, or some of the bulky knitting wools that are on sale today.

Always use wool in short lengths – a thread that is too long will eventually weaken and break from the strain of passing to and fro through the material.

Needles
There are basically two needles which are used in crewel work. The first are crewel needles, which are short with long eyes. The sizes most frequently used are sizes 4 to 10. The second type are chenille needles, which are used for coarser threads. These have large eyes and sharp points and come in sizes 18 to 24.

Remember to choose the size of needle in relation to the thickness of thread and fabric.

Examples of crewel embroidery

***1.** A section of the eleventh-century Bayeux Tapestry, illustrating cavalry men about to do battle at Hastings in 1066, is mostly worked in couched laid wools in earth colours.*

***2.** This medieval scene was in fact worked during the early twentieth century, with simplistic designs of figures, animals and the countryside stitched in sombre colours. The leafy border around the panel is interspersed with heraldic shields reminiscent of feudal times.*

***3.** These bed hangings from Kelmscott Manor were designed by William Morris and worked by his daughter May in the late nineteenth century. They show an interesting mixture of stylization and realism. Extravagant birds of paradise as well as the more familiar shapes of Western birds in bright colours perch on the boughs of an intensely-worked flowering tree, and on a rose-covered trellis amongst a variety of other recognizable plants. The colours are an integral part of the design.*

***4.** A delicate and pretty piece of crewel embroidery, where much of the background is left plain, this is a bedspread worked in about 1910. The centre is stitched with wild flowers in subtle colours, and the borders lined with a thin, geometric pattern.*

1

2

3

e wold and the night is a-cold and thames runs chill
hill but kind & dear is the old house here
s warm midst winter's harm rest then & rest and think

4

I·KNOW·A·BANK·WHEREON
THE·WILD·THYME·BLOWS

The needle should pass through the fabric without any strain. If the thread breaks, the needle is probably too small. If you are working with a fairly fine thread and your stitches are uneven, your needle is probably too big.

Tapestry needles with blunt ends should be used when working a laid filling stitch where threads are woven on the surface, since these needles will not split the thread. If you do not have a tapestry needle, it is also possible to push a crewel or chenille needle through eye-first, which has the same effect. A point to remember when buying needles is that the higher the number, the smaller the size.

Frames

A frame is essential when working most of the techniques associated with crewel work. It is always much easier to keep work neat and even, when the background fabric is held taut. When doing laid work or working the various laid filling stitches, frames are essential – it is impossible to work these stitches in the hand as the threads have to lie flat on the surface of the material. A frame is also preferable when couching or working long-and-short stitch.

Any kind of frame can be used for crewel work. A ring frame is suitable for small pieces, but if this will flatten areas of stitchery, it is better to use a slate or square frame, which enables larger areas of work to be completed at a time. A square frame only governs the width of the stitching area, as any excess length can be wound on the rollers. For a bedspread or another large item, it is easier to work in strips and join them together later, unless you have access to a large quilting frame.

Techniques

Design

There have been many different styles of crewel work over the centuries, from the simple, lively approach of the Bayeux Tapestry, the large Jacobean hangings with their Oriental motifs and the delicate floral designs of the Queen Anne period to the bold naturalistic style of William Morris' hangings. A good deal of crewel work is still based on traditional stitches and the laid fillings used on those wall and bed hangings of the seventeenth century, although your designs should not be straight copies from early techniques. Photographs of gardens and seed catalogues are useful for designing flowers and foliage, and leaves are a marvellous source of design. When you have found a leaf you like, take a tracing and then make a paper cutout. Leaf designs are ideal for pockets or handbags, or you couid cut out several identical leaf shapes and repeat the design as a border on a dress or a pair of curtains.

Crewel work has often been associated with large-scale work such as wall hangings

Right *The leaf motif pictured here is part of a Jacobean bed hanging. The crewel embroidery was worked with long-and-short stitches for the shading, stem and split stitches and block shading. The motif is outlined with couching.*
Far right *This sampler was worked at the Royal School of Needlework. Split and stem stitches, long-and-short and block shading, also French knots, seeding and couching were used to give the work an interesting texture and to add variety to the shapes.*

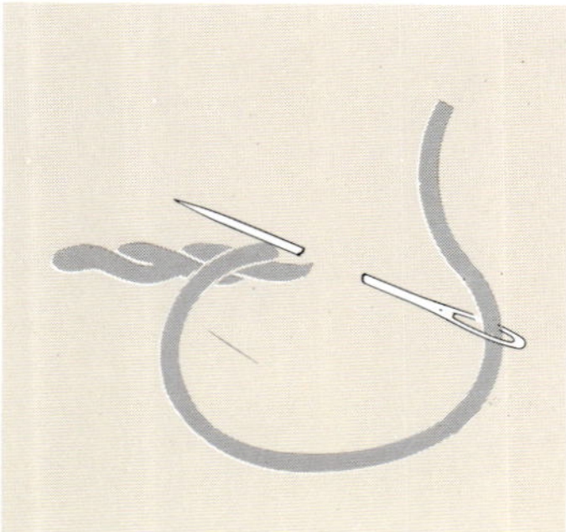

Stem stitch *Make a long stitch and come up again a half stitch back at a slight angle. Repeat the sequence.*

Split stitch *Work this stitch like stem stitch, except, when emerging, point the needle through the thread so splitting it.*

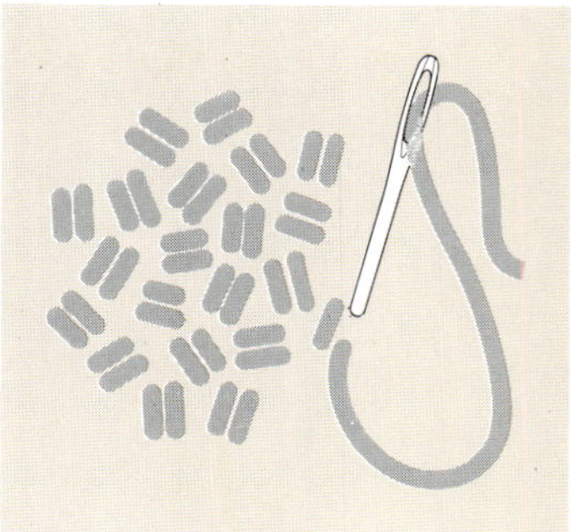

Seeding *This filling stitch consists of tiny straight stitches of even length worked at all angles, sometimes with two stitches together.*

Block shading *Work a line of close satin stitches, then in another shade work a second line with the end of each stitch precisely beneath those of the previous line.*

and panels, but it is also ideal for cushions and curtains, and can be worked on a much finer scale for clothes and accessories. Eyeglass cases, purses and belts are all suitable projects but your first piece of crewel work does not have to be small. Crewel work grows relatively quickly and a wall hanging could be very satisfying to do.

Stitches

Aim to build up a knowledge of stitches. One of the best ways of doing this is to work a spare piece of material as a sampler. This does not have to be an exquisite piece of work, but will serve as a kind of dictionary to which you can refer. Keeping a sampler enables you to decide if the stitch you propose to use is the right size and scale for your work, and it will also show up any advantages or disadvantages.

Many standard stitches can be used in crewel work, and any freehand stitch can also be combined with the special stitches associated with crewel work. These can be worked on different scales, in threads other than wool. The stitches most commonly used in crewel work are stem, split, long-and-short, satin, block shading, coral, laid and couched work, with a variety of fillings. French knots are also frequently used.

Stitches are used to make lines, solid and

semi-solid shapes, and open fillings. Once you have learnt the basic form of each stitch, experiment. Where the whole design is to be worked in wool, it is important to create texture, and apart from choosing stitches to complement each other, this can be done by working the same stitch in different directions, or using different thicknesses of wool. You can change the scale of your work or even combine more than one stitch, possibly to make a new one.

Crewel work does not have to be worked solely in wool. Experiment with different threads, such as stranded cottons, perle cottons, silks or textured yarns.

Stem stitch The first stitch that was used a great deal in crewel work and is still a basic stitch, is stem stitch. It is probably one of the oldest stitches in the world. Stem stitch is effective as an outline and in rows as a filling stitch, when it gives a slightly ribbed effect. When using stem stitch as a filling, remember to work all the lines in the same direction and when working curves, make each stitch slightly smaller. However, this stitch is inclined to pucker the fabric, so practise it first.

Work stem stitch from the bottom of a line to the top, away from you. The thread may be held either to the right or left of the needle, but once a line has been started, always hold the thread to the same side. Bring the needle up at the beginning of the line and take it down a short way forward. Bring the needle up again halfway back. Go forward, ensuring that the second stitch is the same length as the first. Take the needle down and back up to the end of the last stitch. Repeat to the end of the line. If working curves, bring the needle up on the inner side of the curve.

Split stitch is another useful outline stitch, and, like stem stitch, it can be worked in close lines all in one direction, as a filling. As an outline, it can be worked in any direction.

Bring the needle up at the beginning of a line and take it down a short distance away. Bring the needle back up about halfway along the first stitch and through the centre of it, splitting it in two. Repeat, going forward. As for stem stitch, ensure that the stitches are slightly smaller on the curves.

Split stitch is often used as an outline and then covered by another stitch, serving as a padding, and ensuring that you have a sharp edge to your work.

Block shading Satin stitch is a very common stitch in crewel work. Padded satin stitch is also useful. For this stitch, first work a vertical row of satin stitches to fill a shape. Work a few horizontal stitches to hold the first row. Work a second padding row vertically and finish with a row of slanting stitches worked close together.

Block shading has always been popular in crewel work, especially in the eighteenth century, when silk was used to very good effect. It consists of rows of satin stitch worked in tones of one colour or in graduating colours. It is best worked with a single thread of crewel or Persian wool. Start with an outline of split stitch. Bring the needle up into the material and down just over the outline. The following rows are worked by bringing the needle up into the fabric and taking it down into the extreme end of the previous row.

Long-and-short stitch is used for filling areas and gives a smooth effect when worked well. It can be worked all in one colour, but it is more usual to shade the colours. It is advisable to work long-and-short in a frame. As this is a difficult stitch to master, start by working in straight horizontal lines before trying to fill a specific shape.

Experiment first with blending colours and with the size of the stitch. Select three tones of one colour – light, medium and dark. The best effect is probably achieved when you work with one strand of crewel wool. Take the lightest colour and work a line of split stitch across the top. Bring the needle up about ½ inch (1 cm) below the line of the split stitch. Go down just over the split stitch. Then bring it up about a ¼ inch (6 mm) below and work across the line alternately with long-and-short stitches. Then, with the medium tone, work a second line of stitches

Left *A recently embroidered Jacobean sampler was worked with long-and-short, split and stem stitches and French knots.* ***Right*** *Worked in 1930, "St. Francis" involved the embroidering of split, long-and-short, satin and chain stitches with couching on a linen twill.*

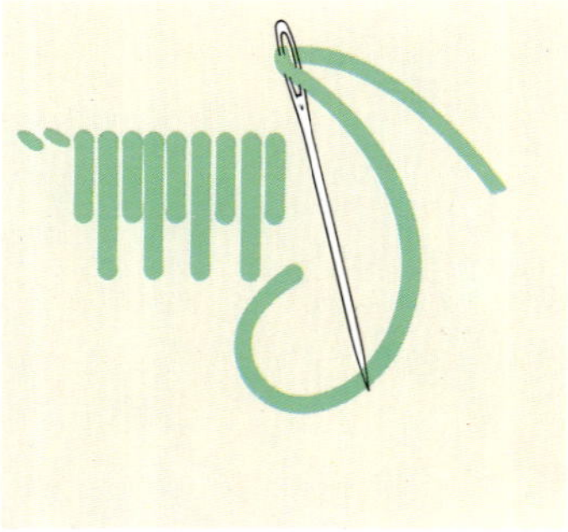

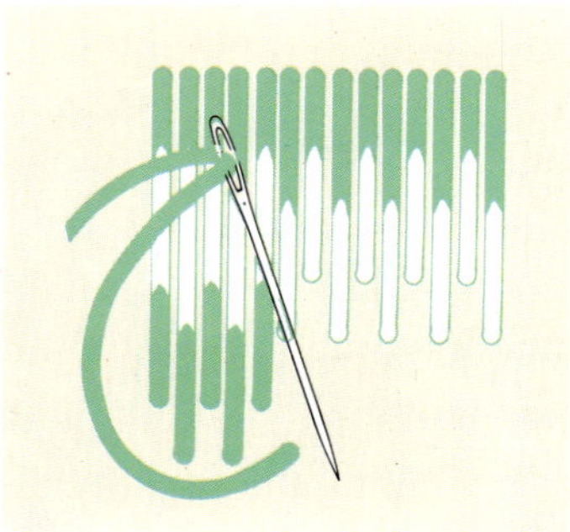

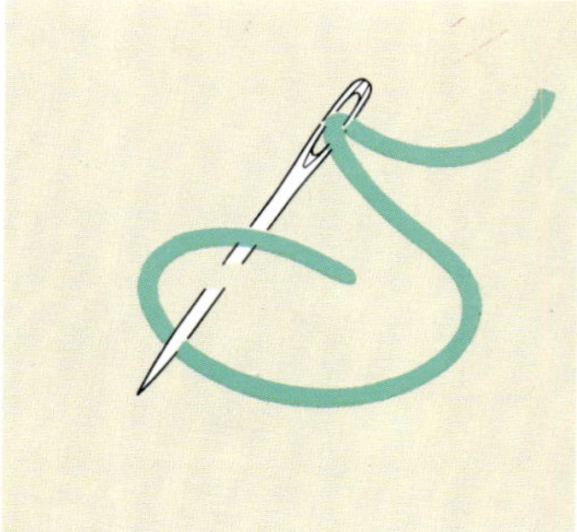

Long-and-short stitch
1. *Having worked a line of split stitch across the top, stitch alternate long and short stitches.*

2. *Work subsequent lines with all the stitches the same length, bringing the needle up into the end of each stitch in the previous line.*

Coral stitch
1. *Bring the needle through the fabric and place your thumb over the thread at an interval. Pierce the fabric and bring out the needle.*

2. *Take the thread from behind and loop it over the end of the needle. Pull the needle and a knot will form at the base.*

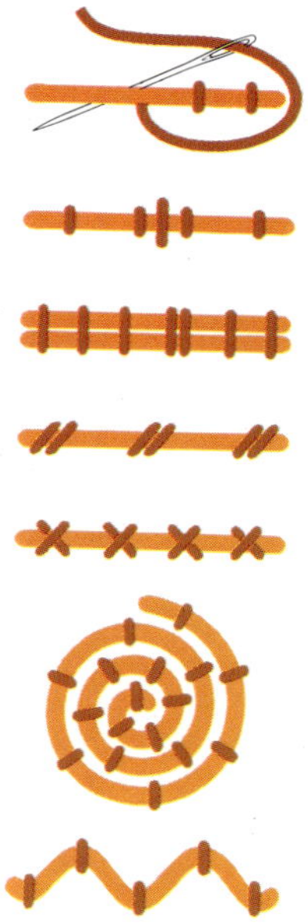

Above *Methods of couching laid threads. A thread is usually couched with small single stitches at regular intervals.* ***Below*** *Laid work is useful for filling large areas of work. The laid threads need to be couched, possibly with another couched thread making a contrasting pattern.*

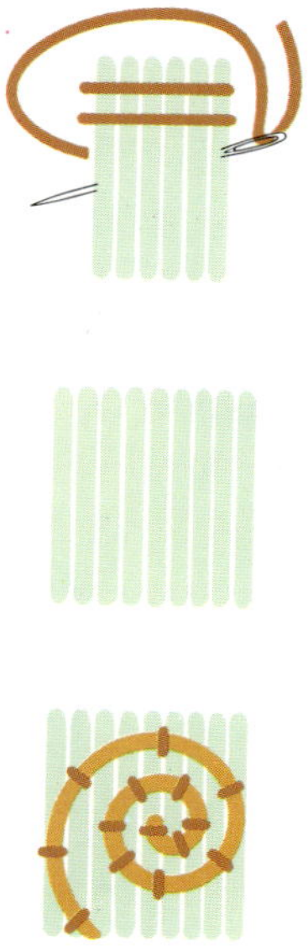

bringing the needle up into the end of each stitch in the first line and down into the fabric. Remember that in the second and subsequent rows the stitches are all the same length, until you come to the last row, when they will once again be long-and-short to fit the space.

When working this stitch within a specific space, it is advisable to mark the direction in which your stitches will be worked and angle the stitches towards the base. Remember not to make your stitches too short or you will not get the right effect. Quite a bit of practice is needed to achieve good results.

Shading is very much a feature of traditional crewel work and it can be achieved with other stitches as well as long-and-short, but good shading once again only comes with practice.

Coral stitch is usually worked from right to left. It is very useful as an edging stitch, and was used a lot in the crewel work of the seventeenth century for the veining of the leaves.

Bring the thread up at the beginning of the line to be worked. Hold the working thread down with the left thumb. With the needle at right-angles to the line, pick up a small portion of the material on either side of the line to be worked and pass the working thread under the point of the needle. The stitch is varied by the angle of the needle, the thickness of the thread and the spacing of the knots.

Couching The simplest method of couching is where one thread is laid on the surface of the material and another thread is used to hold the laid thread in place, with stitches at right-angles to the laid thread. This thread is usually finer, and, if worked in the same colour as the laid thread, can be virtually invisible.

Bring your needle up on one side of the thread to be couched and take it down on the opposite side, making a tiny stitch. Repeat along the line to be worked, leaving about 1/4 inch (6 mm) between the stitches. When you have finished a line, take the laid thread to the back of the work and fasten off with the finer thread. Cut the laid thread, leaving about 1/2

Right *This piece of crewel embroidery shows an interesting and varied selection of textures and patterns made with laid work. The central leaf motif is filled with laid threads, couched in straight lines. Others have been couched producing brick and lattice effects. Split and stem stitches have also been used, with French knots completing some details.*
Far right *This modern crewel work illustrates the strong, and imaginative decorative work that can be achieved with laid fillings. The squares and circles within the scalloped shapes have been filled with a mixture of embroidery stitches including stem, cross and split stitches, couching and knots.*

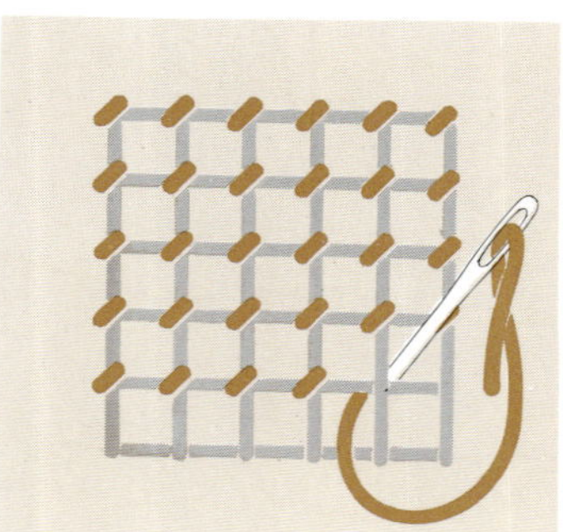

Laid fillings 1. *Work this laid design with long stitches placed to form a lattice, and tiny slanting stitches over the crossings.*

2. *Work straight cross stitches in a contrasting colour into every alternate square of the original lattice to produce this variation.*

3. *To achieve this design, stitch a block of four detached chain stitches into the corner squares of the lattice.*

4. *Over the original lattice, lay diagonal threads, and secure them at the intersections with small vertical stitches.*

5. Lay pairs of diagonal threads to form a diagonal lattice base, then work four small straight stitches at the intersections.

inch (1 cm) at either end. Remember that the laid thread is only taken to the wrong side of the work at the beginning and end of each line to be couched.

Using this method, any thickness of thread can be couched down, including rug wools, strings or cords, and any weaving yarns or threads which would not easily pass through a fabric. To pull a thick thread through to the wrong side of your work, use a large-eyed chenille needle and insert it into your fabric, leaving only the eye showing. Insert the laid thread into the eye and with a firm tug, pull it through to the wrong side. Fasten off securely.

Once you are familiar with the basic form of couching, there are many variations. The thread used to secure the laid thread may be the same colour or a contrasting colour. You can experiment by varying the length between the stitches, or by using other stitches to tie down, such as cross or chain stitch. Couching can also be worked in a circle or to fit any shape, as an outline or as a filling stitch. If the laid thread is pulled up between the stitches, which are then pulled tight, this is pendant couching.

Seeding is used as a filling stitch and involves working tiny straight stitches at all angles and in any direction, but of more or less even length and fairly close together. The stitches should be the same length as the thickness of the thread. Worked in a variety of threads, combining matt with shiny and wool with silk, seeding produces an interesting texture. If it is worked in a variety of colours, the stitches blend well.

Laid work These patterns of stitches were frequently used as fillings for the large leaf shapes so popular on the embroidered bed curtains and hangings of the seventeenth and eighteenth centuries. The Bayeux Tapestry was also worked partly in laid work. Today, laid work can be used to advantage for backgrounds, when economy in time and material has to be considered. It is quickly worked, and as all the threads are on the surface, no materials are wasted. Another advantage of laid work is that the colours can be blended. Designs should be bold, important and large.

It is almost impossible to work these fillings without a frame, as it is essential that the threads lie flat on the surface of the material. When doing laid work for the first time it is advisable to use wool. Threads are laid across the surface and these must be carefully secured with surface stitches.

Use a closely woven fabric, a linen twill or even a firm satin, and a stranded thread rather than a rounded one which does not cover the material quite so well. Thread two strands of crewel wool and start by bringing the needle up on the outline at the widest part of the shape to be worked. Insert it again on the opposite outline. Bring the needle up again close to this stitch, take it across and insert it just above the first stitch. Continue back and forth until the whole shape is filled, always making sure that the threads lie perfectly flat. Do not pull the stitches too tightly. To blend colours, you can either mix the strands of thread in your needle before going on to your next colour, or alternate your colours for a few rows.

After laying all the threads, they have to be couched down. Split, stem, couching, back and chain stitches are all suitable for this. These stitches can be worked at right-angles to the laid threads or in a pattern to complement the shape of your outline. As laid work is not very serviceable, it can be outlined afterwards to hold the shape with couching, or split stitch, or with a cord.

Once you have learned the art of laid work, you can experiment with the numerous laid filling stitches. Once again, long lines are laid across the shape and caught down, but instead of laying threads side by side, leave about 1/4 inch (6 mm) gap from the last stitch and work a series of spaced parallel stitches. Then work a second set of stitches over the first set, and at right-angles to it. Complete the filling by working a small diagonal stitch at the intersection of the crossed threads. These lines can also be set in a diamond pattern and a small upright stitch worked over the intersection. With this basic grid, any amount of patterns can be devised, using straight, cross and woven stitches. Laid fillings can also be worked over laid work, by working the square grid diagonally across the laid threads.

It is worth studying some of the examples of laid work on historical pieces. The veining of the leaves in the seventeenth-century hangings have inspired many fillings.

Left *To show their range of crewel wools, Appletons have produced a box of sample wools, ranged by shade on cardboard mounts.*

Left *Recently worked by Audrey Francini, this piece of American crewel embroidery shows delicate stitchery. She made use of an inventive variety of stitches, so creating eye-catching textures and unusual effects.*

Above *This is a piece of nineteenth-century American crewel work. The designs developed in the United States were often influenced by those prevalent in England, but were lighter, leaving a considerable amount of plain ground fabric, partly due to the fact that wool was not easy to obtain. The preferred stitches were those which used as little wool as possible: laid work was popular. This piece was embroidered in 1851, with a beautiful, fresh floral design in rich yet subtle colouring.*

Whitework, Cutwork, Drawn and Pulled Work

Whitework is a generic term covering the many styles of embroidery carried out using white threads and stitches on white fabrics. These styles of embroidery include surface stitches, cutwork, pulled fabric and drawn thread work. The stitches and methods have developed and become interrelated over the centuries, to produce yet more types of work, many identified by the areas where they originated. These include broderie anglaise, Ayrshire, Ruskin or Langdale linen, Mountmellick, Dresden and Madeira. Hardanger and Hedebo are other disinctive types of white embroidery.

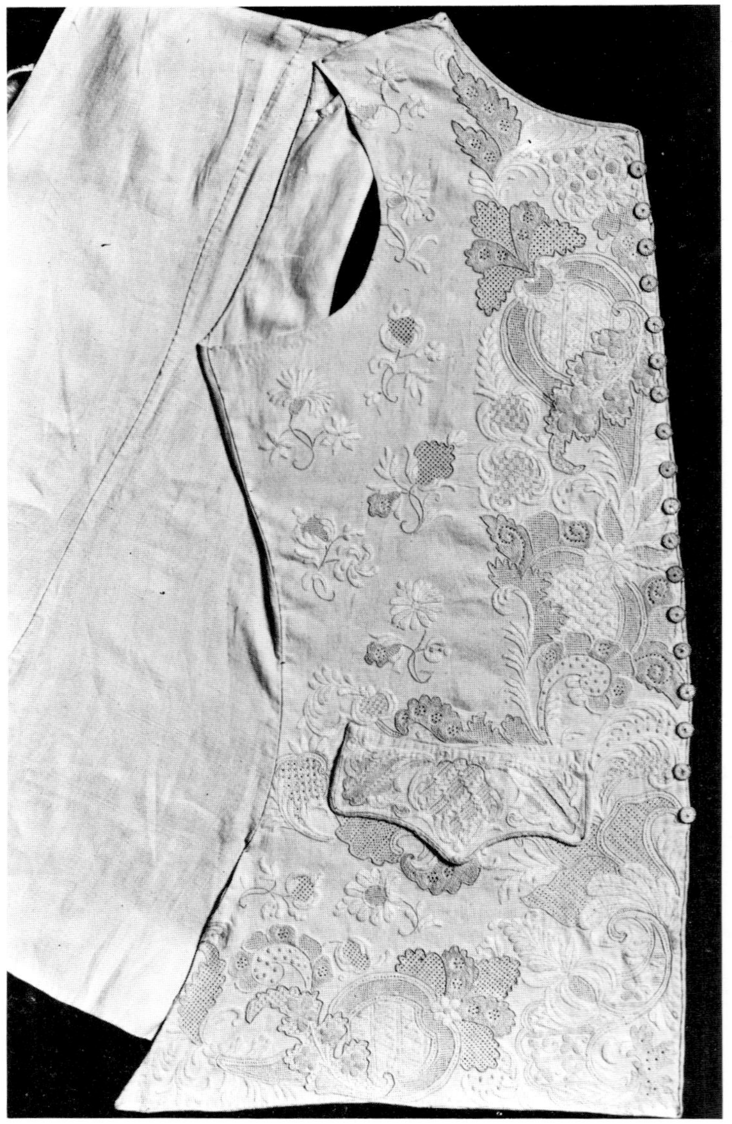

Left *A man's waistcoat in white embroidery and pulled work made in the early eighteenth century. It is a delicate piece of work that has remained in very good condition. Waistcoasts can be very decorative garments, and this is acknowledged in the extravagant curlicues of the design.*

History

Ever since man began to join skins and narrow pieces of fabric, stitches have been created as a form of decoration. As weaving evolved, the structure of fabric played an important part in the development of stitches. Homespun, loosely woven linens presented an obvious ground for drawn thread and pulled fabric work – the pulling together and whipping of ground threads to form lacy effects. Fine, closely woven linens and cottons were used for cutwork and surface embroideries; the beautiful fine muslins of India and the Middle East provided the inspiration for broderie anglaise and Ayrshire work.

From time to time, particularly in the Middle Ages, sumptuary laws banned the use of colour and rich work in embroidery and textiles. When this occurred, needlewomen gave more attention to white embroideries to express richness and delicacy.

Embroidery of the highest order has always been associated with religion, and for a long time whitework was only carried out in convents for church purposes. German whitework – *opus teutonicum* – of the thirteenth and fourteenth centuries was of particular importance as a contrast to the coloured silk and gold work of *opus anglicanum.* One of the earliest surviving pieces is a particularly beautiful Lenten cloth, dating from the thirteenth century and made at Altenburg on the Lahn. It is white stitchery on white linen fabric and shows a fine sense of composition, techniques and varieties of stitches including interlacing stitch.

In 1640, the English poet John Taylor wrote *The Prayse of the Needle,* making a statement on the value of embroidery for decoration and as part of education. He makes reference to "Frost-worke", a perfect name for the whitework of the sixteenth and seventeenth centuries. At this time, the coarse white surface embroidery had evolved to become more delicate, and motifs of flowers and leaves were combined with drawn thread fillings and Italian reticella work. Sometimes part of the work would be quilted, the design being back-stitched through two layers of linen, padding inserted

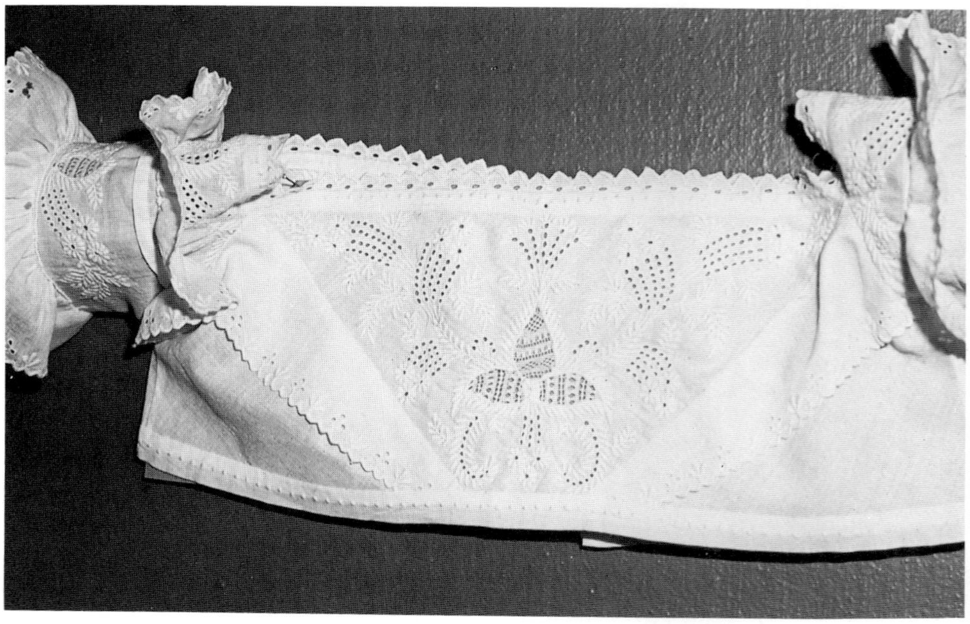

Below *A baby's yoke decorated with Scottish Ayrshire work and made in approximately 1840. It is worked in cotton on muslin and cotton, overcast with raised satin buttonhole in needlepoint lace. This type of work was very popular in Scotland, particularly for embellishing babies' bonnets and christening robes.*

from the back and the second fabric cut away from areas between the quilting. In these areas, pulled fabric stitches were worked, the whole presenting interesting variations of light and shade. Other rich effects were achieved by filling areas with French knots, outlining with fine cord and introducing silver-gilt thread on flowers and stems.

Whitework was now one of three main methods of embroidery used on clothes, the others being blackwork and silk embroidery. There are surviving examples of shirts, richly embroidered with whitework, known to have been worn by Charles I. One shirt of fine white linen had drawn threadwork along both sides of each seam; another had French knots, four-sided stitch, eyelets and double back stitch at the neck opening. Meticulously painted portraits from this period show the use of Italian reticella, and other forms of white embroidery on collars, cuffs and sleeves.

Every item of women's dress carried at least some embroidery. One sixteenth-century woman's coif with a matching triangular forehead cloth survives which is embroidered in whitework, using ladder-work, French knots and cutwork. A coif, usually about 20 x 10 inches (51 x 25 cm) was a small area in which the fashionable needlewoman was able to experiment with her stitches, and there is evidence of a great many variations.

The most interesting details are to be found on samplers, which were a record of design ideas and technical skills. Undoubtedly, much of the work on samplers consists of designs and stitches handed down from generation to generation. However, pattern books also began to appear in the sixteenth century; in 1566, an Italian book, *Giardineto novo di Punto* illustrated geometric and floral motifs, designs for shirt openings and two ABCs. Another, by Federico Vinciolo, was entitled *New and Singular Patternes and Workes of Linnen Serving for Patternes to make all sorts of Lace Edgings and Cut Workes* and was printed in England by John Wolfe in 1591.

Seventeenth-century embroiderers found inspiration in *The Needles Excellency* printed by James Boler in 1631 "At the Signe of the Marigold in Paules Church Yard" in London. Whitework samplers of this time, many of which are now in museums, show a diversity of patterns, and satin stitch, buttonholing, eyelets, French knots as well as cut and drawn borders and alphabets.

By the middle of the eighteenth century, embroidery designs had become much lighter. In particular, quilted waistcoats and petticoats showed whitework floral sprigs in satin, coral and cretan stitches, buttonhole and eyelets.

The development of overseas trade in the eighteenth and nineteenth centuries, brought cotton fabrics and much-prized fine Madras muslins. The demand helped to promote the cotton weaving industry in England and Scotland, and with it the production of very lovely, fine white embroideries for dresses and babywear. This style of white embroidery originated in Dresden work *(Point de Saxe)* which was imported into Britain and copied. It was worked in cotton threads on very fine cotton fabric and characterized by flowing, floral designs in back stitch, coral stitch and pulled fabric fillings. In 1782, and Italian embroiderer, Luigi Ruffini, set up a workroom in Edinburgh and trained apprentices to do fine embroidery in the style of Dresden work. These embroiderers produced the skills which the next generation were able to apply to Ayrshire work.

Ayrshire whitework

This type of embroidery, also known as "sewed muslin" or "Scottish Flowering", originated in the Scottish county of Ayr, where, in 1814, a Mrs Jamieson was lent a French christening robe inset with lace stitches. She copied these fillings and began to teach the techniques to local women, creating a cottage industry. By 1850, thousands of women were employed in factories to produce this type of embroidery. The women were called "flowerers" because the designs they produced were floral motifs. White cotton threads on white cotton muslins, lawns or cambrics were worked in padded satin stitch, stem stitch, eyelets, and fine needlepoint or drawn thread filling stitches so intricate that they resembled lace. Ayrshire whitework is particularly notable on baby clothes, christening gowns and bonnets as well as women's dresses and men's shirts, and was also worked on collars, cuffs and caps.

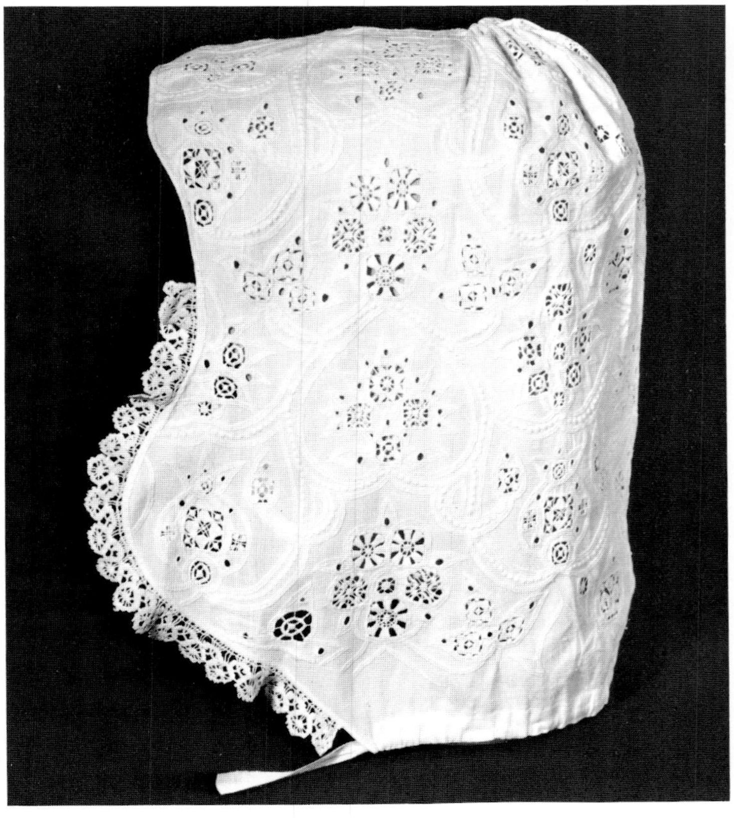

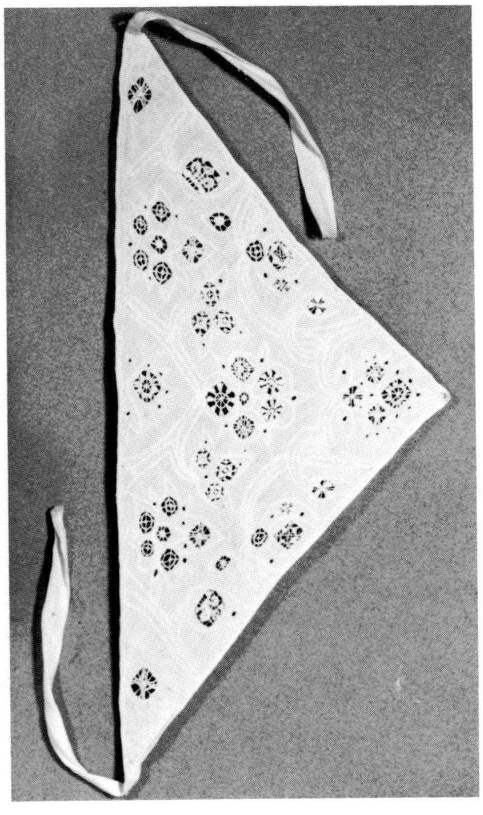

Left *A late sixteenth-century coif with a matching forehead cloth. A variety of different stiches and techniques such as ladder work, French knots and cutwork have been incorporated.*

Mountmellick

This work takes its name from a rural district in Ireland. About 1825, a time of great hardship, a local woman called Mrs Johanna Carter taught unemployed cotton weavers and other impoverished women how to embroider. They produced a distinctive type of whitework using thick white knitting cotton yarn on a heavy cotton sateen. The effect was heavier and more strongly textured than other styles of whitework. Designs for Mountmellick work usually featured wild flowers, leaves and fruits, especially blackberries, embroidered in padded satin stitch, French and bullion knots, coral and herringbone stitches, and a knotted line stitch now called Mountmellick stitch. It was a favourite style of work for bedspreads, nightdress cases, sachets, mats and other household items, and many pieces were finished with a heavy white cotton fringe. By the end of the century, English women's magazines were publishing patterns and instructions for use by amateur embroiderers.

Carrickmacross

Another type of Irish white embroidery, this style is named after the town of Carrickmacross where the technique was established as a cottage industry in the 1820s. It was revived in 1846 to help relieve poverty after the great potato famines. Carrickmacross work resembles lace, and consists of floral designs of fine cambric, cut and applied to a ground of hexagonal net. The cambric motifs are overcast onto the net; sometimes further decoration is added with chain stitches and pulled fabric work. Carrickmacross work is still produced commercially by outworkers who are managed by sisters of a convent in the town. The main items for sale are handkerchiefs, collars and cuffs, and wedding veils.

Other types of white embroidery

Forms of white embroidery are to be found in many countries throughout the world. These styles have either evolved independently or are the result of missionaries and nuns teaching the skills of their home countries to local women. These embroideries are often interpreted using indigenous threads and fabrics. A good example of this is the embroidery found in the Philippine Islands where a fibre is extracted from pineapple leaves and woven into *piña* cloth – a very fine lawn type of cloth. Floral motifs are embroidered in pulled fabric stitches, satin and buttonhole stitches using a matching thread. Table linen, shirts and blouses are produced for export and more use is made of silk threads on fine white cotton fabrics.

In Belgium, white embroidery on fine linen became an important luxury trade from the sixteenth century. There are records of a shop in Antwerp run by Martine and Catherine Plantin. The two sisters commissioned white embroidery from local workers, producing shirts, collars, and handkerchiefs with designs of stars, rosettes, fleur-de-lys and

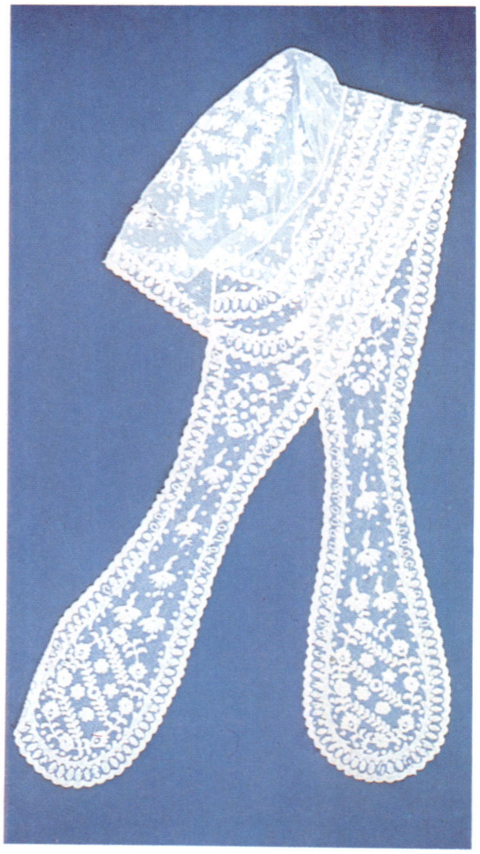

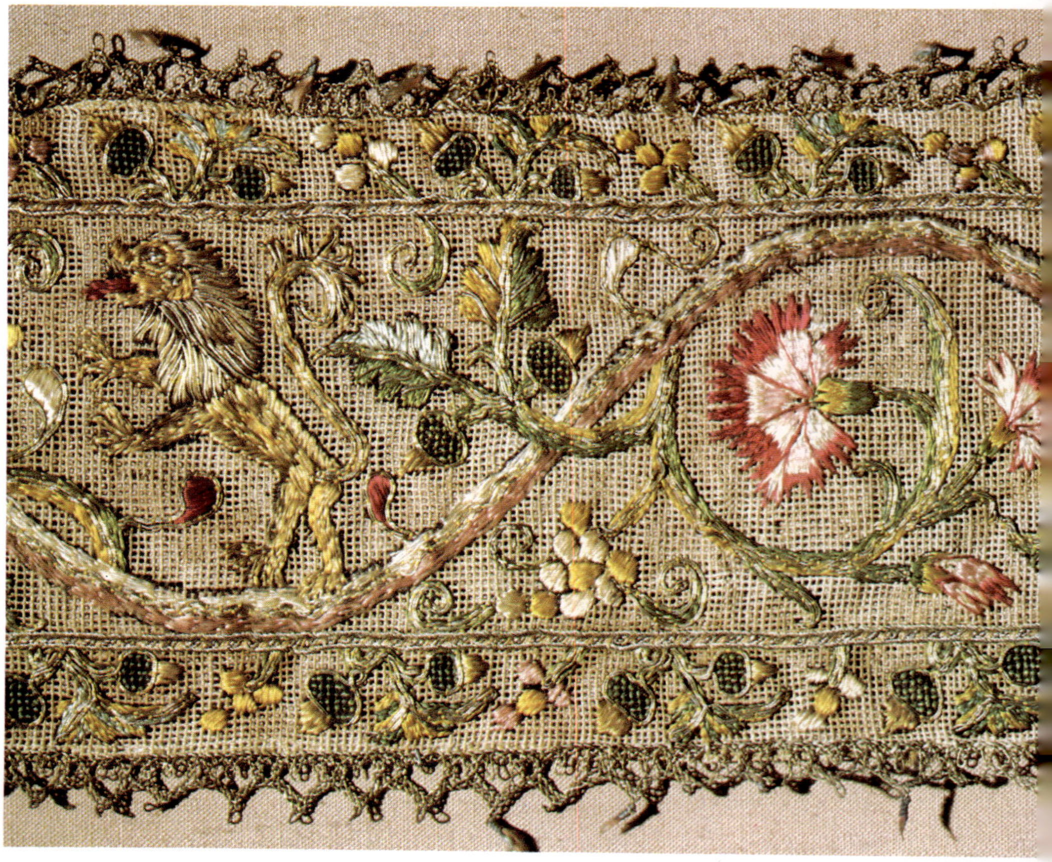

Left *An elaborate sachet made between 1880 and 1890 and decorated with Irish Mountmellick work. It is coarser than most other types of whitework, as it is sewn with thick knitting yarn on heavy cotton sateen.*
Above *A Pina cloth mat from the Philippines. This is one of the finest and most delicate varieties of whitework.*

Below *An Italian sixteenth century cut work border. It is sewn in coloured silks on linen with a border of silver gilt bobbin lace. Split and satin stitches have been used.*
Bottom left *A beautifully worked Carrickmacross bonnet from Ireland. The long lappets display the different techniques used in this kind of whitework.*

flowers in padded white stitches and forms of cutwork.

Crivos embroidery is a type of work produced in the Guimaraes district of Portugal. It features a raised effect achieved by the use of bullion knots and is often combined with drawn threadwork.

National costume, particularly that of Eastern Europe and Scandinavia, is richly embroidered; whitework in various forms may be seen on aprons, blouses, caps and bonnets. Notably, the very decorative regional head-dresses of France display white embroidery, lace and pleating in fine lawns and muslins. White embroidery is also seen in Dutch costume, shirts and bed-linen. The patterns are mostly geometric and worked in surface stitches, drawn thread, needleweaving or cutwork. Settlers from The Netherlands in South Africa wore a traditional poke bonnet made of white cotton and called a "kappie". It had a wide brim and was quilted and richly embroidered with floral sprays in surface stitchery.

White embroideries have flourished throughout the centuries and in many countries, showing great inventiveness in patterns and the use of stitches. Today, great changes in design and the increase of opportunities for experiment have been encouraged by movements like the Rural Industries Bureau, set up in 1921. One of its aims is "to foster rural crafts and revive those that have declined", including the traditions of quilting and whitework. Art colleges have also been encouraged to promote design and drawing, and, in 1934, the Needlework Development Scheme was set up by J.P. Coats of Glasgow to improve embroidery standards, especially in schools. One of their experts was Rebecca Crompton, an important pioneer in twentieth-century embroidery. Her revolutionary ideas promoted the use of abstract designs, unorthodox materials and the use of stitchery *across* a shape as well as to outline a shape. She produced many designs for cutwork and panels of embroidery, using white fabrics, nets, and even buttons. From the 1950s, there has been a revival in embroidery of all kinds, the greatest emphasis being on experiment and the expression of individual style.

Materials

The choice of materials and threads will depend on the purpose of your work, how it is to be used, how durable it has to be in wear and laundering, and the scale of design. It is always a good idea to work a sampler and experiment with threads and fabric.

Whitework usually demands a smooth fabric to emphasize the texture of stitches, and traditionally is worked in fine cotton or linen threads on fine cotton or linen lawn, muslin and cambrics. It is worth considering the contrast of matt cotton threads on a shiny

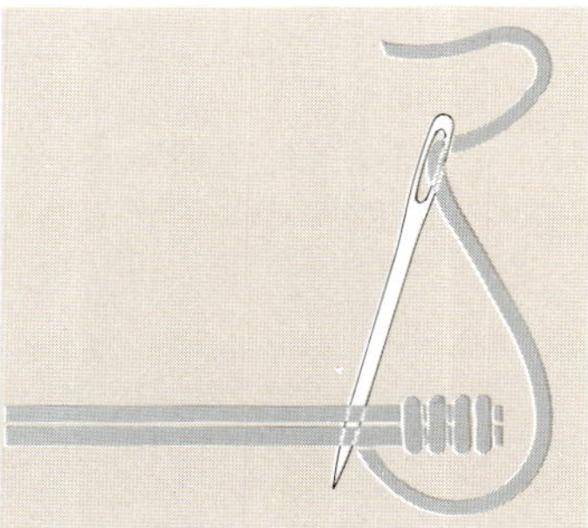

Trailing stitch *Work tiny satin stitches closely over several thin threads that have been brought through the fabric and laid down. Cover these padding threads.*

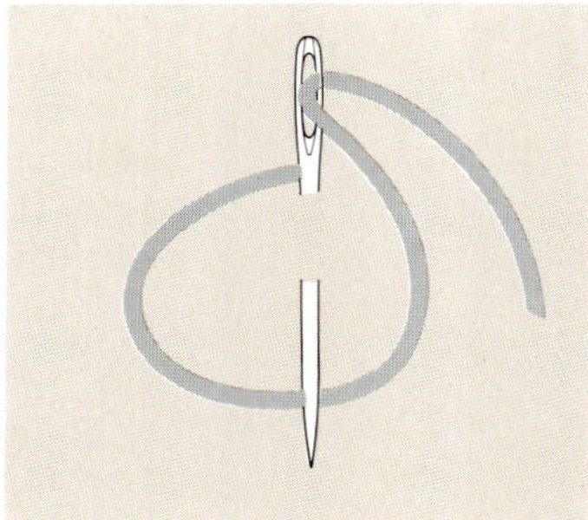

Chain stitch 1. *Work a stitch at the back of the canvas, trapping the thread in an oval loop on the front of the material as shown above.*

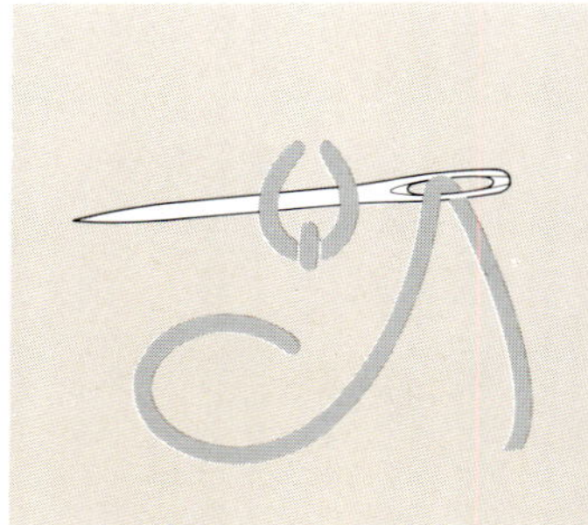

2. *Work subsequent stitches to form an interlocking chain, anchoring the final loop with one discreet overstitch. Use closely worked rows to fill an area.*

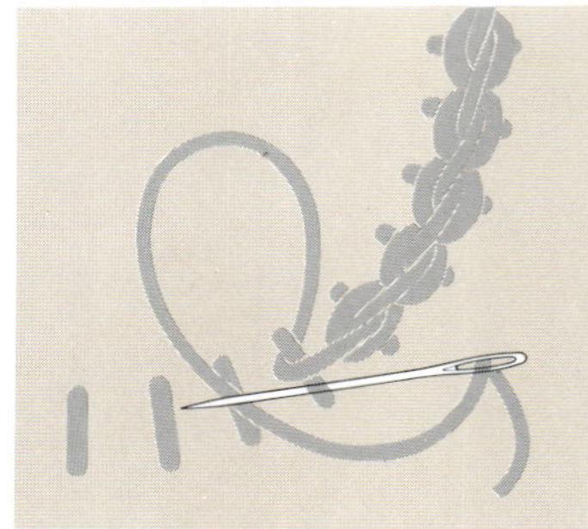

Raised chain band *Work a track of parallel horizontal stitches as shown, and work the chain stitches over these attaching each loop to a horizontal stitch.*

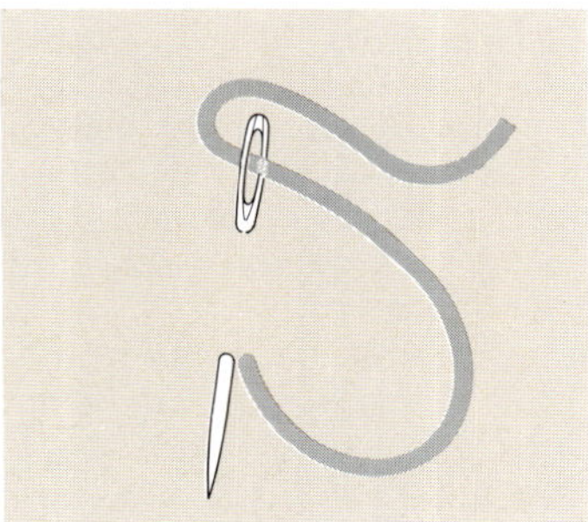

Sheaf stitch 1. *This stitch looks like a wheat sheaf, and each unit is made of vertical stitches worked close to each other and tied across the middle.*

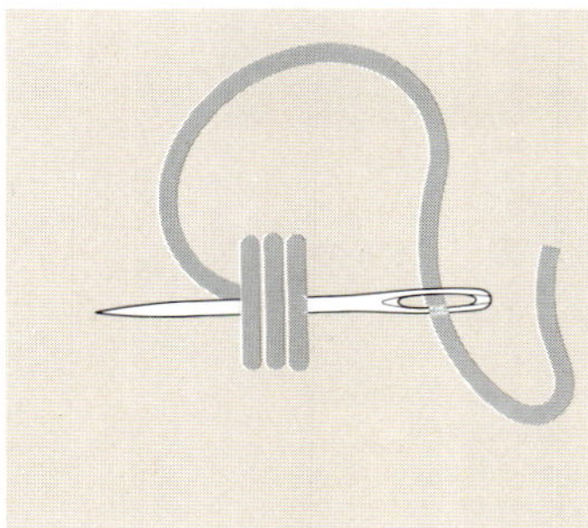

2. *Work three or four vertical stitches, bring the needle back up through the fabric and pass it twice between the threads and the fabric to tie the stitch.*

3. *Anchor it at the back and repeat for next stitch. These units can be scattered at random or arranged in lines. The tying stitches can be worked in a contrasting colour.*

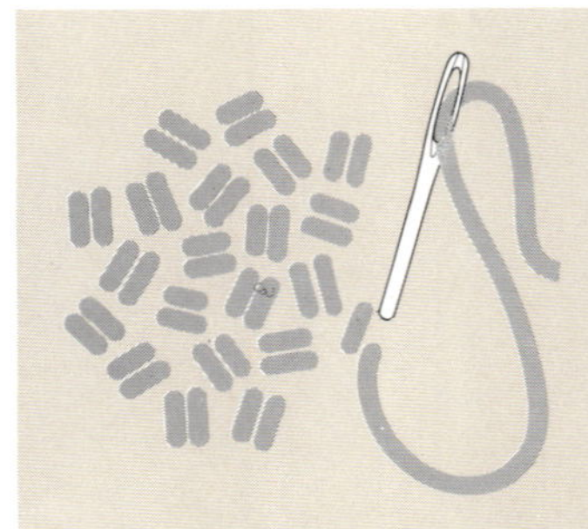

Seeding *This stitch is simple, attractive and useful for filling. Work small back stitches in pairs as shown, spacing them in different directions as required.*

Left *An English nineteenth-century false sleeve, decorated with broderie anglaise and lace fillings. The scalloped edges and simple repeated design are very characteristic of this type of work.*

satin fabric, or a wool fabric stitched with mercerized cotton threads like Sylko perle, especially for Mountmellick work. Several types and weights of thread could be used in one design.

Techniques

The best work is achieved by putting the fabric into an embroidery frame. When the work is completed and ready for pressing, cover the ironing board with a soft cloth or blanket and place the embroidery *face down* so that the pressing is done on the back. This ensures that the raised textures are preserved. Whitework can quickly become grubby if care is not taken to keep hands clean and dry.

Design

The essence of designing for whitework lies in the creation of different areas of light and shade. These are made by padded and knotted stitches and the contrast of textures produced by stitches and threads.

Sources of ideas include natural objects, such as flowers, leaves, tree shapes, lichens and butterflies, and buildings, the texture of brick and stone, and wrought-iron. It is always useful to keep a notebook for cuttings from magazines and sketches.

Using a brush and white paint on a tinted paper is an effective way of producing designs for white embroidery, as is cutting paper shapes and moving them about until a pleasing pattern is achieved. Background spaces are important for emphasizing the design; it is also important to remember that the design can be altered or added to as the the embroidery proceeds.

Stitches

Trailing stitch is a characteristic of whitework and is used for lines, stems, or veins of leaves. It is worked by laying three padding stitches and then overcasting with tiny stitches to completely cover the padding.

Raised chain band is a strongly textured line stitch, also used for finishing edges. The transverse stitches are worked first to provide a foundation for the looped top stitch.

Chain, stem and back stitch are also used as line stitches.

Cretan stitch is versatile and interesting to use because its appearance can be varied by the spacing or closeness of stitching.

French knots and bullion knots can be used as scattered fillings or closely textured as in Mountmellick work.

Seeding and sheaf stitches are just two of many scattered filling stitches. Seeding consists of

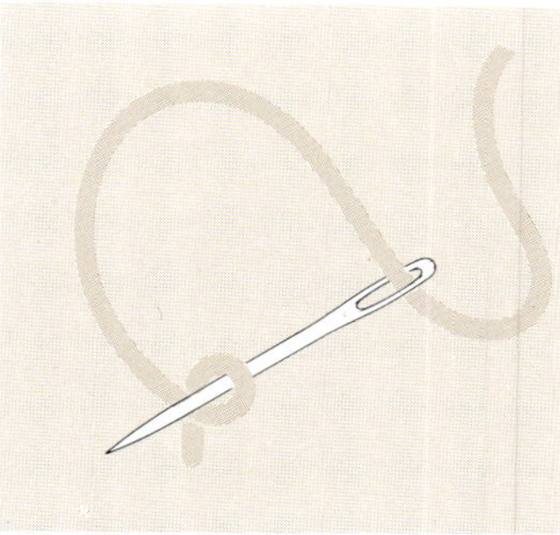

French knot 1. *Wrap the thread firmly round the needle fairly near the point. Use free hand to keep the thread taut, and insert the needle in the fabric.*

2. *Pull the needle through to the back, leaving a neatly formed knot on the right side of the fabric. This filling stitch can be spaced as densely as required.*

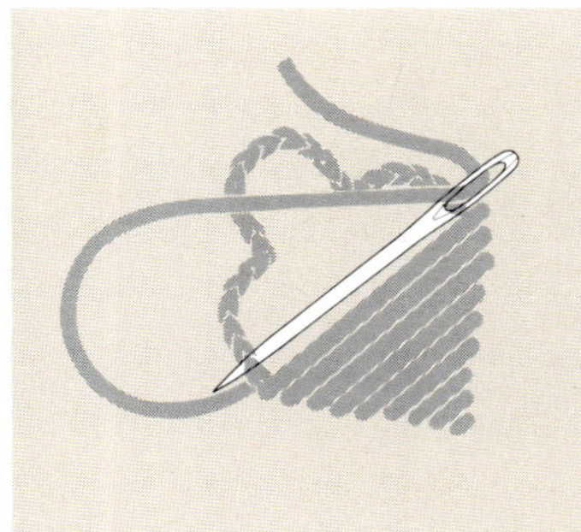

Padded satin stitch 1. *Sew round the shape to be filled with any outline stitch and block it in carefully with horizontal satin stitch covering up the initial outline.*

2. *The second layer of satin stitch can then be worked over the first in whatever direction is desired. The final effect should be of a raised shape, evenly worked.*

Cretan stitch *This stitch, popular for borders, is made up of upside-down interlocking Y-shapes. Work it horizontally, spacing the units.*

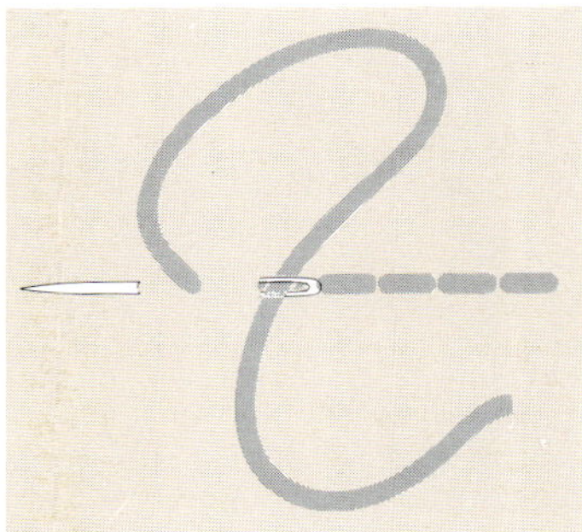

Back stitch *This is one of the plainest outline stitches. Work small horizontal stitches as shown, that do not overlap, although they will on the back of the fabric.*

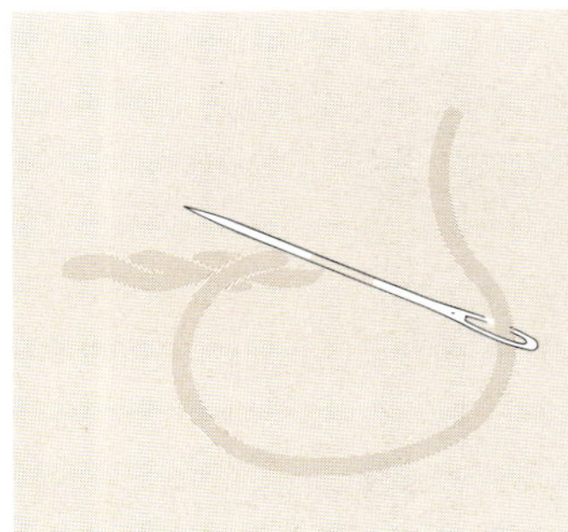

Stem stitch *This outline stitch is formed by working small overlapping back stitches and keeping the thread held below the needle throughout.*

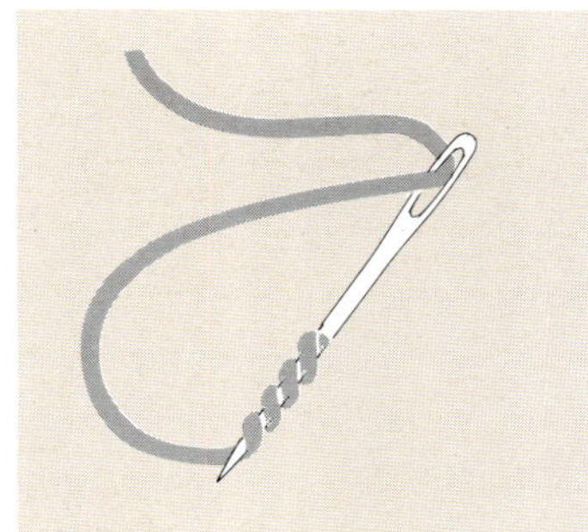

Bullion knot *Work a back stitch leaving enough slack to wrap round the point of the material six or seven times as shown. Pull through carefully and secure.*

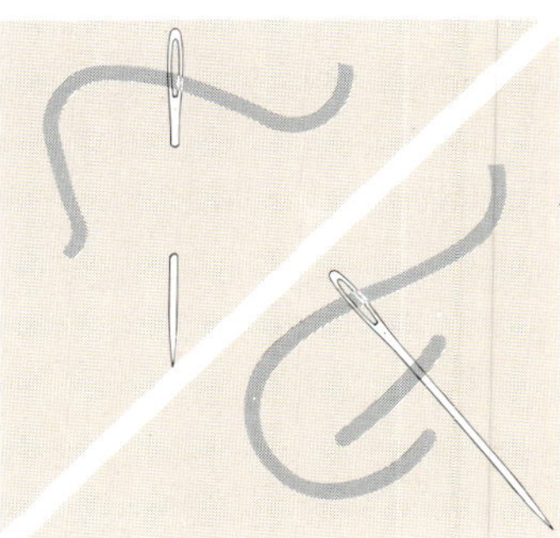

Mountmellick stitch
1. *Start off by working a half cross stitch and bring the needle up as if to complete this cross. Place the needle under the existing stitch.*

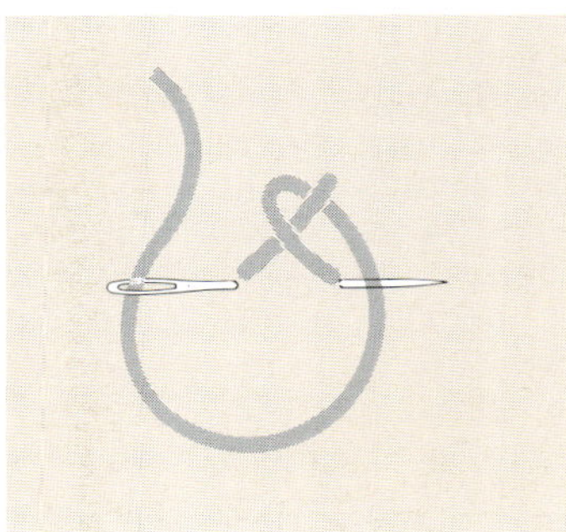

2. *Do not penetrate the fabric; simply pull the needle through as shown and work a stitch at the back of the fabric that spans the base of the cross stitch.*

3. *Pull it through gently. This stitch cannot be worked tightly. Work another stitch vertically at the back of the fabric the same height as the first unit.*

4. *The linking loop between the two units will act as the initial half cross so that the entire procedure can be repeated. Work as evenly as possible.*

small back stitches worked in random directions and spaced as required. Sheaf stitch is composed of groups of three or four long stitches tied across the centre by two back stitches.

Padded satin stitch is an important whitework stitch giving a rich, raised effect. Satin stitches are worked over a padding of rows of chain, running or stem stitches.

Broderie Anglaise

Broderie anglaise, or English white embroidery, is a lovely type of whitework, which, despite its name, occurs in many countries. It is particularly common in Czechoslovakia and Poland for decoration on caps and blouses. In Finland, this type of embroidery was used on household linen and on brides' handkerchiefs, masterpieces of fine work on linen or cotton cambric.

Broderie anglaise became very popular in Britain during the nineteenth century and was used for baby clothes, children's dresses and nightdresses. The Victorian lady found this repetitive style most agreeable to work and produced many yards of broderie anglaise with scalloped edgings, for use on petticoats, drawers, and cotton day-dresses. The white detachable undersleeves called *engageants*, worn under the big sleeves of dresses, were often embroidered with broderie anglaise eyelets, and sometimes there were collars to match. Aprons worn for "show" were decorated with whitework and broderie anglaise.

Broderie anglaise can be distinguished from Ayrshire whitework by the simplicity of its design. It consists of repetitive eyelets, round or oval in shape. Sometimes designs are entirely worked in these open eyelets, but other designs include solid satin stitch spots or simple leaf sprays. Stems and scrolls are worked in overcast or stem stitch, and scalloping is the usual method of finishing edges.

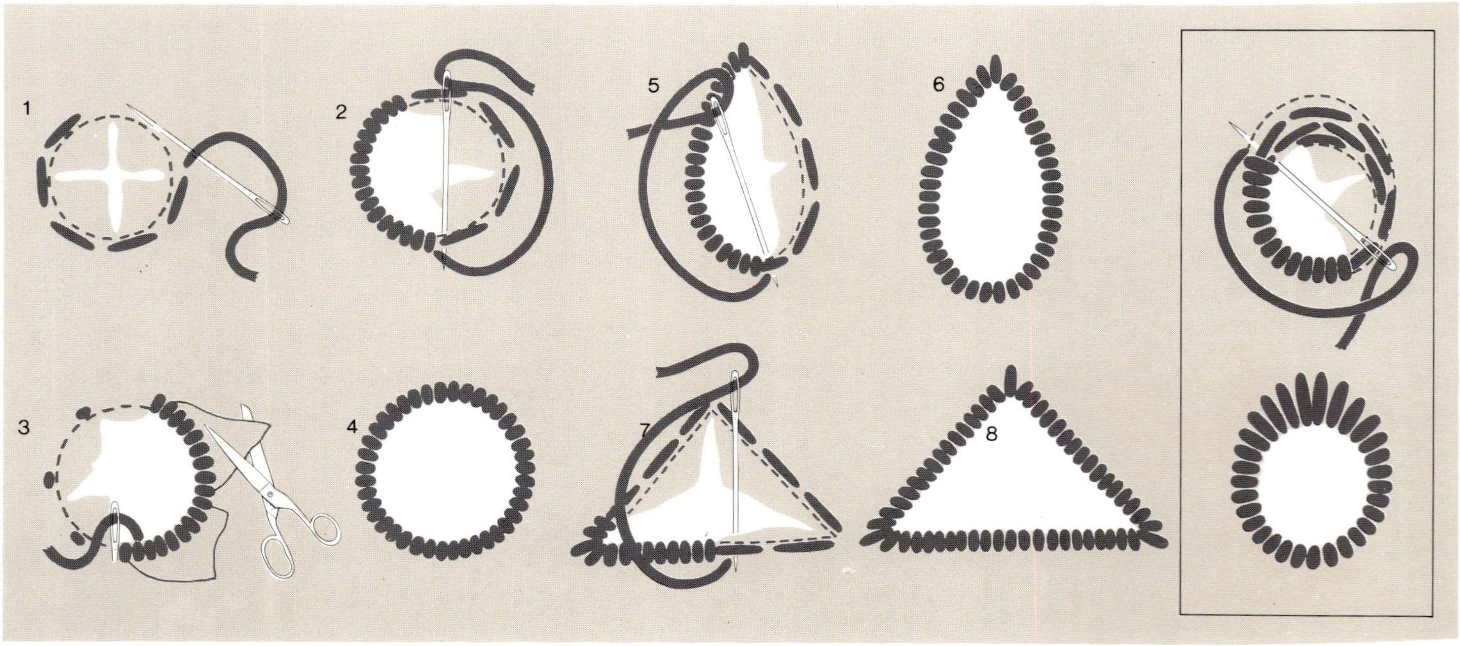

Materials

Use soft, mercerized cotton threads, such as coton à broder, on smooth, closely woven fabrics. An embroidery stiletto is useful for piercing the fabric to work small holes, and a pair of fine, sharp scissors is necessary for cutting larger eyelet holes and scallop edges.

Broderie anglaise is usually worked in the hand, but if the design includes solid forms in satin stitches, a frame would be an advantage.

Techniques

Designs should include round or oval eyelets and can be applied to edgings, or as flowing, free motifs. Eyelet holes should be outlined in running stitches – two rows for large holes. The holes are then cut across and the fabric taken to the back. The hole is overcast with small stitches, and the turnings on the back of the work carefully trimmed. Large holes can be given a raised effect by working the overcasting over padding stitches. For small holes, work a running stitch outline, pierce the centre with a stiletto and overcast the hole.

Buttonhole stitch is used for scalloped edges, the stitches gradually getting smaller towards the top or point of a scallop. Small scallops should be padded with rows of running stitches and deeper curves padded with chain stitches. Lines can be worked in stem or chain stitch but an overcast stitch gives the richest effect.

Madeira work

A development of broderie anglaise, Madeira work was introduced to the island of Madeira, situated off the northwest coast of Africa, by nuns who taught it to the local peasant women. Since 1856, when Miss Phelps, daughter of an English wine merchant, started a small business by giving local girls English designs to embroider, the industry has developed extraordinarily. These embroideries were so successful in London that Miss Phelps was able to start an export business, which is now a principal source of income for the island and employs thousands of women, most of whom work at home. They produce blouses, handkerchiefs and table linen, and the embroideries are collected and finished by laundering and pressing in "factories". As well as the eyelets and buttonholed edges typical of broderie anglaise, Madeira work includes surface embroidery, and cutwork with rich padding and buttonhole bars. It is generally carried out in white or blue threads on white fabrics, but there are also lovely pieces worked in ecru on cream.

Cutwork

Cutwork, or *opus scissum,* is a term given to embroidery in which the background of the design is cut away. Up to the sixteenth century, cutwork was mainly worked in convents, but later it became a popular technique with needlewomen of all classes. There are many beautiful seventeenth-century samplers showing cutwork and drawn thread embroidery, worked on evenly woven fine linens with matching threads. Parchment was often tacked to the back of the ground fabric to ensure ease of working when the fabric was cut. This style is normally carried out in white or natural threads, but there are examples of Italian cutwork where the embroidery is worked in coloured silks.

In England, cutwork appears to have come from Flanders and Italy, and was used a great deal for shifts or chemises, the embroidery showing at the neckline of the dress. Elizabeth I wore a great deal of cutwork embroidery and a reference to this, dated 1586, states "bought 6 yds good ruff lawn well worked with cutwork for 60 shillings". Stephen Gosson, in 1596, wrote of cutwork aprons, "so quaintly cut and richlie wrought".

Greece, particularly the island of Corfu, is long acknowledged to be the source of very fine embroidery. Here, a type of linen cutwork was produced known as Greek Lace. Venetian needlework was much influenced by this; eventually the two styles merged to become puntoreticella, recognized as the first needlepoint lace. Reticella is geometric in character with squares and triangles, and needle-woven bars.

Cutwork continued to evolve in many countries, was produced and worn by all classes of people, and has enjoyed revivals up to the present day.

Langdale linen or Ruskin work

During the nineteenth century, in England, there was a notable revival of needlework in the Lake District, encouraged by the poet John Ruskin (1819-1900) who lived at Brantwood on the shores of Lake Coniston. Ruskin was concerned for the well-being of

Making cut shapes 1. *Sew running stitches round and make cuts across the centre.* ***2.*** *Fold the corners back and overstitch the edges.* ***3.*** *Turn the fabric over and cut off the corners.* ***4.*** *The finished circles should be neat.* ***5, 6.*** *Use the same method for an oval, making one end pointed.* ***7, 8.*** *A triangle must have longer overstitches at the corners with deep cuts.* ***(Inset)*** *Shadow eyelets are made by working rows of running stitches then working graded overstitching.*

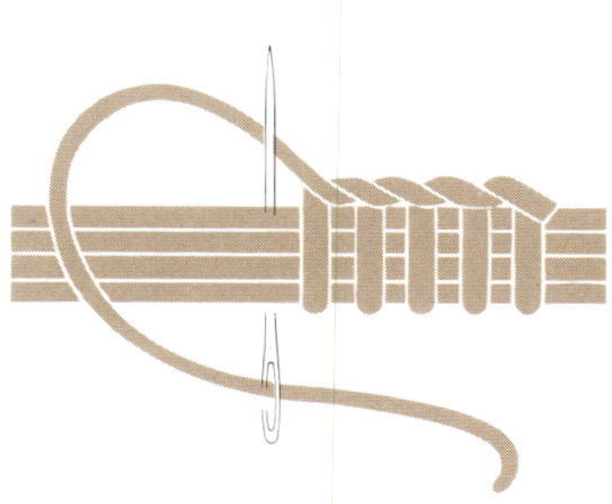

Buttonhole stitch *Used a great deal in cutwork, this stitch is similar to blanket stitch, but the upright vertical stitches are worked closely adjacent with no gaps.*

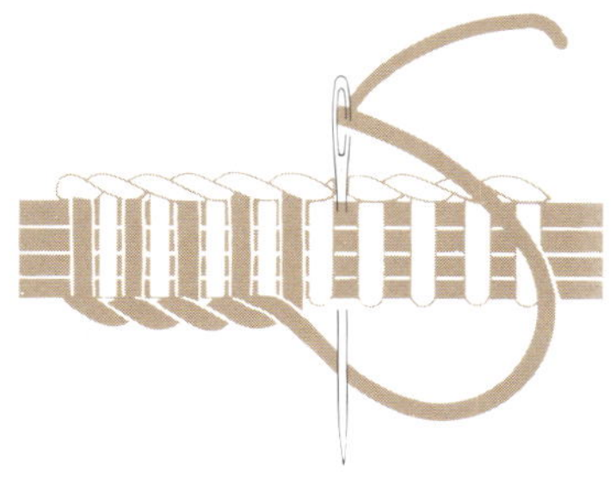

Double buttonhole stitch *For this stitch, small gaps must be left between the stitches in the initial row so that those of the facing row can be slotted in between them.*

Reticella 1. *Select the square and tack round the outline with small even running stitches. Cut out four windows as shown.*

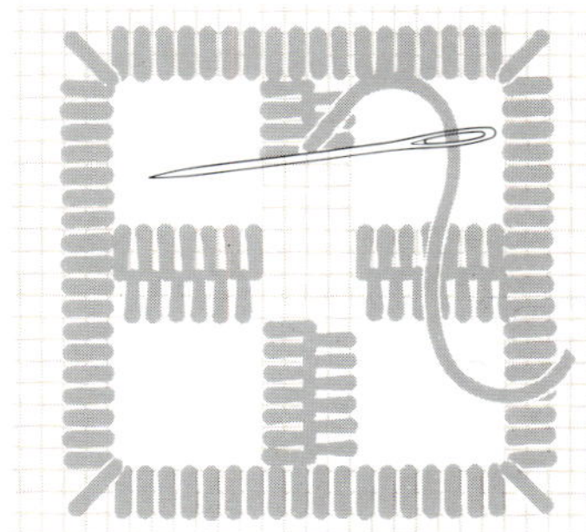

2. Over stitch carefully round the outline, working a diagonal over stitch at each corner, and continuing through the bars as shown.

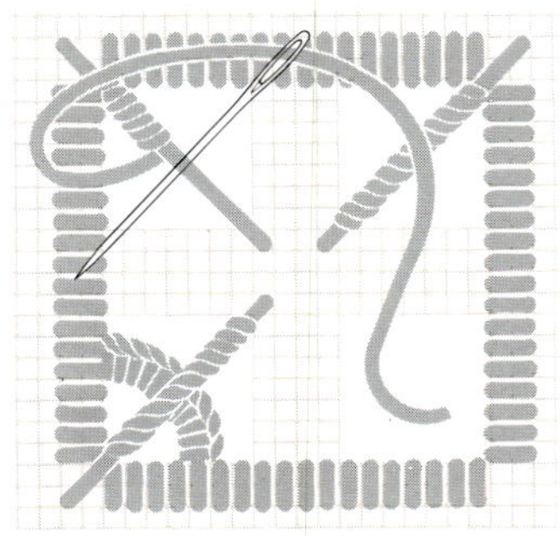

3. Work the bars as woven bars. A small square of canvas will be left in the centre. This basic unit can then be further decorated as required.

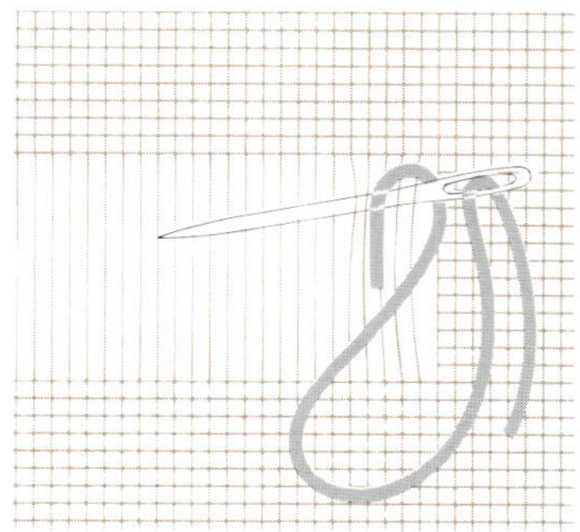

Overcast bar 1. *Align working thread with the vertical threads that will make up the overcast bar. Start to bind them all into a bundle as shown.*

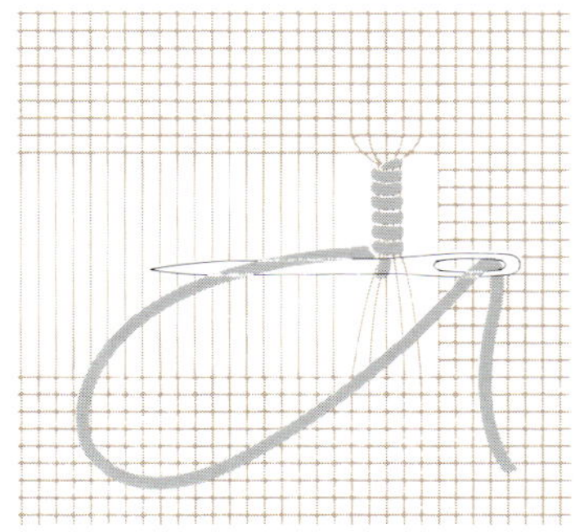

2. Keep coil neat and firm by pushing the wrapping threads close together without letting them overlap. Make sure the remaining thread stays taut.

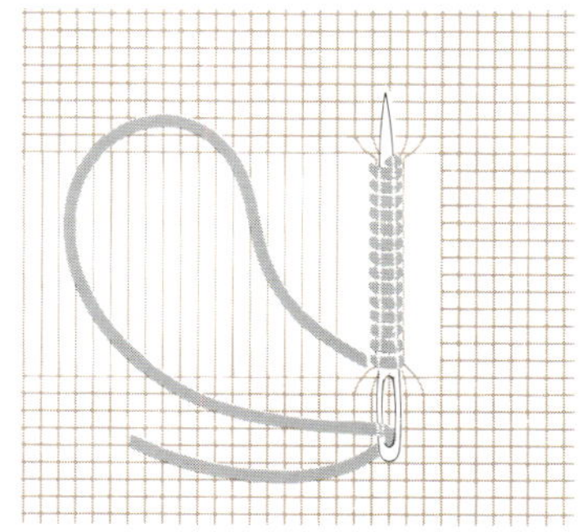

3. Having wrapped the bar to the bottom of the drawn thread area, take the needle straight back up the bundle to anchor it and pull it through.

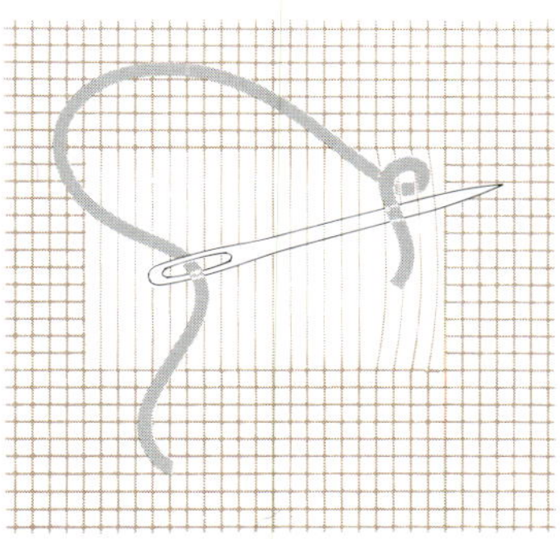

Woven bar 1. *Align working thread with the four fabric threads to be used for the first bar. Work the needle over two, under two and back in a figure of eight.*

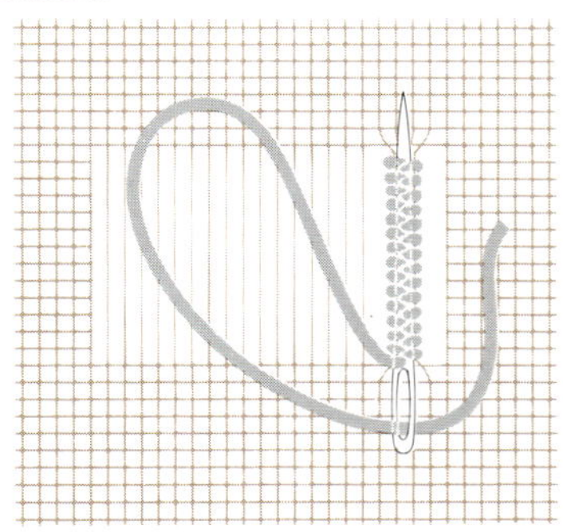

2. Work tightly down to the bottom of the fabric threads, pushing the figures of eight up against each other. End off as for the overcast bar shown above.

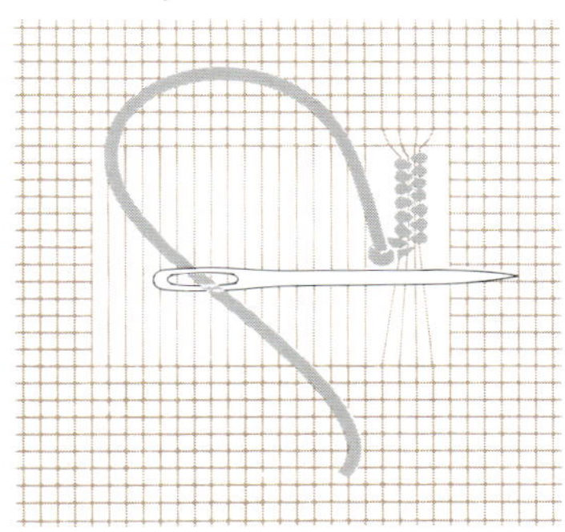

Woven bar with picot 1. *Work half of woven bar in normal fashion, and then form a small loop having brought the needle up in the centre under two threads.*

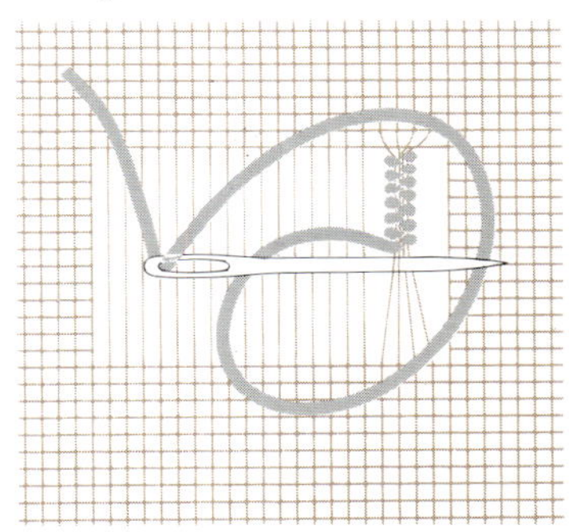

2. Pull it through, and then form another loop or picot in the same way, exactly opposite one the other side. Weave the other half of the bar again as normal.

the local people and wanted them to be "busily occupied in one of the natural pursuits of life; either at home or in the field". Since flax grew well in the Langdale valley, this was a natural source of inspiration, and, when Albert Fleming and his housekeeper, Miss Twelves, came to live near Ruskin in 1883, all three worked enthusiastically to reinstate the old skills of spinning and weaving. Spinning galleries built onto the homes of the villagers became a feature of the Lakeland scene, and village social life was greatly enhanced by spinning "bees" or "tea-parties". Women would sit spinning and weaving while exchanging gossip, and soon were producing evenly woven linen which had about 32 threads per inch.

John Ruskin had close ties with Venice, which may account for the reticella designs which were embroidered on this Langdale linen. The patterns were passed from one generation to another and Langdale linen is still being made and sold today, especially in the district around Grasmere. The geometric patterns are always enclosed in a frame of "open hem" with a padded roll immediately inside it. This roll is important because it carries the foundation threads inside the cut area, on which the needlewoven bars, bullion knots and points are worked.

Modern cutwork

Simple cutwork The cut background spaces are quite small and need no reinforcing.

Renaissance cutwork The design is more open and the larger background spaces are bridged with buttonholed or woven bars. These bars are always worked before the surrounding buttonhole edging to the design motif. The background fabric is cut away last of all.

Richelieu cutwork This is similar to Renaissance work, with the addition to the bars of loop, bullion or buttonhole picots, crossbars and buttonhole wheels. Ladderwork is sometimes introduced.

Venetian cutwork The most elaborate form of cutwork, Venetian cutwork incorporates padding, filling stitches, satin stitch spots and eyelets. Outlines are worked in high relief over rows of chain stitch padding.

Materials

It is important to consider the purpose and relationship of the embroidery to the finished article, how simple or elaborate the work should be and the suitability of different threads and fabrics. Cutwork can be made strong enough for household linen, or elaborate, delicate and lacy for dress wear. Materials are smooth, plain fabrics and threads of coton à broder or stranded cottons.

Techniques

Designs can be repetitive for borders or single motifs. Cut paper shapes are a good way of starting to plan a simple piece. Arrange these on a dark background, remembering that the background spaces are as important as the motif. More elaborate types of cutwork may have more of the background cut away, with bars introduced to connect points and spaces which need strengthening. Bars should be carefully spaced. There is plenty of scope for making interesting effects by adding surface stitches, using coloured threads, or contrasting linings.

Stitches include buttonhole edgings, buttonhole bars, woven bars, picots, knots, surface stitches, and small powdered fillings.

Hardanger

This striking style of embroidery comes from the Hardanger district of western Norway. About the middle of the eighteenth century, the women of Hardanger were spinning flax and weaving linen fabric with a characteristic double thread in both warp and weft. It was on this type of fabric that Hardanger embroidery was developed, using thick cotton or linen threads.

Traditionally, Hardanger was for festive wear, aprons and head-dresses, for sheets and pillowcases, and for shirts for the bride and groom. The regional costume worn by the women of Hardanger, and still seen sometimes on Sundays or at festivals, consists of a long-sleeved blouse, red waistcoat, full-length black skirt and a long white apron. Bands of Hardanger embroidery feature on the apron and on the sleeves of the blouse.

Designs for the embroidery are geometric and composed of drawn thread squares and cross-shapes, edged with blocks of satin stitches called "kloster" blocks. Eight-pointed stars and needlewoven bars are also common. This hardwearing style of embroidery has not changed very much since the

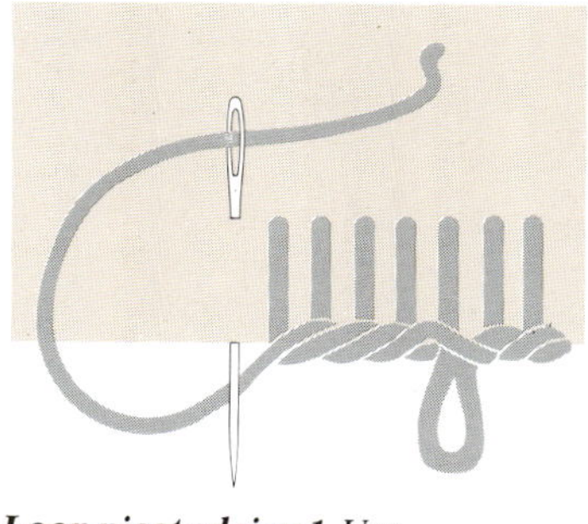

Loop picot edging 1. *Use buttonhole stitch to edge the fabric, and at the desired point place a pin in the edge and loop the thread behind.*

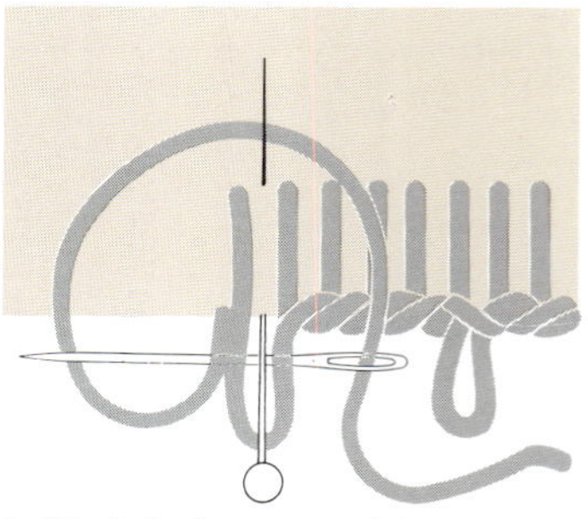

2. Work the long arm of the next buttonhole stitch, and continue working these stitches along the edge.

Above *A child's dress made in about 1870, featuring Richelieu cutwork. This is very similar to Rennaisance cutwork. Both are striking and rather dramatic types of whitework.*
Right *A traditional square of reticella work owned by the Embroiderers Guild. Reticella was originally an Italian technique, and was worked mainly in Venice during the fifteenth and sixteenth centuries.*
Far right *A cutwork mat in the Richelieu style owned by the Embroiderers' Guild.*

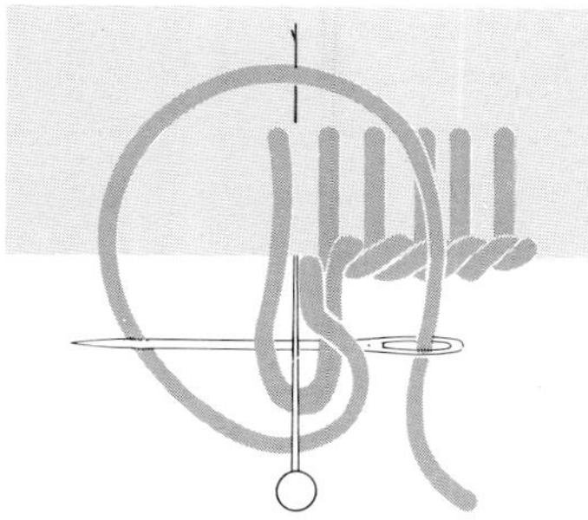

Venetian picot edging 1. *Work buttonhole stitches to the point for the picot and insert a pin in the edge of the fabric. Pass the looped thread behind the pin.*

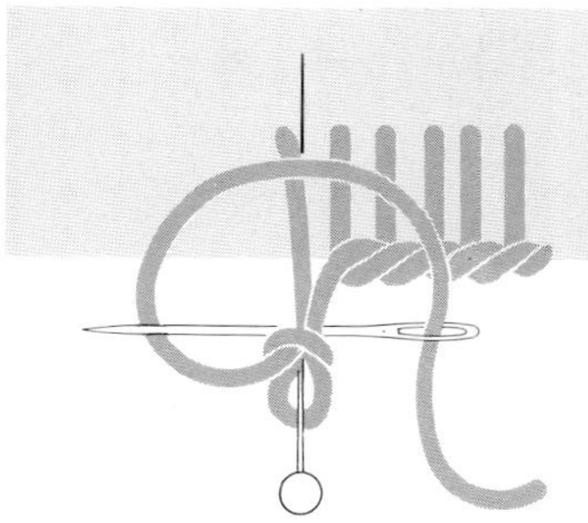

2. *Take the needle behind the loop, and make side stitches up the neck of the loop.*

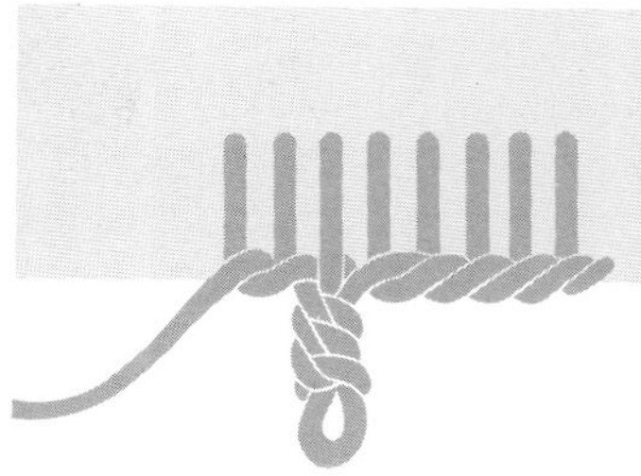

3. *Make about three side stitches, then continue with the buttonhole edging.*

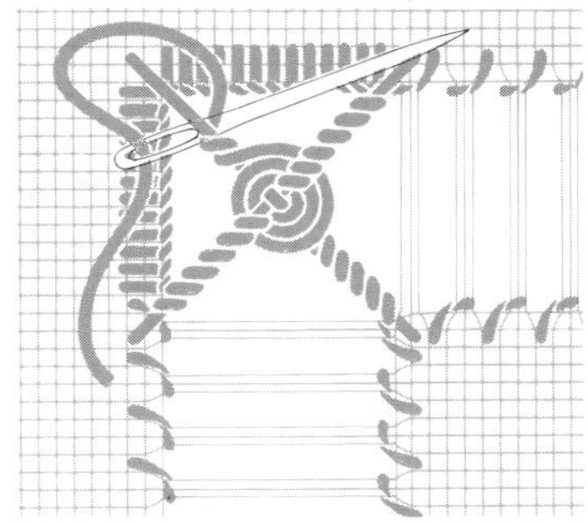

Dove's eye filling *Having oversewn one laid cross thread, oversew half the other then weave the thread round before oversewing to corner.*

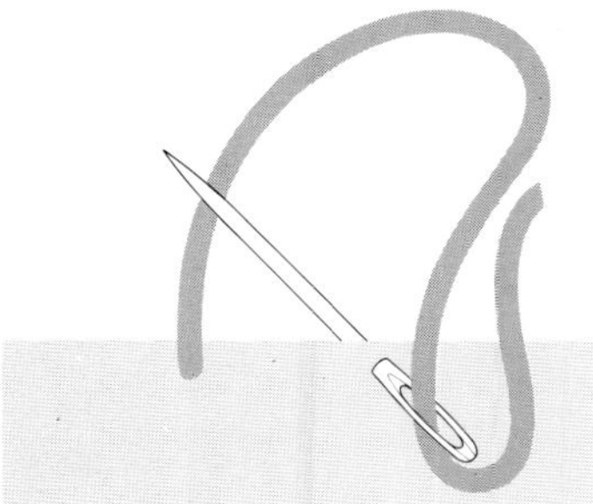

Pyramid filling 1. *This can be used as an edging or a filling. Make a large loop and take the needle through the edge of the fabric.*

2. *Place a pin in front of the loop, and take the thread from behind, through the loop, behind the pin and back through.*

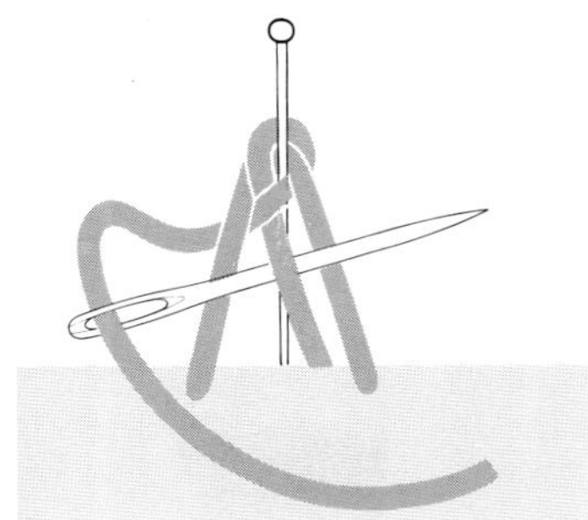

3. *This is the beginning of the woven pyramid, three vertical threads being available for weaving round.*

4. *Continue weaving with the threads worked close together, until you reach the base.*

eighteenth century, and it is still made, often for the tourist trade.

Materials

Fabrics should be of even texture to allow threads to be drawn. Hardanger fabric is available with 18 to 24 threads per inch. Mercerized threads such as perle cotton no. 5 should be used for working kloster blocks and other surface embroidery, while a finer thread – no. 8 – is suitable for needlewoven bars and filling stitches.

Techniques

Designs are based on squares and the counted thread of the fabric, using the same number of threads each way. Graph paper is useful to plan ideas.

The work is always started by outlining the design with kloster blocks of satin stitches. Each block is usually composed of five satin stitches worked over four threads of the fabric, or seven stitches worked over six threads. When all the kloster blocks are completed, the area within each motif is cut away and threads withdrawn. Threads that are left may be overcast or woven.

Other stitches to use are dove's eye filling, ribbed wheel, and star eyelet. Triangles and star motifs can be worked in satin stitches.

Hems on table linen can be finished with mitred corners and hemstitching, while small mats can be finished with cross stitch and fringed raw edges.

Hedebo

Hedebo, or Hedebosyning, is a form of white Danish embroidery, originating in the Hedebo region south of Copenhagen. During the eighteenth century, in certain areas of Denmark, better economic conditions gave women more time for needlework. One such area was Hedebo, where the land was fertile and the farmers prosperous. Here, women produced fine linen fabrics for their embroidery, which subsequently developed into a splendid branch of Danish folk art.

It was considered very important for a girl to have a well-appointed trousseau and work

Hedebo filling 1. *This is created with a mixture of cutwork and needlepoint lace. Using a pencil, wind then secure a ring of threads.*

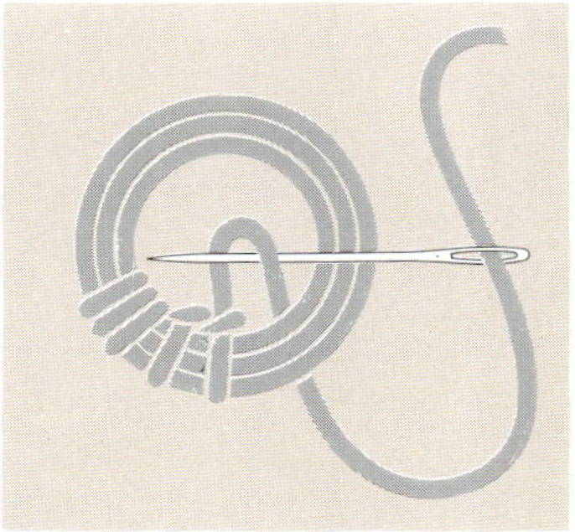

2. *Work around the ring with buttonhole stitches, making them firm but not too tight.*

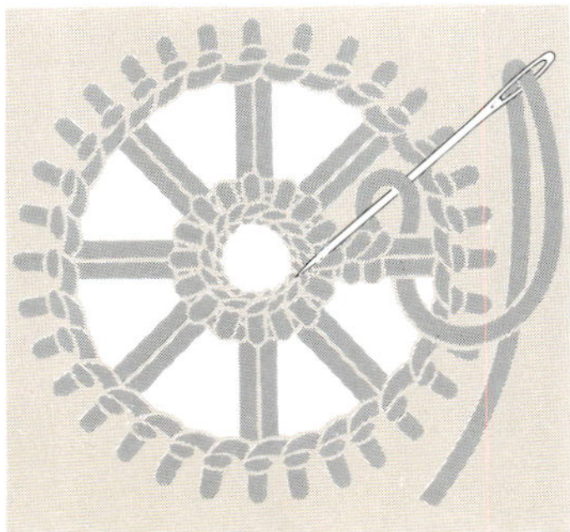

3. *Having made a cutwork circle and outlined it with buttonhole stitches, place the ring in the centre, and work double bars across.*

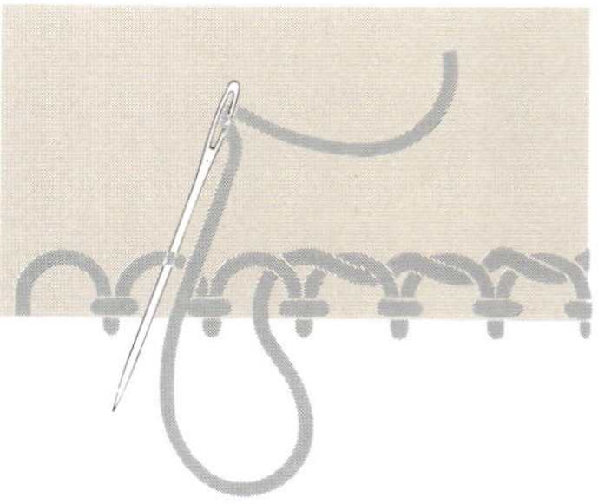

Hedebo edging *This second step, showing an interweaving thread, is made after the Hedebo twisted buttonhole has been worked.*

was begun on household linen and pillow-cases with open-work embroidery, when she was five or six years old.

From about 1760 to 1820, Hedebo embroidery showed a lot of surface embellishment. Floral motifs were overcast or outlined in chain stitch and filled with drawn thread work. During the next 30 years, designs were formal, and included cutwork fillings based on Italian reticella. From the 1850s to the present time, Hedebo embroidery has incorporated circular cut holes with lace fillings, and Hedebo edging.

Materials

Evenweave fine linens and cottons worked with two strands of linen or cotton thread are the traditonal materials, but stranded cottons and coton à broder may be also be used. An embroidery frame is necessary to facilitate the working of filling stitches.

Techniques

Hedebo edging stitch differs slightly from ordinary buttonhole stitch, but is quite simple to do. Stitches should not be too close together or the purl edge will not lie flat and there will be no room for the insertion stitches. When working cut shapes, outline the area with small running stitches, cut the fabric with radial cuts from the centre of the shape to just inside these stitches, and turn the cut fabric to the back of the work. Now the Hedebo edging stitch may be worked. When the edging is complete, trim away any untidy fabric at the back. Surface stitchery may be added, satin stitches, eyelets and so on.

Designs may be quite informal, incorporating flower sprays with large petals which can be filled with circular lace and buttonhole fillings.

Drawn Threadwork

Drawn threadwork is undoubtedly the link between pulled work and cutwork, and the bold geometric patterns of the fifteenth century were also the inspiration for sixteenth-century needlepoint lace. Traditionally, drawn threadwork is carried out on white or natural linen fabrics, in similar threads. Threads of the ground fabric are drawn out and the remaining threads strengthened and decorated by overcasting, binding and weaving stitches. (Early twentieth-century pieces were not always sufficiently overstitched and the weak threads have torn away with wear and laundering.)

History

Drawn threadwork *(opus tiratum)* is one of the oldest styles of embroidery, and dates back to Biblical times. The fine linens, used for the vestments of priests and altar hangings, and which are mentioned in the Scriptures, appear to have been worked in drawn thread embroidery. Many countries have had a tradition of drawn threadwork for centuries, but the technique did not appear in England until the sixteenth century, when members of the Royal Household introduced the style to decorate fine linen and clothes. Many sixteenth- and seventeenth-century English and American whitework samplers survive, featuring drawn threadwork among the exercises. Some of these were obviously intended as records of the technique.

Right *Using a frame, to keep the ground fabric firm and to prevent stretching while working, these filling stitches may be worked to complement the designs on whitework and Florentine or Venetian cutwork. Working satin stitches, cross stitches, in blocks or in floral or geometric shapes, seeding and speckling can produce intricate designs.*

Above *A fine muslin apron made in the early eighteenth century to wear with a lady's yellow silk quilted dress. The lacy border is very fine and delicate and the central pattern of birds and flowers is both lively and elegant in its design.*

Examples of white embroidery and drawn thread work
1. *This little nightcap is embroidered with whitework on the turn-up as well as all over the cap itself. White embroidery has always been very popular for embellishing nightwear.*
2. *The detail of this panel from the Royal School of Needlework shows a combination of geometric and natural motifs.*
3. *Drawn thread work has been used to pattern this dun-coloured rough silk petticoat.*
4. *This nineteenth-century handkerchief has small patterns of white embroidery and scalloped edges. The simple design is appropriate and dainty.*

1

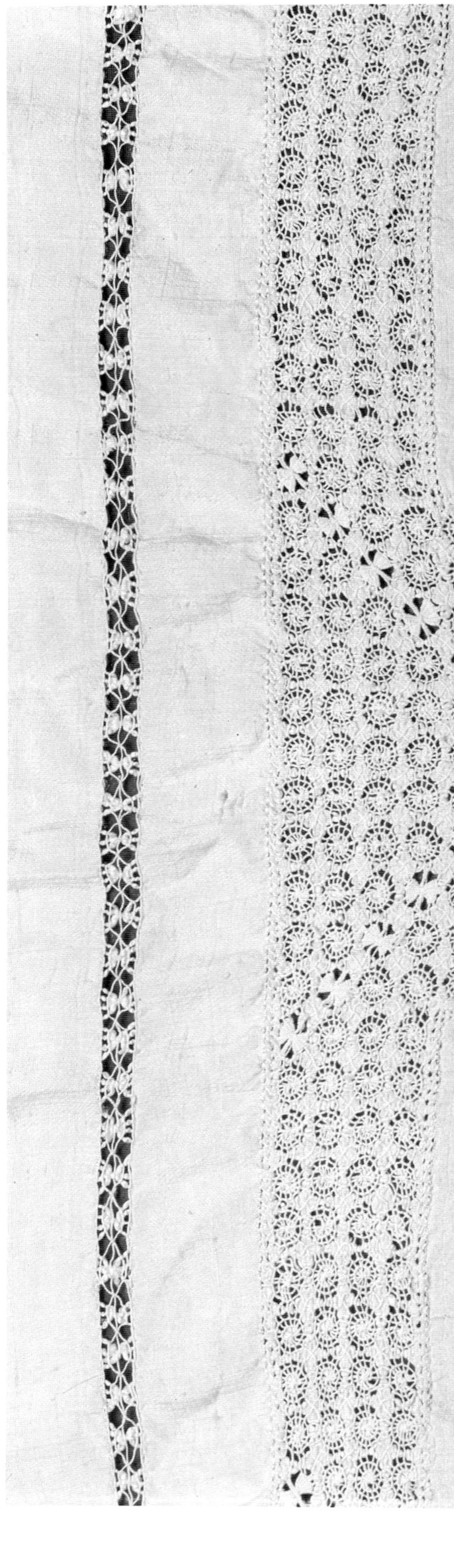

2

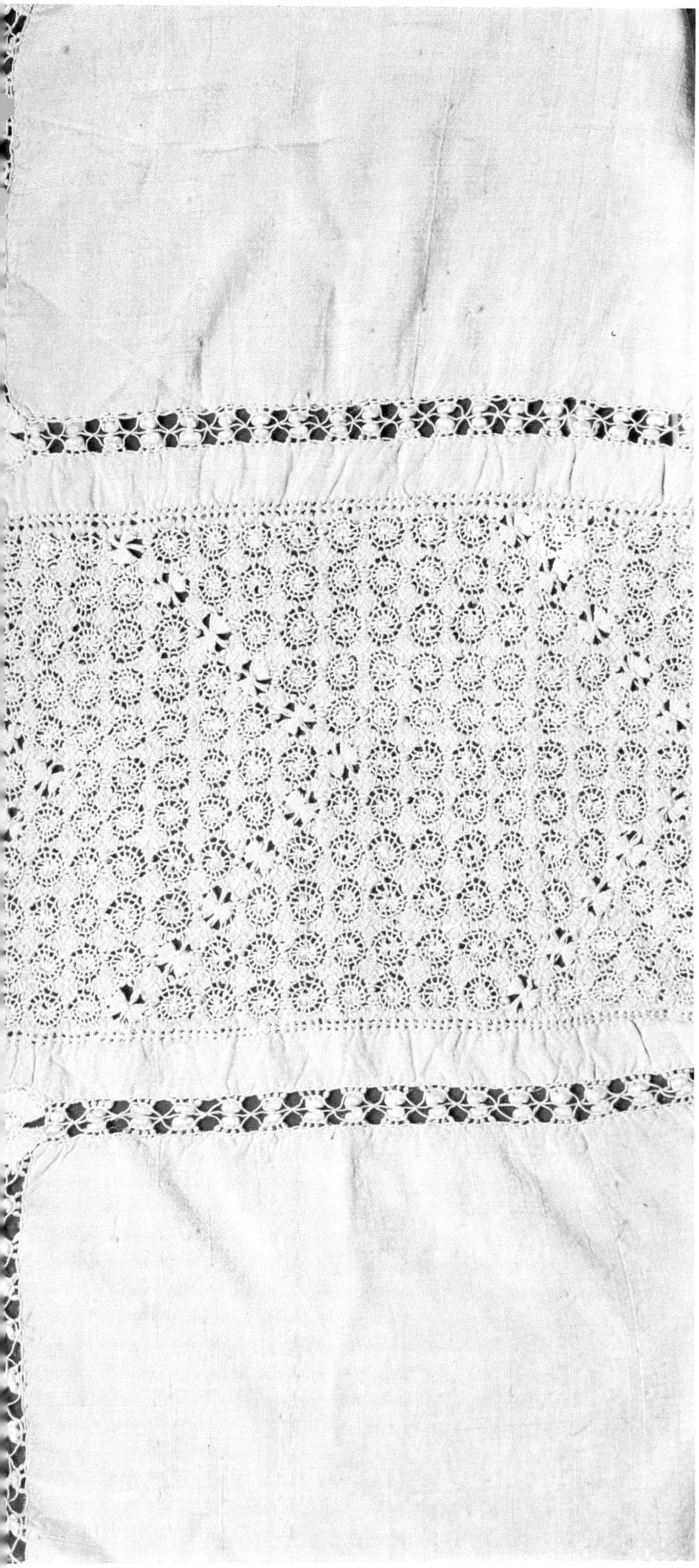

3

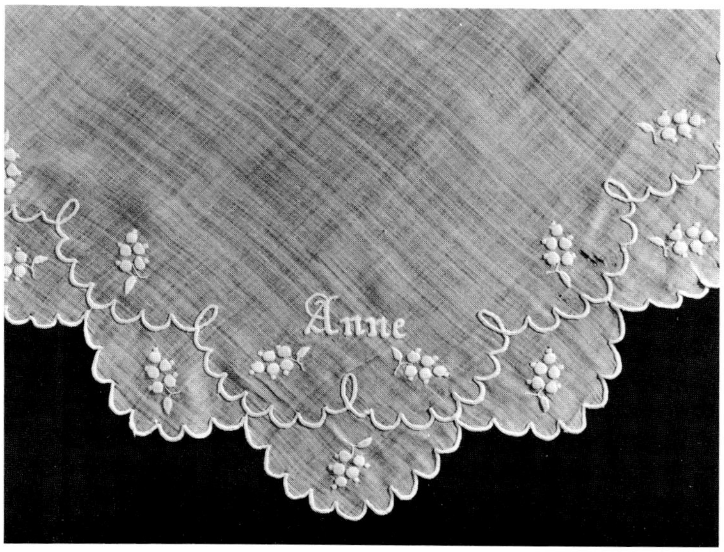

4

5

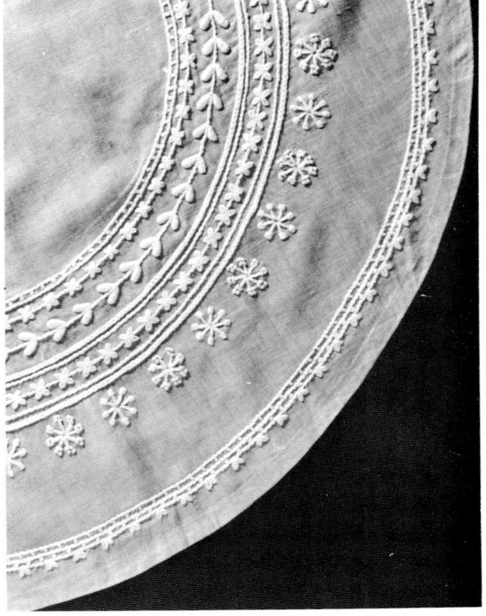

6

__5.__ This cushion cover is embroidered in Mountmellick work. The little blackberries are very characteristic of this style.
__6.__ This Swedish cloth worked in 1947 features different white embroidery stitches arranged in concentric circles. It is almost a sampler of different techniques and was possibly worked as a piece of ecclesiastical linen.

In England, drawn threadwork has enjoyed different periods of popularity. At the end of the nineteenth century, and early twentieth century, the technique was featured in embroidery magazines and was worked on handwoven linen by disabled people employed by the Fisherton-de-la-Mere Industries.

Drawn threadwork is one of the most notable styles of white embroidery in Scandinavia. Telemark in Norway produces drawn threadwork with other surface stitches for table linen.

From about 1760, the peasant women of the island of Amager, near Copenhagen, Denmark, produced their own evenweave linen. On this they worked a lovely style of drawn threadwork. Each motif is outlined with blocks of small satin stitches worked over three or four threads of the ground fabric. Some of the threads within the motif are then cut and drawn out and the remaining threads decorated with needleweaving and overcasting. Sometimes small holes are filled with lace-filling stitches, such as a dove's eye. Amager embroidery features on cushion covers, table and household linen, for domestic as well as commercial use.

The Swedish name for drawn thread threadwork is *Näversöm,* meaning "birchbark embroidery". The name is derived from the fact that the ground fabric was originally stretched over a piece of birchbark, which acted as a flexible frame. This was light to carry about, and girls would tuck their birchbark embroidery into their pockets, when taking flocks to pasture, to work on during the long days. Occasionally the ground fabric would be woven onto the birchbark simply by looping the warp and weft threads over the edges.

Drawn threadwork has been used to decorate clothing and church linen in Sweden since the seventeenth century. In the north, much of the work was carried out in blue, white, pink or red threads, according to the province; in the south, white threads were used. Patterns were geometric squares, triangles, stars, and freely interpreted crowns, flowers and leaves.

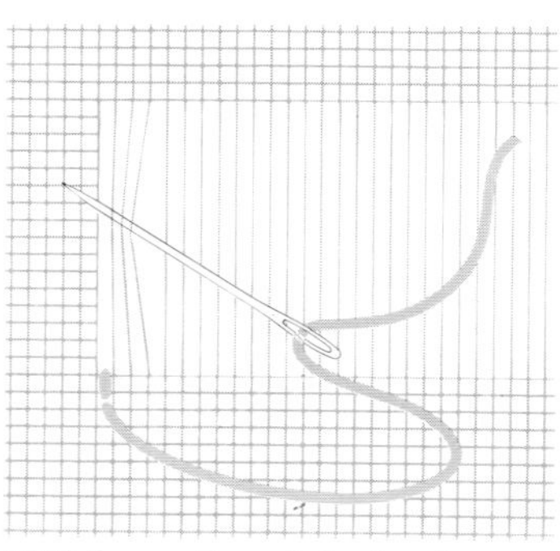

Withdrawn threads for borders
Hem stitch 1. *This stitch is formed from small vertical stitches worked round set numbers of vertical fabric threads tying them into bundles.*

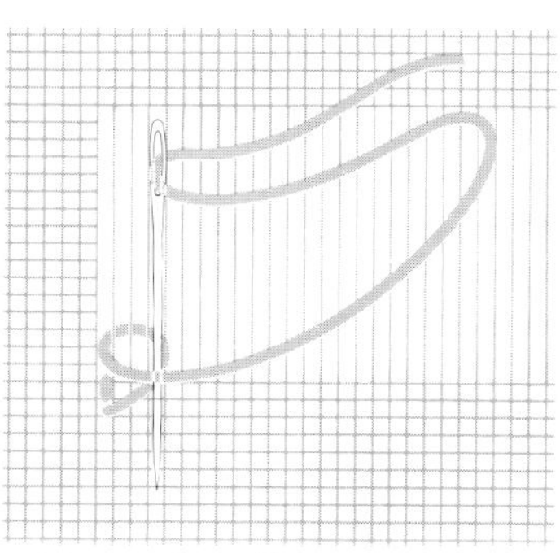

2. *The number of horizontal threads varies from three to five depending on the effect desired. The small vertical stitches must be worked evenly and neatly.*

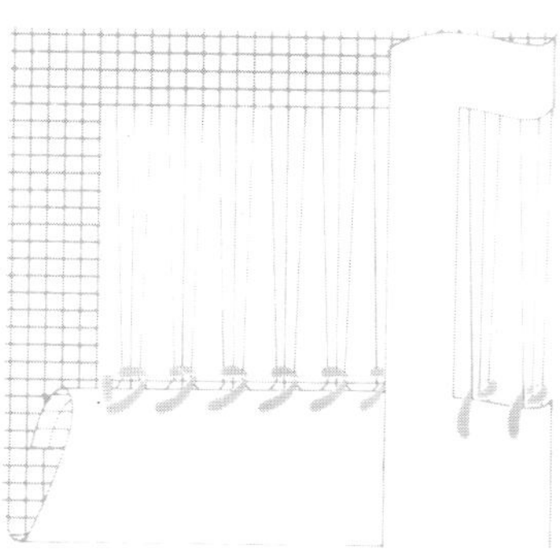

3. *The end result should be a row of sideways Vs at equal distances. This stitch can also be used to hold a hem in position as shown on the back of the fabric.*

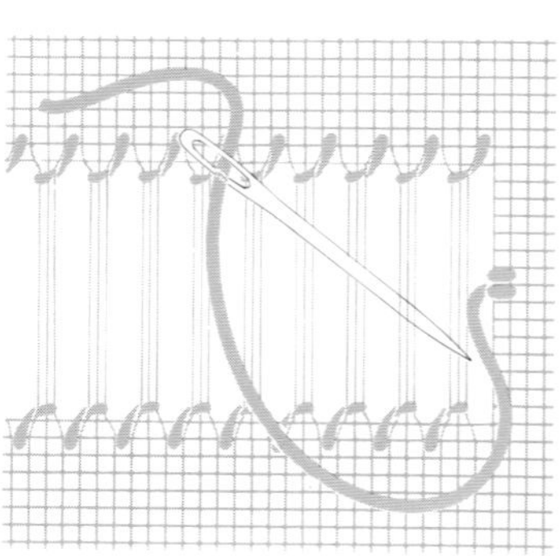

Interlaced hem stitch 1. *Work hem stitch along the top and bottom of the drawn thread area, tying the vertical threads into equal bundles top and bottom.*

Drawn threadwork was revived in Sweden at the end of the nineteenth century by Augusta Gripenberg in Hudiksvall, and modern drawn threadwork is included in Swedish educational syllabuses with real encouragement given to creative designs.

Italy, Armenia and the Ukraine also have strong traditions of drawn threadwork. Italian whitework embroidery has always incorporated drawn thread; in the nineteenth century, particularly in Sicily, conventional animal motifs were depicted in reserve against backgrounds worked in this way. Similar work of very high standard is seen in the embroidery of Nisa in the Alto Alentjo province of Portugal.

In the Caucasian Republic of Armenia, where weavers, dyers and needlewomen often worked together in monastery workshops, there is a long history of skilled embroidery. Geometric designs were carried out in drawn threadwork with needleweaving, satin stitches and buttonhole edgings.

In the Ukraine, drawn threadwork employs the use of kloster blocks, similar to those used in Hardanger embroidery.

Materials

Use strong, evenly woven fabrics and perle or stranded cottons, for stitching with tapestry needles. It is an advantage to have the fabric *loosely* framed while withdrawing threads, and tightened up for the embroidery.

Techniques

The technique of drawn threadwork calls for drawing threads from the ground fabric and working over the remaining threads. It is important to be precise when planning a piece of work. Graph paper is useful for working out designs based on warp and weft of the fabric. Such geometric designs may be applied to bands of decoration.

Hemstitching, and its variations, is used

Far left *A seventeenth-century Italian sampler of cut and drawn work. This type of work has been described as halfway between embroidery and lace, a description well-illustrated by this particular sampler. The centre for Italian cutwork or reticella during the sixteenth and seventeenth centuries was Venice.* ***Left*** *An attractive if fairly crude piece of whitework, probably a handkerchief. Since the Middle Ages, handkerchiefs have reflected trends in needlework, and are often intended to be decorative rather than functional. Needleworkers would work them like samplers, or embroider them with names or initials as gifts.*

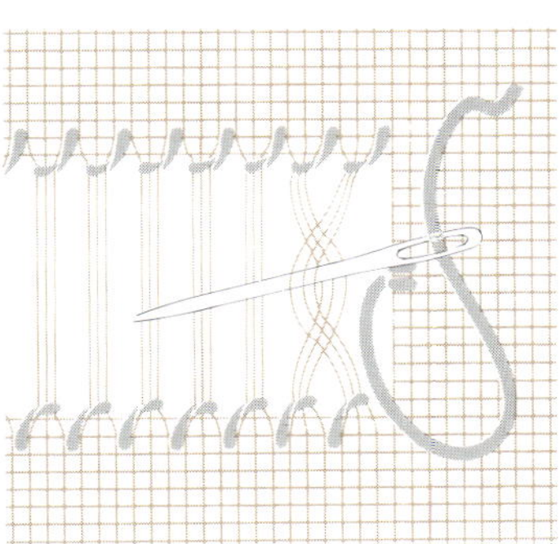

2. *Attach a new thread firmly to the centre of one side, place the point of the needle under the second bundle and over the first, pointing left to right.*

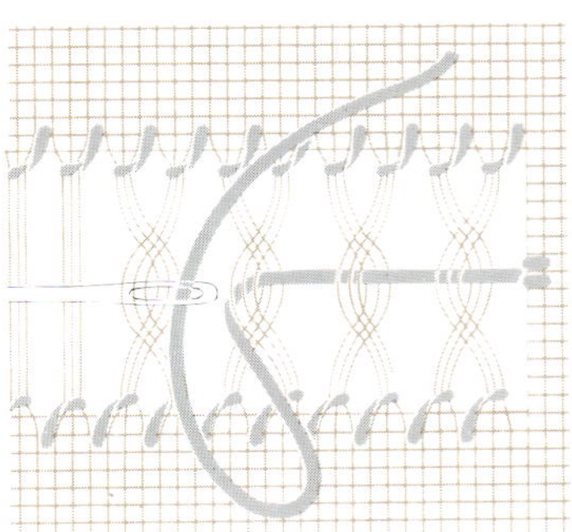

3. *Scooping up the first bundle, pull the needle back through in the opposite direction making up the twist as shown. Repeat for each pair of bundles. Anchor securely.*

Withdrawing threads *Having cut the required threads very carefully down the centre of the area to be worked, unpick them with a needle as shown.*

Tacking down threads *At the edges of this area weave the loose ends of the cut threads back into the wrong side of the fabric leaving straight borders.*

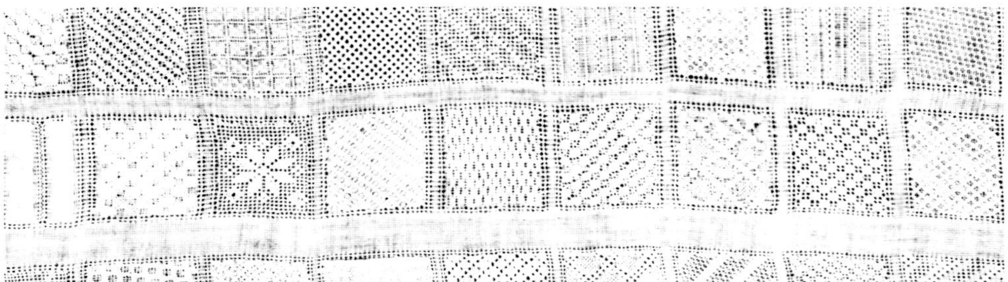

Left A Danish sampler of drawn and pulled work worked in 1758 and signed Rebecke Aasgn. The influence of this squared pulled work can still be seen in contemporary Danish embroidery, although cross stitch is also very popular.
Right These stitch diagrams only represent the shape of the stitches. and do not give an impression of the resulting pulled work.

for edging bands of drawn threadwork and for finishing the hems of articles. Needleweaving and overcasting are the main stitches used. Motifs are outlined with small running stitches. These are then buttonholed over, threads withdrawn and cut within the motif. Needleweaving, overcast or Russian drawn ground are then worked over the remaining trellis of threads.

Pulled Fabric Work

Pulled fabric, sometimes called pulled thread or drawn fabric, is a fascinating style of embroidery. No threads are withdrawn from the ground fabric to weaken it, but instead threads are drawn together to create lacy effects.

These techniques were often combined with other types of white embroidery. This is particularly noticeable in the Dresden whitework of the eighteenth century, where fine pulled fabric fillings were a feature of the flowing floral designs worked on very fine cotton fabrics. Dresden work simulated expensive lace and was used for caps, ruffles, and fichus. Italian seventeenth-century and Russian and Greek Island nineteenth-century work is characterized by faggot stitch backgrounds and simple but vigorous motifs.

In England, during the eighteenth century, men's waistcoats were richly embroidered with surface stitchery, quilting and pulled fabric stitches. Later, pulled fabric stitches were often combined in the designs of Ayrshire whitework.

Scandinavian countries are well-known for their tradition of attractive, unpretentious pulled fabric work. There is an exquisite Danish sampler worked by Rebecke Aasgn in 1758, in which 96 of the squares are embroidered with pulled fabric stitches. Present-day designs show an appreciation of texture, scale and combination of fabric, threads and stitches, and are applied to table linen or more creatively to curtains and wall hangings.

Materials

Slightly open, evenly woven fabrics, handwoven linens, linen scrim, and some contemporary curtain fabrics with open mesh will all produce interesting results. Strong threads of linen, perle cotton, coton à broder, and sometimes threads drawn from the edge of the fabric may be suitable. Untensioned satin stitch needs a thicker thread for the best effect. Wool, fine strings, or slightly textured threads used for handweaving give lively effects in creative pulled fabric work.

Use blunt tapestry needles, as these will not split the threads of the ground fabric. A frame makes the work easier to control.

Techniques

The effect of pulled work is to change the structure of the ground fabric, to enrich and lighten by lacy open area. The use of evenweave fabrics and the need to count threads suggests the precision of formal or geometric shapes, and this type of design is satisfying to produce. Designs may be based on lines, grids, geometric or large simple shapes which will show the filling stitches to advantage. There is also great scope for a spontaneous, creative approach and the use of unusual threads.

Although pulled fabric embroidery is traditionally worked in white or natural threads, it is also worth experimenting with colour. It is a good idea to work a sampler, experiment with various materials and threads, and observe the effects achieved by altering the tension when pulling the stitches together. Consider the contrast of smooth satin stitches with the textures of filling stitches, and try satin stitch in various tensions.

Stitches

The usual outline for pulled fabric work is a whipped stem or whipped chain stitch. Filling stiches include single faggot, double faggot, four-sided, honeycomb, three-sided, step, trellis, and wave stitch. A number of other embroidery filling stitches can be adapted simply by pulling them tightly when working. The edges of household linen and mats should be carefully and neatly finished, especially the corners, which should be mitred. Hemstitching, satin stitch and picot edgings are effective and simple.

Start a new thread at the beginning of a line of stitches, never in the middle. If a long stitch has to be taken across the back of the fabric, darn the thread carefully along the work to prevent it showing through the lacy holes.

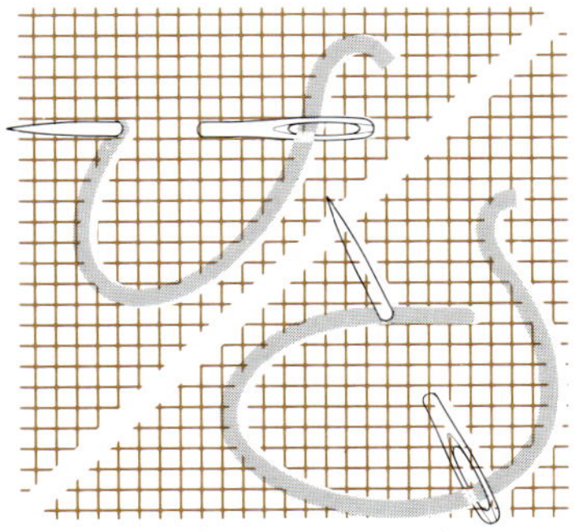

***Three-sided stitch 1, 2.** Working this filling stitch from right to left, make back stitches horizontally and diagonally.*

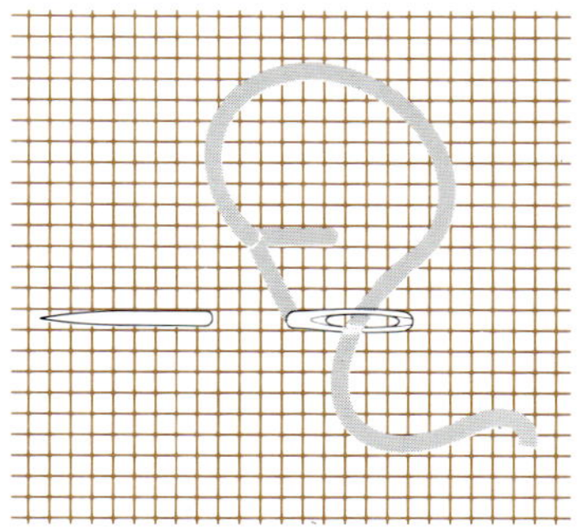

***3.** Pulling the stitches very tight, make a second diagonal stitch over the first.*

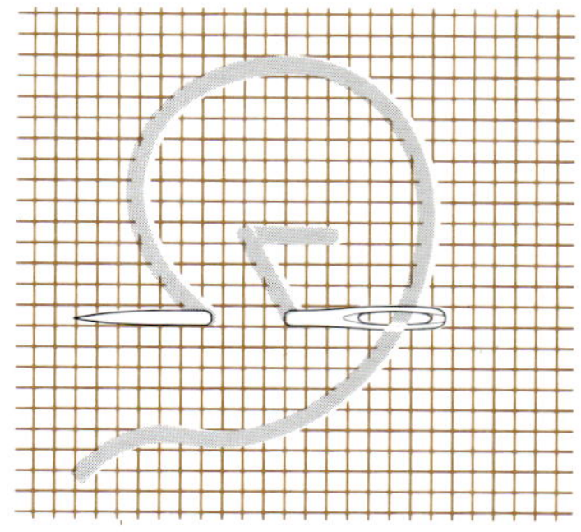

***4.** Again pulling the stitches, make a parallel horizontal back stitch.*

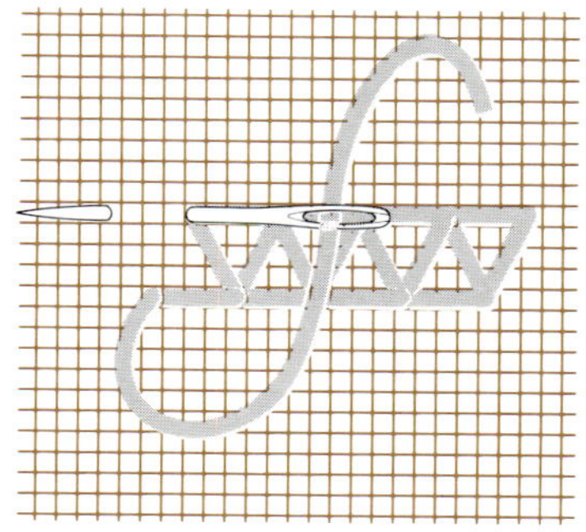

***5.** Drawing each stitch as tight as possible, so pulling the ground threads together, continue with this triangular progression.*

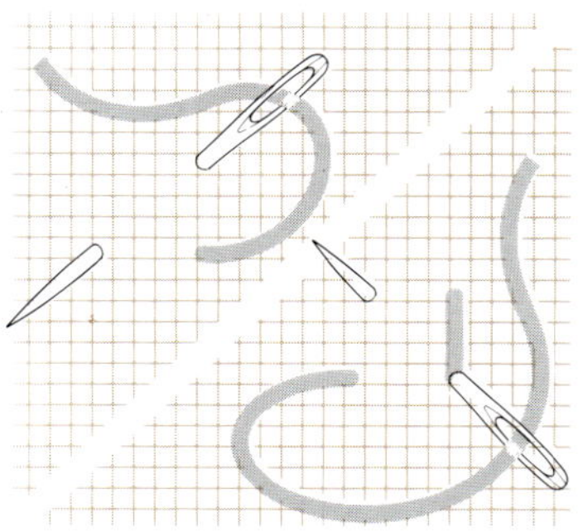

***Four-sided stitch 1, 2.** Working from right to left, make a vertical and a horizontal stitch over a certain number of ground threads.*

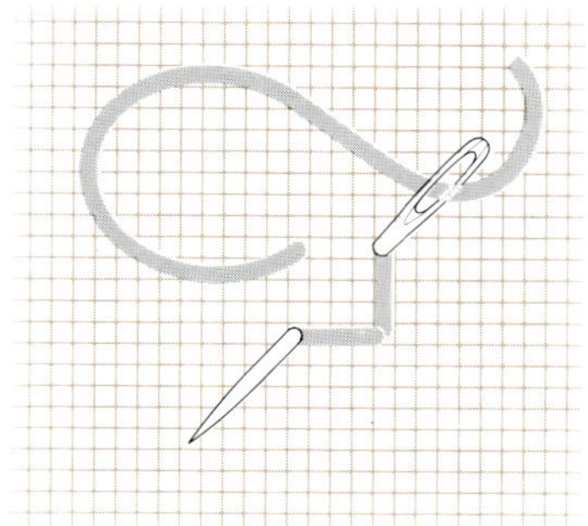

***3.** Drawing the ground threads together by pulling the stitches tight, make the third side of the square.*

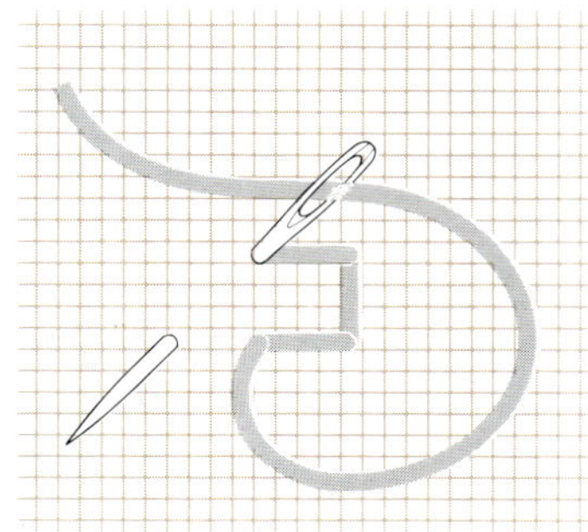

***4.** Stitch the vertical fourth side and pull it tight. You are then in a position to repeat the sequence.*

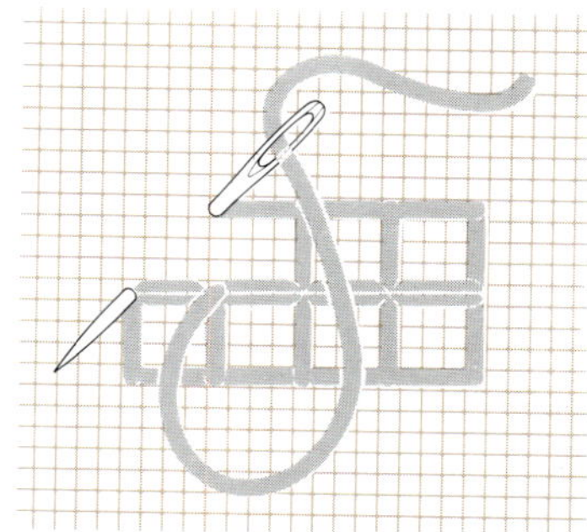

***5.** Return to the right side of the fabric to continue with another row of four-sided stitches.*

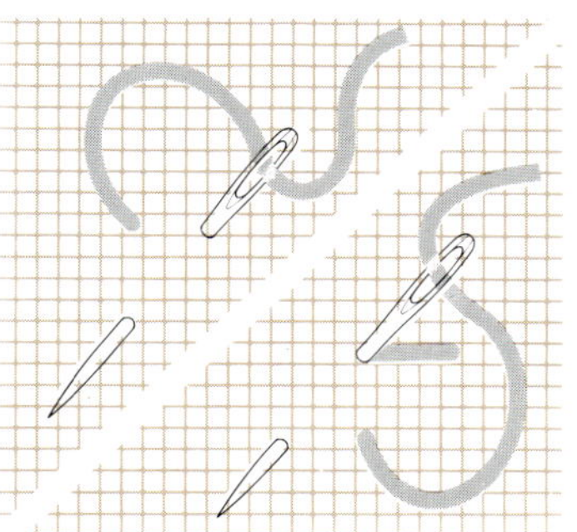

***Faggot stitch 1, 2.** Working diagonally downwards, make alternate horizontal and vertical stitches, and draw them tight.*

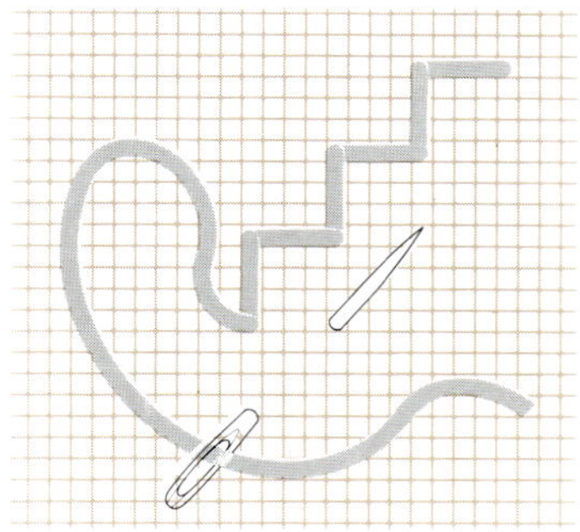

***3.** Having created a step-like pattern, work upwards diagonally making squares with alternate horizontal and vertical stitches.*

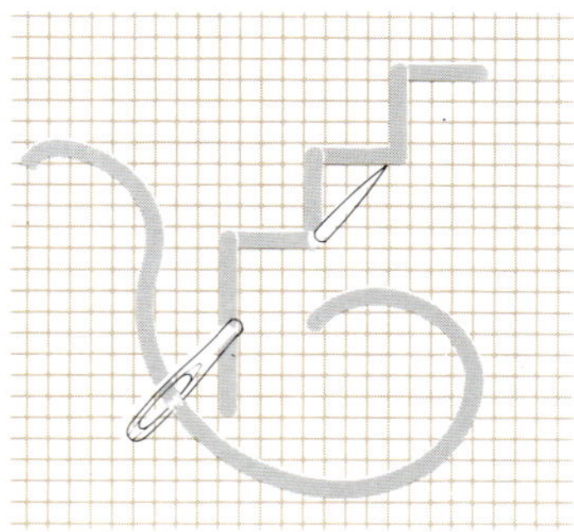

***4.** The stitches behind the fabric are always diagonal. All the stitches should be pulled tight.*

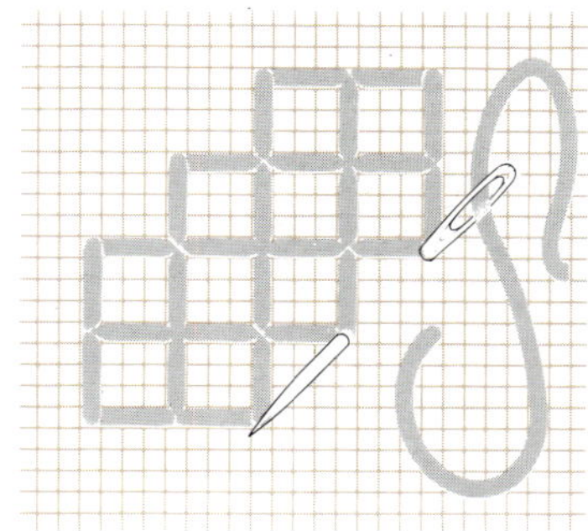

***5.** Continue working down and up until the area to be filled is complete.*

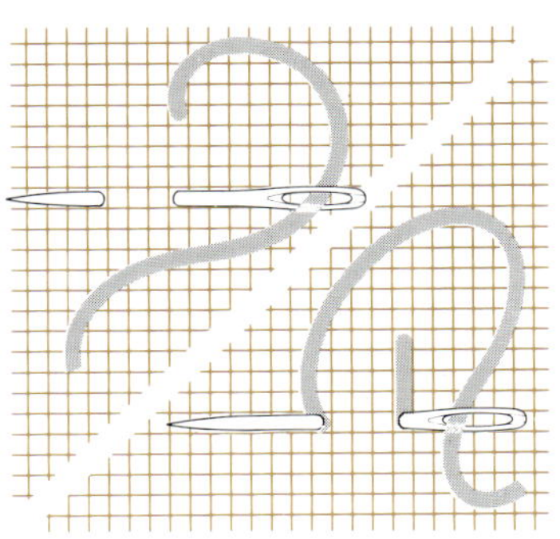

***Honeycomb stitch 1, 2.** Working from right to left, make horizontal and vertical stitches in a U-shape.*

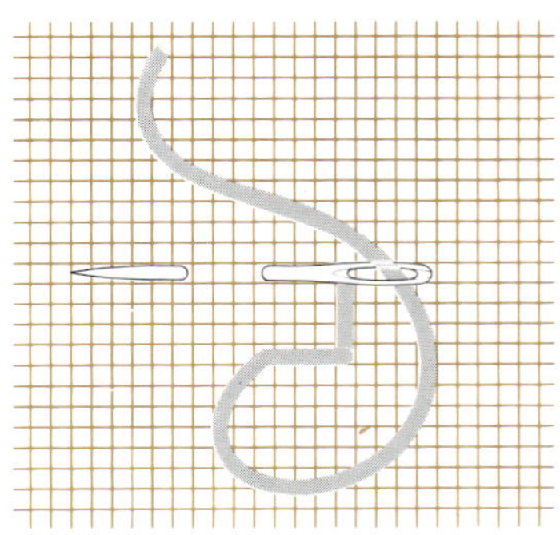

***3.** Every alternate stitch is a back stitch. This is a vertical straight stitch.*

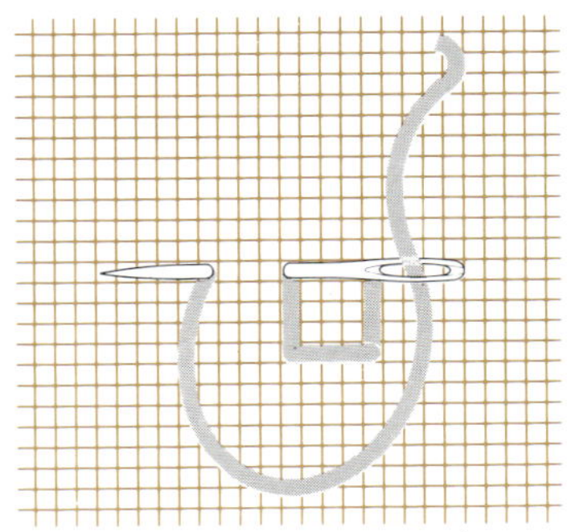

***4.** The back stitch creates a horizontal. Pull all the stitches tight, so drawing the ground threads together.*

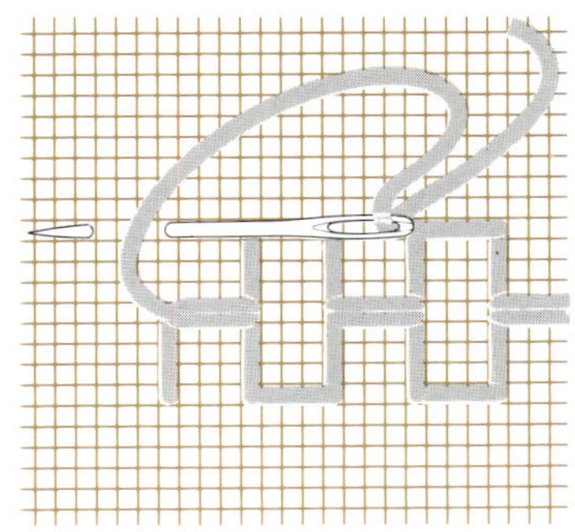

***5.** Continue working in rows for the particular lattice pattern created by rows of this stitch.*

Collecting, Display and Conservation

There has been a considerable resurgence of interest in collecting embroidery, both as an art-form and as a display of technical expertise. A collection of embroidery may be built up from a variety of sources. Antique pieces may be obtained from salerooms and auctions, antique shops and jumble sales, or may be handed down as heirlooms. Modern embroidery is widely available from craft centres, specialist galleries and student diploma shows. There are advantages and disadvantages of each of these sources.

Sources

Auctions and salerooms The sales are normally announced in the press. The sale is usually preceded by what is called a viewing when the items for sale may be examined. This is particularly useful when considering purchasing antique textiles, as it presents an opportunity to handle and examine items carefully.

The major salerooms employ experts who can provide specialist information. Catalogues are usually available which describe the object and indicate the price it may be expected to reach. By regularly attending such sales, it is possible to acquire considerable knowledge of the range of textiles available and their monetary value. The prices reached at auctions reflect the demand on a particular day and so may vary considerably. Auction rooms can only sell those items which are brought to them for sale and, therefore, the range and quality of items available at one sale may be very different from the next.

Antique shops are another potentially rich source of old pieces. The local antique shop may offer a few pieces for sale, but there are not many specialist shops. As with auction rooms, antique shops offer an opportunity to examine the pieces offered for sale closely, with the added advantage that a possible purchase can be considered over a number of days. Dealers may not have specialist knowledge or be able to record the provenance of an object. It is sometimes difficult for a non-specialist to assess the value of an object, with the result that the prices charged may vary considerably from shop to shop. However, it is still possible for textile collectors to acquire an interesting piece at a bargain price.

Jumble sales are another source for items of needlecraft. However, the frantic and disorganized nature of jumble sales may outweigh the possible advantage of acquiring a bargain.

Heirlooms For many people, an heirloom is the start of a collection. Family samplers and other domestic embroideries are often acquired in this way. They are usually of considerable sentimental value and historic interest because of their family associations. The wish to preserve family pieces for future generations underlines the importance of long-term care.

Galleries and shops selling modern embroidery usually support established artists, and should be able to give advice and background information on the embroidery. The costs of running a gallery make these items a little more expensive than when obtained directly from the artist. Locally made hobby embroidery, some of which may be of collectable quality, may be bought from craft fairs and markets.

Diploma shows Pieces may also be obtained from art colleges, which offer specialist courses in embroidery and textiles. On completion of the course, students prepare shows of their work. Items displayed in these degree shows are usually for sale and often represent the most up-to-date and innovative examples of needlecraft. The students are available to talk about their work, which may be offered at a reasonable price. It is often difficult to assess the monetary value of this type of new embroidery, and specialist advice is seldom available. These shows are not usually advertised.

Left *This piece of seventeenth-century canvaswork, which was perhaps used to decorate the border of a bedcover, was stitched in silk on linen. It has retained its bright colours and remained in good condition, with firm, unfraying French knots and tent and cross stitches, and a pleasingly soft texture.*

Left *This child's collar is a beautiful example of Chinese embroidery, c. 1900. The alternate black and red silk panels have been finely decorated with animal, bird and flower motifs in multicoloured satin stitch, then each panel joined with embroidered bars. All the edges are bound in bright powder-blue silk. Being light, the collar would be easy to mount and frame, and the result would be pleasing.*

Above *This ordinary-looking sampler, stitched with linen threads on a linen ground, is interesting for its expertise. The sampler was stitched by a six-year-old, in cross stitch and eyelets. Practising her alphabet was probably more difficult than creating neat stitches.*

Above right *Tiny, transparent glass beads and thick Berlin woolwork on cotton canvas with a cross stitch border combine to decorate this Victorian square. It was probably intended as a cushion cover, but now, backed and framed, it could make an interesting example of the work of its time.*

Examining needlecraft

When looking at a piece of historic or modern embroidery, it is important to consider it from different points of view: aesthetic worth, technical quality or workmanship, and condition. First, consider how the piece was made, whether it is pure stitchery or whether other techniques, such as glueing, have also been used. Try to establish which materials were used, both for the ground fabric, and for the stitching or applied areas. Examine the frame or mount, if there is one, and establish how the piece is held in position. Lastly, make a study of the condition of the needlework, looking carefully for any signs of damage. It may have holes, tears, loose threads, missing areas, stains from dirt or running dye; it may smell dusty.

Types of historic needlecraft

As a guide to recognizing and identifying different types of historic needlecraft, it is useful to acquire some knowledge of textile history. Specialist advice on historic pieces may be obtained from museums. Most private collections of embroidery fall into four categories: samplers, canvaswork, whitework and oriental embroidery.

Samplers are relatively small embroidered panels which were known to have been made from the seventeenth century to the present day. Samplers usually consist of a neutral-coloured canvas decorated with stitching. They often feature the alphabet, a verse and the name of a child, and even the date when the sampler was worked. The canvas is usually linen or wool.

Samplers made of woollen canvas are susceptible to moth damage. It is important

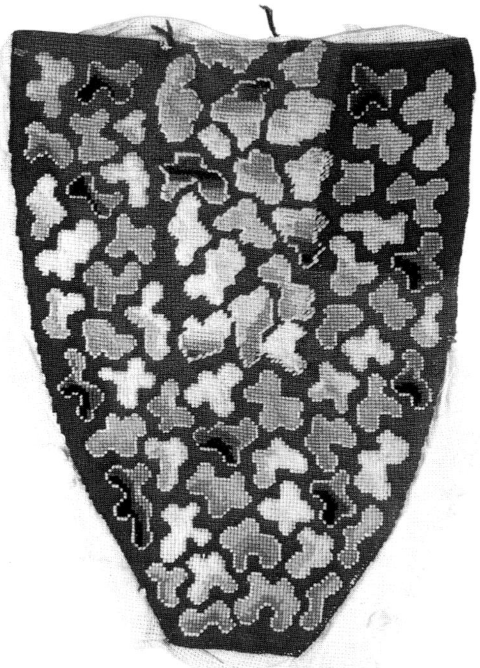

Above *Typically Oriental in design, this inexpensive piece of voided velvet, with borders of ribbon and of silk and couched metal thread embroidery, could now be used as a tray cloth or small tablecloth.* ***Right*** *This piece of Victorian canvaswork, worked in tent stitch, may have been intended as a small firescreen or a decorative hanging. It is worked in wool and silk on cotton canvas. Although the black background has faded, except in one corner, the colourful pattern could well catch a collector's eye in an antique shop or sale.*

to look for any evidence of moth attack in the form of small holes (especially around the edges) and moth frass.

Samplers are usually mounted in some way. Traditionally, they were stretched over a wooden frame and held taut by nailing round the edges. The use of such stretcher frames has often resulted in damage. The nails cause strain and rusty nail holes around the edge. Tears often form along the inner edge of the stretcher frame. Poor framing often results in soiled samplers.

Some samplers have areas of missing

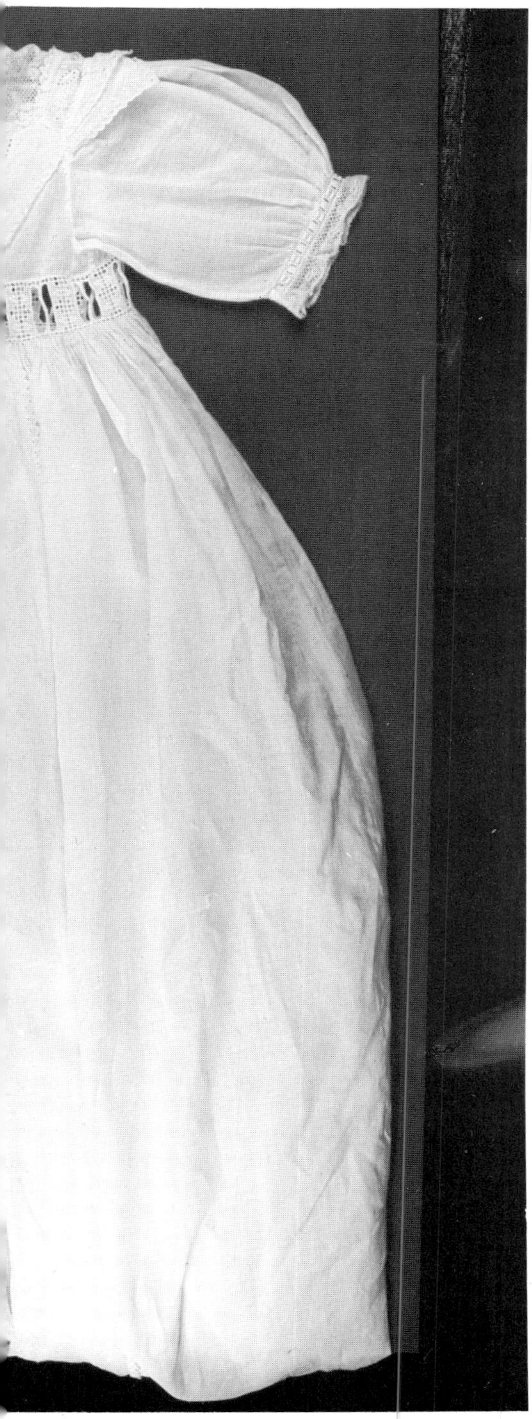

***Left** A baby's christening robe is worth collecting not only for possible use but for its beauty and fine workmanship. The tiny detail of the centre chest is typical of Ayrshire whitework; the lace collar, picot edges and cutwork complement its delicacy.*
***Top** In this very stylized canvaswork design, the only subjects out of symmetry are the man and his dog in the foreground. Possibly because it was not worked on a frame the canvas was pulled and distorted from its rectangular shape. It would be possible to straighten the work a little, by blocking.*
***Above** This piece is a detail from a picture of a fairground worked in colourful wools and cottons. Designed and stitched almost like a painting, with patches of colour built up into a scene, the result is also textured and very unusual.*

embroidery. This is especially noticeable with lettering in black silk thread; unfortunately, very little can be done to prevent this.

Canvaswork is a form of embroidery where the ground canvas is completely covered with stitching. This technique was used for stool and chair covers, firescreens, decorative pictures, and it was particularly popular in the Victorian period. The canvas is usually linen or cotton, with wool and silk used for the embroidery.

If silk has been used for the embroidery, it is often damaged and sometimes even missing. Wool embroidery may have been attacked by moths resulting either in holes or surface irregularities. The canvas itself is sometimes weak and brittle, with small holes. This is a particular problem in canvaswork furnishings where the embroidery is often weaker than it looks, and may become unserviceable. Some canvaswork includes beads worked with the embroidery. The threads holding these beads in place often become weak and disintegrate, resulting in loss of beads.

Oriental embroidery These pieces are normally coloured silk threads worked on a silk satin background. The embroidery technique, usually long-and-short stitch and couched metal thread, often results in overall weakness exhibited by areas of loose stitching. As with samplers, the mounting techniques used should be carefully examined. The dyes used are often not colourfast and sometimes pieces are marred by dye stains.

Whitework is white embroidery worked on a ground of white cotton or linen. Although such items are generally quite strong, they may become weak and worn through much use, and are susceptible to tearing. It is important to examine such items very carefully for signs of this type of damage.

Storage and Display

Owners or collectors of textiles are faced with problems in caring for their collections both in storage and display. Individual pieces may be displayed about the house (hanging framed on a wall, or draped over furniture) or they may be carefully packed away in drawers or trunks. In considering either display or storage it is useful to understand the causes of damage to textiles.

Textiles are usually made from a combination of organic and inorganic materials (wool fibres from sheep, silk filaments from moth cocoons, linen from flax stalks, man-made fibres, metal sequins, glass beads), but because of their essentially organic nature, textiles begin to deteriorate from the moment they are made. This deterioration or ageing process may take a variety of forms, and happen rapidly or very gradually. Most damage is caused by light, excessive dampness or dryness, handling, soiling, insect infestation, and poor mounting. The way in which a particular textile is made can also affect its long-term survival.

Causes of damage

Inherent factors The inherent weakness of all organic materials can be exacerbated by various dyeing and finishing treatments. Some dyestuffs, while satisfactorily colouring a textile fibre initially, may result in damage to the fibre in the long run. A traditional way of dyeing black was to use an iron mordant, which over time in certain conditions causes disintegration of the fibre. In the nineteenth century, there was a fashion for weighting silks with metallic salts to make a cheap, light fabric appear heavier and more luxurious. This weighting process results in rapid deterioration of silk material, often to be seen in the shattered linings of Edwardian pieces.

Light The damaging effect of light on textiles has long been recognized. Its effect takes two main forms: the fading of dyes, and the weakening of fibres.

Some dyestuffs are more susceptible to light-fading than others. For example, many seventeenth-century woven tapestries now show blue foliage, because differential dye fading has taken place. In order to achieve the colour green, two dyes were used – yellow and blue; the yellow dye is more vulnerable to the effects of light and fades more rapidly, so that the foliage now appears blue.

Above *This woven piece of brocade has been so badly damaged by light that the fabric has become very brittle and its fibres have in places almost competely disintegrated.*
Right *The dye run on this Oriental embroidery has ruined a large area. The embroidery was probably made specifically for tourists, with brightly coloured silk raised work and densely couched metal thread embroidery decorating bird and flower motifs. The orange-coloured silk core of the couched gold used to outline the motifs has proved not to be dye-fast, and has run badly in a slightly damp atmosphere. The metal threads have also tarnished.*

Above *Over the years, a fabric left in broad daylight will deteriorate at a different rate than a fabric in the shade or a fabric in the dark. This photograph of pieces of some silk woven curtains illustrates the three rates: on the left the piece has been badly damaged by light – it was probably the curtain edge; on the right, the top section is darker than below – the shine and richness have gone out of the fabric and it shows some signs of deterioration and dirtiness; the section of the same piece which was part of the hem and unexposed to daylight, looks almost new.*

However, dye fading is not the most serious effect of light on textiles. Light also causes an actual weakening of the fibres. This weakening action involves changes in the chemical structure of the fibres which make up textiles, and can sometimes be observed in old curtains, where the exposed folds become weak, brittle and susceptible to tearing.

Light damage is also cumulative. Bright light over a short time will have the same effect as a dim light over a longer time. All forms of light are damaging, whether from natural or artificial sources.

Temperature and humidity Changes in temperature and humidity can also adversely affect textiles. Just as pieces of furniture swell and shrink according to the climate within a room, so do textiles. In a damp atmosphere, textile fibres can swell; in a dry atmosphere, fibres can shrink.

Considered in isolation, as long as a textile remains in a stable condition, little damage is caused. However, the regular swelling and shrinkage of fibres caused by temperature and humidity changes inside a room, can cause fibres to weaken. In ideal conditions, textiles should be stored in stable conditions, where the temperature and humidity do not vary. The recommended climate is a temperature of 55°F (12.8°C) and a relative humidity of 55%.

Soiling and staining can also result in damage. Two different sorts of soiling have been recognized – airborne pollutants and gaseous pollution. The former type causes abrasion to fibres and the latter contributes to chemical changes within the fibre. The effect of gaseous pollutants can be particularly severe especially in the presence of light and is shown by serious weakening of the textile rather than visible surface soiling.

Wear and tear Wear and handling cause damage to textiles. Worn cuffs and chair seats are evidence of this. Soiled textiles are usually affected more by wear than clean textiles, because the prisms of gritty soils between the fibres result in an abrasive action gradually rubbing at the surface of fibres.

Areas of tension are also points of weakness, so, for example, the folded edges of a textile will weaken over a period of time. Similarly, textiles may be mounted under tension, like samplers. Ill-considered mounting techniques often cause the most avoidable damage.

The harmful effect of soils and stains can be very serious. However, greater damage can be caused by inappropriate cleaning treatments. For example, dyes may run and disfigure a piece permanently.

Museum storage and display

Extensive collections of textiles are kept in museums for display, study and reference. Although visitors may be irritated by some of the restrictions which govern the display of such items, these restrictions are intended to preserve the collections for the future. Generally, textiles in a museum collection cannot be touched; they may be behind glass; and they are often displayed in low light.

Museum professionals use a variety of fairly sophisticated equipment to assess whether or not storage and display areas present a suitable environment. These include light meters to measure lux levels and hygrometers to measure humidity.

Storage and display in the home

Owners of more modest collections than those found in museums will not have

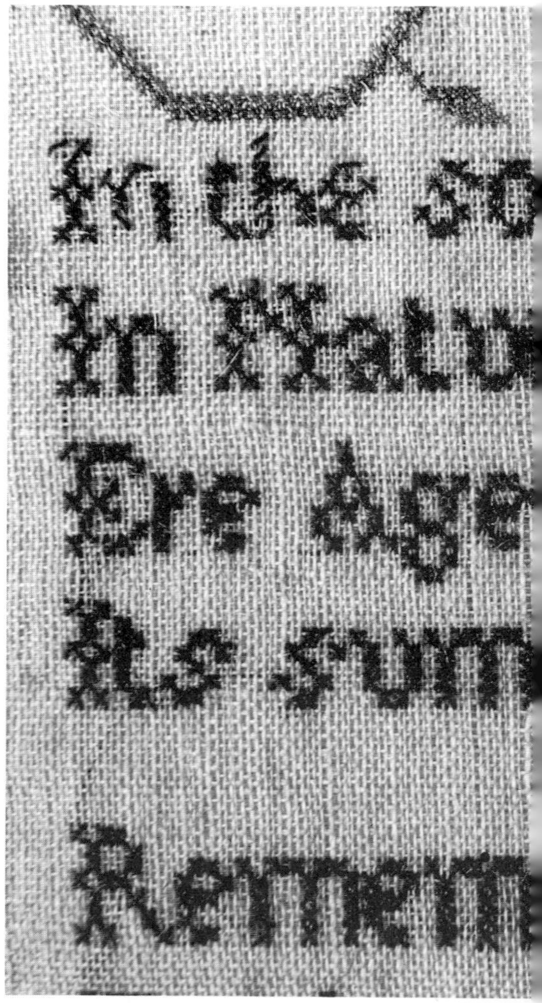

Above *The rusty-looking frayed holes on the binding round this sampler are an example of the damage nails can do, when they are used to back or frame a work.* ***Far right*** *It is obvious from this detail photograph of the reverse side of a Liberty print silk scarf that applying glue to fabric causes damage. Glue will stain or change the colour of a fabric, will cause the fabric to pucker and stiffen and will attract dirt. The glue on this scarf was applied when framing, and would not be easy to remove without causing further damage to the fabric.* ***Above right*** *The silk thread, used in this sampler to delineate the words of a poem, was dyed with an iron-based colourant which has caused the thread itself to disintegrate. The sampler, which was stitched in the mid-nineteenth century by an 11-year-old, may have been displayed near a window, with daylight acting as a catalyst in the deterioration. Other threads used to decorate the plain wool ground, including yellows and greens, have remained strong.*

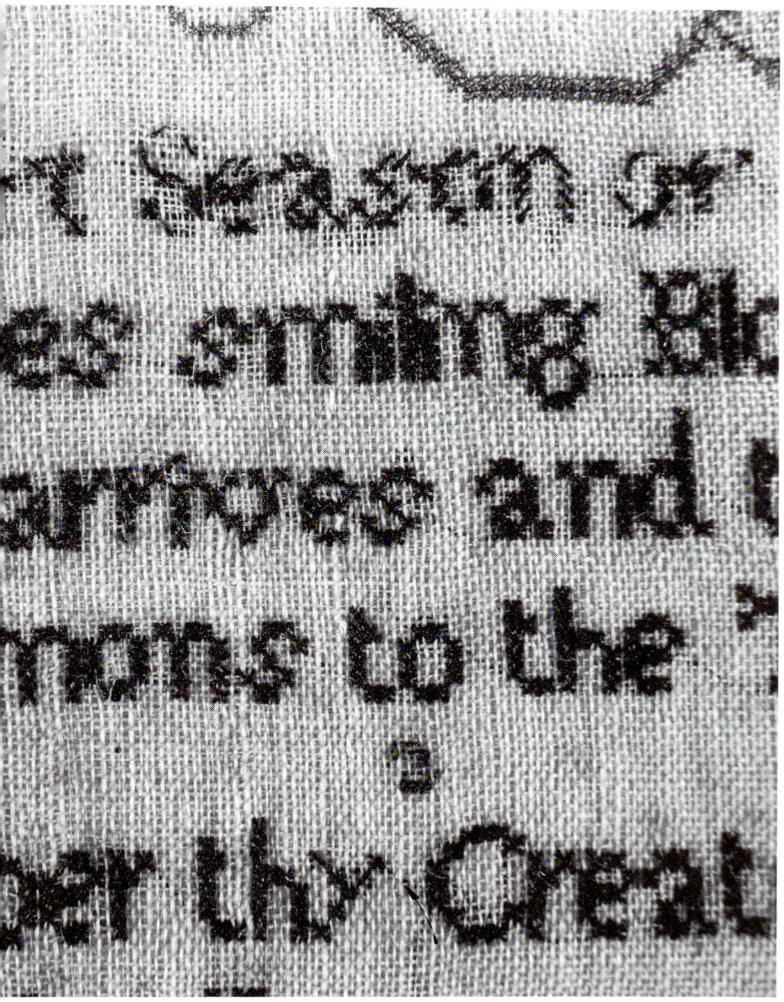

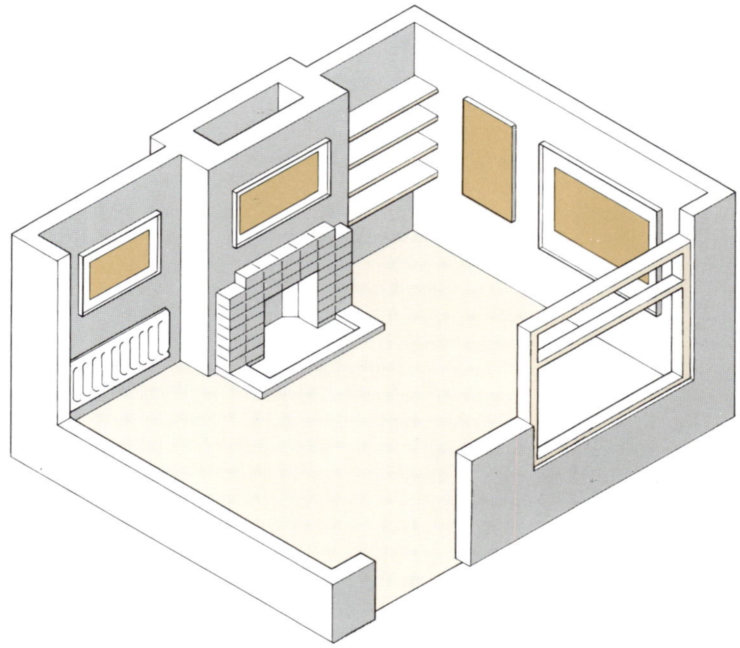

Above *When displaying a textile at home it is important to bear in mind the factors which cause deterioration and to place the textile where it will not be subject to damage. In the room delineated here, the most obvious sources of possible damage are those which are likely to cause changes of temperature and humidity, so the textile will shrink and swell, and its fibres will be weakened. Culprits include the window, which may allow sunlight to stream through so also causing light damage; the outside wall, which may at various times be damp and cold or warm and dry; the fireplace, which produces dust as well as extreme changes of temperature and humidity – particularly damaging if a fire is lit regularly, resulting in frequent expansion and contraction; and the radiator, which causes dryness when it is on. The best place to hang a textile in this room would be on the near wall, as long as there are no bright lights nearby. The room should preferably be well-ventilated, but not draughty, maintaining a moderate and constant temperature.*

access to sophisticated monitoring equipment. However, by following a few basic guidelines and applying them sensibly, it is possible to make a reasonable assessment of conditions at home and decide how suitable they are for the display of a collection.

Prevention of light damage The more light, the more damage. If textiles are not on display, they should be kept in the dark, but light is obviously necessary if textiles are to be looked at. Do not display a textile on a wall which is opposite windows; before you put a valued textile in a room, observe where the sun shines in at different times of the day and avoid those places.

Artificial light also damages, so do not put a textile too near the light source. Tungsten light contains less ultraviolet light (the invisible rays which cause most damage) than fluorescent light.

For special occasions, an extra, small light can be switched on to illuminate a textile hung in a dark corner. A curtain can be hung in front and pulled aside for viewing; this would provide long-term protection.

Controlling temperature and relative humidity It is more important that the temperature be even and not fluctuating, rather than be fixed at any specific level. However, if the atmosphere is too hot, the textile is likely to become too dry, and if the temperature is too low, the textile is likely to become too damp. Avoid putting a textile near a source of heat – a radiator, for example. Similarly, outside walls should be avoided, as these are most liable to damp. A textile in an unused, unheated room is more likely to suffer from damp.

Remember that an old textile may well be more sensitive to conditions than less-valued household furnishings, and may well be the first to show signs of damage from excessive humidity. A room which smells musty when left unused for a time is not a suitable environment for either display or storage. Particular care must be taken with cotton and linen articles which are subject to mould in damp conditions. It is best not to seal textiles in non-porous containers – plastic bags or boxes – as these cannot breathe, then moisture may build up and cause mould if the temperature of the atmosphere fluctuates.

Prevention of soiling, insect attack and handling Textiles are excellent dirt traps. Avoid hanging a textile in the path of a dust-carrying air flow – above a radiator, for example, or near a door. Careful framing of small pieces can help here, as can lining of larger hanging pieces.

The greatest amount of insect damage to textiles is caused by six varieties of moths, the larvae of which feed on wool and other animal fibres, or by the larvae of the carpet beetle. The moth larvae, when fully fed on wool, change into chrysalises, from which the adults later emerge. The female insects generally lay their eggs soon after emerging and before flying, unless suitable egg laying sites (for example wool) are scarce. These insects thrive where left undisturbed, and consequently the most effective way of avoiding infestation is to ensure that wool textiles are not left neglected for long periods. Proprietary moth balls may do a little to discourage moths, but will not prevent attack completely.

Much avoidable damage also occurs in the poor handling of pieces. This includes folding and crushing in storage.

Storing textiles

Most textiles are best stored flat. Even careful folds turn, over time, into unsightly creases which may be difficult or even impossible to remove; and creases can too easily become cracks, where the fabric splits along the line of the fold. This is particularly a problem with silk.

Often, to store a piece completely flat is impractical, as it would take up too much space. In these cases, to avoid the problems caused by creasing, care must be taken to pad all the folds. This is usually best done with acid-free tissue paper which can be crumpled to provide enough bulk to avoid sharply creasing the textile. Wherever possible, the piece should be folded so that the right side is on the outside. This means that the right side is folding over a larger arc than the wrong side, and will consequently suffer less.

Folding a flat textile Place the piece right side down on a flat surface and decide where the piece needs to be folded. Do not fold more than necessary. Place rolled or lightly crumpled acid-free tissue paper along the entire length of the proposed fold line. Fold the textile at this point ensuring that the tissue paper is pushed well into the fold.

Rolling a flat textile It is often more conve-

Right Professional conservators use repair fabrics of various types to back textiles while working on them. Shown here is a variety of fabrics ranging from fine silks and polyesters to linen. Stored on rolls, they are easily visible and accessible.

Below The results of folding and leaving a fabric folded without padding are illustrated by this damaged piece of ecclesiastical embroidery. The silk has become brittle over the years, and where creased and under strain has cracked and worn away.

nient to roll the textile. Large textiles are better rolled rather than folded too many times.

Lay the piece face down on a flat surface. For a large piece, this may well be the floor. It is important that the piece is open flat and not folded in any way. Cover the wrong side of the textile with acid-free tissue.

Choose a roller with as large a diameter as possible, and slightly longer than the width of the textile. Cardboard rolls are readily available: smaller ones can be taken from rolls of aluminium foil and larger ones can be obtained free from many fabric shops. The cardboard should be covered with acid-free tissue, so that it does not come into contact with the textile.

Place the roller at one end of the textile, and roll evenly, smoothing out any creases or folds which appear. Wrap the rolled textile in acid-free tissue, or a piece of washed, undyed cotton (for example an old

Left *To prevent the deterioration of textiles when they are stored, it is important to ensure they are padded, preferably with acid-free tissue paper which cannot affect the fibres of the textiles. This nineteenth-century Paisley shawl is being folded with tissue paper to prevent the layers of the shawl touching and creases forming which could later result in cracking.*

Above *Although textiles should be stored flat, they can be kept rolled if there is a lack of space. The design is rolled with acid-free tissue, the right side of the textile on the outside of the roll.*

Top *To prepare for boxing and storing this handmade Chinese silk robe, acid-free tissue is being used to pad the sleeve. This will help to keep the shape of the garment, and will prevent couched metal threads from touching and possibly damaging other threads or the silk fabric.*

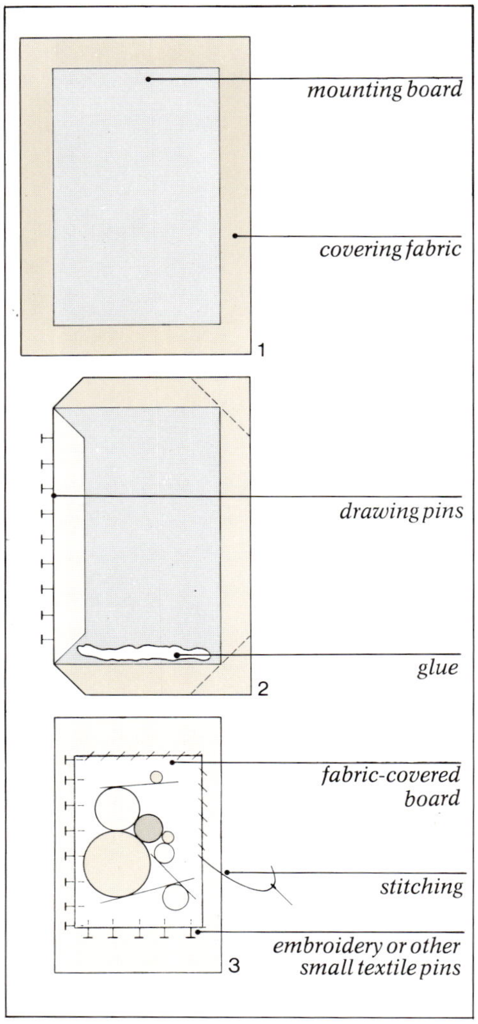

Mounting a textile
1. Cut the fabric to cover the board about 3 inches (7.5 cm) larger than the board, and place it with its right side face down. Place the mounting board, with its smoothest side face down, above the fabric.
2. Use drawing pins to keep the fabric on a straight grain while glueing.
3. Turn the fabric-covered board right side up and place the material centrally on it. Pin the embroidery in position, ensuring it is as flat as possible, and under even tension all round. Slip stitch around the edge.

sheet). If the roll needs to be secured, tie (not tightly) cotton tape or strips of fabric around it, but not string which may eventually bite into the package. Label the package.

Storing shaped textiles The basic principle of padding to avoid sharp folds and creases applies. The inside of a christening robe, for example, should be padded slightly, as should the sleeves.

The container will be either a box or a drawer (or both). When museums use cardboard boxes for storage, they usually insist on acid-free, buffered cardboard. This is obviously the best, but such boxes are not easily obtainable in small quantities. An ordinary cardboard box may be used if the textile is protected by acid-free tissue and preferably wrapped in a piece of washed, undyed cotton. If possible, choose a box with a close-fitting lid, but do not seal it, as this may cause humidity problems. Pack the textile carefully into the chosen box. Pad empty spaces with tissue so that the textile is held in place if the box is moved.

If plastic or metal containers are used, it is important that they are not sealed, as this may cause problems if they are situated somewhere where there is a fluctuating atmosphere. As with cardboard, ensure that the textile is protected with acid-free tissue.

Displaying small flat textiles

Owners often wish to frame their small, flat textiles either to display them to best advantage or to protect them behind glass. Framing can protect a textile efficiently as long as it has been carefully considered and executed.

Mounting Textiles should first be carefully mounted. In most cases this involves attaching the textile to a solid support. In the past, some textiles were nailed or glued onto the mounting board with disastrous results. Samplers, for example, were usually nailed to a wooden stretcher frame with iron nails. Nailing at intervals means the textile is under uneven stress. Over time, the nails become rusty, staining the textile and becoming rusted in places.

Glue has also been used to attach the textile to the mount and is not to be recommended. Traditionally animal glue or starch was used, and more recently, synthetic adhesives. Glues may stain and make the textile brittle, and they also may become ineffective over time. Some of the modern glues contain chemicals whose long-term

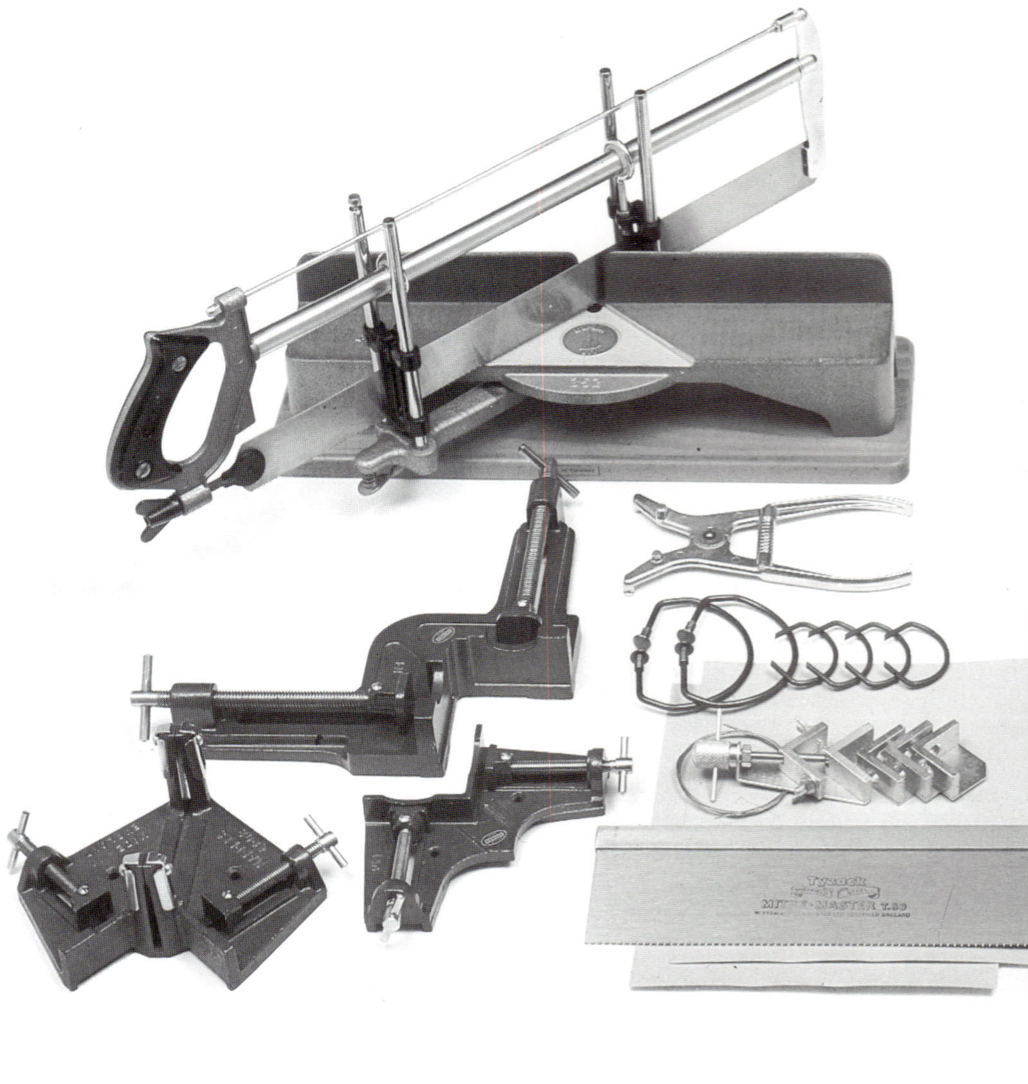

Right *Equipment needed for making and assembling frames* (left to right): *combined mount cutter and clamp; simple clamps for securing mitre; pliers and spring clips for holding mitres together while assembling; corner pieces, wire and screws for clamping mitres together; adjustable mitre saw which runs in grooves for accurate cutting; 45° trisquare; hand drill; panel pin hammer; chisel; staple gun; bradawl; pin punch; glass cutters; pliers; steel rule.*

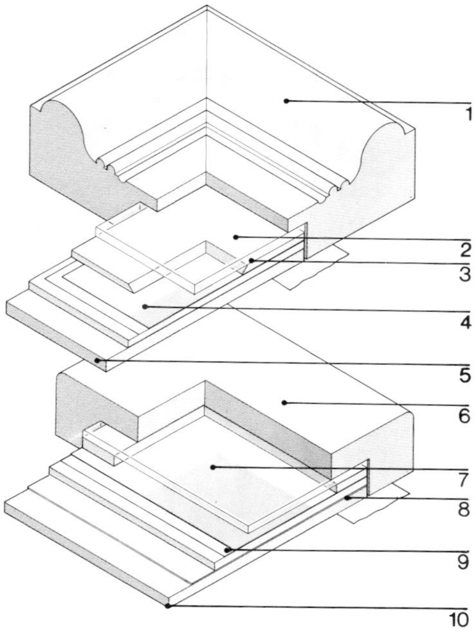

Above *This raised embroidery has a box-shaped, wooden frame specifically constructed so the glass does not touch the fabric. The paint, used to give the frame an impression of age, is of a bronze-gold colour, which picks out some of the detail in the embroidery.*

Above right *Parts of a traditional frame include: moulding* (1); *glass* (2); *mount, probably of a complementary colour* (3); *textile attached to a fabric-covered mounting board* (4); *backing board* (5). *Parts of a modern frame include: moulding* (6); *glass* (7); *fillet or spacer, to prevent the glass touching the textile* (8); *(if a mount is used it should be acid-free); textile attached to fabric-covered mounting board* (9); *backing board, firmly attached to prevent air circulation* (10).

effects on dyes and fibres are not known.

The use of a solid mounting avoids the potentially damaging effects of a stretcher frame. Textiles which are mounted on stretchers and are not framed are particularly vulnerable – becoming, in effect, dust filters. Weak textiles mounted in this way may also break along the inside edges of the stretcher.

To mount a small, flat textile, first measure the piece. The maximum measurements serve as a guide to the size of the mounting board and frame. Remember to include any fringes. It is usually advisable to allow at least an extra inch all the way around for the framer's filet.

The mounting board is a flat piece of card or board which will support the textile and keep it rigid for framing. Thick cardboard or hardboard are commonly used. Select and cut the board to the required size. Prepare the board by smoothing the cut edges and sharp corners with sandpaper.

Next, the mounting board should be covered with suitable fabric. Choose a fabric which either matches or complements the specimen. Cut the fabric slightly bigger than the board all the way round. Place the fabric face down on a table and centre the smoother side of the mounting board on top, with the grain of the fabric as straight as possible. Bring the excess fabric to the rougher side of the board and glue in place, taking care not to allow the glue to spread. Leave until the glue is dry.

Centre the textile on the board and pin in place. It will probably be necessary to adjust and readjust the pins to get the piece correctly and satisfactorily placed. The piece should then be sewn in place using a matching thread and suitable stitch.

If you want to display a textile in a glazed frame, a framer has to be contacted. Remember that if you take an unmounted textile to a framer, he is unlikely to mount it using this method.

Framing You must ask the framer to ensure that the glass does not rest on the textile. This is easily achieved by inserting a wooden filet between the glass and the mounting board. Alternatively, a picture mount of coloured acid-free card may be used. The depth of the filet or picture mount will depend on the thickness of the embroidery; normally ¼ inch (6mm) is sufficient.

The back of the frame must be properly sealed to prevent airborne pollutants soiling the textile. This can be achieved by placing a sheet of paper, traditionally brown wrapping paper, across the back of the frame and sealing the edges with sticky brown paper tape.

Displaying large textiles

Large textiles, such as patchwork quilts or appliqué pictures, are often better displayed by hanging. Traditionally, large textiles were hung using brass rings and hooks, or a rod passed through a fabric sleeve sewn to the back of the textile. For strong pieces, these methods may be satisfactory, although the uneven tension created by using hooks and rings may eventually cause damage.

Delicate pieces are best displayed using a strip contact fastener (for example, Velcro). This has the advantage of giving even support, and the hang and drape of the piece can be easily adjusted.

Velcro consists of two strips – one soft with a looped pile, the other with a rough barbed surface. A piece of contact fastener should be cut to fit the entire length of the top edge of the hanging. For ease of handling, the soft strip may then be machine- or hand-stitched to woven tape, wider than the contact fastener itself. The tape, with the Velcro attached, can then be hand-sewn along the top edge of the hanging. Two lines of stitching are necessary – one along the upper edge of the tape, and one along the lower edge. For effective support, the stitching should go through to the front of the hanging, or be fixed as an extension of the lining, and care should be taken to use matching thread and even stitching. The matching barbed strip can be nailed to a wooden batten which is then fastened to the wall. The textile is then hung from the batten by pressing the two strips firmly together.

Large hangings often benefit from being lined, as this helps to prevent soiling of the textile. Curtain lining materials and techniques are normally suitable.

Treating damaged textiles

If you discover a piece which is damaged, the cause must be identified and a decision made whether the preventive measures could arrest the damaging effects, or whether specialist help will be needed. Sometimes by taking carefully considered action, irreparable damage can be prevented. On the other hand, hasty and inexperienced treatment can result in permanent disfigurement of a valued piece. Some simple yet effective treatments can be carried out in the home.

Light damage Textile dyes or fibres damaged by light have undergone a chemical change which cannot unfortunately be reversed. A professional textile conservator may, however, be able to treat such a damaged textile so that it can be safely displayed.

Touch-and-close fastening is useful for hanging textiles, particularly if they are large. One of the two strips of the fastener is fixed with tacks or staples to a batten attached to the wall and the other strip is stitched to the upper edge of the textile, and along the width if necessary. This results in an even weight distribution, so the textile will not be pulled or strained at any one particular point.

Right *The staining on this piece of embroidery has resulted from the cotton ground being in direct contact with the wooden frame. Part of the centre strut of the frame is below the section shown in this photograph; its width is clearly visible in the stain between the two central leaves.*

A frame should be chosen to match and enhance the textile to be displayed. Its shape will probably depend on the outline shape of the textile. A large, bold textile may probably need a wide frame in high relief to set it off; a smaller textile probably requires a narrow, flat moulding not to be over-powered. A wooden frame can be left plain or it can be stained and varnished, gilded or painted. Metal and plastic frames are also available in different colours and finishes.

Top *The machine-stitched embroidery of a young Edwardian lady is set in a commercially manufactured plastic frame which has been moulded and treated to produce a finish similar to that of an antique wooden frame.* ***Above*** *The frame displaying Grandma and Grandpa, a pair of machine-embroidered portraits, was made from a small block of untreated yew, cut in half and joined with a leather strip at the back. The frame can be closed and clasped like a locket.*

Dryness If a textile feels very dry and brittle, and seems to have set in creases and crumples, it may well be suffering from excessive dryness. The fibres may regain their moisture content, and relax satisfactorily if they are allowed to do this naturally. This means leaving the piece in a normal room environment until it becomes supple. In extreme cases, an old textile will no longer be able to regain the necessary moisture.

Damp The first sign of mould growth is a musty smell. Textiles which smell or feel damp should be dried in a warm room with plenty of clean air circulation. If there is visible evidence of mould, this should be carefully brushed off after the textile has dried. Mildew attacks cellulose fibres, so cotton and linen may be permanently stained and weakened.

If dyes have run due to damp, it is unlikely that this process can be reversed. A professional textile conservator may be able to give advice.

Moth attack Clean away by brushing or gently shaking all moth frass. Vacuum all areas where a build-up of lint may provide refuge for other larvae.

Soiling Such pieces as canvaswork chair covers which are in good conditon may be quite effectively cleaned with a vacuum cleaner. The vacuum nozzle should be covered with a piece of open-weave fabric such as nylon net to prevent the canvaswork being pulled and sucked. Areas with loose threads should be avoided. Brushing with a soft brush is also quite effective. Washing a valued piece is not to be recommended: dyes may run, finishes may be lost, the material may shrink, beads and sequins may begin to dissolve. Damage may equally occur through drying. A piece which has been damaged by inexpert washing may be irreversibly damaged.

Specialist Textile Conservation

Some textiles require special treatment. A large embroidery may become soiled while on exhibition, or much-loved heirloom may require treatment beyond the scope of the amateur. In these cases, treatment must be carried out by a conservator.

It is useful to distinguish between repair, conservation and restoration. Repairing a textile involves mending a damaged area so that the piece can be reused. Restoration involves restoring a textile to its former appearance. It may involve re-embroidering a missing or worn area or replacing a missing part. Repairing and restoration are not normally carried out by textile conservators. The aim of textile conservation is to treat textiles so that they are preserved for the future. This is often difficult to distinguish from restoration, but if by restoring a piece its long-term preservation is adversely affected, this treatment will be avoided by a textile conservator. Normally, missing or worn areas are not renewed, but are supported to help prevent future damage.

Textile conservation treatments are suitable for particular pieces where the aim is to preserve them for display rather than use. This means that normally textile conservators treat historically valuable or rare pieces from museums or private collections.

Items used in the home often require repair or restoration, rather than conservation. An embroidered chair cover, for example, may become worn and need to be repaired or restored before it can continue

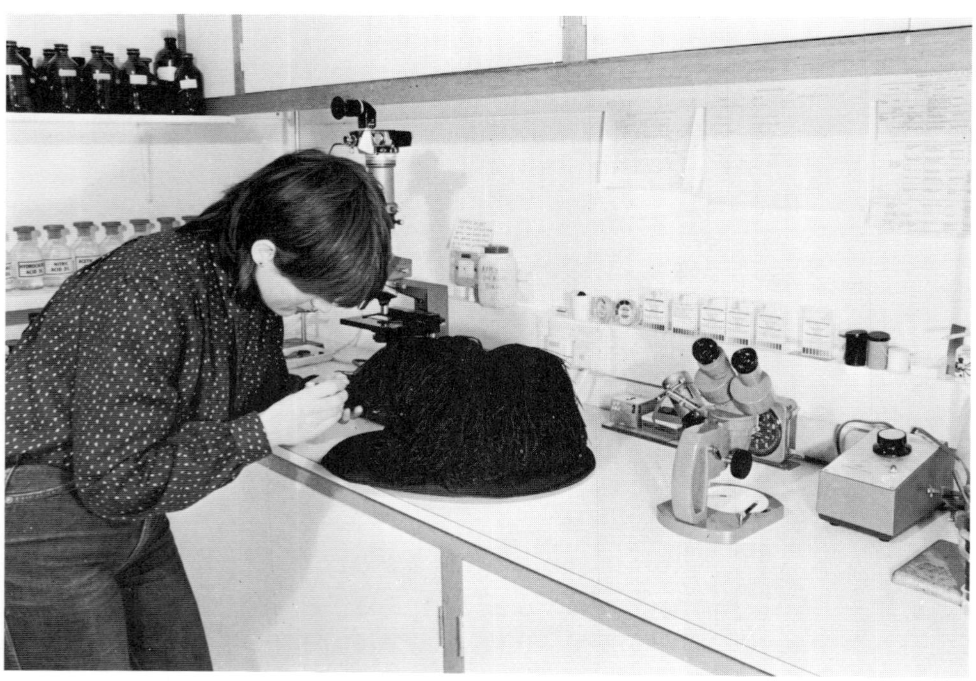

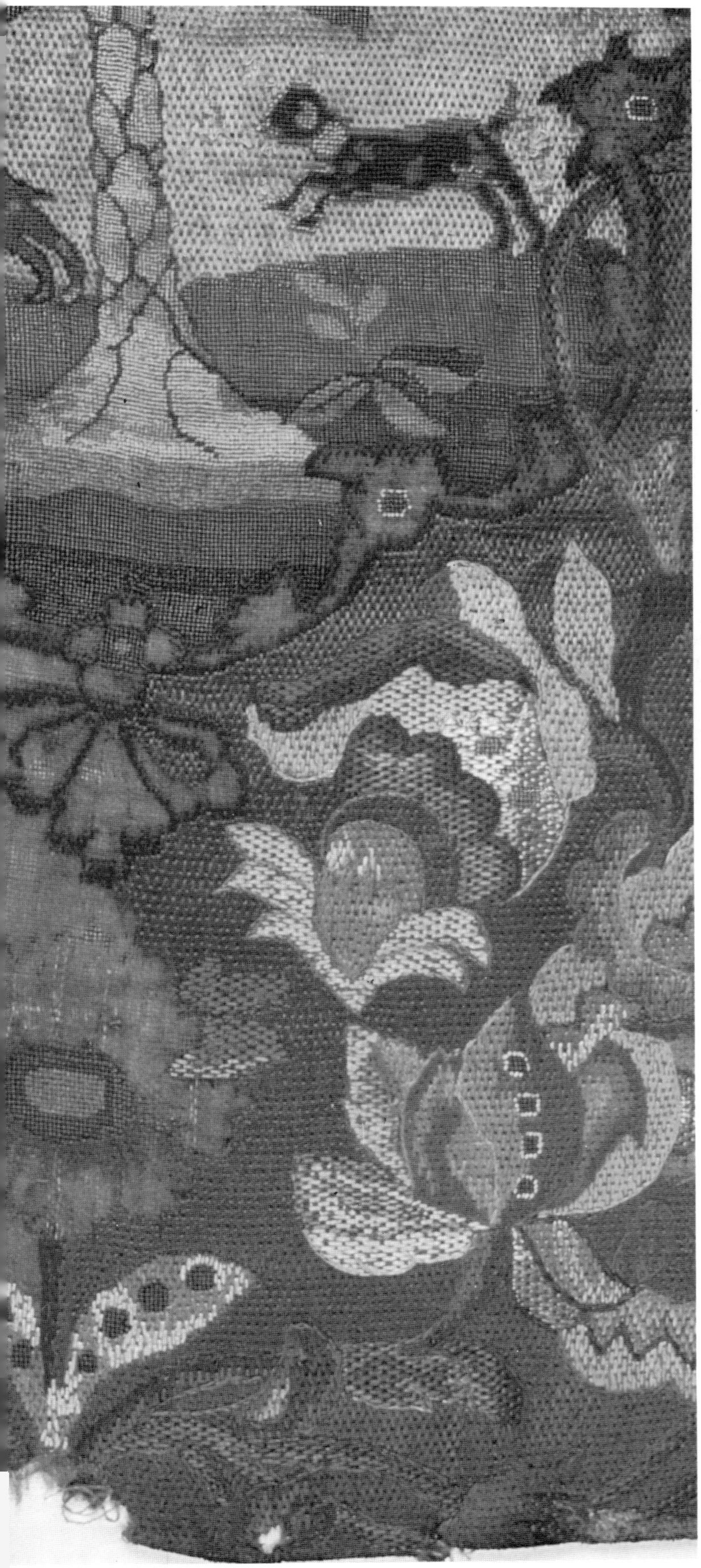

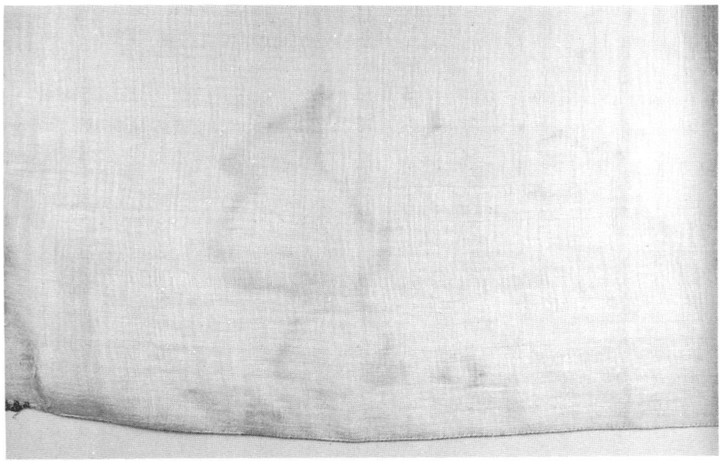

Far left *Here, a professional conservator is scrutinizing an object to ascertain its age and makeup before deciding how to approach its conservation. The equipment available includes microscopes and a lightfastness tester.*
Left *This piece of canvaswork, worked* c. *1700, on an openweave linen with silk threads, has been partly restored. Most of the stitches on the right are firmer and slightly shinier and brighter than those on the left.*
Top *Recently, some crude repairwork was done, the quality of which can easily be seen on the reverse side. This includes the white stitching and the applied patch of new canvas presumably intended to strengthen a frail area.*
Above *This piece of silk has been badly stained as a result of being rolled damp and left for some years. The structure of the fibres themselves has changed during this time.*

__Right__ The large holes and other damage to this early nineteenth-century sampler, which was worked by an eight-year-old in silk, were caused by moths attracted to the wool ground. No restoration or conservation work has been done on this piece.
__Below__ The baby's bonnet, with fine Ayrshire whitework leaf motifs, has worn especially in the corners, where there must have been strain during its use, caused by the tying strings. It has been washed and subsequently supported with some fine silk gauze to prevent further wear.

Left *Here, conservation work is in progress on an eighteenth-century dress which is thought to have been converted in the last century into a masque or effigy robe. Over the years the fabric has been worn bare in places, so the conservator has supported it with a backing fabric. She has started restoring the dress and is mending the fabric by sewing it with single silk thread to the backing.*
Top *Before textiles are washed, they are supported with backing fabrics or interfacing. They are kept flat on a washing table, sponged gently with non-alkaline detergent and rinsed in deionized water.*
Above *A low-power vacuum cleaner can be used to remove particles of dust from textiles. Working over a mono-filament netting, and sometimes placing muslin on the nozzle, ensures there is no loss of threads.*

to be used. In contrast, a piece which is kept for display purposes only may benefit from conservation treatment. The decision to choose between conservation or restoration should be made by the owner. It is unlikely to affect the cost of treatment. However, for rare or valuable pieces it is worth finding out whether the proposed treatment will affect the historical or monetary value of the piece.

Textile conservation is a relatively new profession and there are a limited number of trained textile conservators, employed by museums and museum's services, or working privately. Museums with large or important textile collections employ textile conservators, and some of the larger national museums may employ more than one. Some of the regional area museums service agencies provide a textile conservation service to member museums. There are also a number of private textile conservators.

Conservation demands special skills. Conservators need to have a thorough knowledge of the techniques of conservation together with a sound grounding in the history and science of the fibres, dyes, finishes and other materials which make up textiles. There are still no internationally recognized qualifications for textile conservation, but a trained conservator will normally possess a qualifying certificate or diploma.

Before consulting a textile conservator, it is useful to have thought out exactly how you wish to use your piece after it has been treated. A conservator is likely to ask many questions about where the item is kept, how it has been displayed, where it is to be displayed in the future, and so on. This questioning may be quite detailed, and it provides the conservator with the information necessary to make the appropriate recommendations for treatment.

Textile conservation workshops are normally equipped with specialist equipment. For cleaning, it is usual to have water purifying equipment (a water softener or water deioniser) and a washing table. Washing tables are used to support textiles during the cleaning process and they usually consist of a large, shallow stainless steel or plastic tray, with hose pipe connections and a drain. Aids for drying are also usually available, such as dehumidifiers or cool air fans. The use of dry-cleaning solvents and other chemicals means that conservation workshops should have adequate safeguards to protect the conservator and the premises.

Conservators provide two main services: advice and conservation treatment. If an item is submitted to a conservator for advice, he or she will be able to examine it and advise on its conditon, suggesting suitable methods of display and storage. Objects may be taken to a conservator, or alternatively, the objects may be examined where they are, which is often more convenient if a whole collection is to be examined. In many cases, conservators are able to advise owners that their collection is in a stable condition and that the methods used for its

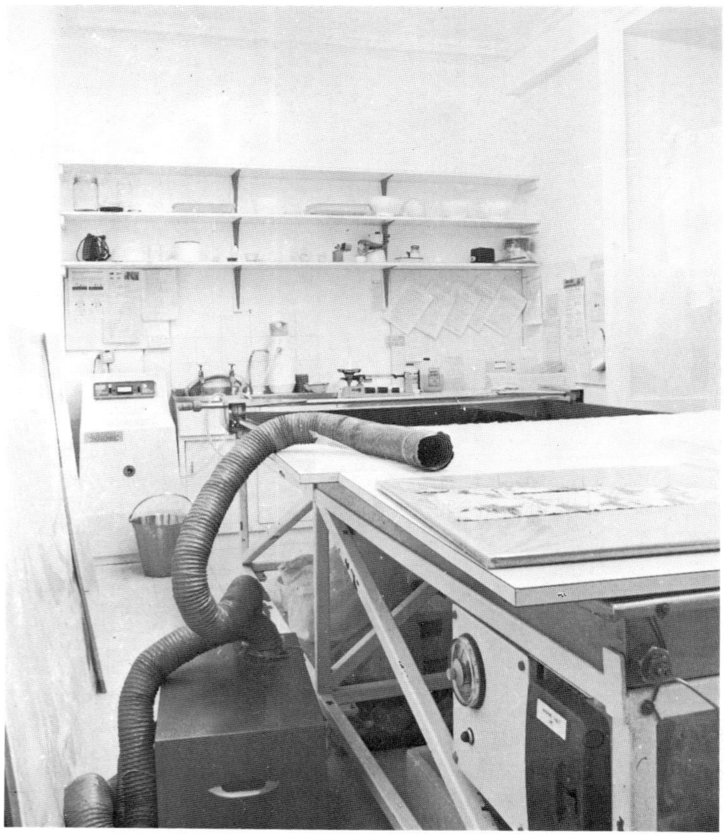

***Above** This photograph of a washing room shows some of the equipment necessary for efficient conservation. In the foreground is a dehumidifying unit which removes damp air from around drying textiles. A water deionizing machine stands at the back, ready to be used for purifying water for rinsing. The large washing table is especially useful for large textiles. Washing agents and other apparatus are at hand.*

display and storage are satisfactory.

The conservator's recommendations will normally be given in written form. If it is felt that specialist conservation treatment is required, an estimate of the cost of this will be included. The report may propose a number of different options for treatment which often require further discussion between conservator and client. As each object has to be treated individually, it is usually very difficult for a conservator to suggest treatment, or give an idea of the treatment's cost without close and detailed examination.

Conservators may often need to keep a specimen for much longer than expected. This is because time is needed to do the initial work of examination and documentation. Similarly, once the treatment has been completed, a final report must be compiled.

Conservation procedures

Examination Once accepted for treatment, a textile will be thoroughly examined to establish the precise nature of the fibres, dyes, finishes and other materials used to make it,

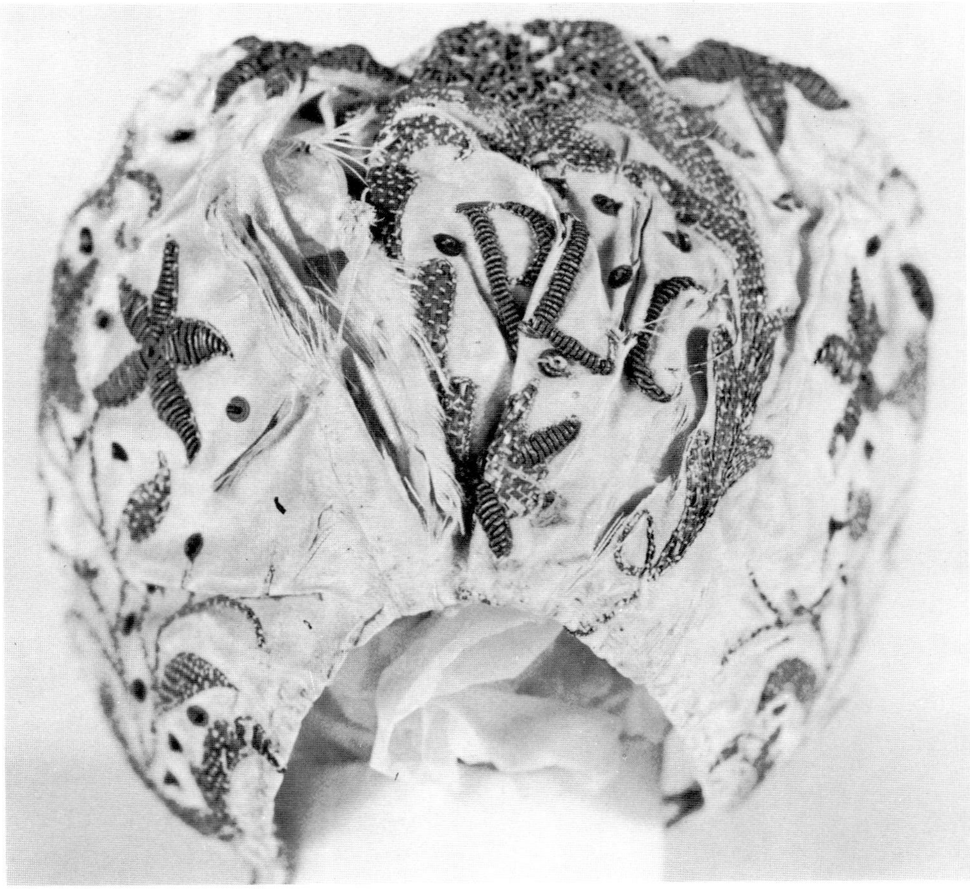

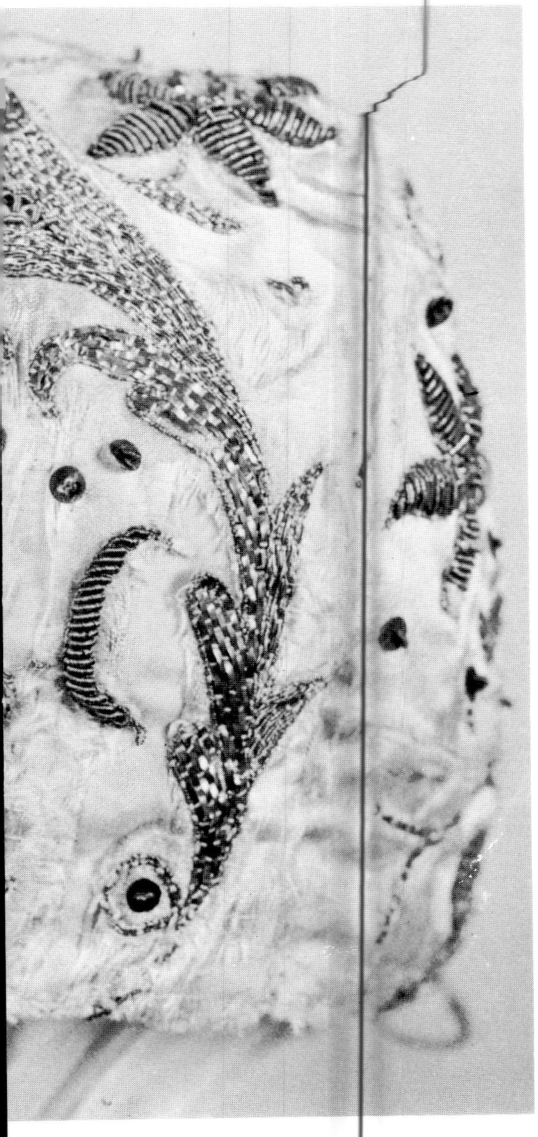

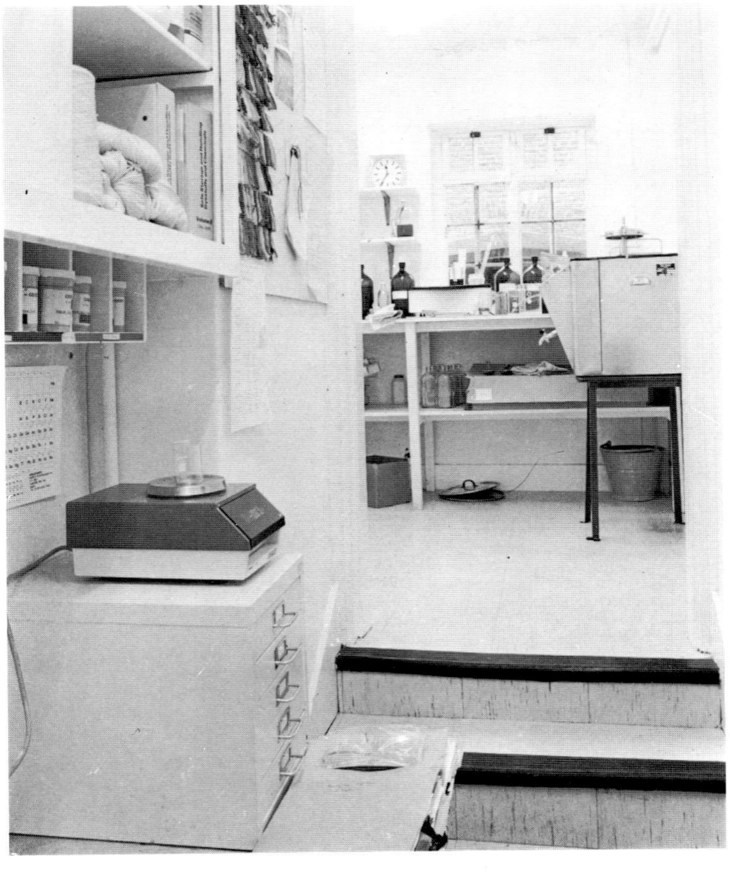

Left *The dye room in this photograph includes an electronic balance, seen in the foreground, and, on the right, a dying machine which is used for dying up to eight different support fabrics and yarns at one time.*

Above and far left *The German seventeenth-century child's cap is shown here before and after conservation. It is embroidered with silk and metal threads on silk satin and has initials at the back. The damage seen above was caused by bad storage—the fabric was crushed and had cracked in the folds. It was cleaned, then pieces of suitably dyed silk were inserted behind the weak and damaged areas, which were also supported with stitching and carefully shaped.*

as well as the type of damage. The conservator will probably use a microscope and a variety of chemical tests to aid the investigation. All stages of the treatment, from the examination onwards, are recorded – with notes, diagrams and usually photographs. This recording procedure is extremely important.

Cleaning is usually the first treatment to be carried out; it is usually regarded as the most critical stage of the treatment. The type of cleaning depends on the nature of the textile – the fibres, dyes, finishes, construction and also the type of soiling and condition of the piece. Careless or inappropriate cleaning can cause irreversible damage.

Loose dust and dirt may be removed with a soft brush or low suction vacuum cleaner through nylon filament screening. Ingrained soiling and stains may require further cleaning with water or dry-cleaning solvent. Washing or dry-cleaning a damaged textile needs special care to avoid further damage, such as shrinkage or distortion of the fabric, dye runs, fibre loss, or tearing through excessive handling. Sequins or bead decorations may also be adversely affected by cleaning.

In most cases, considerable preparation is needed before washing or dry-cleaning can be carried out, and usually involves giving temporary support to weak and damaged areas. In wet-cleaning the conservator uses pure, not tap, water and prepares a detergent solution which varies according to the soil and the type of textile being cleaned. Considerable space is needed, as the piece, no matter how large, has to be kept completely flat while it is wet.

The method of drying is also extremely important and needs to be carried out with equal care. Damaged pieces can obviously not be hung to dry, nor can they be ironed to smooth out creases.

Support Damaged and weak textiles usually require some form of support to enable them to be displayed.This will involve attaching the piece to a new fabric, in most cases by stitching, although occasionally a thermoplastic adhesive technique may be employed.

The support fabric may be of a natural or synthetic fibre. The choice will depend on the nature and condition of the damaged piece, the colour, the weave and quality of the support fabric available. In many cases, the new support fabric will have to be dyed especially to match. The conservator is careful to use dyes which are colour-fast and may spend a long time matching colours. Once cleaned and supported, the piece will be made ready for display, whether by mounting a solid support ready for framing or by lining so that it can be hung. Before the piece can be returned to the owner, the detailed description of the treatment will be completed and the piece will probably be photographed.

After conservation The success of the conservation treatment depends on how the textile is treated after it has been returned to its owner. No treatment can be given which

Left *These fragments of an eighteenth-century embroidery, worked with silk and metal threads on silk, may have been part of an ecclesiastical robe or cloth. The background fabric has deteriorated badly; also, some outlines of the fragments that remain suggest that the fabric was cut away at some time.*

Above *After conservation, the piece probably looks much as it did originally. The fragments were cleaned and carefully supported on a matching silk backing fabric. They were then mounted on a board covered with cream-coloured silk, ready for framing.*

makes a piece immune to the effects of light, damp or soiling.

Textile conservation is a specialist skill much in demand, and it usually takes a very long time to treat a damaged piece. The cost of conservation often seems quite high, but is calculated to cover the costs of labour and materials. Conservators are often asked whether it is worth treating an individual piece. Conservators are not usually qualified to give valuations and are not able to compare the value of an object with the cost of conservation. This decision must rest with the owner, for whom sentimental value is often an important factor. Sadly, the cost of conserving a much-loved heirloom may exceed its monetary value.

It is worth noting that textiles, like other art-forms, fetch the best prices at auction if they are in good condition. As the cost of preventive conservation is much cheaper than the cost of remedial conservation, it is crucial to care for items by careful storage and display.

Top and above *These two photographs show restoration work in progress on an early nineteenth-century military colour. When work was begun, the silk was very fragile and had torn and split. It was cleaned, and slowly pieced together, supported on a backing fabric through which repair stitching was executed.*

Index

Italics indicate illustrations

A

B

C

D

E

F

G

H

I

J

K

L

M

N

O

P

Q

R

S

T

U

V

W

Y

Z

Acknowledgements

The illustrations are reproduced by kind permission of the following:

6(bl) Welsh Folk Museum; **6–7**(c) Marion Appleton; **7**(br) Caroline Jubb; **8–9** Victoria and Albert Museum; **14–15**(c) Marion Appleton; **17** Margaret Hall; **19**(c) Victoria and Albert Museum; **21** Marion Appleton; **23** Belton House (photo Martin Gostelow); **24** Victoria and Albert Museum; **25**(t and b) National Trust Property, Hardwick Hall; **26–7**(c) (photo J. Whitaker); **26**(b) National Trust Photographic Library; **27**(t) National Trust Property, Hardwick Hall; **27**(c) Parham Park (photo Martin Gostelow); **27**(b) (photo Edwin Smith); **28–9**(t),**28**(b) National Trust Property, Hardwick Hall (photo J. Whitaker); **29**(tr) Victoria and Albert Museum; **29**(b) (photo Martin Gostelow); **30**(bl) The Dean and Chapter of Winchester; **30**(br) Sir John Carew Pole; **31**(l) Freda Clinch; **31**(r) Ruth Levy and Anna Pearson; **34,36–7**(c)**38–9**(c),**39**(r),**39**(b) Anna Pearson; **40,41** Parham Park (photo Martin Gostelow); **42,42–3**(c),**44,46–7**(c),**47** Anna Pearson; **48,49**(t) Victoria and Albert Museum; **49**(b),**50**(bl) National Trust Property, Hardwick Hall; **50**(r),**51**(b) Victoria and Albert Museum; **51**(t) Belinda Montagu; **52**(t),**53**(t) The Dean and Chapter of St Paul's Cathedral, London (photo *Country Life*); **52**(b) Whitbread Museum, London; **52–3**(b) Victoria and Albert Museum; **54** Bath City Council; **55,56** Julie Athill; **56–7**(c) Victoria and Albert Museum; **58**(t) Kunstgewerbe Museum, Zurich; **58**(b) Carla Hunt (photo Martin Gostelow); **59**(tl) Julie Athill; **59**(tr) The Embroiderers' Guild; **59**(b) Denman College, Abingdon (Thomas Photos, Oxford); **61** Julie Athill; **62**(b) Bayerisches Nationalmuseum, Munich; **62–3**(c) The Syndics of the Fitzwilliam Museum, Cambridge; **63**(br) Burrell Collection, Glasgow Museum and Art Gallery; **64**(t) Victoria and Albert Museum; **64**(b) A. Augustus Healy Fund, Brooklyn Museum; **65** Cluny Museum, Paris (photo Musées Nationaux); **66** private collection; **67**(t) Catherine Riley; **67**(b) Victoria Bartlett; **68,69**(t) American Museum in Britain; **68–9**(b),**70**(l) (photo Kilkenny Design Workshops); **70–1**(c),**71**(r),**72,74,74–5**(c),**75,76–7**(c),**77** American Museum in Britain; **78** Cheltenham Art Gallery and Museum; **78–9** Sir John Carew Pole; **80** Beamish, North of England Open Air Museum; **82** Mrs Faucet's Embroidery students, Warrington; **83**(l) Francesca Kemble; **83**(r) Mrs Helen Kelley; **84**(b) Beamish, North of England Open Air Museum; **84–5**(b) American Museum in Britain; **86** Goldsmith's College, London; **87**(t) The Tate Gallery, London; **87**(b) Museum of Costume and Textiles, Nottingham; **88** Victoria and Albert Museum; **89** Somerset Rural Life Museum, Glastonbury; **90**(l) Buckinghamshire County Museum, Aylesbury; **90–1**(c) Hereford City Museum and Art Gallery (photo Derek Evans); **91** Welsh Folk Museum; **92**(t) Luton Museum and Art Gallery; **92**(b),**93**(l) *Lady's World*, 1887 (photo Ray Gardner); **93**(t and b) Hereford and Worcester County Museum, Hartlebury Castle; **95,97,98–9,100,101** Beverley Marshall; **102** Victoria and Albert Museum; **103**(t) The Embroiderers' Guild; **103**(b) Marion Appleton; **104**(t) Victoria and Albert Museum; **104**(b) Lady Lever Art Gallery; **105** Victoria and Albert Museum; **106**(t) the 6th Marquis of Bath, Longleat House (photo Derek Balmer); **106**(b) National Army Museum; **107**(l) Marion Appleton; **107**(r) Royal Scottish Museum (photo Martin Gostelow); **109** Royal Albert Memorial Museum, Exeter; **111**(t) Marion Appleton; **111**(b) Kathleen Chester; **113** Marion Appleton; **114**(t and br) Victoria and Albert Museum (photo Martin Gostelow); **114**(bl) Gulbenkian Museum of Oriental Art, University of Durham; **115**(l) The Embroiderers' Guild; **116–7,117**(t and b) Victoria and Albert Museum; **119**(tl) British Museum (photo Michael Holford); **119**(tr) American Museum in Britain; **119**(b) The Syndics of the Fitzwilliam Museum, Cambridge; **120** The Embroiderers' Guild; **121**(l) Museum of Costume, Bath; **121**(r) Helen L. Allen Collection, Department of Domestic Studies, University of Wisconsin, Madison; **122**(t) Christine Risley; **122**(b) Victoria and Albert Museum; **123** Christine Risley; **126**(l) Ruth Tovey, Goldsmith's College; **126**(r) Ariella Rosen, Goldsmith's College; **127** Fiona Ede, Goldsmith's College; **128,129** Hazel Chapman; **130**(t) Diana Thornton, Goldsmith's College; **130**(b) Margaret Hall, Goldsmith's College; **131**(t) Christine Risley; **131**(bl) Sally Freshwater, Goldsmith's College; **131**(br) Denziel Grant, Goldsmith's College; **132**(bl) Sarah Whitely, Goldsmith's College; **132**(br) Hazel Chapman; **133**(t) Diana Thornton, Goldsmith's College; **133**(b) Hazel Chapman; **134**(l and c) Diana Thornton, Goldsmith's College; **135** Thomasina Beck; **136** Hazel Chapman; **137** Goldsmith's College; **138**(t) National Trust Property, Hardwick Hall; **138**(b) Victoria and Albert Museum; **139** The Brotherton Library, University of Leeds; **140,141** Victoria and Albert Museum; **142** Marion Appleton; **143** Lady Simpson; **144–5** Mrs Beckford (photo Martin Gostelow); **145** The Trustees, The Wallace Collection, London; **150**(b) The Embroiders' Guild; **150–1**(t) Royal Scottish Museum (photo Martin Gostelow); **151**(b) Christie's Fine Art, London; **152,153**(tl) Sir John Carew Pole; **153**(tr) The Warden and Fellows of Wadham College, Oxford (photo Martin Gostelow); **153**(b) Aramco World; **154–5** Episcopal Museum, Bayeux (photo Giraudon); **155**(r),**156,156–7,157,158,158–9,159** Victoria and Albert Museum; **161** Parham Park (photo Martin Gostelow); **162** Episcopal Museum, Bayeux (photo Giraudon); **163**(t) J. E. Knowles, Wareham, Dorset (photo Martin Gostelow); **163**(bl) Society of Antiquaries (photo A. F. Kersting); **163**(br) The Embroiderers' Guild; **165,166** Dorothea Nield; **167**J. E. Knowles (photo Martin Gostelow); **168** Dorothea Nield; **169** Vicky Lugg; **170**(br) Audrey Francini (photo Martin Gostelow); **171** The Helen L. Allen Collection; **172**(t) Victoria and Albert Museum; **172**(b) Royal Scottish Museum; **173,174–5**(t and b) Victoria and Albert Museum; **174**(bl) Valentine Museum, Richmond, Virginia; **175**(tr) Honiton Museum (photo Martin Gostelow); **176** The Embroiderers Guild; **180** Victoria and Albert Museum; **181** The Embroiderers' Guild; **182–3**(c) Victoria and Albert Museum; **184**(t and b) Royal Scottish Museum; **184–5**(c) Caroline Courtney; **185** The Embroiderers' Guild; **186–7**(c) Victoria and Albert Museum; **187**(r) Marion Appleton; **188** Victoria and Albert Museum; **190**(b) Marion Appleton; **190–1**(t),**191,192,193**(t) Textile Conservation Centre, Hampton Court Palace; **193**(b) Lynn Fetterington, Goldsmith's College; **194,195,196,197,198,199** Textile Conservation Centre; **201** Margaret Hall, Goldsmith's College; **202–3**(c) Textile Conservation Centre; **203** Goldsmith's College; **204,205,206,207,208,209,210,211** Textile Conservation Centre.

Key – (t) top (b) below (l) left (r) right (c) centre